LIVE & WORK IN

SCOTLAND

Nicola Taylor

Distributed in the USA by
The Globe Pequot Press, Guilford, Connecticut

Published by Vacation Work, 9 Park End Street, Oxford
www.vacationwork.co.uk

LIVE & WORK IN SCOTLAND
by Nicola Taylor

First edition 2001
Second Edition 2005

ISBN 1-85458-334-4

Cover design by mccdesign ltd

Title page illustration by Mick Siddens

Typeset by Brendan Cole

Cover photograph: cottages overlooking Glencoe

Printed and bound in Italy by Legoprint SpA, Trento

LIVE & WORK IN

SCOTLAND

CONTENTS

SECTION I - LIVING IN SCOTLAND

SECTION II - WORKING IN SCOTLAND

EMPLOYMENT

STARTING A BUSINESS

PERSONAL CASE HISTORIES

MAPS

PREFACE

This is the second edition of *Live and Work in Scotland*. The first edition proved immediately popular with people from all around the world, in particular other parts of the UK, Europe and the USA, who wished to experience the unique Scottish way of life for themselves.

Since the first edition was published, just a year after the people of Scotland elected their first devolved parliament to sit in the country since 1707, many changes have taken place. In their first session, 62 bills were passed by the Scottish Parliament, on a wide range of issues, several of which directly affect the process of setting up home in Scotland. In particular, legislation on Land Reform and Abolition of Feudal Tenure will have far-reaching effects on the buying and selling of land and property in the country.

Scotland has always been much more than just a northern region of England, with a different accent and more rain – now it is making those differences obvious in a more formal way. For example, the historic decision recently taken to ban smoking in all public places, and the equally dramatic decision to scrap the swingeing tolls on the Skye Bridge, introduced by the Westminster-based Scottish Office when the bridge was built in 1995.

What hasn't changed is the great quality of life offered by this beautiful country. As modern life becomes increasingly stressful and urban areas more crowded and polluted, many people are looking for a place where they can escape to a calmer, cleaner way of life. Scotland, with an area of over 30,000 square miles and only five million people, has around one-tenth of the population of England living in three-fifths of the area. The feeling of having room to breathe is tangible, especially to those from the overcrowded south-east of England. Even in the Scottish central belt, where around 90 per cent of the population live, the towns and cities have not developed the urban sprawl which bedevils many industrial nations, and the countryside is still close by even if you live in the centre of Edinburgh or Glasgow.

The principle of freedom of movement within Europe means that it has never been easier for European nationals to relocate in Scotland, either temporarily or permanently. UK regulations do, however, make immigration from other parts of the world quite difficult if you do not have British ancestry. You will be required to demonstrate that you have qualifications, skills and experience which are of benefit to the country, or that you have the resources to make a substantial investment in the local economy. For those who wish to study or gain work experience in the UK on a short-term basis, the opportunities are greater now than they have been in the past. Foreign students are encouraged to study in the universities and to stay on afterwards while they look for work which will keep them in the country, using their new-found skills and qualifications in the new industries, such as IT and electronics, which are making Scotland a desirable home for many international companies.

Scotland has always been attractive to the English, many of whom spend their holidays there every year, eventually moving there permanently, often when they reach retirement age. Some may have the impression that Scotland is not much different from England. This is not the case, however. The legal and political systems are different, the education system is distinct, land and property ownership are governed by different rules. These differences are explained clearly in this book, and advice is given as to the best way to proceed with the move. Whether you dream of buying a holiday home to visit a few times a year, with the idea of retiring there one day, or whether you wish to move permanently to Scotland while you are still of working age, this book will help you achieve your aim.

It is difficult to talk about Scotland as a whole, because the way of life in the crofting areas of the north is very different from that further south. In this book, emphasis is laid on the peculiarities of life in the Highlands and Islands. There is no doubt that if you are searching for a slower pace of life in beautiful surroundings, the Highlands and Islands is the part of Scotland which will appeal. This has been the case for many years, but only recently has this been a realistic option for those without independent means of support, such as a retirement pension. The big change is, of course, the internet. Across the Highlands and Islands people are making a comfortable living working from home in an amazing range of occupations. The one common factor is that they can find work and clients, and can market their products, whether they be traditional consumer goods or knowledge-based skills, through the wonders of the world wide web.

The pattern of work in the rural areas of Scotland is rather different from that in the central belt. People are more likely to have a number of part-time, possibly seasonal, jobs than to have a single full-time source of income. Tourism is a very important part of the economy in these areas with most people making some part of their income from the thousands of tourists which visit the country each year. As a result of this pattern of work, the rural areas of Scotland have the highest proportion of small one-man businesses in the UK. Contact details are given here of local and national government agencies which encourage and assist such ventures.

Whether you prefer the crystal clear rivers and lush pastures of the lowlands, or the mountains, lochs and glens of the Highlands, Scotland is a beautiful country. The opportunities to enjoy the outdoor life are many and varied. Even if you just want to put down roots and watch the world go by, there are few better places in the world to do it. So why not take the high road to Scotland? This book will guide you on your way.

Nicola Taylor
January 2005

ACKNOWLEDGEMENTS

The author would like to thank all those people who provided advice and encouragement during the writing of this book. In particular, Clare, Ally, Callum and Ruairdhri Wright; Bob Grayson; Rainer Thonnes; Samuel White, Stuart and Sandy Nairn; and Pam and Tony Shinkins who kindly served as case studies; Ric and Jill Holmes, Janis MacLean, my sons Adam and Matthew Taylor, whose experiences feature elsewhere in the book. Finally, as always, for his encouragement and support, warm thanks are due to my husband Derek Taylor.

Telephone Numbers

International Telephone Codes. Throughout this book, UK telephone codes have been used. For those calling UK numbers from abroad, the international code is +44 (or 00 44) and the initial 0 is dropped. So 0131-222 5555 is +44 131-222 5555 when calling from outside the UK.

While every effort has been made to ensure that the information contained in this book is as up-to-date as possible, some details are bound to change within the lifetime of this edition, and readers are strongly advised to check facts and credentials themselves. Readers are invited to write to the author c/o Vacation Work, 9 Park End Street, Oxford OX1 1HJ, with any comments, corrections and first hand experiences. Those whose contributions are used will be sent a free copy of the next edition.

SECTION I

LIVING IN SCOTLAND

GENERAL INTRODUCTION

RESIDENCE AND ENTRY REGULATIONS

SETTING UP HOME

DAILY LIFE

RETIREMENT

GENERAL
INTRODUCTION

CHAPTER SUMMARY

○ **Scotland** is not just England with a different accent and more rain
  – it has its own distinct legal, political and education systems.
○ **Mainland Scotland** covers over half the area of Great Britain,
  with a population only a tenth of that in England and Wales.
○ Over five million acres of Scotland's scenic areas are protected
  under environmental designations.
○ **The Highlands** has a population density of just 8 people per
  square kilometre.
○ **Edinburgh** is the nation's capital, although its second city,
  Glasgow, is much larger.
○ In **May 1999** the Scottish people elected the first parliament to sit
  in Scotland since 1707.
○ The **new Scottish Parliament building** opened in 2004, three
  years late and costing 11 times more than the original estimate.
○ **Whisky** accounts for 15 per cent of Scotland's exports.
○ **The Scottish education system** is widely agreed to be the best in
  the UK.
○ **The Highlands** is known as the last great wilderness of Europe.

DESTINATION SCOTLAND

As other parts of Britain become more crowded, more polluted and the pace of life ever faster, increasing numbers of people are seeing the attractions of moving to Scotland. Although it is often the wild scenery of the Highlands and Islands that attracts them, there is a new interest in moving to the lowland and urban areas since the establishment of the Scottish Parliament, which promises new opportunities now and in the future. Scenically too these areas have much to offer. Even in urban areas the beauty of this essentially still rural country is evident, if not quite on one's doorstep, then not many paces down the road.

Scotland is a favourite holiday destination for Europeans and Americans. Many of the latter, indeed, come in search of their Scottish ancestors. Some fall in love with the country and visit regularly, and dream of one day moving there permanently or buying a holiday home. For those from the EEA (European Economic Area) there are few regulations preventing them from taking up permanent residence, but for those from elsewhere in the world, there are tough entry regulations to satisfy before making the move.

It is difficult to talk about Scotland as a whole, because the way of life in the Highlands and Islands is very different from that in the more populated areas further south. For those moving from elsewhere in Britain, Southern Scotland is not very different, in many respects, from what they are used to. Moving to the lowlands is just moving house; moving to the Highlands is more like emigrating, as there is a far greater sense of it being a 'different country', socially, culturally and economically. However, it is a mistake to think that even the south of Scotland is just England with a different accent and more rain. Legal and political systems are different, the education system is distinct, land and property ownership are governed by different rules.

PROS & CONS OF MOVING TO SCOTLAND

There is no doubt that Scotland provides a beautiful environment in which to live. Over five million acres of the land are protected under various environmental designations including National Parks, National Scenic Areas, Sites of Special Scientific Interest, National, Local and Forest Nature Reserves. Together they make up over 25 per cent of the land mass. The downside of this is that there is comparatively little in the way of industry, with implications for the quantity and type of employment available. 90 per cent of land usage is classified as non-urban, which means that there is a preponderance of small companies or 'one-man' businesses.

With only five million people in an area of 30,420 square miles, there is plenty of elbow room. The low population density combined with the lack of heavy industry means that there is little air pollution, and in the remote rural areas, where even street lights are few and far between, light pollution is rare, so better views of the stars can be seen than elsewhere in Britain. When conditions are right, the Northern Lights (*aurora borealis*) can be seen in the more northerly parts of the country.

With the modern trend to work harder over longer hours, stress related illnesses seem to be reaching epidemic proportions. The attractions of moving to a remote area with fewer people and a slower pace of life are obvious. However, it is recognised that there is a high rate of suicide in the Highlands. Isolation, social deprivation and even the landscape can have a deleterious effect on those with depression, so moving to escape such problems may actually make them worse.

However, there are plenty of opportunities to relax in 'the great outdoors', taking part in activities which many find ideal for lowering stress levels, as well as affording simple enjoyment. Fishing, golf, watersports, walking, climbing and cycling are all widely available.

Good education and a low crime rate are added benefits, particularly for those with children. The Scottish education system has long been perceived by many as the best in the UK. In rural areas it is still possible to leave your house and your car unlocked without fear of theft. Parents can let their children out on their own without undue anxiety. In smaller rural communities, anyway, the children know everybody and everybody knows them so there is an efficient, if unofficial, 'neighbourhood watch' system.

A move to a new country or a new area inevitably means moving away from the family and social support networks one may have enjoyed previously, and in rural areas with little or no public transport and less easy access to various services, this can make life harder to organise. However, in areas where people are reliant on private transport, for instance, or where the doctor's surgery or the shop are some miles away, neighbours are always ready to assist when your car is at the garage, or if you are ill. After all, they may need you to return the favour some time.

There is a good network of social services in the remote areas, but it is inevitable that there may be a long way to travel to a doctor's surgery or a hospital. Doctors are far more geared up to home-visiting as a result, and in emergency where time is crucial, transport to hospital will be supplied by helicopter.

Public transport is patchy in rural areas. Often there will only be one bus a day, or maybe every other day, to the larger towns. Royal Mail post buses provide a valuable local service in many areas. In large areas of the Highlands, and the whole of the Islands, there is no train service. Reliance on the private car is therefore heavy. Petrol and diesel are more expensive in the Highlands and Islands than anywhere else in Europe, making fuel a large element of the weekly budget. Shopping too will be more expensive, due to high transport costs and low demand. Throughout Scotland, the cost of living is generally higher the further you live from centres of population.

Of course, it is wonderful to dream of living in a remote rural area, but without a means of earning an income it may not be feasible. The unemployment rate in Scotland is slightly higher than that for the UK as a whole – in the fourth quarter of 2003 it was 5.8 per cent, compared with 5.1 per cent for the whole of the UK – and in the rural areas there are fewer opportunities for the traditional nine to five, long term job. Many people have two or more part-time jobs, often supplemented by one-off jobs they pick up here and there.

Paradoxically, for the innovative and adaptable, there can be greater opportunities to set up your own business than you might find in the centre of a town. With advances in computer technology, and new high speed internet links promised to all communities in Scotland by the end of 2005, it is more feasible now to move to a remote area and run a business from home. From a house on a remote island one can do business with the rest of the world. At the same time, there are more openings to supply services to the local community. Big companies don't

REGIONS OF SCOTLAND

*Atlantic
Ocean*

**Shetland
Islands**

Unst

Yell

Fetlar

Hillswick

Muckle Roe

*Out
Skerries*

Papa Stour

Whalsay

Foula

Bressay

Isle of Noss

Lerwick

Shetland

Mousa

Sumburgh

*Papa
Westray*

*North
Ronaldsay*

**Orkney
Islands**

Westray

Rousay *Eday*

Sanday

Stronsay

Kirkwall

Shapinsay

Stromness

Orkney

Flotta

Hoy

*South
Ronaldsay*

Thurso

John O'Groats

Wick

*North
Sea*

Handa

Stornoway

Highland

Summer Is.

Priest I.

Ullapool

*Shiant
Is.*

Tain

Gairloch

Rona

Dingwall

Elgin

Banff

Portree

Peterhead

Raasay

Scalpay

Inverness

Skye

Kyle of Lochalsh

Grampian

Aviemore

Mallaig

Aberdeen

Fort William

0		50 km
0		25 miles

find it economically viable to concentrate their efforts on the sparse populations of outlying districts, but those people still need the same services town-dwellers do. They need someone local who can fix their computer when it goes wrong; they want someone to professionally photograph or video their wedding or 21st birthday party without having to pay for someone to travel up to one hundred miles to do so; they would like to club together with other families to order groceries through the Internet and have them delivered to their door. These opportunities are waiting for those with the equipment and skills to provide such services.

Since devolution on 1st July 1999, the new Scottish Parliament was determined to make its mark, to show it would not be just a poor relation of Westminster. The second general election for membership of the Scottish Parliament was held on 1st May 2003, with the 129 Members of the Scottish parliament (MSPs) elected for a fixed term of four years. In its first session (1999-2003) 62 bills were passed by the Scottish Parliament, on a wide range of issues including Fur Farming, Homelessness, Land Reform, Mortgage Rights, Protection of Children and Protection of Wild Mammals. This compares with the two or three Scottish bills per year previously passed by Westminster before devolution. So in that sense, the new parliament has had a great effect. Further details and summaries of all bills can be found on the Scottish Parliament website; www.scottish.parliament.uk.

However, public perception is somewhat different. A survey in November 2004 found that while 66 per cent of people in Scotland thought the Scottish Parliament should have most influence over how the country is run, only 17 per cent of people believed that it did. But devolution is generally seen as an improvement on the government of Scotland – 56 per cent were still in favour of devolution, and 59 per cent thought that the Scottish Parliament should have more powers.

Bob Grayson moved from Ireland to Edinburgh for a six month contract, and loved it so much he stayed
I find Scotland, and Edinburgh in particular, a great place to live. I often have friends visiting from Ireland, and they really enjoy the city and the surrounding countryside. I found it quite easy to settle, helped by having a good friendly social crowd in work...I'd recommend moving to Scotland – even if you don't have a particularly pressing reason. The pace of life in Edinburgh is unlike that in other capital cities, but gives access to far greater amenities. Living and working here is easy to do – plenty of jobs and accommodation available if you look at the right time of year.

On the downside, the first thing many people think of in connection with Scotland, is the weather. It always rains, allegedly, and the sun rarely shines. Although it is true one must expect a relatively high rainfall in a country of mountains and vast inland waters, even the wettest areas of Scotland boast a similar rainfall to parts of the Lake District or Cornwall. Snow too is less of a problem than commonly perceived. On low ground in most coastal areas of Scotland, snow lies for less than ten days a year, rising to 15 to 20 days in the north and north-east. It is rare for roads to be blocked by snow, the ones most susceptible being those on high ground. As for the sun, the island of Tiree is claimed to be the sunniest place in Britain, while Nairn marketed itself to the Victorians as the 'Brighton of the North'.

From June to September, whether it rains or is fine, a local resident not to be underestimated is the midge. They may be tiny, but at a density of ten million per acre they make up in number what they lack in size. Although some people prove to be allergic to their bite, generally their irritation value is greater than their propensity for harm. There are many proprietary and home-made insect repellents to try, plus the new breed of 'midge machines' which claim to capture and kill vast quantities of the pests, but the final best line of defence is to do what the locals do – if the midges get too bad, go indoors and shut the windows.

A move to Scotland may entail a drop in one's standard of living, but the benefits of the potential improvement in one's quality of life may compensate for that. The point at which one side of the standard of living/quality of life equation balances or outweighs the other is different for everyone. You need to balance what you are prepared to sacrifice financially against what you expect to gain in other areas of your life through the move.

When Pam and Tony Shinkins gave up their jobs to move to the Highlands, although they assumed that their standard of living would drop, this didn't prove to be the case

We've come to see that it costs a great deal of money to go to work. The costs of what you wear to work, travel expenses, attendance at social functions and, if you're in a stressful occupation, the costs of holidays to get away from the daily grind. Now we're here, we rarely go away on holiday – we don't find the need for them.

Pros

- Beautiful scenery
- Less crowded than other parts of UK
- Less pollution
- Quietness
- Wildlife
- Easy driving
- Remote areas
- A time of change
- Good education system
- Safety

- Neighbourliness
- New business opportunities
- Plenty of recreational opportunities

Cons
- The weather
- Unemployment
- Isolation
- Lack of services in some areas
- Cost of living higher
- Distance to hospitals
- Distance to large shops
- Lack of public transport
- Lack of family/social support groups

POLITICAL & ECONOMIC STRUCTURE

Government

A huge change in the governing of Scotland took place on 6th May 1999. On that day the people of Scotland voted for devolution, electing the first parliament to sit in Scotland since the government of Scotland was transferred to Westminster in 1707 under the Act of Union.

Prior to the establishment of the Scottish Parliament under the Scotland Act, 1998, there was a measure of autonomy from Westminster, with the Scottish Office, under the Secretary of State for Scotland, providing various government departments in Scotland. These included local government, economic development, home affairs, law and order, education, health, housing and agriculture and fisheries. An annual allocation of funds called the 'Scottish Block' was given by Westminster, within which overall budget the Secretary of State could set his own spending priorities.

Despite this, there had long been a movement for Scottish home rule. This was given new impetus in 1928 when the Scottish National Party was set up with the aim of working towards that end. The SNP, viewed with suspicion by many, gradually became a stronger force in UK politics, and in 1974 they returned 11 MPs to Westminster, a signal to the UK government of a growing feeling within the Scottish people that the country should have greater control over its own affairs.

Legislation was put in place to establish a Scottish assembly and a referendum was held in 1979. The required majority in favour of the move failed to emerge. The movement for a measure of home rule continued, however, and another referendum was held in 1997. This time the Scottish people were overwhelmingly in favour of the establishment of a Scottish Parliament with tax-varying powers and a measure of proportional representation.

The Scottish Parliament

On 9th October 2004, the new Scottish Parliament building at Holyrood in Edinburgh was officially opened by the Queen. The construction of this building was a cause celèbre in Scotland ever since the first estimate of cost was put forward in September 1997. This initial estimate was a very conservative £40 million, and the building was expected to be completed by 2001. By the time MSPs first began to use the building in July 2004 it was over three years late and the cost had soared to over £430 million. The building was not expected to be entirely completed until 2005 with the final bill close to £500 million.

The Scottish Parliament is subordinate to Westminster and is empowered to legislate only on those matters devolved to it. These include local government, planning and economic development, criminal and civil law, criminal justice and prosecution system, police and fire services, education, health, social work and housing, environment, natural and built heritage, forestry, agriculture and fisheries, food standards, tourism, some aspects of transport, sport and the arts.

The Scottish Executive, which governs Scotland in respect of all devolved matters, comprises the First Minister, the Lord Advocate and the Solicitor-General for Scotland and other Scottish Ministers appointed by the First Minister. There are in addition junior ministers appointed to assist the Scottish Ministers.

DEPARTMENTS OF THE SCOTTISH EXECUTIVE

- Development
- Education
- Enterprise, Transport & Lifelong Learning
- Health
- Justice
- Environmental & Rural Affairs
- Finance & Central Services
- Corporate Services
- Legal & Parliamentary Services

The Scottish Parliament has a single chamber with 129 members (MSPs). 73 of these represent constituencies and are elected on a first past the post basis. An additional 56 regional members are elected on a proportional basis. The parliament has a fixed term of four years, elections normally held on the first Thursday in May. It has made a commitment to operate in an open, accessible and transparent manner, and allows public access to meetings of the parliament and most of the committees.

By November 12th 2004, the Scottish Parliament Building had seen the 100,000[th] visitor through its doors, making it well on target for its aim of attracting 780,000 visitors per year.

There are sixteen committees covering all aspects of government business, made up of MSPs from all political parties. Their role is to consider and report on policy; conduct enquiries; initiate and scrutinise primary, secondary and proposed legislation; and scrutinise Parliamentary procedures.

COMMITTEES OF THE SCOTTISH PARLIAMENT

o Audit	o Health
o Communities	o Justice I
o Education	o Justice II
o Enterprise & Culture	o Local Government & Transport
o Environment & Rural Development	o Procedures
o Equal Opportunities	o Public Petitions
o European & External Relations	o Standards
o Finance	o Subordinate Legislation

In relation to all devolved matters, the Scottish Parliament can pass primary legislation (Acts of the Scottish Parliament) and Scottish Ministers can in addition make secondary legislation.

Relationship with the UK Government
Westminster retains control over a range of reserved matters, including the constitution, foreign affairs, defence, financial and economic matters, social security, employment, equal opportunities, and the civil service.

The Secretary of State for Scotland is a member of the UK Government and is not a member of the Scottish Executive. The Scottish Secretary's main role is to represent Scotland's interests in respect of reserved matters.

In addition to MSPs, Scotland still elects representatives to Westminster (MPs), currently in 72 constituencies.

A system of non-statutory agreements, called concordats, aims to ensure good working relationships and communications between the Scottish Executive and the UK Government.

Political Parties
The main political parties are the Scottish Conservative Party, the Scottish Green Party, the Scottish Labour Party, the Scottish Liberal Democrats, the Scottish National Party (SNP) and the Scottish Socialist Party.

The make-up of the Scottish Parliament after the election in May 2003 was as follows:

Party	Constituency MSPs	Regional MSPs	Total
Labour	46	4	50
SNP	9	18	27
Conservative	3	15	18
Liberal Democrats	13	4	17
Green	0	7	7
Scottish Socialist	0	6	6
Scottish Senior Citizens Unity Party	0	11	
Independent	2	1	3
Total	73	56	129

Source: *Whitaker's Scottish Almanack* , *4th edition A&C Black*

The European Parliament

Scotland constitutes a region with eight members (MEPs) within the European Parliament. After the election of June 1999 these comprised three Labour, two Conservative, two SNP and one Liberal Democrat. European Parliament elections take place every five years.

Relations with the European Union are a reserved matter, so it is the UK Government that represents Scottish interests in the European Council of Ministers. This is the case even with those matters which are devolved to the Scottish Parliament within the UK – farming and fishing, for example. The Scottish Parliament and Executive have a responsibility, therefore, to scrutinise EU proposals to ensure Scotland's interests are taken into consideration in these areas.

Economy

Scotland's economic standing is below average compared to that in the UK as a whole. In 1999, with 8.6 per cent of the UK population, Scotland accounted for 8.5 per cent of total UK employment and 8.3 per cent of UK gross domestic product (GDP). GDP per head was £12,512 compared with £12,972 for the UK, or 96.5 per cent. The gap between Scotland and the rest of UK is increasing: in 1996, Scotland had the third highest GDP per head among UK regions, while by 1999 Scotland had fallen to fifth position.

Within these figures there are broad differences between regions within Scotland. In 1998 GDP per head was 27 per cent higher in North Eastern Scotland than in Scotland as a whole, while in the Highlands and Islands it was 23 per cent lower than average. The comparative standing of the Grampian region, however, has fallen in recent years due to the fall in north sea oil prices, with its knock-on effect on employment both directly and indirectly attributable to the oil industry. Despite this, the revenues from oil and gas are expected to continue to make a significant contribution to the Scottish economy. The picture is somewhat distorted, however, as oil and gas output from the continental shelf is treated as a separate region in the national accounts.

Scotland's economy has been characterised for many years by fluctuations in the fortunes of its regions as industries have come into prominence and declined. In the first half of the 20th century heavy industry, in particular shipbuilding, was the mainstay of Scotland's economy, but in the second half of the century a substantial restructuring has occurred.

Today service industries account for over 70 per cent of output and around 78 per cent of employee jobs. Of these, financial services such as banking and insurance have grown significantly in recent years. Inward investment has, over a similar period, stimulated rapid growth in the hi-tech electronics and IT industries. At the same time agriculture and construction have both decreased in importance.

Tourism, an important sector of Scotland's economy, is 'hidden' in official statistics which do not identify tourism as an industry because areas such as food and drink, hotels and catering, for example, are not exclusively devoted to visitors to the country. However, they are heavily reliant on them. It is estimated that tourism injects over £4 billion per year into the Scottish economy and that up to 197,000 people are employed in tourism.

Scotland's economy follows the characteristic pattern of most small economies in its openness to trade. Both imports and exports are relatively more important than in the UK as a whole. The majority of Scotland's exports are to other regions of the UK, with the other main export markets being the European Union and North America. Scotland's food and drink industry is very important to the economy, with annual sales of £7.3 billion and employing over 48,000 people in more than 1,500 businesses. This sector, of course, includes Scotland's most famous export, whisky which alone accounts for 15 per cent of all Scottish manufactured exports, with Japan among the biggest buyers of the 'amber nectar'.

Outlook

Scotland is currently undergoing great structural change. It is difficult, therefore, to predict very far into the future. The longer-term picture, however, is of a significant contraction in the traditional heavy industries, while service provision will increase substantially in importance.

GEOGRAPHICAL INFORMATION

Area

Scotland, which is bordered to the south by England, comprises the mainland and many islands including the Hebrides, the Orkneys and the Shetlands. Its area is 30,420 square miles (78,789 square kilometres) of which 653 sq. miles (1,692 sq. km) are inland water. Although its population is only about one tenth of the population of England and Wales, the mainland covers over half the area of Great Britain. The greatest length of the mainland, from the Mull of Galloway to Cape Wrath, is 274 miles (441 km), compared with the total distance from Land's End to John O' Groats which is 603 miles (965 km) as the crow flies.

Mainland Scotland is divided into three basic topographical regions: the southern uplands, bordering England; the central lowlands formed by the valleys of the Clyde, the Forth and the Tay; and the northern Highlands, which are themselves divided into a northern and southern system by the Great Glen, a major geological fault running between Inverness and Fort William. The Grampian Mountains cover the southern Highland area and include the Cairngorm Mountains in the east and Ben Nevis, the highest mountain in the British Isles (1,343m) in the west.

There are 284 Scottish mountains over 3000 feet (914m) high, known as the Munros since Sir Hugh Munro listed them in 1891.

The western coast is characterised by its islands and sea lochs. The longest is Loch Fyne at 42 miles (26 km) long. The largest inland loch is Loch Lomond at 27.46 sq. miles (71.12 sq. km), while the longest and deepest is Loch Ness at 24 miles (38 km) long and 800 feet (244m) deep.

Scotland's most important river commercially is the Clyde, while the Tay, the Dee and the Spey are renowned for their salmon.

Population

The current population of Scotland is approximately 5.06 million. Edinburgh, the capital, has a population of around 448,000, while Glasgow is much larger at 577,000. The population of Scotland as a whole has fluctuated over the years, from 1.6 million at the 1801 census, to an all-time high of 5.2 million in 1971. It decreased steadily to 4.9 million in 1991 but has since shown signs of recovery. However, the trend is for the population to fall, with the projected figure for 2021 at 4.9 million. This includes a net loss in the younger age groups while the 60 plus age group shows an increase. Only between one and two per cent of the population are from ethnic groups, and these are concentrated in the Glasgow and Edinburgh areas.

First Minister Jack McConnell has said that demographic change is the greatest threat to Scotland's future prosperity. His first priority is to prevent the population falling below five million, and to that end he has introduced the 'Fresh Talent' initiative designed to encourage an additional 8,000 migrants a year between 2004 and 2009. The problem with encouraging immigration from other countries is that immigration is not, and could never easily be, a devolved matter. England and Wales are currently trying to cut down on immigration – if Scotland encourages more foreign graduates and others to stay in Scotland, there is no easy way, with open borders, to ensure they remain in Scotland and do not move elsewhere in the UK.

During 2003, it is interesting to note, Scotland's island communities recorded the highest birthrates, exceeding those in inner-city areas significantly. 251 babies were born in Shetland, giving a general fertility rate (GFR) of 61.4 per 1,000 women of child-bearing age. And in the Western Isles 255 babies were born, a GFR of 57.3. This compares with Edinburgh having 4,577 births, a GFR of 42.2, and Aberdeen having 2,003 births, a GFR of 43.1. Rural areas surrounding the cities all recorded higher rates than in the cities, which suggests that the high proportion of young students or professionals in the cities are delaying having families, while those people who want to start families prefer to move to more rural areas with gardens and a perceived better atmosphere to bring up children in. Despite these variations, Scotland's birthrate last year was still the lowest in the United Kingdom and the major cause of the nation's falling population.

Regional Divisions

Scotland's local government is currently divided into 29 unitary authorities and three Islands councils, which in 1994 replaced the previous two-tier system of nine regional and 53 district councils. Geographically, Scotland is divided into 12 larger regions: Shetland, Orkney, Western Isles, Highland, Grampian, Tayside, Fife, Lothian, Borders, Central, Strathclyde, Dumfries & Galloway. However, socially, economically and to some extent culturally, the more important divide is that between east and west. This has arisen historically through the topography of the country, with the lower, less mountainous, land on the eastern side. This has made access to the east far easier than to the west. Indeed, until relatively recently, large areas of the west coast were only accessible by sea.

Although today there are reasonable road systems throughout the west, the main road arteries run from Carlisle and Berwick-on-Tweed, in the far north of England, to Glasgow and Edinburgh, and then northwards along the A9 to Thurso. The largest clusters of population and industry are found to either side of this corridor. Only in the Glasgow area does the concentration of people reach as far as the west coast, around the Firth of Clyde.

This divide is clear from population density figures. While the population density for the whole of Scotland is around 65 people per square kilometre, the average density for the eastern and Glasgow area councils is 656, while for those on the west and the Islands the average is 41. Even in the rural, mainly agricultural areas of the east, the population is denser than in the rural areas of the west, largely due to the more accessible and fertile land. On the west and the Islands the mountainous terrain, together with the excessive cost of transporting produce to more populous areas, means that any agricultural efforts are less economically viable.

The Highland Council region is the lowest populated area in the whole of Scotland, at eight persons per square kilometre, lower even than the Western Isles at nine. The figures for Highland are distorted by the inclusion of Inverness, 'the capital of the Highlands', which is currently undergoing something of a boom in population and economy generally. As Inverness accounts for nearly one third of the total population of the Highlands, the population density for the remainder is significantly lower than eight.

The sparsity of population and low GDP per head means the Highlands and Islands has for some time qualified for European Commission structural funds. However, as this funding has to be matched pound for pound by domestic funds, the amount of European money coming into the country is dependent on political decisions. With comparatively few voters in such a large area, the perception has been in the past that the Highlands and Islands have come low down the list of government spending priorities.

Culturally, there are distinct north/south differences. This is based almost exclusively on the crofting system still extant in the northern counties. Now less important economically – few are now full-time crofters, but use it to supplement their income from other sources – culturally the traditional crofting lifestyle retains a hold. The influence of the Church is still strong, with many areas still resistant to Sunday opening of shops and other attractions. Gaelic is still spoken, to a far greater extent than elsewhere in the country. The language is strongest in the Western Isles, where at the 1991 census there were 19,546 Gaelic speakers, 68 per cent of the population. This compared with 7.4 per cent in Highland and only 1.4 per cent for Scotland as a whole. The total number of Gaelic speakers in Scotland at this time was 65,978. Full results from the 2001 census are not yet available, but overall there was an 11 per cent drop since the 1991 census, with the total number of Gaelic speakers at 58,560.

This picture is changing, however. With the loss of indigenous population and a corresponding influx of new residents from elsewhere, the influence of the Church is weakening and, despite efforts to revive the language, few young people are brought up speaking Gaelic.

The Shetland Islands only became part of Scotland in 1469, previously being part of the kingdom of Norway. The Viking heritage continues to influence the culture and traditions of Shetland today, with the residents feeling their Norse roots are as important as their Scottish connections. The local dialect is almost a language of its own, with many words finding their origins in Scandinavian languages, and Lerwick's annual fire festival 'Up Helly Aa' culminates in the burning of a full-size replica Viking longboat.

Climate

It is a common misconception that the whole of Scotland suffers from very high rainfall. In fact, although the mountainously scenic areas of the country are very wet, the Highlands have a comparable rainfall to that of the English Lake District, the Welsh Mountains and Cornwall, while Edinburgh's rainfall is similar to London's.

Scotland actually experiences far fewer thunderstorms and hailstorms than many areas of England. Edinburgh and Glasgow have about seven days with thunder annually, the Moray Firth only three or four, while many places in England have 15 to 20 days.

Scotland is generally cloudier than England, but because of the lack of pollution the country enjoys extremely good visibility. Poor visibility on the east coast and in the northern isles during April to September is frequently caused by fog coming in off the North Sea, known locally as *haar*.

Another misconception is that the whole of Scotland suffers from very severe snowy winters. In fact, although snow may lie for months on the mountains of the north east, the west coast, due to the influence of the Gulf Stream, is characterised by comparatively warm and wet winters with snow rarely lying on low ground for more than a couple of days at a time.

The difference in hours of sunshine between Scotland and England is small when areas in similar geographical locations are compared. Because of its latitude, winter days in Scotland are short, but this is more than compensated for by the long days of summer. On the longest days of the year, the north of Scotland does not go completely dark, experiencing an extended twilight.

In Great Britain, the major temperature divide is from west to east, rather than from north to south. The Gulf Stream has an influence on the seas off the west coast, making them warmer than the North Sea. This makes areas of the west coast suitable for the growth of many plants originating in far warmer regions of the world. The world-famous Inverewe Gardens at Poolewe in Wester Ross, despite being on the same latitude as parts of Greenland, is home to exotic plants from around the world, including South Africa and the Americas.

INFORMATION FACILITIES

Visit Scotland (formerly The Scottish Tourist Board) promotes the attractions of the country throughout the world. They can advise on and arrange holiday accommodation in Scotland through a countrywide network of Tourist Information Centres. Visit Scotland can be contacted at Thistle House, Beechwood Park North, Inverness, IV2 3ED; ☎01463-716996; fax 01463-717233; www.visitscotland.com.

Unitary councils in Scotland also have 'drop in' centres situated about their areas, giving advice and assistance on local council services. All councils are now on-line. A full list of websites can be found at the end of the chapter.

GETTING THERE

The UK Public Transport Information website (www.pti.org.uk) gives details of all forms of public transport available in each area.

Plane. The main airports are situated at Edinburgh, Glasgow, Aberdeen and

Inverness. Domestic and international flights operate from Edinburgh and Glasgow, or via connections at London. Aberdeen has direct flights to Scandinavia, Amsterdam and the Northern Isles, as well as to Central Scotland, the major English cities and all the London airports. Inverness flies regular services to London (Gatwick) and London (Luton), Kirkwall (Orkney) and Stornoway (Lewis).

Inverness Airport is part of Highlands and Islands Airports Ltd (HIAL) which also has airports at Barra, Benbecula, Campbeltown, Islay, Kirkwall, Stornoway, Sumbrugh, Tiree and Wick. They fly frequently between the mainland and the islands, and also operate regular inter-island services. For further details, see *Daily Life*.

Traditionally, domestic flights throughout the UK have been expensive. In recent years, low-cost airlines such as *easyJet* and *Ryanair* have introduced no-frills economy flights which have forced the larger airlines to compete, so prices are tending to fall generally. However, it is still comparatively expensive to travel between Inverness and English cities other than London, and there are large variations in price for flights to London. Generally, the longer in advance tickets are booked, the cheaper will be the price.

Sample prices for return flights in December 2004 (booked 1 month in advance)	
Inverness – Manchester	£159.20 (British Airways)
Inverness – London (Luton)	£34.48 (easyJet)
Inverness – London (Gatwick)	£92.50 (British Airways)

Train. Within Scotland, rail services are run by First Scotrail Railways, Great North Eastern Railway and Virgin Trains. However, there is a large area of the Highlands, to the north and west of the line from Kyle of Lochalsh to Thurso, where the railway has never reached and in other rural areas branch lines are scarce.

Trains between Glasgow, Edinburgh, Aberdeen and Inverness and London run from either Kings Cross or Euston. For information about train times and fares telephone the national rail enquiries service on 08457-484950 or see www.firstgroup.com/scotrail. Train tickets for all UK services can be bought on-line at www.thetrainline.com.

Scotrail run the Caledonian Sleeper service from London Euston to Glasgow, Edinburgh, Fort William, Aberdeen and Inverness. www.firstgroup.com/scotrail.

For further details of train operators and services, see *Daily Life*.

Eurostar (Eurostar House, Waterloo Station, London SE1 8SE; ☎08705-186186; www.eurostar.com) runs passenger train services linking England and Europe via the Channel Tunnel. They run from London, Waterloo and Ashford International, Kent to Paris, Brussels and Lille. There are connecting services running from Edinburgh to London. Through-tickets between Scotland and

France on Eurostar and the Caledonian Sleeper are available. ☎08457-550033. Eurostar tickets can also be purchased online through www.raileurope.co.uk.

Bus. Bus and coach services run throughout Scotland, but their availability and frequency vary greatly between areas with the least populated areas having the most restricted services. In the western Highlands and Islands it is impractical not to have access to a private car. To rely on public transport would mean one's movements would be severely curtailed. Many more or less informal 'car-sharing' schemes have grown up in these areas, to enable everybody access to essential local services. Paradoxically, it is in these areas where the private car is a lifeline that petrol and diesel are most expensive.

For long distance coach travel between the UK and Europe contact National Express. ☎08705-808080; www.nationalexpress.com. Scottish Citylink runs services in Scotland, England and Northern Ireland. ☎08705-505050; www. citylink.co.uk. For further details regarding local and national services, see *Daily Life*.

Ferries. There are a number of passenger ferry operators sailing to Great Britain from continental Europe and Ireland, including Brittany Ferries, DFDS Seaways, Fjord Line, Hoverspeed, P&O Ferries, Sea France, Stena Line. A few sail into Scottish ports, but most sail to England or Wales.

FERRY ROUTES BETWEEN BRITAIN & EUROPE

Country	Routes Available
Belgium	Hull-Zeebrugge
	Rosyth-Zeebrugge
Channel Islands	Poole-Guernsey-Jersey
	Weymouth-Guernsey-Jersey
	Portsmouth-Guernsey-Jersey
	Penzance-St Mary's
Denmark	Harwich-Esbjerg
France	Dover-Calais
	Newhaven-Dieppe
	Portsmouth-Caen/St
	Malo/Le Havre/Cherbourg
	Poole-Cherbourg/St Malo
	Plymouth-Roscoff
Germany	Harwich-Cuxhaven
Holland	Harwich-Hook of Holland
	Hull-Rotterdam

	Newcastle-Amsterdam
Irish Republic	Fishguard-Rosslare
	Pembroke-Rosslare
	Holyhead-Dublin/Dun Laoghaire
	Liverpool-Dublin
	Swansea-Cork
N. Ireland	Stranraer-Belfast
	Cairnryan-Larne
	Liverpool-Belfast
	Stranraer-Belfast
	Troon-Belfast/Larne
Norway	Newcastle-Bergen/Stavanger
	Lerwick-Bergen
	Aberdeen-Bergen
Spain	Plymouth-Santander
	Portsmouth-Bilbao
Sweden	Newcastle-Kristiansand-Gothenberg

Comprehensive details of routes and operators, plus links to ferry operators' websites are on www.seaview.co.uk.

For details of ferry services within Scotland see *Daily Life*.

USEFUL BOOKS, ADDRESSES & WEBSITES

All the books which follow should be available through Amazon at www.amazon. co.uk or from good bookshops.

Guides & Maps

The Rough Guide to Scotland (Rough Guides 2004)

Scottish Islands – Skye & The Western Isles (Vacation Work 2004)

Scottish Islands – Orkney & Shetland (Vacation Work 2004)

Collins Scotland Touring Map (Collins 2000)

Ordnance Survey Travel Maps - Roads (1:250 000 scale) Sheets 1, 2 & 3 cover Scotland.

Ordnance Survey Landranger Maps (1:50 000 scale – 2cm to 1km/1¼ inches to 1 mile) Sheets 1-85 cover Scotland. For index to specific sheets, see their website. Ordnance Survey maps can be bought online through their website www. ordnancesurvey.co.uk

General

Whitaker's Scottish Almanack 2004 (A&C Black)

Collins Encyclopaedia of Scotland, ed. John and Julia Keay (HarperCollins 2000)

The Highland Clearances, John Prebble (Penguin Books 1969)

The Scottish Nation:1700-2000, T.M. Devine (Penguin Books 2000)

Gaelic Dictionary, Malcolm Maclennan (Acair and Mercat Press 1993)

Teach Yourself Gaelic Complete Course (book and CD pack) (McGraw-Hill 2003)

Two practical cookery books with interesting narrative about food in Scotland: *A Feast of Scotland*, Janet Warren (Lomond Books 1997) and *Classic Scots Cookery*, Catherine Brown (The Angel's Share 2003)

The Malt Whisky File: The Connoisseur's Guide to Single Malt Whiskies and their Distilleries, John Lamond and Robin Tucek (Lyons Press 1997)

The Bluffer's Guide to Whisky, David Milstead (Oval Books 2000)

Scottish Literature

A Journey to the Western Isles of Scotland: The Journal of a Tour to the Hebrides, Samuel Johnson and James Boswell (Penguin Books 1993). Contains both Johnson's and Boswell's accounts of their travels in Scotland in 1773.

Leaves from a Journal of our Life in the Highlands 1848-61. Queen Victoria's only writings published in her lifetime, which appeared in 1868. An audio cassette reading from the book is available from Mr Punch Audio Books, 1996.

Kidnapped, Robert Louis Stevenson (Penguin Books 1994) Classic tale of kidnap, murder and fleeing across the Highlands.

Whit, Iain Banks (Abacus 1996) Another perspective on Scotland, from one of the most successful and prolific contemporary Scottish novelists.

The Highland Omnibus, Compton MacKenzie (Penguin Books 2000) Three classic comic novels, *The Monarch of the Glen*, *Whisky Galore* and *The Rival Monster*.

The Irvine Welsh Omnibus, (Jonathan Cape 1997). Notorious modern writer presenting an uncompromising view of the seamy side of Scottish life. Includes *Trainspotting*, *The Acid House* and *Marabou Stork Nightmares*.

The Picador Book of Contemporary Scottish Fiction, ed. Peter Kravitz (Picador 1999) Includes work from James Kelman, Alasdair Gray, Candia McWilliams, Janice Galloway, A.L. Kennedy.

Websites

Directgov: www.direct.gov.uk Links to most UK public sector websites.

Scottish Executive: www.scotland.gov.uk.

*Scottish Parliament:*www.scottish.parliament.uk.

European Union: http://europa.eu.int.

British Council: www.britishcouncil.org. Includes information about British Council schemes and links to their websites worldwide.

Hi-Ways: www.hi-ways.org. Public service information for the Highlands and Islands.

Convention of Scottish Local Authorities: www.cosla.gov.uk. Includes links to all Scottish local council websites.

There are a number of Scottish newsgroups worth visiting:
soc.culture.scottish
alt.scottish.clans
scot.general
uk.local.scot-highlands

LOCAL COUNCILS

Throughout this book, reference will be made to local council or local authority services (the two terms are interchangeable). This is the full list of contact details for all Scottish councils.

Aberdeen City Council: Town House, Broad Street, Aberdeen AB10 1FY; ☎01224-522000; fax 01224-644346; www.aberdeencity.gov.uk.

Aberdeenshire Council: Woodhill House, Westburn Road, Aberdeen AB16 5GB; ☎01467-620981; fax 01224-665444; www.aberdeenshire.gov.uk.

Angus Council: The Cross, Forfar, Angus DD8 1BX; ☎01307-461460; fax 01307-461874; www.angus.gov.uk.

Argyll and Bute Council: Kilmory, Lochgilphead, Argyll PA31 8RT; ☎01546-602127; fax 01546-604349; www.argyll-bute.gov.uk.

City of Edinburgh Council: Wellington Court, 10 Waterloo Place, Edinburgh EH1 3EG; ☎0131-200 2000; fax 0131-529 7477; www.edinburgh.gov.uk.

Clackmannanshire Council: Greenfield, Alloa, Clackmannanshire FK10 2AD; ☎01259-450000; fax 01259-452230; www.clacks.gov.uk.

Dumfries and Galloway Council: Council Offices, English Street, Dumfries DG1 2DD; ☎01387-260000; fax 01387-260034; www.dumgal.gov.uk.

Dundee City Council: 21 City Square, Dundee DD1 3BY; ☎01382-434000; fax 01382-434666; www.dundeecity.gov.uk.

East Ayrshire Council: Council Headquarters, London Road, Kilmarnock, Ayrshire KA3 7BU; ☎01563-576000; fax 01563-576500; www.east-ayrshire.gov.uk.

East Dunbartonshire Council: Tom Johnston House, Civic Way, Kirkintilloch, Glasgow G66 4TJ; ☎0141-578 8000; fax 0141-777 8576.

East Lothian Council: John Muir House, Court Street, Haddington, East Lothian EH41 3HA; ☎01620-827827; fax 01620-827888; www.eastlothian.gov.uk.

East Renfrewshire Council: Council Offices, Eastwood Park, Rouken Glen Road, Giffnock G46 6UG; ☎0141-577 3000; fax 0141-620 0884; www.eastrenfrewshire.gov.uk.

Comhairle nan Eilean Siar/Western Isles Council: Council Offices, Sandwick Road, Stornoway, Isle of Lewis HS1 2BW; ☎01851-703773; fax 01851-705349; www.cne-siar.gov.uk.

Falkirk Council: Municipal Buildings, West Bridge Street, Falkirk FK1 5RS; ☎01324-506070; fax 01324-506071; www.falkirk.gov.uk.

Fife Council: Fife House, North Street, Glenrothes, Fife KY7 5LT; ☎01592-414141; fax 01592-414142; www.fife.gov.uk.

Glasgow City Council: City Chambers, George Square, Glasgow G2 1DU; ☎0141-287 2000; fax 0141-287 5666; www.glasgow.gov.uk.

Highland Council: Glenurquhart Road, Inverness IV3 5NX; ☎01463-702000; fax 01463-702111; www.highland.gov.uk.

Inverclyde Council: Municipal Buildings, Clyde Square, Greenock, Renfrewshire PA15 1LY; ☎01475-717171; fax 01475-712731; www.inverclyde.gov.uk.

Midlothian Council: Midlothian House, 40-46 Buccleuch Street, Dalkeith, Midlothian EH22 1DJ; ☎0131-271 7500; fax 0131-271 3050; www.midlothian.gov.uk.

Moray Council: Council Office, High Street, Elgin, Morayshire IV30 1BX; ☎01343-543451; fax 01343-540399; www.moray.org.

North Ayrshire Council: Cunninghame House, Irvine, Ayrshire KA12 8EE; ☎01294-324100; fax 01294-324144; www.northayrshire.gov.uk.

North Lanarkshire Council: PO Box 14, Civic Centre, Motherwell, Lanarkshire ML1 1TW; ☎01698-302222; fax 01698-275125; www.northlan.gov.uk.

Orkney Islands Council: Council Offices, School Place, Kirkwall, Orkney KW15 1NY; ☎01856-873535; fax 01856-874615; www.orkney.com.

Perth and Kinross Council: 2 High Street, Perth PH1 5PH; ☎01738-475000; fax 01738-475710; www.pkc.gov.uk.

Renfrewshire Council: Council Headquarters, North Building, Cotton Street, Paisley PA1 1BU; ☎0141-842 5000; fax 0141-840 3335; www.renfrewshire.gov.uk.

Scottish Borders Council: Council Headquarters, Newtown St Boswells, Melrose, Roxburghshire TD6 0SA; ☎01835-824000; fax 01835-825142.

Shetland Islands Council: Town Hall, Hillhead, Lerwick, Shetland ZE1 0HB; ☎01595-693535; fax 01595-744509; www.shetland.gov.uk.

South Ayrshire Council: County Buildings, Wellington Square, Ayr KA7 1DR; ☎01292-612000; fax 01292-612143; www.south-ayrshire.gov.uk.

South Lanarkshire Council: Council Offices, Almada Street, Hamilton, Lanarkshire ML3 0AA; ☎01698-454444; fax 01698-454275; www.southlanarkshire.gov.uk.

Stirling Council: Viewforth, Stirling FK8 2ET; ☎0845-277700; fax 01786-443078; www.stirling.gov.uk.

West Dunbartonshire Council: Garshake Road, Dumbarton G82 3PU; ☎01389-737000; fax 01389-737700; www.west-dunbarton.gov.uk.

West Lothian Council: West Lothian House, Almondvale Boulevard, Livingston, West Lothian EH54 6QC; ☎01506-777000; fax 01506-775099; www.wlonline.org.uk.

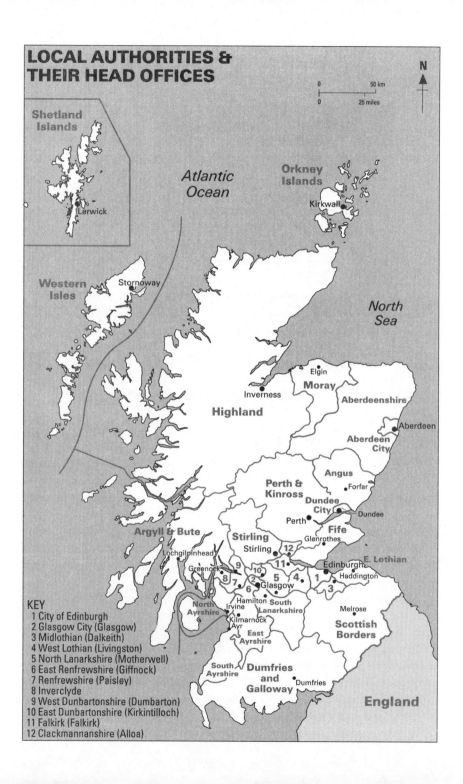

LOCAL AUTHORITIES & THEIR HEAD OFFICES

N

0   50 km
0   25 miles

Shetland Islands

Lerwick

Atlantic Ocean

Orkney Islands

Kirkwall

Western Isles

Stornoway

North Sea

Elgin

Inverness

Moray

Aberdeenshire

Highland

Aberdeen

Aberdeen City

Angus

Perth & Kinross

Forfar

Dundee City

Dundee

Perth

Fife

Argyll & Bute

Stirling

Stirling

Glenrothes

Lochgilphead

Greenock

12

11

Edinburgh

E. Lothian

9

10

Haddington

8 7

2

5   4   1

6

Glasgow

3

Hamilton

Melrose

North Ayrshire

Irvine

South Lanarkshire

Kilmarnock

Ayr

East Ayrshire

Scottish Borders

South Ayrshire

Dumfries and Galloway

Dumfries

England

KEY
1 City of Edinburgh
2 Glasgow City (Glasgow)
3 Midlothian (Dalkeith)
4 West Lothian (Livingston)
5 North Lanarkshire (Motherwell)
6 East Renfrewshire (Giffnock)
7 Renfrewshire (Paisley)
8 Inverclyde
9 West Dunbartonshire (Dumbarton)
10 East Dunbartonshire (Kirkintilloch)
11 Falkirk (Falkirk)
12 Clackmannanshire (Alloa)

RESIDENCE AND ENTRY REGULATIONS

CHAPTER SUMMARY

- Immigration rules are consistent across the whole of the United Kingdom.
- Immigration to the UK is on the increase.
- Nationals of countries in the European Economic Area have a right to live and work in the UK.
- Many Commonwealth citizens with British ancestry have a right of abode in the UK.
- Nationals from USA may have difficulty gaining the right to live and work in the UK.
- You may need a visa or a work permit before you can enter the UK.
- Scotland's universities welcome overseas students.

THE CURRENT POSITION

The following comments necessarily relate to the UK as a whole. Separate statistics regarding entry to Scotland are fairly meaningless because, once you have gained admittance to the UK, residence in its different countries is, of course, unrestricted.

All overseas nationals who wish to enter the UK must satisfy the Immigration Officer at the point of arrival that they meet the requirements of the UK Immigration Rules. These rules allow or deny entry under a number of different categories and for varying lengths of stay.

Since the Maastricht Treaty was signed in 1993, nationals of the European Economic Area (EEA), which comprises the member states of the European Union plus Iceland, Norway and Liechtenstein, have a right to live and work in the United Kingdom. Other visitors need to obtain entry clearance in the form of a visa or an entry certificate before they can gain admission. However, there are different rules for those who can claim British Citizenship or other connection with the UK, such as by ancestry. In addition, those intending to work in the UK may need to obtain a work permit.

There is currently an upward trend in most categories of entry to the UK, a recovery from a period when entry figures fell. 139,675 people were granted settlement in 2003, 20 per cent more than in 2002. 21 per cent of those granted settlement originated from the Indian sub-continent, 18 per cent from the rest of Asia, 32 per cent from Africa, 12 per cent from the Americas, 11 per cent from Europe and 5 per cent from Oceania. This figure will inevitably underestimate the number of permanent residents from Europe, because there is no legal requirement for EEA nationals to apply for settlement, so the figure for Europe includes only those from outside the EEA plus those EEA nationals who chose to apply for formal settlement.

In 2003 the total number of admissions of work permit holders and their dependants was 119,180,935 (1 per cent) less than in 2002. However, in 1999 only 76,000 were granted work permits, so despite what may be a temporary small fall, the overall trend over recent years is upward. In addition, 83,990 extensions of stay from work permit holders or trainees were also granted in 2003, 22,905 more than in 2002. Persons from the Americas accounted for 25 per cent of the total of new work permit holders, while 15 per cent were from Europe, 12 per cent from Africa, 21 per cent from the Indian sub-continent, 21 per cent from the rest of Asia and 6 per cent from Oceania. Of the total number, 44,480 came for 12 months or more, 36,870 came for less than 12 months, and 37,830 were dependants.

The latest accurate figures for the ethnic make up of the population of Scotland come from the 2001 census. At that time, 98 per cent of the population was classified as white, with Pakistanis being the next highest ethnic group identified, at 0.3 per cent of the population. Scotland has a much higher proportion of white residents than the rest of Britain, with most non-white groups clustered in the cities of southern Scotland. It is rare to see a non-white face in the Highlands.

At the 2001 census 87 per cent of the population were born in Scotland. Of the rest, the largest group were, perhaps not surprisingly, born in England. These numbered 408,948, 8 per cent of the total population of 5,062,011.

UK IMMIGRATION RULES

The Right of Abode

Those with the right of abode are completely free from UK immigration control and do not need to have their passports stamped by an immigration officer on entry to the UK. They may also live and work there without restriction.

All British citizens have the right of abode and can apply for a British Passport, possession of which will be sufficient proof of their right of abode.

Commonwealth citizens with a parent who was at the time of their birth a citizen of the UK and Colonies by dint of being born in the UK, and those whose husbands have the right of abode, may also have the right of abode.

> **The following countries are members of the British Commonwealth:**
> Antigua and Barbuda, Australia, Bahamas, Bangladesh, Belize, Brunei, Cameroon, Canada, Cyprus, Dominica, The Gambia, Ghana, Grenada, India, Jamaica, Kenya, Kiribati, Malaysia, Malawi, Maldives, Malta, Mauritius, Mozambique, Namibia, Nauru, New Zealand, Nigeria, Pakistan, Papua New Guinea, Saint Kitts and Nevis, Saint Lucia, Saint Vincent and the Grenadines, Seychelles, Sierra Leone, Solomon Islands, South Africa, Sri Lanka, Swaziland, Tanzania, Tonga, Trinidad and Tobago, Tuvalu, Uganda, Vanuatu, Western Samoa, Zambia, Zimbabwe.

Nigeria's membership of the Commonwealth was suspended in 1995 because of the country's human rights abuses, but the country was reinstated in 1999 following its election of a democratic government.

In order to prove you have the right of abode, you may apply for a Certificate of Entitlement. This may be applied for by Commonwealth citizens who satisfy the above conditions, and by those British Citizens who are travelling on a foreign or Commonwealth passport. Application forms are available from any British mission (Embassy or Consulate) offering a visa service. There is a non-refundable fee payable.

Entry for EEA Nationals

> The European Economic Area comprises the EU countries, viz. Austria, Belgium, Cyprus, Czech Republic, Denmark, Estonia, Finland, France, Germany, Greece, Hungary, Ireland, Italy, Latvia, Luxembourg, Malta, Netherlands, Poland, Portugal, Slovakia, Slovenia, Spain, Sweden and the UK. In addition it includes Iceland, Liechtenstein and Norway. Since 1st June 2002, Swiss nationals have had the same rights as EEA nationals.

Nationals of these countries have a right of residence (i.e. a right to live and work) in the UK if they are working in the UK or if they are not economically active in the UK but do have sufficient funds to support themselves during their stay without needing financial assistance from UK public funds such as income support, housing benefit, council tax benefit, family credit, job seeker's allowance, attendance allowance, severe disablement allowance, invalid care allowance, disability living allowance and disability working allowance.

Ten new states joined the EU on 1st May 2004. There us a requirement for nationals of the following new member states to register with the Home Office and obtain a workers registration certificate: Czech Republic, Poland, Lithuania, Estonia, Latvia, Slovenia, Slovakia, Hungary. Nationals from Malta and Cyprus have full free movement rights and are not required to obtain a workers registration certificate.

Individuals must register under the scheme as soon as they start work in the UK. They must complete an application form and send it together with a copy of a letter from their employer confirming their employment; two photographs; a valid passport/ID card; payment of £50 to: Worker Registration Team, Home Office, Walsall Road, Cannock WS11 0WS. The application form is available on the internet at www.workingintheuk.gov.uk/working_in_the_uk/en/documents/all – forms.html.

Family members, including one's spouse, dependent children or grandchildren, and dependent parents or grandparents who are also EEA nationals have the same right of residence. Family members who are not EEA nationals need to obtain a visa or an EEA family permit, before entering the UK.

> **Rainer Thonnes, the son of a diplomat, came to Scotland aged 18 in the 1970s**
> *Diplomatic status had its advantages, of course, and I'm not sure how easy it would have been without it in those days. All this business about equal rights for EEC nationals was just starting then, but today there should be no difficulties whatever in that respect for nationals of EU member states, though it's more difficult for non-EU Europeans and for Americans.*

An EEA family permit can be obtained from the British mission in the country where you are living. The application must be supported by your passport, two recent passport-sized photographs, your family member's passport plus proof of the relationship between you and your family member such as a marriage certificate or birth certificate.

After entry to the UK, the family member may obtain confirmation of their right to reside from the Home Office, Immigration and Nationality Directorate, Lunar House, 40 Wellesley Road, Croydon CR9 2BY. If everything is in order they will be issued a residence document, normally valid for five years.

Entry for US Citizens and Non EEA Nationals

The general position under the Immigration Rules is that overseas nationals (other than EEA nationals) coming to work in Britain must have work permits before setting out. The employer (**not** the employee) has to apply to Work Permits (UK), which administers the scheme. Permits are issued only for specific jobs requiring a high level of skill and experience for which resident or EEA labour is not available. In other words, a UK employer will not receive a work permit for a non-EEA citizen unless it is a job for which there is no EEA National available.

In 2003 Work Permits (UK) introduced a new low-skilled work permit scheme. The Sectors Based Scheme (SBS) operates in the food manufacturing sectors (fish, meat and mushroom processing) and the hospitality sectors (hotel and catering). The scheme operates in the same way as the existing work permit arrangements. A limited number of permits are available where employers can show that they have been unable to recruit resident workers in certain posts, which are below NVQ level 3. Individuals employed under this scheme must be aged between 18 and 30. Again, it is the employer and **not** the employee who is responsible for obtaining the appropriate documentation. Further details about the SBS are available at www.workpermits.gov.uk, and any queries should be directed to Work Permits (UK)'s Customer Relations Team on 0114-259 4074.

Entry Clearance

An entry clearance is a visa or an entry certificate issued to a passenger prior to travel to the UK. A person who has an entry clearance will not be refused admission as long as there has not been a material change of circumstances since the entry clearance was obtained.

Holders of entry clearances may be refused entry if they have a criminal record or if they are subject to a deportation order. They may also be refused entry on medical grounds. With few exceptions, visitors to the UK are not entitled to free medical treatment and a charge will be made for any treatment received. Visitors should make sure they have adequate medical insurance to cover their stay.

Application for entry clearance should be made through the British Mission in the country in which the applicant is living, or through the Immigration & Nationality Directorate website www.ind.homeoffice.gov.uk. Downloadable leaflets and application forms on all aspects of visa information are available on that site.

It should be noted that in all cases, long or short term visitors to the UK must be able to support and accommodate themselves in the UK without recourse to public funds.

It is advisable to allow two to three months for a visa or work permit to be approved.

British Visas

Nationals of the following countries or territories must have a visa to enter the UK:
Afghanistan, Albania, Algeria, Angola, Armenia, Azerbaijan, Bahrain, Bangladesh, Belarus, Benin, Bhutan, Bosnia-Herzegovina, Bulgaria, Burkina Faso, Burma, Burundi, Cambodia, Cameroon, Cape Verde, Central African Republic, Chad, China, Colombia, Comoros, Congo, Croatia, Cuba, Djibouti, Dominican Republic, Ecuador, Egypt, Equatorial Guinea, Eritrea, Ethiopia, Fiji, Gabon, Gambia, Georgia, Ghana, Guinea, Guinea Bissau, Guyana, Haiti, India, Indonesia, Iran, Iraq, Ivory Coast, Jamaica, Jordan, Kazakhstan, Kenya, North Korea, Kuwait, Kyrgyzstan, Laos, Lebanon, Liberia, Libya, Macedonia, Madagascar, Mali, Mauritania, Moldova, Mongolia, Morocco, Mozambique, Nepal, Niger, Nigeria, Oman, Pakistan, Peru, Philippines, Qatar, Romania, Russia, Rwanda, Sao Tome & Principe, Saudi Arabia, Senegal, Sierra Leone, Somalia, Sri Lanka, Sudan, Surinam, Syria, Taiwan, Tajikistan, Tanzania, Thailand, Togo, Tunisia, Turkey, Turkmenistan, Uganda,

> **Ukraine, United Arab Emirates, Uzbekistan, Vietnam, Yemen, Yugoslavia, Zambia, Zimbabwe.**
> People from these countries are known as visa nationals.

In addition, the following also need visas: persons who hold passports or travel documents issued by the former Soviet Union or the former Socialist Federal Republic of Yugoslavia; stateless persons; persons who hold non-national documents.

If entering as a visitor, you must show that you are able to support and accommodate yourself without working in the UK. This support and accommodation may be provided by family and friends in the UK but not from public funds. A visitor is not allowed to work in the UK, but may conduct business, and must intend to leave the UK after a maximum stay of six months.

Nationals of any other country do not need a UK visa for a visit or to study but must obtain a visa or an entry certificate if they wish to settle, work or set up a business in the UK. There is a fee payable.

Students

In 1999, the UK Prime Minister Tony Blair announced the start of a world-wide campaign to attract more international students to the UK. As part of this, certain changes in visa and work rules were introduced, to the benefit of students.

You may enter the UK for study or training as long as you can support and accommodate yourself and pay for your studies without recourse to public funds. Students will be given leave to enter and remain in the UK for the full length of their studies, unless there is a specific reason why they should not stay so long. Previously, students had to apply annually to the Home Office for an extension to remain in the UK.

Students whose studies in the UK are longer than six months can work up to 20 hours per week during term time and full-time in vacations. Students whose studies involve a period of work placements, as in a sandwich course, do not need to obtain a work permit. The income from part time work provided and guaranteed by a publicly-funded institution of further or higher education in the UK at which you are studying may be taken into account when assessing your financial means.

Any course of study followed should occupy at least fifteen hours per week of organised daytime study and the student must intend to leave the UK on completion of their studies. When applying for entry clearance a letter from the educational establishment confirming acceptance on the course of study must be provided.

> **Sam White found no difficulty coming from the US to study at St Andrews University**
> *Immigration was pretty easy, but it's important to bring written proof of your*

acceptance to university and financial details proving you can pay your own way without taking full-time employment. I received a one-year visa to start with, extended to a four-year visa the next year. None of the other Americans I have talked to have reported any difficulties passing immigration.

Settling in the UK

There is no requirement to apply for settlement if you can claim British Citizenship or other connection with the UK, by ancestry, for example, nor if you are a national of another member state of the EEA.

Those who may apply for settlement from other countries are certain family members of a person who is already settled in the UK. These include their husband, wife or unmarried partner (including same sex partner); fiancé(e); children; parents, grandparents or other relatives dependent on them. There are different rules for these different family members. For instance, a husband or wife will be allowed to stay in the UK and work for one year initially, at the end of which time they may apply to stay in the UK permanently, whereas a fiancé (e) will only be allowed initially to stay for six months without working and may only apply to stay for a longer period once he/she is married. Children will not normally be allowed to settle in the UK while one parent lives abroad.

Special concessions outside the Immigration Rules have been made to allow overseas nationals to settle in the UK as a common law spouse or homosexual partner, where it can be shown that the couple are legally unable to marry under UK law and have been living together in a relationship akin to marriage for two years or more.

Commonwealth Citizens

Commonwealth citizens with a grandparent born in the UK, Channel Islands or the Isle of Man qualify for UK ancestry. If they can show they are able to work and intend to seek work in the UK they will be granted entry for a period of four years and will not need a work permit.

Entry as an Employee

There are various categories of people entering the UK as an employee who do not need a work permit. These are EEA nationals, Commonwealth citizens with a grandparent born in the UK and Islands (see above) and those whose employment falls into one of the following categories: a working holidaymaker or au pair; a Minister of Religion, a missionary or a member of a religious order; the representative of a firm with no representative in the UK; a representative of a an overseas newspaper, news agency or broadcasting organisation on long term assignment to the UK; a domestic worker of a member of the staff of a diplomatic or consular mission; a domestic worker in a private household; a teacher or language assistant coming to a UK school under an exchange scheme; a member of the operational ground staff of an overseas airline; a postgraduate doctor or dentist coming for training; a seasonal worker at an agricultural camp.

US students seeking temporary work in the UK can benefit from the 'Work in Britain Program'. This allows full-time college students and recent graduates over the age of 18 to look for work in Britain, finding jobs through BUNAC listings or through personal contacts. Jobs may be pre-arranged, though most participants wait until arrival in Britain to job hunt. US students on study abroad programmes through an American University overseas are also eligible for the programme. To qualify for the scheme, students must first obtain a BUNAC 'Blue Card' recognised by the British Home Office as a valid substitute for a work permit. The Blue Card must be presented to immigration on arrival in the UK. It is valid for six months and cannot be extended, although it is possible to obtain a second Blue Card in another calendar year if they again fulfil the eligibility requirements. The Blue Card costs $250 from BUNAC, PO Box 430, Southbury, CT 06488 ((1-800 GO BUNAC; e-mail wib@bunacusa.org; www.bunac.org).

All other intending employees will need a work permit, which must be applied for on their behalf by their intended employer in the UK. Your work permit must be obtained before travel to the UK or you will be refused entry. Visa nationals need a visa in addition to a work permit, and the visa cannot be issued until they have a work permit to show to the visa officer.

For further information on work permits, see *Employment*.

Entry as Self-Employed

Visitors to the UK are free to transact business during their stay. You may come to the UK permanently to set yourself up in business or self-employment, or to join as a partner or take over an existing business, if you satisfy the following requirements. You must bring at least £200,000 of your own money to invest in the business and your investment must create new, paid, full-time employment for at least two people who are already settled in the UK. In addition you must show that there is a genuine need for the services you will be offering.

Writers, artists and composers who intend to support themselves by self-employment in their field may be admitted to the UK as long as they can satisfy the immigration authorities that they are bona fide and have a proven track record in their field in the country in which they have been living.

The Innovator Scheme, originally introduced as a two year pilot scheme from September 2000-2002, has now become permanent. It is aimed at those who have a new business idea that will bring considerable economic benefits to the UK, particularly in the areas of information technology and telecommunications. To apply under the scheme you must have a business idea that is new and innovative; you must bring exceptional economic benefit to the UK; you must have sufficient funding in place or agreed in principle to establish the business; you must create employment for at least two people; you must have significant business experience; you must maintain at least a 5 per cent shareholding of the equity capital in the business.

If you are a citizen of Bulgaria or Romania it may be possible to enter the UK and establish yourself in business under the EC Association Agreement. The requirements under this agreement are less onerous than under others. You need to show that you will be the owner, or have a controlling interest, in the business, and will be actively involved in trading or providing services on your own account or in partnership in the UK.

Investors

If you intend to come to the UK as an investor, you must have documentary evidence to show that you have capital of at least £1 million and that you intend to invest not less than £750,000 in approved UK government bonds or companies. The UK must become your main home.

Useful Address

UK Trade & Investment, operating through the commercial sections of British Embassies, High Commissions and Consulates-general, can assist firms with all aspects of locating or relocating a business in the UK or expanding existing facilities. UK trade & Investment Enquiry Service, Kingsgate House, 66-74 Victoria Street, London, SW1E 6SW; ☎020-7215 8000; www.uktradeinvest. gov.uk/ukti/appmanager/ukti/home.

Retired Persons

Retired persons of at least 60 years of age must be able to show that they have an annual income of at least £25,000 which must be disposable in the UK. You must be able to support and accommodate yourself and any dependants indefinitely without working, without assistance from anyone else and without recourse to public funds.

In addition to the financial requirements you will also need to show that you have a close connection with the UK.

Sponsors

Visitors intending a limited stay in the UK may get a sponsor within the UK who will provide their support and accommodation during their stay. A sponsor may be in receipt of public funds, but must not seek additional public funds to support the foreign visitor. The period for which the visitor is admitted is at the discretion of the Immigration Officer and will normally be for six months.

Working Holidaymakers

The working holidaymaker scheme allows young Commonwealth citizens the opportunity to come to the UK for an extended holiday which they may help fund by working in the UK for up to a maximum of two years. To qualify you must be a Commonwealth citizen, be aged 17 to 30 inclusive and either be unmarried, or married to a working holidaymaker who is taking the holiday with you.

During the period of stay, you may take employment incidental to a holiday but not engage in business or pursue a career in the UK. A working holidaymaker may engage in some part-time study and short periods of full-time study while in the UK.

Council Exchanges and BUNAC run schemes which allow US and other citizens to work in Britain for limited periods. See *Entry As An Employee* above.

Au Pairs

The au pair scheme allows single people to learn English by living with an English speaking family. In return for working in the home the au pair must be given a reasonable allowance and two days off each week.

To qualify as an au pair you must be aged between 17 and 27, be unmarried and have no dependants, be taking up a pre-arranged placement and be a national of the EEA or one of the following countries: Andorra, Bosnia-Herzegovina, Bulgaria, Croatia, The Faroes, Greenland, Macedonia, Monaco, San Marino, Turkey.

The maximum time you may stay as an au pair is two years.

British Citizenship

Anyone who does not automatically qualify for British citizenship may apply, if over the age of 18, to become a British citizen. This process is also called naturalisation. To qualify the applicant must have lived legally in Britain for at least five years without being absent for more than 450 days and with less than 90 days absence in the year preceding the application. In addition the applicant must intend to continue living in Britain, have a good knowledge of English, Welsh or Gaelic and have no criminal record.

Anyone over 18 and married to a British citizen may apply for naturalisation if they have lived in Britain legally for at least three years without being absent for more than 270 days.

It is not necessary to give up your original nationality as you may have dual nationality under British law.

Entry Clearance Fees

Fees vary depending on the length of your proposed stay and the category under which you enter the UK. At time of writing they vary between £22 and £260, and are subject to periodical review and amendment. For a full list and latest fee schedule see www.skillclear.co.uk/services_pricing.asp. Entry fees are payable in the local currency of the country in which you are currently residing, so contact your nearest British mission, embassy or consulate for the fee currently charged. These are listed on the Foreign & Commonwealth Office website: www.fco.gov.uk.

Arrival In Britain

Even if you have all the necessary visas and entry clearances for you and your family before arrival in Britain, you will still have to satisfy an Immigration Officer that you are entitled to enter Britain under whichever category of the rules you applied to enter. You must present your passport together with whichever of the following are applicable: your visa or entry clearance; a work permit; a completed landing card if you are a non-EU national (this can be obtained or will be handed to you on the plane, ship or ferry bringing you to Britain); a letter from a bona fide educational establishment confirming you have been accepted on a course of study; a letter stating you have been offered work as an au pair, trainee or voluntary worker; evidence that your qualifications are adequate for such a job or course of study; evidence that you will be able to support yourself and your dependants during your stay without recourse to public funds. Acceptable evidence includes such things as a bank statement or letter from a bank, cash, travellers cheques and credits cards; if your stay is for a limited period you may have to confirm that you will leave at the end of that period.

If you leave Britain during your period of stay, you will be required to produce the same documents before you are readmitted to the country. EU nationals are given a form on arrival in Britain which they must produce if they stay for longer than six months. If entering from some countries you may need to have immunisation certificates. The requirements will be explained in your country of origin.

The Immigration Officer can send new arrivals for a routine heath check before allowing them to have their passport stamped, permitting entry to Britain.

If you are refused entry into Britain, as long as you have entry clearance such as a visa, entry certificate, letter of consent or work permit, you cannot be sent immediately back to your home country. You can appeal to an independent adjudicator and will be allowed to remain in Britain until the appeal has been heard. Appeals can take several months to be heard, so if you entered Britain for work or study it may be sensible to continue with your plans, although any long-term commitments, especially those involving substantial financial outlay or the signing of a binding contract – say, a long term lease on a property – would be unwise in case you lose your appeal.

If you arrive in Britain without entry clearance you will either be sent home immediately or will be given temporary admission of between 24 hours and a week or more while a final decision is made. This period allows you to gather any evidence you need to support your application to stay. If you are refused temporary admission you will be kept in an immigration detention centre or may be allowed to stay in private accommodation, until you can be deported.

If you are granted temporary admission you must surrender your passport, provide the immigration officer with an address where you will be staying, and will be told to report back to immigration at a certain date and time.

Useful Addresses
If you are refused entry to Britain, contact the Immigration Advisory Service (IAS), 3rd Floor, County House, 190 Great Dover Street, London, SE1 4YB; ☎020-7967 1200. Students may also contact UKCOSA: The Council for International Education, 9-17 St. Albans Place, Islington, London, N1 0NX; ☎020-7288 4330; fax 020-7288 4360; www.ukcosa.org.uk.

Asylum Seekers and Refugees
Refugee status will be granted if you can prove that you have a 'well-founded fear of persecution in your own country for reasons of race, religion, nationality, membership of a particular social group or political opinion'. Each case is considered on its own merits, a process which can take months. You are then entitled to appeal, which can take further months.

In recent years it has been recognised that is something of a 'refugee crisis' in the UK concerning the processing of applications for asylum. Measures have therefore been taken to cut down the number of asylum seekers and to speed up the process of hearing cases. Figures for 2003 indicate that these measures have had some effect: applications for asylum fell by 41 per cent to 49,405. To put this in context, the figure for 1999 was over 60,000, which easily beat the previous record figure of 48,000 in 1998.

USEFUL ADDRESSES AND WEBSITES
For immigration, citizenship and nationality enquiries: *Immigration and Nationality Directorate:* Lunar House, 40 Wellesley Road, Croydon CR9 2BY; ☎0870-606 7766 (Mon-Fri 9am-4.30pm); www.ind.homeoffice.gov.uk/ind/en/home/html.

Immigration Advisory Service (IAS): County House, 190 Great Dover Street, London SE1 4YB; ☎020-7967 1200; fax 020-7403 5875; www.iasuk.org.

Immigration Appellate Authority (IAA): The Arnhem Support Centre, PO Box 6987, Leicester LE1 6ZX; ☎0845-6000 877; www.iaa.gov.uk.

There are British Consulates and British Missions around the globe, far too many to list here. For a full list see www.fco.gov.uk and follow the link under Directory/UK Embassies Overseas or contact *Foreign and Commonwealth Office:* Consular Division, King Charles Street, London SW1A 2AH; ☎020-7008 1500.

Detailed information and advice on UK immigration, visas and work permits, www.workpermit.com.

Cooper Tuff Consultants: 146 Buckingham Palace Road, London SW1W 9TR; ☎0870-990 9480; fax 0870-990 9483; www.uk-immigration.co.uk.

SETTING UP HOME

CHAPTER SUMMARY

○ **Housing.** Home ownership in Scotland is rising and about 64% of Scots own their own homes.
  ○ Two-thirds of people in Scotland live in houses, one-third in flats.
  ○ The average house price in Scotland in 2004 was £107,377 compared to £177,023 in England.
○ **Crofting.** The crofting system is unique to Scotland.
  ○ There are around 17,700 crofts in the Highlands, occupied by an estimated 10,000-12,000 households with a total population of around 33,000.
○ **Housebuying.** Mortgages can be obtained for up to 95% of the value of a property.
  ○ When buying a property, you must use the services of a Scottish solicitor.
  ○ The Scottish legal system and the process of housebuying are different in Scotland from the rest of the UK.
  ○ VAT is not charged on the costs of building a new house.
○ Many rural areas do not have mains sewerage or piped gas.
○ Pets may travel between the UK and Europe on a Pets Passport.

One of the major concerns for people wishing to move to a new area is finding a new home. In Scotland, there is the usual choice: private rented; local authority and housing association rented; purchased ready built property; and new build on a purchased plot.

In Scotland as a whole accommodation accounts on average for around 20 per cent of a family's budget, with households or individuals living in rented accommodation spending around 23 percent of their income on housing costs, while mortgage payers spend only 15 percent, so buying is the cheapest option in the long run. These averages, however, hide a large variation in price depending on the area in which one lives. House prices and rentals are higher in Glasgow and

Edinburgh, for instance, than in the Highlands, but this may be offset by other items of the family budget, such as transport and fuel costs, being lower in the more populous areas where competition drives prices down.

The amount of property available to buy or rent varies depending on the area. Although it is accepted that there is a shortage of houses in various parts of Scotland, this refers in the main to low-cost 'social' housing provided by councils or housing associations. The picture is different for private houses, and can fluctuate quite significantly from area to area, and from time to time.

> **The author bought a house in the north west Highlands in 1994**
> *The house, like others we looked at in the area, had been on the market for a long time – over two years, in fact. Since we moved here, there has been a noticeable improvement in the speed of turnover of properties, with most selling fairly quickly. The demand to move to the Highlands has grown significantly in the last ten years, as more people are attracted by moving away from over-crowded urban areas and find that new technology makes it easier for them to continue to earn a living in remote areas. This reached a peak by 2003 when there was a shortage of houses and land for sale, and any houses that did come on the market were snapped up within a couple of weeks, at prices well over the asking price. Now, in late 2004, there are signs that property is taking longer to sell again.*

Home ownership in Scotland is rising, and currently is around 64 per cent, catching up with England and Wales at 70 per cent. The United Kingdom as a whole comes third in the league table of European countries, after Ireland and Italy. Germany and France have lower levels of home ownership at 43 per cent and 54 per cent respectively, while in the United States, 65 per cent own their homes.

There is plenty of property available to rent in urban areas, less in rural areas. However, because of the large number of self-catering holiday cottages in the countryside, it is often possible to negotiate with holiday cottage owners a temporary long term let of up to six months during the off-season.

There was an unprecedented boom in the UK house market during the 1980s, culminating in house prices rising by 30 per cent during 1988. By the early to mid-nineties, house prices were, in contrast, falling rapidly in real terms. By the end of the nineties, prices were starting to rise again. At time of writing in 2004, after a period of rising prices and a large volume of house sales across the UK, prices seem to have peaked and are now levelling out, largely due to interest rate rises. Experts are divided as to whether house prices will fall significantly – at present they are simply rising at a lower rate – but it is generally agreed that there is most unlikely to be another crash. Most experts are predicting that the house market will 'calm down' to a more sustainable level.

HOW DO THE SCOTS LIVE?

In Scotland as a whole, two out of three people live in houses and 1/3 in flats or apartments, In larger cities there is a higher proportion of flat or apartment dwellers, either living in purpose-built apartment buildings, or conversions of older properties. A feature of Scottish cities is the tenements, (low quality apartment buildings) constructed in the 19th century for workers in the various industries where many families lived in often appalling conditions. Many of those that were not demolished in the more enlightened years of the mid-20th century, have now been upgraded into desirable apartments. Prices for these can be at a premium in the more upmarket areas of cities.

The cities of Scotland are surrounded by suburban residential areas where many who work in the cities choose to live, commuting on a daily basis. New building in the 50 mile 'corridor' between Glasgow and Edinburgh is slowly turning this area into a suburban conglomeration which is destined to blur the edges of Scotland's two main cities if it continues at the same pace. Although such ribbon development is common throughout England, the other cities of Scotland are still surrounded by essentially rural areas. New building occurs on the edge of them all, but the relatively small population of the country means that once outside a city you will quickly find yourself in distinctly rural areas.

There has been an increasing trend in recent years for residents of either houses or flats to be owner-occupiers, due both to easier access to home loans and the increasing numbers of council tenants buying their properties. Rentable properties, furnished or unfurnished, are available in both the public and the private sectors. Traditionally, local councils provided the only public sector housing, but in recent years these have been augmented in many areas of Scotland by housing association properties, provided via a mixture of public and private funding.

Since the UK government introduced legislation in 1979 giving council tenants the right to buy their council house at less than the market value, there has developed a shortage of council housing in many areas. Since that date, 40% of council stock has been sold. In June 2004, South Ayrshire became the first council to ban tenants from buying their homes, in order to safeguard their dwindling stock of social housing. It may be that other councils will feel forced follow suit as they find they cannot satisfy the demand for social housing with their existing house stocks.

As a result of right to buy legislation and loss of council housing stocks, the low-cost housing offered by Housing Associations became more important. In 2001 the Scottish Executive introduced legislation to extend the right to buy to certain Housing Association tenants, a move which concerned many in Highland areas in particular, including the Highland Council, local Housing Associations and charities for the homeless. To address these concerns, the Housing (Scotland) Act 2001 allows 'pressured' areas to be ruled out of the right to buy, pressured meaning there is a shortage of affordable rented housing. Both Edinburgh and the Highland Council are considering applying for pressured status for some areas. Their concern is that the loss of rented accommodation could have a detrimental effect on vulnerable areas, where local people may not be able to find affordable housing and may therefore leave the area.

There has been a significant change in the balance between owner-occupied and rented accommodation in Scotland between 1991 and 2001, a trend which seems set to continue.

Type of dwelling	1991	2001
Owner occupied	52.4%	64.2%
Private rental	7.1%	6.7%
Housing association	2.6%	6.3%
Local Authority	37.8%	22.8%

Crofts

In the north of Scotland and the Islands, the pattern of land use is rather different from that elsewhere. Here large estates are still owned by private individuals or, increasingly, companies, often foreign, which are taking the place of the lairds of the past. Areas of these estates are divided into crofts of an average size of five hectares (12 acres) and rented out at a tiny annual rent – between £10 and £30 – to tenant crofters. Crofters have the right to build a house on their croft. In crofting areas many crofters' cottages of up to one hundred years old still stand. While some have been modernised and are lived in today, and others have been turned into holiday accommodation, sadly the majority have been left to decay. This sorry state of affairs came about as a result of a laudable, but in hindsight possibly misguided, government initiative introduced in the 1970s to give crofters generous grants and loans to build new houses to replace the traditional tiny stone-built, often asbestos-roofed, croft houses in which their parents and grandparents had raised large families. Consequently, many of the houses in these areas are variations on the relatively cheap timber-framed 'kit house', while nearby stands the remains of the original croft house. Belatedly the Scottish Executive have come to recognise this folly and are, at the start of the 21st century, beginning initiatives to bring these older properties back into the housing market.

Not all land in these areas is croft land. Crofters have the right to 'de-croft' patches of land which are then sold on to outside purchasers to build on. These decrofted areas tend to be between 1/4 acre and 1/2 acre in size. Larger areas of land have been sold off by the estate for private or public sector housing schemes.

Whereas in suburban commuter belts the tendency is for large houses to be built on relatively small plots of land, the situation is reversed in rural areas. Houses tend to be small but are situated in a comparatively large patch of land.

The typical suburban garden is a rarity in the Highlands. Although most crofts have an area of 'garden ground' immediately round the house, this is usually just a lawned area with perhaps a few shrubs and a vegetable patch, the rest of the croft being left wild for sheep and cattle to graze. Even houses on decrofted land tend not to be surrounded by a typical 'cottage' garden. Who needs a garden, after all, when you are surrounded by some of the most stunning scenery in the world?

It is somewhat of a paradox that because of the crofting system, the Highlands are unique in that many of those who have the largest areas of land, albeit rented, and own their own home, are classed as economically and socially deprived because their incomes are low. In fact, because of the nominal rents they pay and the fact that few have mortgages, in many cases crofters' disposable income is actually equivalent to those earning rather more but paying off a large mortgage.

Their income is often derived from several sources, with that made directly from crofting becoming a smaller part of the whole as prices for sheep and cattle from these areas continue to fall. The payment of subsidies per head of livestock, which has long been a useful source of income for the crofter, is being replaced in 2005 by the Single Farm Payment (SFP). This subsidy cuts the direct link between livestock numbers and the level of payment, so those crofters who have relied on high stock numbers to boost their income will have to adopt a different approach. The SFP aims to improve the environment by taking into account environmental aspects of crofting. The idea is that crofters should not get rid of all their stock, but that they keep stock at a level which is most productive and beneficial for the land, as it is the interaction of livestock with the various habitats that has created the mix of wildlife and plants which make the Highlands and Islands so unique. It is recognised that this balance should be maintained to keep the ecosystem thriving. As a result of this new emphasis, there is an increasing number of regulations connected to the environment, covering activities such as management of unimproved land, overgrazing, heather burning and so on – 'green tape' to add to the red tape they already have to deal with.

Almost all crofters today also have at least one other source of income, working in areas such as the construction industry, or for the utilities companies, often living away from home for a week or more at a time on contracts in other parts of Scotland. Crofters or their wives will often also be involved in tourism in some way, whether by offering bed and breakfast, renting out a holiday cottage, or working in local hotels during the summer season.

Crofters have the right to buy their crofts, but even owner-occupiers do not need to be wealthy in the conventional sense as they can buy their croft for 15 times the peppercorn annual rent. It is only when these are sold on to incomers that 'market prices' start being charged.

In rural Scotland you rarely see the conspicuous consumption of urban areas. Houses are small, with the biggest ones tending to be those purpose built as guest houses. People are likely to have more than one vehicle, but expensive new cars are thin on the ground, and these will be augmented by working vehicles such as ancient pick-ups and Land Rovers.

It is predicted, however, that the average size of houses will grow. With increasing numbers of people working from home, an extra room for use as a home office is becoming a necessity. Many new houses now provide these as standard, while older properties are being extended to include office space.

Although the typical 'nuclear family' – Mum, Dad and children living together – is still the commonest type of household in Scotland, the demographic make-up is changing here as elsewhere. There are greater numbers of single parent households than ever before and it is predicted that the number of single person households – people who have opted to live alone from choice – will grow for the foreseeable future. This means that a higher proportion of dwellings for the population will be required and increasing strain will be put on the existing supply. For this reason, councils in various parts of the country offer 'empty house' grants to assist owners to bring derelict and semi-derelict croft houses back into the housing stock.

RENT OR BUY?

The first decision you need to make is whether to rent or buy a property. This will partly depend on financial factors: whether you have obtained equity from a property you have sold, whether you will need a mortgage, whether you can satisfy the financial criteria of a lender and so forth.

Even if the money side of things is not an issue, there are also practical considerations. The timing of your move can be significant. If you are committed to moving to Scotland at a certain date, to take up employment, for example, you may find that you still have a property to sell elsewhere. If you are selling a property elsewhere in the UK, do not assume that you can just go ahead and make an offer on a property north of the border while you are in the process of selling your own property.

Because the house-buying system in Scotland works under different rules from those south of the border, it is strongly advised that you do not make a firm offer on a house in Scotland before you have signed contracts on the sale of a house in England, say. Once your offer on a Scottish property is accepted, that is an agreement legally binding on both parties, whereas in England or Wales either party can pull out of the deal without penalty at any time until contracts are signed and exchanged. The situation could arise that your house sale in England could fall through after your offer on the Scottish property has been accepted. In this case you may find you can only get out of buying the Scottish property by paying a severe financial penalty. For this reason, it is sensible to rent accommodation until the deal on the house in England is completed. Unless you can afford for things to go wrong, don't take on the risk of buying in Scotland before selling elsewhere.

If you have the choice, a sensible approach is to sell in England (or wherever your property happens to be), move to Scotland into a long-let property in the area of your choice and purchase a new house from there. If you have to move at a certain date in order to take up a job, you would still be best advised to rent a property until your own home is sold. If you are moving up at the behest of an employer, of course, they may be prepared to cover the cost of any bridging loans on your original house. In some circumstances they may even buy your house from you and arrange to sell it on their own behalf. This will depend on your value to them, of course – negotiation of such relocation packages is an individual matter.

It may be advisable to rent for a while anyway, until you find your feet and can have a long, well-considered look at the properties available to buy in your chosen area of Scotland. Indeed, if work, schooling and the like do not commit you to any particular area, it is a good idea to look at all corners of Scotland and decide where you like best. You may find yourself changing from a committed lowlander to a newly-converted enthusiastic Highlander!

You should bear in mind that it is harder to find rentable accommodation in the more remote rural areas, although because of the number of cottages let during the summer for holiday accommodation, it is often possible to negotiate a long let in one of these during the winter months, and maybe during the summer as well.

Unfurnished properties are very thin on the ground in these areas. The bulk of unfurnished properties are those owned by the local authority or housing associations. There is a shortage of these in rural areas so there will be a waiting list and there may well also be residence criteria you would have to satisfy before you could get such a place.

If you are setting up a new business you may find it difficult to get a mortgage. Many lenders are reluctant to give a loan to the self-employed, and will at any rate generally ask for three years' accounts, so you may not be able to get a mortgage in less than this period of time. Those lenders who will lend to a person in this situation will charge a high rate of interest because of the higher perceived risk of defaulting. So again, in these circumstances renting could be the better option.

Once you have decided on the area where you want to stay, you have sold any property elsewhere you need to, and are reasonably financially secure, it is sensible in the longer term to buy a property. Bricks and mortar is the best, relatively risk-free, investment you can make in Scotland.

FINANCE

As far as the basic rules and criteria required for taking out a mortgage in Scotland are concerned, you will find little or no difference in practice from taking out a similar mortgage in England or Wales.

In the UK, mortgages can be taken out through a number of different types of institutions. Traditionally, building societies were the sole source of mortgages, and were available only to those who saved regularly with them. Today, due to changes in the law relating to financial institutions, banks, insurance companies and others can supply mortgages, and building societies will lend to anyone who satisfies their criteria regarding security – you no longer have to be an established saver with any particular building society. In recent years the distinction between building societies and banks has become blurred, with each taking on functions of the other. Indeed, increasing numbers of building societies are now formally converting to banks.

A recent phenomenon, with the advent of telephone and online banking, has been the 'direct mortgage' company which does not do business face to face with the customer. As they will arrange mortgages over the phone, through the post, and over the internet, their overheads are low compared with companies with expensive High Street properties and staff to maintain, so they can offer mortgages at a competitive rate.

These changes have meant that financial services generally in the UK are becoming more and more competitive and the range of choices is becoming larger. It is important to be aware of all the different options available when borrowing money to buy a property or a building site and to understand the advantages and disadvantages of each.

MORTGAGES

Although there are many different mortgages on the market, there are just two main types available, the repayment mortgage, where both the interest on the loan and the capital are repaid over a period of years, and the interest only mortgage where only the interest on the loan is paid, and another payment is made into some sort of investment plan which is used to repay the capital amount at the end of the mortgage period.

In Britain borrowers can usually borrow up to 90 or 95 per cent of the value of a property. This percentage is usually termed the 'maximum loan to value' (LTV). It may be possible to get a 100 per cent mortgage, particularly if you are a first-time buyer, but most lenders will want a deposit of at least five per cent of the cost (i.e. they would allow you a 95 per cent mortgage). A 100 per cent mortgage is likely to attract high interest rates. If you have other savings or security, you may take out a mortgage for a portion of the house value, so you may buy a house for £100,000 with a £70,000 mortgage with the remaining £30,000 paid for from other sources.

The amount any particular borrower will be allowed is calculated on the basis of their annual income. Lenders will usually offer around 3 times your annual salary, or 2.5 times the joint income of a married couple. So, someone earning £34,000 per year could take out a mortgage of around £102,000, another earning £15,000 would be allowed up to £45,000.

During the height of the housing boom, mortgages were available for up to six times one's annual salary, but this led to many people defaulting on their mortgages with a huge increase in house repossessions. Since the housing market crashed, mortgage lenders have been far more wary and stringent in their criteria.

Many people are denied mortgages because of bad credit ratings or uncertain incomes. Self-employed people in particular may have problems finding a mortgage. Many lenders will not lend to the self-employed. They will at the very least need to produce three years' accounts so a lender can determine the risk they may pose. These groups of people very often can only resort to lenders who charge relatively high interest rates and impose large penalties if borrowers fall into arrears. If you are in this position, it is worth trying to persuade mortgage lenders you are a good credit risk by using other means, for instance, by showing them evidence of paid bills and invoices, direct debit agreements which you have never defaulted on, and so forth.

For those who are self-employed or have variable incomes, it may be possible to obtain a 'self-certification mortgage', which enables you to set up loan without the need for payslips, bank statements or accounting records. The interest will almost certainly be higher in this case.

Useful Address
Any mortgage lender or broker should agree to follow the guidelines laid down in 'The Mortgage Code'. A copy of this should be given to you on request or can be obtained from the *Council of Mortgage Lenders* 3 Savile Row, London W1S 3PB; ☎020-7437 0075. It can also be seen online on their website www.cml.org.uk.

Repayment Mortgages. The loan is repaid gradually over the length of the mortgage, usually 25 years, but this could be longer or shorter, depending on circumstances. Monthly repayments comprise interest on the outstanding loan and repayment of part of the loan. As the outstanding loan reduces the interest element decreases while the repayment element increases. The amount of interest paid fluctuates according to the periodic rise and fall in interest rates. The loan is fully repaid at the end of the mortgage term.

Interest-only Mortgages. The loan amount remains the same throughout the mortgage term, again usually 25 years. Interest is paid on the total amount of the loan for the whole of the mortgage period, the interest fluctuating with changes in interest rates. Alongside the mortgage, regular payments are made into an investment plan, and at the end of the mortgage period the capital is repaid in a lump sum from the money accrued in the investment plan.

There are three main types of interest only mortgage, depending on the type of investment plan involved: ISA, Pension or Endowment Mortgages.

Endowment Mortgages. Alongside the interest payments to the lender, a life insurance endowment policy is taken out. The monthly premiums, less charges, are paid to an insurance company which invests them in shares, bonds and other assets. Premiums are set at a level which should ensure that the accumulated investment funds pay off the loan at the end of the mortgage period. There is no guarantee, however, that the final sum will pay off the mortgage in full – you may end up with a shortfall. If the insurance company is doing its job properly it should monitor the progress of investments and, if necessary, increase the monthly premiums payable. It is also possible that you may end up with a surplus, which is payable as a lump sum at the end of the mortgage period.

It is strongly advised that you get good advice from a mortgage broker before deciding on an endowment mortgage. There has been concern in recent years that some endowment mortgages may not be performing well enough in the current low inflationary environment to pay off the full amount of the mortgage.

Part of the monthly premiums payable on an endowment mortgage, typically around five per cent, goes to provide life insurance cover. In the event of the death of the mortgagee, the mortgage is paid off in full. Where there is more than one party to the mortgage, for instance, if a married couple take out a joint mortgage, the mortgage may be paid off in the event of the death of either party, so the surviving mortgagee owns the property outright even if the mortgage still has a period to run.

There are no longer any tax advantages to an endowment mortgage, another reason for their decrease in popularity.

Pension Mortgages. Monthly interest is paid off on the loan but premiums are paid into a pension plan which pays off your mortgage on retirement and also pays you a pension. There are tax advantages with this type of mortgage, as payments into the pension plan qualify for tax relief. There are, however, disadvantages, including the fact that you may no longer be eligible to make contributions to the pension scheme if you should join a pension scheme at work or you become unemployed. In this case, another means of building up capital to pay off the mortgage would be required.

ISA Mortgages. With these, the loan is linked to an Individual Savings Account (ISA). An ISA can be used to invest in a wide range of investments including cash in the form of bank, building society and National Savings accounts; investment-type insurance plans; and stocks and shares. The ISA is used to build up a capital lump sum which pays off the loan at the end of the term. These are more flexible than other endowment mortgages because profits can be taken from the ISA at any time, rather than having to wait for any surplus to be paid at the end of the mortgage period. The disadvantage is that the value of the ISA may be depressed as a result of low share prices at the time repayment of the loan is due. There is no life insurance included in an ISA mortgage, so a policy must be taken out separately if life cover is required.

At present ISAs are the most tax-efficient way to invest, as all the income for the investment is tax-free. The disadvantage of this sort of mortgage is that it is up to the individual to ensure that sufficient payments are made into the ISA to cover the capital cost of the loan at the end of the period.

Foreign Currency Mortgages. It is possible to obtain a mortgage in a foreign currency such as Swiss francs, US dollars, Deutschmarks or Japanese yen. The way they work is that instead of lending you British pounds, a bank lends you Swiss francs, for example. You then sell the Swiss francs for British pounds and use the sterling to buy your house. Your debt is still in Swiss francs and you pay Swiss franc interest rates, not British pound interest rates. When you get your interest charge in Swiss francs you simply sell some British pounds, buy some Swiss francs and pay the interest in Swiss francs.

With historically low interest rates, these have provided large savings for borrowers in the past. The downside is that interest rate gains can be lost due to currency swings. However, by shifting your mortgage between a variety of currencies you should be able to minimise losses.

These are usually only available to very high earners and for a maximum of 60 per cent of a property's value. You should consult a financial advisor before deciding whether to apply for this kind of mortgage.

The ECU Group are specialists in this variety of mortgage (73 Brook , London EC2N 1AR; ☎020-7245 1010; e-mail ecu@ecu.co.uk; www.ecu.co.uk). Please note that the ECU website is only for use by internet users from the UK and other countries where the services they offer are legal. US internet users are not authorised to enter the website.

Buy To Let Mortgages

Some lenders have special mortgage schemes for those who wish to invest in a residential property for letting purposes without paying commercial rates. These work out more expensive than those for buying your own home. However, they have the advantage that when deciding how much you can borrow, they take into account a percentage of the expected rental income on the property.

Flexible Mortgages

A comparative new-comer to the mortgage scene, a flexible mortgage allows the borrower to pay off varying amounts depending on current financial circumstances. By paying increased monthly payments for a period, you can later take a break in their monthly repayments, reduce them, or borrow back any money you have previously overpaid. By overpaying each month you can pay off your mortgage far more quickly and cheaply because less interest will be charged.

The Scottish Building Society has introduced a 'Flexible Guest House Mortgage' designed for those who wish to buy or refinance a guest house or bed and breakfast business.

Self-Build Mortgages

These are new products reflecting the increasing popularity of self-building. One of the biggest problems faced by self-builders is managing cash flow during the course of the build. With a self-build mortgage, stage payments can be made in advance of each stage. The mortgage can be used for both traditional and timber frame builds, as well as for renovation and conversion projects. Typical stage payments will include land, foundations, wall plate or erection of the timber frame, watertight/roof on, plastered and completion. As with a traditional mortgage, how much a lender will be prepared to advance you will depend upon your ability to repay. The usual calculation will be worked out on multiples of the incomes of the people who will be responsible for repaying the loan. Generally, you may borrow up to 95 per cent of land purchase price; up to 95 per cent of the building costs; up to 95 per cent of the end value.

Building Societies and Banks

These are some of the largest lending institutions active in Scotland, but there are many smaller ones. A full list is available from the *Council of Mortgage Lenders* 3 Savile Row, London W1S 3PB; ☎020-7437 0075; www.cml.org.uk.

Addresses and phone numbers of local bank and building society branches can be found in local Phone Books or Business Pages.

Head offices of the main ones are:

Alliance & Leicester PLC: Customer Service Centre, Carlton Park, Narborough, Leicester LE19 0AL; www.alliance-leicester.co.uk.

Bank of Scotland: The Mound, Edinburgh EH1 1YZ; ☎0131-470 2000; www.bankofscotland.co.uk.

The Royal Bank of Scotland: Customer Relations Manager, Freepost, PO Box 1727, Edinburgh EH12 9JN; www.royalbankscot.co.uk.

Scottish Building Society: 23 Manor Place, Edinburgh EH3 7XE; ☎0131-220 1111; fax 0131-220 2888; www.scottishbldgsoc.co.uk.

Internet banks include Egg www.egg.com and Smile (part of the Co-op Bank) www.smile.co.uk.

Mortgage Rates

The Bank of England reviews its base interest rate every month. They may move it up or down, or leave it at its existing rate It applies to the whole of the UK. A long period of low rates, bottoming out at 3.5 per cent in July 2003, contributed to the rising prices in the house market between 2000 and 2004. In order to prevent a potential property market crash, a series of small rate rises were imposed by the Bank of England during 2004. By August 2004 the base rate had risen to 4.75 per cent and there was a noticeable slowing in the UK property market.

Banks and building societies set their own interest rates on the basis of the Bank of England rate, generally somewhat higher than the base rate. Their various mortgage products will offer differing rates depending on the particular conditions of the mortgage and the situation of the borrower.

Fixed or Variable Rate. Whether you choose an interest-only or a repayment mortgage, you can also choose between a fixed rate and a variable rate. With a fixed rate, the interest rate is fixed for a number of years. The longer the fixed rate period, the lower the interest rate offered. The advantage is that you will know exactly what your repayments will be every month for that period. The disadvantage is that you need to make a gamble that interest rates do not fall significantly during that period, as this would mean you would end up paying over the odds. Of course, if interest rates rise appreciably in that period, you can save yourself a great deal of money. At the end of the fixed term, the normal variable rate is paid.

With a variable rate mortgage, as the name suggests, your interest payments will fluctuate as the Bank of England base rate, and therefore mortgage rates, move up and down.

Discounted Rate. In this case a borrower pays a lower rate of interest in the earlier years, which can be useful for people such as first time buyers where money may be tight for the early years of the loan. These deals should be approached with caution, however, as sometimes the discount is not genuine and the interest saved in the earlier years is just added to the outstanding loan.

Capped Rate. This varies in line with general interest rates, but has an 'interest rate collar' which means it will not rise above or fall below an agreed rate. The capped rate is in force for a fixed length of time, after which the variable rate is paid.

Tracker mortgages. The interest rate 'tracks' the Bank of England base rate. There are three basic types of tracker mortgage: those which track the base rate for the whole life of the loan; those which run at an agreed differential to the base rate (either above or more rarely below it) for a set period before reverting to the standard variable rate; and finally those in which the lender promises that the margin between the base rate and the mortgage interest rate will not go beyond a set level.

SAMPLE VARIABLE RATE MORTGAGES IN NOVEMBER 2004

Lender	Rate	Max LTV
Bank of Scotland	5.74%	95%
Woolwich	5.6%	95%
Egg	5.8%	95%
Royal Bank of Scotland	6.04%	95%
Scottish Building Society	5.7%	95%

Redemption Charges

Although it may be desirable, as circumstances change, to pay off your mortgage early, or to switch to a more competitive mortgage, in many cases a redemption charge will be charged by the lender, to offset their loss in interest payments over the remaining period of the loan. This may be five or six per cent of the loan, or 12 months interest. The charges are higher the earlier you repay the loan. High redemption charges are particularly likely with mortgages offering low fixed-interest rates for the first few years or those with discounts of standard variable rates.

After adverse publicity about the punitive redemption charges made by some lenders when borrowers have tried to pay off their mortgage early, or move their mortgage to another lender, some lenders have started offering mortgages which claim to have 'no redemption fees'. Although this may be strictly true, the other costs need looking at carefully: you may find you have to pay an 'application fee' of around £300 which is not payable with a scheme which does attract a redemption fee.

Non-Mortgageable Properties

Before a lender will give you a mortgage they need to be satisfied that the property is worth the money you intend to pay for it. They will have a survey carried out on their behalf – at your cost – and estimate a value for the property. Any amount they agree to lend you will take this into account. In some cases, particularly if you wish to buy a run-down or semi-derelict property which requires a great deal of renovation, or is not of approved construction, it may be that some lenders will refuse to mortgage it. If you shop around you may, however, find another institution which is prepared to lend the money.

The author bought an old croft cottage in Wester Ross and the surveyor's report included the following comment
Due to the nature of construction of various parts of the building (i.e. the timber

> *framed front wall covered with metal lath and roughcast; and the corrugated asbestos roof covering), this structure would not be acceptable for security purposes by a Building Society. However, some banks may have a more relaxed attitude.*

In a case such as this, a lender may agree to mortgage a property with conditions attached – e.g. that the asbestos roof is replaced with a more acceptable alternative.

Buying Land

If you satisfy requirements regarding income and so forth, there should be no difficulty getting a mortgage if you wish to buy a plot of land and build a house on it immediately. The amount of the mortgage would be based on the combined value of the land and the house you build, together with the cost of running services such as mains water and electricity to the site. However, if you wish just to buy a building site, with the intention of building on it at some later date, you would not be granted a mortgage on the land alone. In this case you would have to find the cash or look for some other form of loan, probably at a higher rate of interest, to purchase the land.

Buying from Abroad

You are unlikely to get a loan in your home country for the purchase of a property in Britain, but it may be possible to use your existing property as all or part security for a loan or mortgage if you currently reside in Belgium, Cyprus, Denmark, France, Germany, Gibraltar, Greece, Holland, Ireland, Italy, Portugal, Spain, the Caribbean or the USA.

The situation for buyers within Europe may change in years to come, as the European Commission recommended in December 2004 that there should be a single European market for home loans. There will be a lot of difficulties to overcome before Euromortgages are possible, among them language and legal barriers, fluctuating exchange rates and different rules on early repayment, but once these issues are addressed, a single market could mean cheaper and better loans for all Europeans, regardless of where they obtain their mortgage.

Grants and Loans

There may be other sources of funding towards a property, particularly if you are building from scratch. Crofters have access to various grants and loans from the Crofters Commission for both domestic and business/agricultural buildings, so if you are buying a croft you may be eligible for some of these. There is a wider range of grants available to tenant crofters than to owner/occupiers. For full details of schemes currently available, contact the Crofters Commission.

Scottish Enterprise in the south of Scotland, and Highlands and Islands Enterprise in the north, have various grant and loan schemes which are generally administered through their subsidiary Local Enterprise Companies (LECs). (Further background on the enterprise companies can be found in *Starting A Business*.) If you are building or extending a property to run a business from, or will be using part of your house for business purposes, you may be eligible for some funding from your LEC.

In addition, both the Crofters Commission and LECs may be able to assist with funding towards ancillary elements of a house build, such as fencing, the provision of access to a property and so forth.

The economic development department of the local council may also be able to assist with funding towards a business, but generally this is unlikely to be available for the bricks and mortar. The assistance they can offer is more likely to be for equipment and other elements of the day to day administration of the business.

Useful Addresses
Crofters Commission 4-6 Castle Wynd, Inverness IV2 3EQ; ☎01463-663450; fax 01463-711820; www.crofterscommission.org.uk.
Scottish Enterprise: Atlantic Quay, 150 Broomielaw, Glasgow G2 8LU; ☎0141-248 2700; fax 0141-221 3217; www.scotent.co.uk.
Highland and Islands Enterprise: Cowan House, Inverness Retail and Business Park, Inverness IV2 7GF; ☎01463-234171; fax 01463-244469; www.hie.co.uk.
See contact details for all Scottish local councils in the *General Introduction*.

Advice
There is a variety of mortgage products available for house buyers in Scotland, designed to suit a wide range of people in different circumstances. It is important that you find the one that is best for you in your individual circumstances, so it is strongly advised that you get the advice of an independent mortgage broker, who will be able to source the best mortgage for you. On the internet, Find Financial Directory has links to mortgage brokers. www.find.co.uk.

Always treat mortgage advice given by lenders with caution. They will be on commission for the numbers and types of mortgages they sell, so the temptation for them to 'mis-sell' mortgages – i.e. to sell you a mortgage which is not the best one for you in your circumstances – is often there. There is evidence that the mis-selling of mortgages is not an uncommon phenomenon, so you must do your homework carefully.

It is wise to ensure that anybody you borrow or take advice from is a member or associate member of the Council of Mortgage Lenders. Any complaints you have regarding the advice or service you are given can then be reported to them for investigation.

The Times and *Sunday Times*, plus most other weekend papers, publish lists of the best variable, fixed-rate and discount mortgages. The on-line *Electronic Telegraph* publishes them at www.telegraph.co.uk. The website www.aboutmortgages.co.uk has tables of the best value mortgages currently available.

An excellent website giving information, advice and current facts and figures on all aspects of house-buying, including current mortgage rates and links to other useful sites, is www.houseweb.co.uk. It includes an exhaustive list of links to mortgage services on the web. This includes all the main UK banks and building societies plus some smaller ones and some 'direct mortgage' companies (see below).

High Street banks and building societies have free leaflets outlining the mortgages they have to offer. The same information is also explained on their websites.

For some years, a number of building societies have operated without High Street branches, conducting their business through the post and through the internet. Because of their lower overheads they have been able to offer competitive rates for savers and borrowers. Rates payable by postal accounts are published in the newspapers.

Internet banks have their own mortgage products available. The rates they offer are competitive with more traditional banks and building societies. Direct mortgages through the internet, where the process is fully automated and no face to face contact is needed between lender and borrower, will doubtless be available soon. Currently, however, this sort of service is in its infancy – there are so many variables to check, so much concrete proof of income, security and so forth required that, for the time being at least, it will not be possible to purchase a mortgage with the click of a mouse.

Useful Address
A full list of members of the *Building Societies Association* can be obtained from them at 3 Savile Row, London, W1S 3PB; ☎020-7437 0655; fax 020-7734 6416; www.bsa.org.uk.

FINDING A HOME

The law relating to property generally, and house purchase in particular, is different in Scotland from the rest of the UK. The legal procedure attached to the purchase or the sale of houses is called conveyancing, a process which in Scotland can only be undertaken by a solicitor. In the rest of Britain, there are certain stages of the conveyancing process that a purchaser can undertake himself or can engage a licensed conveyancer to do on his behalf, but in Scotland the entire process must be carried out by a solicitor qualified to do so.

The other main difference between the system of house purchase north and south of the border is that in Scotland conveyancing is carried out only after an offer has been accepted. Once an offer has been made and accepted, this forms a contract which is legally binding on both parties. If either side wishes to withdraw after this stage there can be substantial financial penalties and legal costs payable.

Finding a Property

Details of properties for sale can be found from a number of sources. Most property in Scotland is sold through solicitors (lawyers) or estate agents.

Solicitors

In Scotland, unlike in England and Wales, many solicitors also act as estate agents – i.e. they advertise properties for sale and act for the vendor during the conveyancing procedure.

The involvement of a solicitor in these aspects of house purchase might be somewhat disconcerting to people from south of the border who are familiar with a demarcation of interests between the legal side of house purchase and the sales side. The Scottish system seems not to cause any undue problems, though, and it should be borne in mind that the purchaser will always choose a solicitor who is not acting in any way for the vendor.

It is necessary to secure the services of a Scottish solicitor: a solicitor qualified only in the English system is not qualified to practice in the Scottish legal system. Ensure that any solicitor you use is a member of the Law Society of Scotland. Remember, solicitors are selling a service and you would be well advised to obtain written quotes for their service before engaging one to act for you – their charges and efficiency can vary.

Details of the properties for sale they have on their books will generally be displayed in their offices or may be sent to you by post. Most of them now have their own websites with details of the properties they currently have for sale.

As the average firm of solicitors will have a comparatively small number of properties on its books at any one time, groups of solicitors in various areas of Scotland have banded together for advertising purposes and set up 'Solicitors' Property Centres' (SPCs) with town centre premises. These are 'one-stop shops' which keep details of all the properties on the books of the participating solicitors. In addition, they will have a duty solicitor accessible during opening hours who can advise on all aspects of buying a property. This service is particularly helpful to first time buyers and to buyers from outwith Scotland.

The SPC acts as a joint enterprise estate agency on behalf of the individual member firms of solicitors. Each solicitor acts on its own vendor-client's behalf in the sale of particular properties advertised through the SPC. Once you have identified a property to buy, you will need to engage the services of a different solicitor to represent your interests as the purchaser. Regional SPCs produce free newspapers which contain a selection of properties and building sites on their books.

To cut down on the costs of producing and distributing print newspapers, fewer of their properties are shown in these. Instead, brief details of their complete selection are available via their websites and most of the properties have full details online. For those which do not, you can request online for full details to be sent to your home address. You can arrange to have the newspaper sent to your home address every month, for three months at a time. If you wish to continue after three months, simply contact them and they will send it for another three months. This is a completely free service.

To find the properties of those solicitors who do not belong to their local SPC you will need to visit their offices, phone them direct, or visit their websites. You can ask to be advised of suitable properties as they come onto their books, in which case they will send details of any new properties which fit your specified requirements.

SOLICITORS' PROPERTY CENTRES

Aberdeen Solicitors' Property Centre: www.aspc.co.uk.
   40 Chapel Street, Aberdeen AB10 1SP; ☎01224-632949.
Borders Solicitors' Property Centre: www.bspc.co.uk.
Dumfries & Galloway Solicitors' Property Centre: www.dgspc.co.uk.
   14 Queensberry Street, Dumfries DG1 1EX; ☎01387-252684; fax 01387-250585.
   48 King Street, Castle Douglas DG7 1AB; ☎01556-503245.
   24 High Street, Annan DG12 6AD; ☎01461-204459.
Edinburgh Solicitors' Property Centre: www.espc.co.uk.
   85 George Street, Edinburgh EH2 3ES; ☎0131-624 8000; fax 0131-624 8570.
   25 Whytecauseway, Kirkcaldy KY1 1XF; ☎01592-597929; fax 01592-597969.
   24 Newmarket Street, Falkirk FK1 1JQ; ☎01324-886000; fax 01324-886005.
   8 King Street, Stirling FK8 1BD; ☎01786-449201; fax 01786-449202.
Fife & Kinross Solicitors' Property Centre: www.f-kspc.co.uk.
   PO Box 10034, Dundee DD3 8WA; ☎/fax 01334-880593
Glasgow Solicitors' Property Centre: www.gspc.co.uk.
   Kilpatrick House, 145/147 Queen Street, Glasgow G1 3BJ; ☎0345-229922; fax 0141-248 9055.
Highland Solicitors' Property Centre: www.hspc.co.uk.
   30 Queensgate, Inverness IV1 1DA; ☎01463-231173; fax 01463-715292.
North East Solicitors' Property Centre: www.nespc.com.
   31 Duff Street, Macduff AB44 1QL; ☎01261-832491; fax 01261-833444.
Perth Solicitors' Property Centre: www.pspc.co.uk.
   6 South St. John's Place, Perth PH1 5SU; ☎01738-635301; fax 01738-621168.
Solicitors' Property Centre Moray: www.spcmoray.com.

29/31 High Street, Elgin IV30 1EE; ☎01343-548755; fax 01343-550053.
Tayside Solicitors' Property Centre: www.tspc.co.uk.
9 Whitehall Crescent, Dundee DD1 4AR; ☎01382-228770; fax 01382-228650.
The Scottish Solicitors Property Centre website has links to all these websites.
www.sspc.co.uk.

Estate Agents

Estate Agents advertise and attempt to sell properties on commission for owners. It has to be said that estate agents have, on the whole, a bad public image. It often appears that they charge a lot of money for very little other than advertising a property. In most cases, their fees are a percentage of the amount they sell the house for, so it is in their interest to inflate the price of houses. This may be counter-productive, putting off prospective purchasers, and in the longer term the advertised price may have to be reduced to generate some interest.

Using an estate agent is likely to add to the costs of house selling, because once the vendor finds an interested buyer he has to engage a solicitor to deal with the legal aspects of the sale, as estate agents have no legal qualifications. Indeed, they are not required to have any professional qualifications nor be a member of any professional body. Anybody can set themselves up in business as an estate agent so it is essential to be sure they are trustworthy before doing business with them.

However, this is more of a problem for the vendor – the buyer should incur no financial cost in respect of the estate agent he is buying a property through. They should provide details of and arrange visits to houses for free.

There is one large estate agency, *Your Move*, which has branches throughout Scotland. Smaller estate agencies operate in some areas.

Your Move has a website from which you can download details of properties or can ask for details to be sent to your home address. www.your-move.co.uk.

Each 'Your Move' branch deals with properties in its area, not all of which will be listed on the internet, so are best contacted direct with your requirements.

YOUR MOVE BRANCHES

213 Gorgie Road, Edinburgh EH11 1TU; ☎0131-313 333; fax 0131-313 3344.
295 Leith Walk, Edinburgh EH6 8PD; ☎0131-554 6222; fax 0131-5536219.
51 High Street, Dalkeith EH22 1JA; ☎0131-660 3033; fax 0131-654 2491.
13A Tay Walk, Cumbernauld G67 1BU; ☎01236-780818; fax 01236-780969.
2 Queensberry Street, Dumfries DG1 1EX; ☎01387-257666; fax 01387-

248390.

4 Bank Street, Falkirk FK1 1NB; ☎01324-632266; fax 01324-612149.

22 Friars Street, Stirling FK8 1HA; ☎01786-451555; fax 01786-450416.

Almondvale Centre, Livingston EH54 6NB; ☎01506-440440; fax 01506-440400.

9 High Street, Linlithgow EH49 7AB; ☎01506-844993; fax 01506-848073.

2 King Street, Bathgate EH48 1AX; ☎01506-655802; fax 01506-630069.

87 High Street, Kirkcaldy KY1 1LN; ☎01592-205432; fax 01592-640123.

61 Crossgate, Cupar KY15 5AS; ☎01334-656533; fax 01334-656131.

11 Regents Way, The Bay Centre, Dalgety Bay KY11 9YD; ☎01383-824242; fax 01383-825164.

11 New Row, Dunfermline KY12 7EA; ☎01383-739729; fax 01383-620595.

North House, North Street, Glenrothes KY7 5NA; ☎01592-759653; fax 01592-610307.

41-45 George Street, Perth PH1 5LA; ☎01738-636064; fax 01738-643533.

51 Murray Street, Montrose DD10 8JZ; ☎01674-672979; fax 01674-674491.

22 Whitehall Crescent, Dundee DD1 4AU; ☎01382-224333; fax 01382-202285.

60 Academy Street, Inverness IV1 1LP; ☎01463-221166; fax 01463-710166.

59 High Street, Dingwall IV15 9HL; ☎01349-864848; fax 01349-861479.

75 High Street, Elgin IV30 1EE; ☎01343-548861; fax 01343-549703.

2A Righead Gate, East Kilbride G74 1LS; ☎01355-248133; fax 01355-248136.

70 Cazdow Street, Hamilton ML3 6DS; ☎01698-891799; fax 01698-891895.

8 Hill Street, Wishaw ML2 7AT; ☎01698-355920; fax 01698-358599.

As with solicitors, estate agencies will keep you updated with details of suitable properties if you inform them of your requirements. Note that all these services are free to the prospective purchaser. In all cases, it is the vendor who foots the bill.

The Internet

There are a growing number of websites advertising property for sale country-wide, either privately or through estate agents. Some of these also allow you free advertising of your own property for sale.

Gairloch & Loch Ewe Action Forum: www.highlandwelcome.co.uk. This is a small site run by a charitable local action group. It advertises properties and building sites in the Wester Ross area.

Property Live: www.propertylive.co.uk.

The Property Market: www.propertymarket.co.uk.

Property Window: www.propertywindow.com.

UK Homes For Sale: www.homes-uk.co.uk.

Asserta Home: www.assertahome/com.

Property Finder: www.propertyfinder.co.uk.

The House Hunter: www.thehousehunter.co.uk.

Home Hunter: www.homehunter.co.uk

As there are so many similar sites on the internet, and because new ones are coming online all the time, this can only be a selection of some of the most useful. A search for 'Scottish property' through any of the search engines will lead you to more.

Listed Buildings

Any building which is considered of special architectural or historic interest is 'listed' by the Scottish Executive. Buildings on the list are assigned a category, A, B or C, according to their relative importance. If you are looking for something out of the ordinary, such as a church, a castle or other historic building, there are a number of listed buildings for sale in Scotland.

There are fairly stringent controls placed on the alterations which can be made to listed buildings and their immediate surroundings, so you must take these restrictions into account when considering buying a listed building. The planning authorities must always be consulted before doing any work on a listed building – it is a criminal offence to undertake unauthorised works to demolish, significantly alter or extend a listed building. There are also obligations on the owner to keep the building in a reasonable state of preservation. On the plus side, grants towards the repair, maintenance or sympathetic improvement of listed buildings may be available through central or local government. Contact the local authority planning department for advice and for the full rules and regulations relating to listed buildings.

Useful Address

There is an estate agent which specialises in the buying and selling of listed buildings. *Pavilions of Splendour Ltd* 22 Mount View Road, LondonN4 4HX; ☎020-8348 1234; fax 020-8341 9790; www.heritage.co.uk.

New Property

There may be certain advantages in buying a new house. They tend to be built to higher standards than older houses and come with thermal insulation, double glazing, modern central heating and adequate ventilation, which may not always be the case with an older property. They are often sold complete with luxury fitted kitchens, bathrooms and bedrooms, together with the full range of kitchen appliances such as fridges, freezers, dishwashers and so forth. They tend to be built as small 'estates' or 'developments' of from around a dozen up to scores of similar houses, which may be a disadvantage if you prefer some 'elbow room' from your neighbours. In rural areas, new developments are correspondingly smaller – maybe half a dozen or so houses – because of the smaller population.

Around 60 per cent of new homes in Scotland are built with brick and block cavity walls, the remaining 40 per cent being of timber frame construction. New properties are generally sold directly by the builders, most of which are large concerns with developments in various parts of the country. You can contact them direct for details of properties currently available or under construction.

The process of buying a new house is exactly the same as buying any other property but it has the advantage that you will not find yourself caught in a chain of buyers – i.e. where the house you want to buy will not be available until its current occupants can take occupation of the house they are buying. If the owners of that house are negotiating on a house which is also still occupied – and so on ad nauseum – you can find yourself in a chain of several different parties, who are all waiting on the party at the top of the chain reaching the stage of vacating their property. If any one of the 'links' in such a chain pulls out, this can result in all the other sales falling through. Because of the binding nature of an accepted offer in Scotland, this situation is far less likely to arise than in England and Wales, where either party can pull out of the deal at any stage until the contract is actually signed – normally only days before the move actually takes place.

When the housing market collapsed in the early nineties, builders found themselves left with properties on their hands. They were desperate to sell, and customers were desperate to buy, but found they could not sell their own houses at the right price because there were so many on the market that prices were depressed. At this time, some large building firms bought houses from their potential customers so they could sell their newly-built developments. The biggest building companies could afford to put these older properties with estate agents and leave them for months or years before they sold. Some smaller building firms which did not have the financial resources to absorb that short term loss went to the wall during that period.

With the current slowing of the house market there are some fears that another crash could be on the horizon, but the general consensus among experts seems to be that this will not occur, and that house prices will level out and rise less quickly, but that there will not be a fall in property prices in real terms. Mortgage lenders learned from their own mistakes during the period when repossessions were running at a high rate, and now set far more stringent criteria for borrowers, so a similar high rate of repossessions is less likely to arise in the future.

Useful Publications & Addresses

New Home Locations Scotland Adaptive House, Quarrywood Court, Livingston EH54 6AX is a quarterly publication available by subscription though the website www.new-home-locations.net. Subscription costs £3 for one issue, £5 for the next two issues, £8 for the next three and £10 for the next four. This publication contains details of new developments around the country in addition to articles on all aspects of buying a new house.

Scotland's New Homebuyer Pinpoint Scotland Ltd, 9 Gayfield Square, Edinburgh EH1 3NT; ☎0131-556 9702; fax 0131-557 4701; www.snhb.co.uk. Another quarterly publication, available free from estate agents and SPC offices.

There are a large number of building companies with new developments throughout Scotland. Some of the largest are listed below, but there are smaller companies operating regionally. For a full list of current developments with contact details see *New Home Locations Scotland* and *Scotland's New Homebuyer.*

Barratt Construction: Golf Road, Ellon, AB41 9AT; ☎01358-724174; fax 01358-724043; www.barratthomes.co.uk.

Bett Homes: Argyle House, The Castle Business Park, Stirling FK9 4TT; ☎01786-477777; fax 01786-477666; www.betthomes.co.uk.

Alfred McAlpine Homes: Linnaird House, 1 Pall Mall East,London SW1Y 5AZ; ☎020-7930 6255; www.alfred-mcalpineplc.com.

Redrow Homes: Redrow House, 3 Central Park Avenue, Larbert, Falkirk FK5 4RX; ☎01324-555536; fax 01324-574890; www.redrow.co.uk.

Self-Build

This is a popular option in Scotland, especially in crofting areas. Crofters have long had the right to build a house on their croft, so the pattern of house building tends to be of individual properties rather than developments of several houses.

Of course, the term 'self-build' does not mean that you have to physically design and construct the house yourself – although those who have the skills may do all or part of the building or fitting-out work themselves. You may hire a building contractor to undertake all the work, or you may wish to employ a number of different tradesmen and craftsmen to do various parts of the project. But it means that you have overall control of the build from start to finish and you can work with an architect or builder to produce a building to suit your individual requirements. You will end up with a unique house which is tailored to your specific needs and, especially if you can do part of the work yourself, may end up with a property costing less.

One thing which might make building a new house preferable to the alternative of buying an existing small house and extending it is that, at the time of writing, there is no value added tax (VAT) charged on the building of a new house, whereas VAT at the standard rate (currently 17.5 per cent) is charged on extending, improving and repairs to an existing house. With new build, the VAT regulations allow you to claim back all the VAT paid on materials as a single sum on completion of the project and without having to register as a VAT trader.

Despite this, self-build is not necessarily a cheaper option. In addition to the cost of the building there are the costs of buying the land and of installing services such as electricity, water and sewerage on site to take into consideration. There are also likely to be other unforeseen costs that arise due to the topography of the land and to changing planning regulations. For instance, in recent years more stringent specifications in regard to domestic sewerage and drainage arrangements have been introduced, particularly in the many rural areas which are not on mains drainage and sewerage systems. Septic tanks which were previously approved are no longer deemed suitable for the purpose in some areas where the ground is particularly boggy, so new houses are only being granted planning permission if they specify a modern and more expensive form of septic tank termed a 'sewage treatment plant' which can process waste more efficiently. These can add several thousand pounds onto the cost of the build.

On the other hand, as the re-sale value of your self-built house can be at least 25 per cent greater than the cost of the project including the purchase price of the plot, it is an option worth considering. Providing you occupy the house for at least a year before selling on, it will be classed as your principle residence and any profits made on the sale will therefore be tax-free.

You may find self-build a frustrating process, due to the notorious difficulties of getting tradesmen to stick to agreed timescales. This and the vagaries of the weather can delay the completion of the project, with the associated extra costs of accommodation in the meantime. If you decide to build your own home, remember there are only two things that you can be certain of: it will take longer and cost more than you bargained for!

There has been a boom in self-build throughout the UK in recent years (although it has long been a feature of the Highlands) and to satisfy the increased interest, there are a number of periodical magazines which deal specifically with building one's own house.

Useful Publications

Homebuilding & Renovating Magazine and sister publication *Plotfinder* are both available via newsagents or by subscription from Ascent Publishing Ltd . Subscribe by telephoning 01527-834406 or via their website at www.homebuilding.co.uk The website includes a self-build directory which lists products, suppliers and services. It also has a database of plots for sale throughout the country.

Build It Inside Communications Ltd, 19th Floor, 1 Canada Square, Canary Wharf,

London E14 5AP; ☎020-7770 8300; fax 020-7772 8584; www.self-build.co.uk. Available through newsagents or by subscription. 12 issues around £40.

Prices of plots vary widely, as with every other aspect of property-buying, depending on location.

	SINGLE HOUSE PLOT PRICES, NOVEMBER 2004	
Price	**Town**	**Region**
£20,000	Westray	Orkney
£85,000	Newtonmore	Cairngorm
£63,000	Airth	Falkirk
£40,000	Peterhead	Aberdeenshire
£40,000	Bridgefoot	Perth & Kinross

Other Sources of Property

Property for sale and to rent can also be found advertised in local newspapers. In addition to adverts regularly run by estate agents and solicitors with a selection of their current properties, local newspapers in particular are a good place to find properties which are being sold privately without the services of estate agents or solicitors.

If money is no object, very expensive and exclusive properties and large country estates are advertised for sale in glossy magazines such as *Scottish Field*, www. scottishfield.co.uk; *The Countryman*, www.countrymanmagazine.co.uk; *Country Life* www.countrylife.co.uk or in the quality national daily or Sunday newspapers such as the *Telegraph*, www.telegraph.co.uk; *The Observer*, www.observer.guardian. co.uk; *Scotland on Sunday*, www.scotlandonsunday.com.

It can be very difficult to find a property in a rural area from a distance. It is hard to believe in this day and age, but some vendors seem to think they can sell property without advertising it beyond their local area. Some houses or crofts for sale are only advertised in small local newspapers, often run voluntarily, which have a circulation of only those people in the local area. Others one can only find out about by looking on the noticeboard in the local shop or by word of mouth. So it is useful to have a contact 'on the ground' who can sniff out these properties for you. Failing a 'spy' in the area, there are a number of relocation agencies in Scotland who will, for a fee, search out properties which suit your requirements.

RELOCATION AGENCIES

Location Highland: www.locationhighland.co.uk; ☎01463-234422. Based in Inverness.
Compass Relocation: 19A Ruisaurie, Beauly, Inverness-shire IV4 7AJ; ☎/fax 01463-783242; www.compass-reloc.co.uk.

Scott's Relocation: 23 Queen's Avenue, Edinburgh EH4 2DG; ☎0131-539 5367; www.scottsrelocation.co.uk.

Rural Relocation: Main Street, Dalguise, Dunkeld, Perthshire PH8 0JU; ☎01795-2970388; www.ruralrelocation.com. Covers Perthshire, Angus, Fife and Kinross.

The Association of Relocation Agents (ARA) can provide a full list of their members.PO Box 189, Diss IP22 1PE; ☎08700-737475; fax 08700-718719; www.relocationagents.com.

House Prices

Because of the variation in house prices between different areas of Scotland, it is difficult to give a true picture using average figures. However, along with the rest of the UK, the general overall trend is upwards, after a long period of stagnation and even some downward movement in parts of Scotland. In the late 1990s house prices started to move again in the south east of England. This trend has slowly percolated through the rest of the country and now shows strong signs of having reached Scotland, noticeably in Edinburgh, Aberdeen, parts of Glasgow and, to a lesser extent, Inverness.

It is a feature of the UK housing market that there is a cyclical trend, with periods of rising prices followed by stagnation or even falling prices. By late 2004 the UK as a whole was seeing a dramatic slowdown in prices after a five year boom, the slowdown brought about largely by a series of five interest rate rises since Autumn 2003. Again, following the historic pattern, the boom and the later slowdown came first in the South East of England and was followed by other areas of England, Wales and Scotland. House price growth in Scotland continued to outpace the UK average, remaining at above 20 per cent late on in 2004.

Overall there was a huge 56 per cent rise in Scottish house prices during 2001-2004. This still left Scotland with the lowest average house price of all countries in the UK – £107,377 compared with a UK average of nearly £170,000.

Scottish towns with the fastest increase during 2004 were Hamilton and Kilmarnock (both in the Glasgow commuter belt) which saw rises of 39 per cent during the year. House prices in Inverness also rose strongly during the year, up 28 per cent to an average of £128,439, higher than the average price in Glasgow. The fastest regional price rise was in the Borders, at 36 per cent, followed by both Dumfries & Galloway and Highland at 33 per cent.

AVERAGE HOUSE PRICES IN THE FOUR COUNTRIES OF THE UK

Country	1999	2004
Scotland	£60,678	£107,377
England	£75,817	£177,023
Wales	£59,263	£135,162
Northern Ireland	£63,514	£112,806

AVERAGE HOUSE PRICES IN SCOTLAND BY LOCAL AUTHORITY AREA IN 2004

Region	Price
City of Edinburgh	£162,446
East Renfrewshire	£157,498
East Lothian	£139,183
East Dunbartonshire	£137,714
Stirling	£129,943
Borders	£118,719
Perth & Kinross	£117,615
Midlothian	£112,835
Glasgow City	£110,417
Aberdeenshire	£105,433
Inverclyde	£102,308
Argyll & Bute	£101,338
Highland	£100,722
West Lothian	£100,662
Dumfries 8 Galloway	£100,603
South Ayrshire	£100,111
South Lanarkshire	£98,704
Aberdeen City	£96,682
Fife	£93,523
Clackmannanshire	£92,021
Renfrewshire	£91,650
Angus	£89,219
Falkirk	£87,847
North Ayrshire	£85,142
Moray	£84,734
North Lanarkshire	£82,075
West Dunbartonshire	£80,880
East Ayrshire	£80,060
Orkney Islands	£75,054
Dundee City	£74,207
Western Isles	£64,777
Shetland Islands	£62,717

The following tables give an indication of the range of prices asked for various properties in various parts of Scotland in late 2004

Property	Area	Price (offers over)
4 bed detached house	Hawick	£162,000
2 bedroom flat	Edinburgh	£149,995
4 bed terraced house	Edinburgh	£455,000
3 bed flat	Glasgow	£229,000
6 bed detached house	Paisley	£285,000
5 bed detached house	Moffat	£575,000
3 bed detached house	Inverurie	£128,000
1 bed flat	Aberdeen	£40,000
5 bed semi-detached house	Forres	£238,000
3 bed detached house	Nairn	£160,000
3 bed flat	Inverness	£82,000
3 bed detached house	Poolewe	£190,000
2 bed semi-detached cottage	Lairg	£55,000
Building plot 0.15 hectares	Castle Douglas	£75,000
Building plot 0.27 hectares	Lochinver	£40,000
Building plot 0.225 hectares	Wester Ross	£40,000

NEW HOUSE PRICES

3 bedroom detached houses	Aberdeen	£196,000
4 bedroom detached houses	Angus	£197,995
2 bedroom semi-detached houses	Falkirk	£96,475
2 bedroom flats	Glasgow	£164,000
3 bedroom semi-detached houses	Inverness	£120,995

Values placed upon houses in the Highlands in particular owe much to outright arbitrariness. First of all, there are fewer houses in total, so comparisons with similar properties in a similar location are extremely difficult to draw. Secondly, there is very little standardisation of housing types (with the possible exception of the more recently-erected 'kit' houses) so, once again, comparisons between properties are difficult to draw. Thirdly, any estate agent will tell you that the single most important factor in house purchases and sales is 'location, location, location'. Such a maxim might be fine when applied in the south but how does one compare the (relative) convenience of living in Ullapool with the splendour of the views across the Inner Sound from Applecross? Given that a house, like anything else, is worth only what somebody will pay for it, would you, for example, pay more or less for living in Ullapool or Applecross?

So it is impossible to answer the question: Is this or that house price fair? All you can say is whether you would be willing to pay that price to live in that house in that location. This, quite simply, is the test you must apply to your own prospective dream home.

PURCHASING & CONVEYANCING PROCEDURES

Offers

There are two points about house valuations in Scotland which sometimes confuse buyers from elsewhere: requests for 'offers over'; and closing dates for offers.

In Scotland, most houses are advertised for sale at a price 'Offers Over £X'. This is to encourage higher bids. However, if you can't afford £X, this does not mean that you are precluded from making another, lower offer. Follow the test above and offer only the amount you think that a property is worth. Many properties are sold at less than the 'offers over' price, and the longer the property has been on the market, the cheaper you are likely to get it. Take the 'offers over' point only as the point at which bargaining starts.

However, you may have to offer over the price to secure a property. It is impossible to say exactly how big a percentage over you should offer, as this varies by area, type of property, and the state of the housing market at the time. Exceptional cases where houses have sold at double or more than double the asking price hit the headlines, but the vast majority will sell at a more sensible price. Your solicitor should be able to advise you on the average percentage over the asking price expected in the area at the time you are bidding.

An increasing number of properties are now being advertised for sale at a fixed price, similar to the system in England and Wales. This is partly because people from outwith Scotland are put off by offers over, and it can also make the buying of property difficult – you could find you are outbid by other buyers on a series of properties, and as you would normally get a survey on each property before you know it is yours, this can be an expensive process. An indication of the increasing popularity of the fixed price is shown by the fact that between 2003 and 2004 the number of fixed price properties advertised in Edinburgh increased by 70 per cent.

Where a property has excited interest from more than one prospective purchaser, the vendor might decide to hurry the process along a little by advising all those who have 'noted their interest' in the property that a closing date for offers has been set.

The onus is thus shifted to the prospective purchaser(s) to make a formal offer on the property by the date set – a sort of blind auction. Once again, as in all types of auctions, follow the test above and offer only the amount you think that a property is worth, not the amount that you think might beat all other offers – unless, of course, you have decided that it is the only house for you, at whatever cost!

If you anticipate that a closing date for offers on a property might be set in the near future, this will not preclude you from hurrying the process along yourself by making an offer first. This is a way of shifting the pressure from purchaser to vendor. You may even be able to negotiate with the seller that you will add a premium on your offer if they agree to sell it to you without going to a closing date.

Sellers are not obliged to accept the highest offer they receive after the closing date: they may be prepared to accept a lower offer where, for instance, the buyer has not got his own property to sell and can move quickly.

Noting an Interest and Making an Offer

If you are interested in a property you have viewed, although you may not be ready to make an offer on it, you should note your interest with the seller's solicitor or estate agent. You would be well advised to obtain the services of a solicitor prior to making a formal offer on a property because of the complexity and the binding nature of certain contracts under Scottish law.

However, you can ask that your interest in a property be noted by the vendor's solicitor or estate agent without employing the services of a solicitor yourself (although a solicitor would be pleased to undertake this notification for you). Notification of interest does not commit you to buy. It ensures, however, that you will be kept informed of matters such as withdrawal of the property from the market or the fixing of a closing date for offers.Acceptance of your offer creates a legally binding contract and you will be provided with a copy of the formal offer for future reference. However, your offer can be made subject to certain conditions, and if these conditions are not agreed or met by the seller, you are no longer committed to the sale.

Surveys

An offer should be made only after a survey of the property has been carried out because this can affect the offer you make. Your solicitor will advise you about the reasonableness of the offer in the light of a survey's findings and will also take note of the requirement to confirm the existence of building warrants, planning permissions and completion certificates in respect of past changes to a building.

At time of writing, there is a voluntary 'single survey' pilot scheme underway in parts of Glasgow, Edinburgh, Inverness and Dundee. Under the single survey scheme, the seller of a property is obliged to obtain a survey of the condition of the property before the sale, and supply this to prospective purchasers. Depending on the results of this pilot scheme, it may be that the single survey will be made mandatory at some time in the future, but for the time being it is up to prospective purchasers to arrange their own surveys.

As there is currently no requirement for a property seller to tell prospective buyers about any defects in a property, it is advisable to obtain a survey on a property you contemplate buying. There are three main types of survey available, which vary in how detailed an inspection of the property is made.

Valuation Survey. If you are applying for a mortgage, your lender will carry out an independent valuation on the property to ensure that it provides sufficient security for the loan. This is paid for by the mortgage applicant, whether the purchase eventually goes through or not.

A valuation must be carried out by a qualified surveyor, but it is simply an assessment of the value of the property, not a structural survey. You can go ahead with the purchase on the basis of just the valuation report, but it gives no guarantee that the property is structurally sound.

Homebuyer Report. This is a more in-depth survey on the condition of a property, together with a valuation. Any major defect in the property will be listed, including such items as whether the property displays evidence of dampness, rot or woodworm. Recommendations for remedial work and any further investigations may be made. Together with a valuation for mortgage purposes it should also include the current market value.

Building Survey. Previously termed a full structural survey, this is advisable for older properties and those which are particularly large or unique. The surveyor will inspect everything that is accessible. It may involve negotiations with the vendor to allow the surveyor access to the roof space, to pull up carpets to examine floorboards and so forth.

You may employ your own surveyor to carry out either of these latter options, or may instruct your lender's surveyor to combine a homebuyer report or a full structural report with their valuation. This may reduce the overall cost.

If the surveyor's report shows that a property is in poor condition or has structural faults you may be able to negotiate a reduction in the price to cover the cost of remedial work. If a property is particularly poor, the lender may refuse to provide a mortgage on it.

If you go ahead and purchase, and later discover the house has faults which were not identified in the survey and which should have been discovered by the level of survey you commissioned, you may be able to sue the surveyor for damages. It should be noted, however, that they are very careful to cover themselves in the small print of their contracts against any potential claims. You may find they include 'escape clauses' designed to reduce your rights to claim if the surveyor should fail to notice such things as damp, rot or subsidence, so you may not be successful.

Even more detailed specialist surveys may be carried out if it is an especially old or unique building, or if there is particular cause for concern in a specific area.

Useful Address

Property surveys must be undertaken by a qualified surveyor who is a member of the *Royal Institution of Chartered Surveyors in Scotland* (9 Manor Place, Edinburgh EH3 7DN; ☎0131-225 7078; fax 0131-240 0830; www.rics-scotland.org.uk).

Acceptance of the Offer

Just as the offer to purchase might have been conditional (for example, upon acquiring the assignment of a crofting tenancy along with the purchase of a croft house), so the acceptance might also be conditional (for example, upon completion by a specified date). Those conditions are described as 'qualifications' and the vendor's acceptance of your offer as 'qualified acceptance'.

Your solicitor will advise you about those qualifications and subsequent negotiations between your own and the vendor's solicitor has much to do with 'bargaining' about those qualifications. The negotiations take place through the exchange of letters known as 'missives'.

The offer, acceptance and missives form part of the legal contract between vendor and purchaser. When the final acceptance has been issued, the bargain is concluded and a binding contract exists between vendor and purchaser.

Title Deeds

The title deeds of a property name its owner, describe its exact extent and include any conditions relating to the property, such as any restrictions on business use, or a requirement to contribute to the maintenance of common ground with a neighbour.

Your solicitor will examine the title deeds to ascertain a) that the seller is actually the owner of the property and that there are no restrictions on his or her right to sell; b) that the property and the land upon which it stands as described in the deeds are precisely what you think you are buying; c) that any conditions in the title are acceptable to you. If there are deemed to be unnecessary or unfair restrictions, it may be that steps can be taken to amend or remove those conditions.

There are strong elements of the feudal system still extant in Scotland which disappeared long ago in the rest of Britain. The crofting system is the most noticeable expression of this, but historically other properties have been subject to the rights of other bodies or individuals, termed 'feudal superiors', which restricted some of the uses to which you can put that property. The Abolition of Feudal Tenure Act was passed in the first session of the Scottish Parliament, and came fully into force in November 2004. This means that house owners will no longer have to abide by restrictions placed on the use of their properties imposed by feudal superiors. These can cover a variety of different issues, including such items as whether owners can build an extension to the house or run a business from home.

In some cases, the feudal superior had a right of pre-emption on a property, which meant they could buy land or a house which was put up for sale, under the noses of the seller and a potential buyer. Just before the new legislation came into force, a young couple in Strathspey were denied a plot of land in just this way. They had agreed to buy an unserviced plot of land from a farmer for £20,000, but the Laird of the estate exercised his right of pre-emption and bought the land for the same amount. Then he put it on the open market for sale at offers over £125,000.

It is not uncommon for some old Highland properties to have no deeds. In such a case it may be advisable to insist the vendor have some drawn up, at his expense. Be wary and take your solicitor's advice in these matters.

Settlement

After the bargain is concluded, all outstanding matters are settled and entry is gained to your new house, your solicitor will forward the title deeds for registration in the Land Register of Scotland. On their return, the solicitor will forward them to you or your lender. If you have bought the property outright, the deeds then remain in your possession. If you have taken a loan or a mortgage to buy the property, the deeds will usually be lodged with the lender until such time as you have paid off the loan.

Buying a Flat

The foregoing sections apply in most respects to buying a flat. There may be additional conditions in the deeds in respect of obligations regarding sharing the cost of repair and maintenance of the fabric of the building. For instance, in a building which contains several flats or apartments, there may be a requirement for all tenants to share the costs of such things as repairs to the roof or to communal car parking areas.

The Crofting System

Much of the Highlands and Islands is made up of traditional crofting townships which are subject to crofting law. This applies to the following areas which together make up the seven former crofting counties.

FORMER CROFTING COUNTIES

East & West Mainland. Area covered: Caithness, Sutherland, Ross-shire, East Inverness.

Argyll, Skye & Lochalsh. Area covered: Skye & the Small Isles, Glenshiel, Kintail & South from Lochalsh, Argyll & Argyll Islands, South & West Inverness.

Shetland & Orkney. Area covered: All the islands of Shetland & Orkney.

Western Isles. Area covered: Lewis, Harris, North & South Uist, Barra..

There are around 17,700 crofts occupied by an estimated 10,000-12,000 households with a total population of around 33,000. This number has risen over recent years, after a decline in numbers. The Crofters Commission is committed to increasing the number of active crofters and has various schemes to help with this, in particular the Croft Entrant Scheme. Currently, 3,600 crofts are owner-occupied, but this figure is predicted to rise as more are sold on the open market.

It is absolutely vital that, when considering the purchase of any property in these areas, early enquiries are made to determine whether the land in question is croft land or de-crofted land. If it is croft land, it is essential that the identity of both the landlord and the assigned crofting tenant is determined. It is quite possible for the croft to be owned by a private individual (as distinct from the local Estate), yet the crofting tenure be assigned to another individual.

Along with considerations of crofting tenure, each croft will normally be entitled to a share in the common grazing rights enjoyed by a township. The continuation of such rights demand the payment of an annual nominal rent (£1 or so) to the landlord and the transfer of rights to any new crofter.

Crofting legislation is a specialist area and advice should always be sought from a solicitor well-versed in crofting law. Advice is also available from the Crofters Commission.

In addition, crofting is inextricably linked with cultural identity. People croft not simply because of economic benefits. They croft because their parents crofted and because it is as much a social activity as a part-time job. In truth, they are 'crofters' rather than 'people who croft'. Incomers who acquire a croft will often be regarded as people who croft rather than as crofters. Before rushing headlong into croft purchase, you would do well to discuss the implications of acquiring a croft with someone who is resident in the area already and who can give impartial advice about both the general complexion of the larger community and the specific crofting township within which the proposed purchase lies.

As an example of a problem which could arise, a croft might be acquired which is subject of an official sub-let, an unofficial sub-let or occasional grazing rights. Whilst a new croft owner might be legally entitled to avail him or herself of all crofting rights in respect of the croft, the dispossession of a neighbour's habitual rights of access to that croft might have certain social implications.

If you are interested in moving to a crofting area you do need to understand a little about the crofting system. It is very complicated and is hedged about by rules and regulations, administered by the Crofters Commission, which affect access and rights to land and the uses to which it can be put.

Put simply, most croft lands are areas of privately-owned estates, which are divided into many crofts of around four acres in size and rented out at a tiny annual rent to tenant crofters. Tenant crofters have the option to buy their croft, in which case they become owner-crofters. A group of crofts in any particular area is called a 'crofting township' which has its own Common Grazings Committee to discuss and administer anything relating to crofting matters in that township.

In crofting areas house sites come on to the market from time to time – crofters often have the option to de-croft portions of their croft of between about 1/4 and 1/2 acre to sell off for a house. Many more would doubtless be available if permission to de-croft sites were not dependent on agreement from the entire crofting township. If it is felt that a house site would unjustifiably cut down on good grazing for sheep or cattle permission to de-croft is often not granted. De-crofting can be a time-consuming and expensive process, which also puts some crofters off the idea. If you are interested in buying a site, you should always ensure it has both outline planning permission and is de-crofted before you buy, or you could find yourself the proud possessor of a piece of land you can do nothing with, while your neighbour has the right to graze his sheep on it or work it in other ways.

If buying a house, you need to ascertain the status of the ground it stands on. If it is a tenanted croft, it is often the estate which owns the land and the tenant crofter who has the rights to use it. The situation is different if it is an owned croft – in this case you buy the land outright. However, even then you need to make sure there isn't a crofter who is already assigned your croft as a tenant, and can therefore work it.

In many cases, crofters have built modern houses on their crofts, leaving the original dwelling standing. Although some of these old properties have been renovated and are let out as holiday cottages, others are left unused, in a state of semi-dereliction. These are crying out to be renovated and lived in, but sadly, because the existing crofting system guarantees that a croft can be passed down through a family, many of these old buildings are being 'saved for the children' so it is rare that they come on to the open market. In many cases these children are adult and have lived and worked far away for many years, with no intention of coming back. But despite this, it can still be difficult for anyone, whether a young local or an incomer, to get hold of that building or that croft.

There have been significant changes to the land tenure system since the advent of the Scottish Parliament. Legislation has been passed to give community bodies the right to buy land as and when it comes on the market, and to give crofting communities the right to buy land at any time.

Owner-Occupied Crofts

Because tenanted crofts are generally passed on through families, the best chance an incomer is likely to have to obtain possession of a croft is to buy an owner-occupied croft, where the land has been bought from the estate. In this case, both the croft land and the buildings which stand on it become the property of the buyer.

However, it is necessary to investigate closely your rights before buying even an owned croft. Despite owning the land outright, there are still restrictions on the rights to work that croft. The Crofters Commission have the duty to ensure that any croft, owned and tenanted, is occupied by a 'suitable' person. You cannot just buy a croft and treat the land as a garden, for example, without using the croft in a productive way, as defined by the Crofters Commission. If you buy a croft and are then told by the Crofters Commission that you do not satisfy their requirements to be classed as a crofter, they have the right to give the tenancy of your croft to another person who is using it in an approved way. It is essential that you sort out these issues before committing yourself to buy.

You should of course take the advice of a solicitor conversant in crofting law, but the way they would probably advise proceeding would be to put in an offer on the croft with the condition that you are granted the tenancy. If the Crofters Commission decide that you are not a 'suitable' person you could then withdraw your offer without financial penalty.

So, if you are contemplating buying a croft you will need to have a viable plan for using the land productively. In the past, the range of activities you could carry out under the heading of 'crofting' was limited to agricultural activities. However, today the definition has been widened to include, not just such traditional activities as keeping livestock and growing crops, but also environmental and tourism activities and the catch-all phrase 'any activity which is of community benefit.'

In 1999, two English couples bought crofts in Wester Ross, and were granted the tenancies of their respective crofts on the basis of a variety of activities they proposed carrying out. These included re-foresting areas of the crofts with indigenous trees, producing and selling organic produce such as vegetables and herbs, and planting an area in order to attract wildfowl to the area which could then be opened to visitors. They also both proposed building a new house for their own accommodation and renovating and renting out the original croft cottage for summer visitors. In addition, they were involved in other business activities which did not involve using the land in a traditional way.

Clare O'Brien was a successful freelance writer and editor, while her husband Ally Wright had been a professional musician and composer in the past. Clare's workload was increasing and she found herself having to turn down work, so she had the potential to employ a local person to help her with the administrative and secretarial side of her work. Ally proposed building a music studio in his new house which would allow him to compose and produce music on CD, for videos and television, as well as to train local people in sound engineering skills.

> **Clare found her work opportunities actually increased**
> *Don't come to Scotland looking for a quiet life, whatever you do! I'm working harder than I ever have. My work as a journalist is as healthy as ever, I've taught an evening class in teleworking skills at the local school, and we're growing organic*

> *vegetables on the croft for sale locally. I'm also making craft items to sell in the local*
> *market and through shops in the district. I'd only ever made things for amusement*
> *before, but here there are so many natural materials – driftwood, shells, feathers,*
> *stones – that it's really easy to have good ideas.*

The other couple, Ric and Jill Holmes, had a greetings card design and production company which again would need to employ people locally. In addition, Ric was a qualified sailing instructor who had run a successful sailing school for some years. He transported this from his original base in northern England to Wester Ross, and offered boating and sailing courses and cruises to visitors. He was qualified also to train local people to run such courses themselves, so he could offer both training and employment locally, as well as providing added tourist attractions.

> **Ric and Jill too found there was plenty to keep them busy**
> *The biggest problem is finding time to do all the things we planned to do. Between*
> *producing artwork for commissions, running sailing courses and looking after the*
> *croft and the various animals we now keep – from hens to horses – there just aren't*
> *enough hours in the day!*

The Crofters Commission agreed that these many and varied activities added up to an attractive package which would overall be of community benefit and therefore granted them the right to take on the tenancies of their respective crofts.

Five years on, and it has to be said that not all these projects have come to pass, nor are they likely to – in particular the promised local employment has not emerged – but possession being nine-tenths of the law, they would be unlikely to have the crofts taken away from them!

Timescale

Whichever kind of property you buy, because of the legal process in Scotland, it is likely to be a minimum of two months from making an offer before you could legally take possession of your new property.

Finding a Solicitor

The Law Society of Scotland will provide lists of their members. Members of the area Solicitors' Property Centres are listed in their free newspapers and on their websites. If you are contemplating buying a croft, ensure that the solicitor you choose is expert in crofting law – not all of them are. Many firms will have one partner who specialises in this area.

Conveyancing Marketing Services can provide competitive quotes for conveyancing, negotiated with their large database of solicitors, all Law Society members, www.conveyancing-cms.co.uk.

Further Information

The Law Society of Scotland: 26 Drumsheugh Gardens, Edinburgh EH3 7YR; ☎0131-226 7411; fax 0131-225 2934; www.lawscot.org.uk. The Law Society of Scotland produces a booklet called *Your Solicitor and House Purchase and Sale.* It is obtainable from the Law Society direct, the Citizens Advice Bureau in Scotland and from individual solicitors. It provides in slightly more depth some of the information reproduced here but bear in mind that the Law Society also represents the interests of the legal profession and it is consistent of the society to advise you to engage the services of a solicitor at the earliest possible stage in the house purchase process.

Citizens Advice Scotland: 1st Floor Spectrum House, 2 Powderhall Road, Edinburgh EH7 4GB; ☎0131-550 1000; fax 0131-550 1001; www.cas.org.uk. Citizens Advice Bureaux are situated throughout Scotland and provide free advice and information on all sorts of legal, civil and social matters.

Scottish Crofters Union: Old Mill, Harapool, Broadford, Isle of Skye IV49 9AQ; ☎01471-822529; fax 01471-822799; e-mail crofters.union@talk21.com; www. scu.co.uk. Advice on crofting matters.

Crofters Commission (Ughdarras Nan Croitearan): 4/6 Castle Wynd, Inverness IV2 3EQ; ☎01463-663450; fax 01463-711820; www.crofterscommission.org. uk. The Crofters Commission produce a number of useful free booklets relating to crofting.

PUBLICATIONS AVAILABLE FROM THE CROFTERS COMMISSION

Title	Publisher
Purchasing Your Croft	Crofters Commission
Owner-Occupied Croft Land	Crofters Commission
Becoming a Crofter	Crofters Commission
Decrofting	Crofters Commission
Crofting Counties Agricultural Grants Scheme:	
Guidance Notes	Crofters Commission
Scottish Agriculture: Guide to Grants and	
Services	Scottish Executive
Biodiversity on Croftland & Common Grazings	Scottish Biodiversity
	Agriculture Working Group

THE COSTS OF BUYING PROPERTY

The cost of buying property in Scotland involves the paying of separate fees to most of the parties involved. Often the amount payable bears little relationship to the amount of work involved, as the fees are generally a percentage of the selling price of the property, so the larger the house, the higher the total fees payable. This is a rough breakdown of the level of fees for various elements of the transaction.

Solicitors

Their fees cover the preparation of legal documentation, exchange of missives with the sellers' solicitor, plus the administration involved in such things as arranging for stamp duty to be paid, setting up a mortgage and passing monies to the mortgage lender. The level charged is usually between 1 and 1.5 per cent of the purchase price, plus value added tax (VAT), currently at 17.5 per cent. It is worth 'shopping around' for the best deal as charges vary between solicitors.

Estate Agents

The buyer of a house should not have to pay anything to the estate agent or solicitor who is selling it. They charge fees only to the vendor, which vary depending on the company, but generally fall within the range of 1.5 to 2 per cent of the selling price. For this they will produce a brochure with a photograph and details of the property, advertise the property in their offices and newspapers, place an advertising board outside the house, show prospective purchasers round and act as an intermediary between buyer and seller when an offer is made. An insidious additional cost has emerged: some agents and solicitors are charging a separate fee for advertising on their websites.

Again it is worth shopping around as estate agents' fees and the service provided do vary.

Stamp Duty Land Tax

This is a government tax levied on the buyers of all property valued at over £60,000. The rate charged is 1 per cent of the total purchase price of any property costing between £60,000 and £250,000, 3 per cent on properties of £250,001 to £500,000 and 4 per cent on those of £500,001 and over.

Land Registry Registration Fees

Once a property has changed hands, the details of the new owner are recorded in the Land Registry. There is a sliding scale of charges for this depending on the value of the property. See www.ros.gov.uk/solicitor/feestable.html For example, registration fees on a house sold for £100,000 would be £220.

Valuation Fee

You must pay for a lender to value a property before they offer you a loan. Fees vary depending on the lender and the value of the property, but typically are around £10-15 for each £10,000 value of the house, with a minimum fee of between £50-200.

Survey Fee

Homebuyer reports too vary depending on the lender, so it is worth while 'shopping around' for the best deal. For example, the Scottish Building Society charge £300 for a property costing £80,001-100,000 while Nationwide charge £400 for a property costing £50,001-100,000. You may get a better deal if you go direct to your own surveyor rather than using the building society or bank's surveyor, but remember you would then have to pay separately for a valuation for the lender. A building survey varies depending on type and value of the property. As a guide a survey of a three bedroom semi-detached house valued at £150,000 will cost around £325 + vat. This should be arranged directly with a surveyor, but your solicitor or estate agent will be able to provide you with details of recommended surveyors.

Arrangement Fee

Variously called an arrangement, application or acceptance fee, this is charged by a lender for arranging a mortgage and is typically around £250 to £300. However, there are many different mortgages available, each with different fees. You may find a single building society, for example, offering a range of mortgages, some of which have an arrangement fee, others which have none.

Lender's Legal Fees

Any legal fees charged by your lender's solicitor are payable by the borrower. If the same solicitor acts for both lender and borrower the fees may be lower.

Buildings Insurance

A condition of any mortgage is that the property is fully insured against structural and other damage for the full term of the loan. Premiums payable vary depending on individual circumstances, the area in which you live, the size and type of the property and the insurance company, so it is difficult to give a meaningful guide. It is sensible to shop around.

Your mortgage lender may offer you insurance 'in-house' but you have no obligation to take this. You may arrange insurance with another company.

Life Insurance

You may be required to take out a life insurance policy to pay off your mortgage in full in the event of your death. The lender may arrange life insurance, but the borrower is entitled to arrange the necessary cover elsewhere, and this may work out cheaper.

Negotiating Reduced Fees

Note that currently there is great competition within the mortgage market, so it is in your interests to shop around and compare fees. Most lenders are open to negotiation on different elements of the fees charged, if they understand that you can get a better deal elsewhere. For instance, if one lender does not charge an arrangement fee, you may want to try negotiating with another lender who is giving a better deal on other elements that they waive the arrangement fee, to prevent you taking your business to that other lender. It often works!

RENTING PROPERTY

It is a far less complicated process to rent a property than to buy one so it should not take more than two to four weeks to arrange. The part of the process that is likely to take the longest is finding a suitable property. The rental market in Britain is comparatively small – less than ten per cent of private homes. There is a shortage of properties to rent in many areas, particularly those with three or more bedrooms. One bedroom flats or one-room bedsits (sometimes called studios) are easier to come by, especially in cities.

The vast majority of rental properties are let furnished. The reason for this is historical: until the law was changed in 1989, landlords had greater legal protection if their properties were let furnished. Although this is no longer the case, in many areas unfurnished properties are hard to come by. Unless you are looking at the luxury end of the market, the furnishings in a property are often not of a very high standard. Generally, unfurnished properties do include carpets, curtains and kitchen appliances such as cooker and fridge.

In order to find which properties are to let, you should contact all the estate agents and letting agents in the area you are interested in, in addition to looking in the local papers where you may find privately-advertised properties. 'Free-ads' papers, where private sellers and lessors can advertise items and property free of charge carry details of rental properties as well as building sites and houses for sale. *Scot-ads* is one such, covering the north of Scotland.

Rental costs will vary considerably depending on the size and age of a property, its condition and most importantly, its location. In city areas, rents tend to be high. In rural areas they will be far lower, but the saving on rent may be offset by other costs, such as higher fuel costs and higher prices in local shops. As a rule of thumb, the more remote a property is, the lower the rent will be.

Sources of Rental Properties

Scot Ads: ☎08457-434343; www.scot-ads.com.

Letting Web: A very useful website which advertises properties to let via letting agents throughout Scotland. www.lettingweb.com.

Relocation Agencies: You can employ a relocation agency to find a suitable property for you, but it is wise to compare the costs of different agencies, as these can be quite high. *The Association of Relocation Agents* (ARA) can provide a full list of their members. PO Box 189, Diss IP22 1PE; ☎08700-737475; fax 08700-718719; www.relocationagents.com.

Tenancy Agreements

When a property is rented, a tenancy agreement must be signed by both the landlord and the tenant. It is a legal contract, so both parties who sign it agree to abide by the conditions contained within it and if they fail to do so the other party can take legal action against them. For this reason it is essential to read the tenancy agreement closely, and to obtain the advice of a solicitor if there is anything you are unsure or unhappy about.

Rental Costs

The tenancy agreement will detail how often and in what form the rent is to be paid. This is normally payable in advance for one or three months at a time. You may need to set up a UK bank account to make the payments. The agreement will state the length of time the tenant agrees to take the property, and rent is payable for the whole of this period. If the tenant leaves early he/she will have to continue to pay the rent and outgoings for the property until a new tenant is found. The tenancy agreement may state a period after which your rent may be reviewed or increased.

The landlord should issue you with a rent book, in which all rental payments made are recorded. If you are not given a rent book, it is wise to pay only by cheque and insist on a receipt. This provides evidence if there is ever a dispute about rental payments.

In addition to the monthly rental, tenants are responsible for paying for other outgoings such as council tax, contents insurance, as well as for gas, electricity, water rates and telephone bills. Buildings insurance will normally be paid by the owner.

Deposits

In addition to the rent, a tenant pays a deposit to the landlord or letting agent at the commencement of the tenancy. This is a sum of money, usually equivalent to about four or six weeks rent, which is kept in an account until the end of the tenancy when it will be used to pay for any rent arrears or any damage to the property during the tenancy. The balance, if any, is then returned to the tenant. It is important to ensure that the deposit is placed in a separate interest-bearing account and that the tenant receives the interest. The tenancy agreement should state these conditions. This will help to ensure that, in the event that a letting agent or landlord goes bankrupt, you do not lose your deposit.

The tenancy agreement will require the tenant to hand the property back to the landlord in the same condition it was in at the start of the tenancy. The tenant will need to prove that he did not cause any damage, so it is important to ensure that you get an inventory at the outset which outlines the state of the property and what items were provided.

Generally, tenant and landlord are required to give a period of notice (usually a month) if they wish to terminate the agreement. However, depending on the sort of tenancy, the tenant may be protected from eviction. (See *Assured Tenancies* below.)

Letting Agents

Many rented properties are let through letting agencies, which act as an intermediary between the landlord and tenant. They collect rents from tenants and pass them on to the landlord. However, you should check any letting agent out carefully as they have a worse reputation than estate agents. Anybody can set up as a letting agent and there are numerous tales of unscrupulous letting agents collecting rents and deposits and keeping them in their own accounts rather than passing them on to the landlord. Amazingly, there is very little redress in law against such behaviour, and any legal action you do take is likely to be protracted and expensive, so the best way to protect yourself against this is to make enquiries about the agents first before entering into an agreement with them. Try only to deal with a member of the Association of Residential Letting Agents (ARLA), which insists that members have insurance cover to safeguard rental income and deposits. They have a website which includes a searchable database of letting agents by area.

Some properties are run by property management companies where the owners pass over responsibility for the day to day maintenance as well as administering and collecting of rents. These are particularly often found in connection with buildings containing a number of flats owned by different people. The management company will charge service charges to both owners and tenants for maintenance and repairs to the building, in addition to administration charges to the owner for collecting and passing on rents from the tenants to the owners.

Letting agents usually ask for a reservation fee, deductible from the deposit when you sign a rental agreement.

Useful Address

Association of Residential Letting Agents: Maple House, 53-55 Woodside Road, Amersham, Bucks HP6 6AA; ☎0845-345 5752; fax 01494-431530; www. arla.co.uk.

Assured Tenancies

The Housing (Scotland) Act 1988 introduced the concept of assured and short assured tenancies.

An assured tenancy gives greater rights to a tenant as it is for an indefinite period. As long as the landlord does not live on the premises and the tenant observes the terms of the tenancy agreement, the landlord cannot evict the tenant unless he obtains a court order on certain grounds specified in the Act. These include such things as unpaid rent, damage or otherwise breaking the contract with the landlord.

A court may serve you with written notice to leave if the landlord offers you similar property, needs the property for himself or needs vacant possession in order to sell the property.

If there is no written tenancy agreement, the tenant has the same rights as under an assured tenancy, as long as the landlord does not live on the premises in which case different rules apply.

Short Assured Tenancies

These are tenancies of not less than six months. There must be a written notice to the effect that it is a short assured tenancy. The landlord then has the right to regain possession on giving notice to the tenant, whether or not the tenant has observed the terms of the tenancy agreement.

Council Housing and Housing Associations

Low cost 'social' housing is provided throughout Scotland by local authorities and by housing associations which build properties using a mixture of public and private money. Council housing is rented, although tenants have the right to buy their property at below market value. In order to qualify for council housing, you would have to show you had a right to avail yourself of public resources – i.e. that you were not precluded from doing so under the immigration rules (see above.)

Housing association properties are available under various arrangements, ranging from full rental, to shared ownership schemes where part rental/part mortgage is paid until such time as the tenant has paid the full value of the property, to full ownership. Scottish Homes, the central body for Scottish housing associations, is now Communities Scotland, part of the Scottish Executive Development Department.

Useful Addresses

Communities Scotland: Thistle House, 91 Haymarket Terrace, Edinburgh EH12 5HE; ☎0131-313 0044; fax 0131-313 2680; www.scot-homes.gov.uk.

Scottish Federation of Housing Associations: 38 York Place, Edinburgh, EH1 3HU; ☎0131-556 5777; fax 0131-557 6028; www.sfha.co.uk.

Income from Holiday Homes

In areas of Scotland which attract a lot of tourists, a useful income can be made from letting out a property as holiday accommodation. Self-catering cottages in rural areas, and flats in the cities, are in short supply during the holiday season. Highest demand is during the summer months of June to August, but if the property is of a good standard and is marketed well, there should be no difficulty in filling a property for 26 weeks or more each year. Weekly rentals for self-catering cottages vary depending on the size, type and situation of the property and time of year. In the high season (July and August) rents of between £300 and £450 per week are typical.

VisitScotland (formerly The Scottish Tourist Board) markets tourist facilities nationally and internationally. The organisation is currently (in late 2004) undergoing a wholesale review and restructuring, following on from bad performances over recent years. The final restructuring will not be in place until Spring 2005, but the main changes will be that the 14 Area Tourist Boards will be scrapped, and replaced with 14 'hubs' of the central VisitScotland body. Membership fees for belonging to VisitScotland will be scrapped, replaced with a system where tourism providers simply pay for the facilities and services they wish to buy from VisitScotland – mainly advertising in brochures and on their website. All accommodation owners who buy services must have their properties graded. Inspectors will visit all properties in the scheme once a year and award a grading of one to five stars depending on the standard of the accommodation. Membership of the scheme is charged depending on the number and type of properties owned.

With the advent of the internet, more and more owners are opting out of VisitScotland and advertising their own properties directly via their own, or collective, websites. In many cases this proves far cheaper and more effective than marketing via the tourist board. This has caused the falling membership ad therefore falling revenues, which has led to the restructuring. It remains to be seen whether tourism businesses will return to the VisitScotland fold, now they have found that they can advertise their businesses more effectively and more cheaply elsewhere.

There are a number of holiday letting agencies which take a percentage (as much as 33.3 per cent in some cases) of rental income as their fee for advertising properties in their glossy brochures and on their websites, and dealing with bookings for the owner. In some cases there is also an initial fee payable when joining such an agency, which makes this an expensive way to proceed. The high fees charged mean that in some rural areas property owners may find they price themselves out of the market, unable to compete with the lower rental which can be charged by their neighbours who are not paying agency fees from their income. These agencies have also been hit by the increase in owners setting up their own websites, which has forced the agencies to compete for a smaller number of advertisers.

Rates payable on holiday properties take account of the fact that their occupancy is limited. In the Highland Council region, for example, non-domestic (i.e.

business) rates are charged at 50 per cent of the full amount on self-catering cottages. Many of these properties are owned by people who live in the area permanently, although others are owned by people living elsewhere. In some cases, these second home owners use the properties themselves for a number of weeks each year and let them out for the remainder of the time. Others leave them empty apart from the two or three weeks each year when they stay there. There has been a 50 per cent discount on Council Tax for second homes. There is some resentment of this in rural areas where housing for local people is in short supply and expensive. In response to such criticism, from April 2005 local authorities will be able to charge council tax on second homes at a discount of just 10 per cent rather than the existing 50 per cent discount.

Income from Long Term Lets

Rents chargeable on long term lets are far lower than on holiday lets, particularly in rural areas. As a rule of thumb, the further a property is from a large town, the lower will be the rent.

In order to maximise income from a holiday property, some owners let it out during the winter months on a long term let of between two months and six months. In this case, the tenant would be expected to pay the council tax, insurance and other household bills such as telephone, electricity and so forth.

Because of the desperate shortage of council housing in some rural areas, some authorities lease properties from private landlords to house council tenants. The Highland Council, for example, runs the 'Rural Leasing Scheme' under which it leases property from private owners, normally over a period of five or seven years, on a sliding rental scale depending on the size, type and condition of the property. This rental is paid to the owner six-monthly in advance, and the council takes on all costs including buildings insurance, repairs and maintenance, council tax and so forth. Payment of the rental is guaranteed even when the property is empty, for instance during a period between one council tenant leaving and the next taking up residence.

SAMPLE PRIVATE PROPERTIES TO RENT LATE 2004

Area	Type	Cost Per Month
Aberdeen	Studio flat	£275.00
Glasgow	2 bed penthouse apartment	£795.00
Paisley	4 bed house	£850.00
Edinburgh	1 bed flat	£600.00
Borders	2 bed detached house	£400.00
Loch Ness	2 bed cottage	£550.00
Inverness	3 bed flat	£475.00

SAMPLE LOCAL AUTHORITY AVERAGE WEEKLY RENTS 2004-05	
Scotland	£40.70
Inverclyde	£52.80
Edinburgh City	£49.44
Highland	£47.42
Orkney Islands	£39.82
Perth & Kinross	£37.59
Midlothian	£33.77

Useful Websites

Letting Web: www.lettingweb.co.uk. Properties to let via lettings agents across Scotland.

Better Renting Scotland: www.betterrentingscotland.com. Advice and information on all aspects of renting property, for both landlords and tenants.

Capital Gains Tax

Where a property has been let, either long term or as holiday accommodation, capital gains tax (CGT) may be payable when the property is sold. If you have two homes, living for part of the year in one, part in the other, you must nominate your 'main residence' (generally the one with the highest value) for CGT purposes. Husbands and wives each have an annual CGT exemption, thus generating a larger exemption than for single owners (this was £8,200 in 2004/05, therefore £16,400 in total). If the profit made on the second property is in excess of this amount, CGT may be payable. Full details are available from the Inland Revenue.

It is always best to obtain advice from an accountant, because you may be able to reduce your tax liability. Choose an accountant conversant with Scottish legislation which is different in some instances from that elsewhere in Britain.

Useful Addresses

Inland Revenue: Capital Taxes Office (Scotland), Meldrum House, 15 Drumsheugh Gardens, Edinburgh EH3; www.inlandrevenue.gov.uk.

Institute of Chartered Accountants of Scotland: CA House, 21 Haymarket Yards, Edinburgh, EH12 5BH; ☎0131-347 0100; fax 0131-347 0105; www.icas. org.uk.

Association of Chartered Certified Accountants: 83 Princes Street, Edinburgh EH2 2ER; ☎0131-247 7510; fax 0131-247 7514; www.accaglobal.com.

INSURANCE AND WILLS

Insurance

Most mortgage lenders insist that you have buildings insurance as part of your agreement. Buildings insurance policies are usually index-linked which means they rise automatically every year to match the retail price index (RPI). Premiums are usually paid monthly. This can be set up as an automatic 'direct debit' payment from your bank.

Buildings insurance normally protects the structure of the property from severe weather (storms, lightning, floods); theft and vandalism; fire, smoke and explosions; subsidence; burst pipes; civil commotion; water or oil leakage; impact from vehicles, falling trees, aircraft, masts, aerials.

The amount guaranteed by the policy must cover the cost of rebuilding the house, should the worst happen. Your house survey will give an idea of reinstatement costs and recommend the level of buildings insurance to be taken out.

There is no legal requirement to take out contents insurance on the movable objects inside your house. It is estimated that around 25% of all houses in the UK are not covered. Contents insurance normally covers you for the same risks as buildings insurance, listed above. Your policy will cover your possessions for up to a certain total value, either on a 'new-for-old' basis, where items are replaced at their current market value, or 'indemnity cover' where the insurance company will take into account general depreciation on items claimed for.

Most residential insurance does not meet the requirements for let property. For example, it is unlikely to cover for accidental damage caused while your house is let to a tenant. If you are letting a property, you will need to get insurance specifically tailored to your requirements. There are special 'landlords' policies' for long term lets, and also policies designed specifically for self-catering holiday properties, where it is assumed the property will be empty for parts of the year.

Certain types of mortgage require you to take out a life assurance policy which will cover all outstanding mortgage repayments in the event of your death. You may also wish to take out 'mortgage protection insurance' which will cover mortgage repayments for a limited period (usually up to a year) in the event of the mortgagee becoming unemployed, ill or injured.

Useful Address

Association of British Insurers: 51 Gresham Street, London EC2V 7HQ; ☎020-7600 3333; fax 020-7696 8999; www.abi.org.uk.

Wills

When somebody dies it will usually be necessary for someone to deal with the property owned by the person who has died. This is called 'winding up an estate' and the person responsible for dealing with assets of the estate is called the executor. An executor may be named in the deceased person's will. If none is named, or if there is no will, an executor will be appointed by the sheriff court of the sheriffdom (the Scottish equivalent of the English and Welsh magistrates court) in which the person died. This is usually a close relative or friend, or may be a solicitor. In either case, it will usually be necessary to consult a solicitor.

If you move from England or Wales to Scotland, it may be wise to make a new will, because the law relating to the disposal of an estate is different in Scotland. A solicitor will you advise you the best way to proceed in your personal circumstances.

In Scotland, any person over 12 and of sound mind can make a will. They can only freely dispose of part of the estate because members of the deceased's family have certain legal rights which must be satisfied, as follows:

The spouse has the right to inherit one-third of the estate if there are children or other descendants, and one-half of it if there are not.

Children are entitled to one-third of the moveable estate if there is a surviving spouse, and one-half of it if there is not.

Legacies and bequests are payable from the remaining portion. Any debts, inheritance tax (also called death duty), solicitors' and other legal fees are payable out of the whole estate before any division.

If a person dies intestate (i.e. without making a will) their estate passes to certain members of the family. A surviving spouse has 'prior rights' which must be satisfied before the remainder of the estate is divided up. The spouse has the right to inherit the matrimonial home up to a value of £130,000 or one matrimonial home if there is more than one; the furnishings and contents of that home up to the value of £22,000; £35,000 if the deceased left children or other descendants, £58,000 if not (these figures are increased from time to time).

Once these prior rights have been satisfied the remaining portion of the estate is divided between the surviving spouse and children as specified above.

Where there are no surviving spouse or children, half of the estate is taken by the parents and half by the brothers or sisters of the deceased person.

COUNCIL TAX

All Scottish residents must pay council tax, which is levied by local councils to pay for services such as education, road maintenance, police, refuse collection and so forth. Each council fixes its own tax rate based on the number of residents and the income needed to supply those services.

The amount payable is based on the value of your home as rated by your council. This is not necessarily current market value as the valuation bands were set according to open market value on 1st April 1991.

PROPERTY VALUATION BANDS

Band	Property Value
A	£27,000 or under
B	£27,000 to £35,000
C	£35,000 to £45,000
D	£45,000 to £58,000
E	£58,000 to £80,000
F	£80,000 to £106,000
G	£106,000 to £212,000
H	over £212,000

Council tax rates can vary considerably between different council areas. In the tax year beginning April 2004 the lowest rates were in Borders, where the basic council tax was £656.67 (Band A) to £1970 (Band H), and the highest were in Glasgow City: £790 (Band A) to £2370 (Band H).

When a property changes hands, the new occupant takes over payment of the council tax. It may be necessary to contact the local council to arrange this. In rented accommodation it is the tenant, not the landlord, who is liable for the council tax. It is not included in the rental.

Council tax is payable by weekly or monthly instalments or a lump sum. It can be paid by standing order or direct debit through your bank account, by cheque or postal order through the post, at post offices or in person at council offices.

UTILITIES

For many years utilities in Britain were nationalised (state-owned) industries. This changed from 1986 onwards when, over a period of years, they were privatised. Since then a number of regional companies supplying electricity, gas, water and telephone supplies have emerged. It is a booming area for entrepreneurs as it has been recognised that the utilities can be very lucrative businesses, earning potentially large profits. In recent years, there have been a number of mergers and take-over bids as companies in the UK and abroad have grabbed their slice of the pie. In some areas, different utilities are provided by one company, so you may be billed for electricity and gas on the same bill, for instance.

Electricity, gas and telephone are generally billed quarterly, but payments may be made by monthly direct debit payments through a bank account. This allows for easier budgeting as regular equal payments are made throughout the year, levelling out the fluctuations of large fuel bills in the winter and smaller bills in the summer months. They all levy a standing charge for their services in addition to the payments for actual consumption. This is added to the quarterly bill.

When moving into a property, you will need to have the meters read and new accounts set up in order to ensure that you do not pay for electricity, gas or telephone calls used or made by the previous owner or tenant. You should give the company two weeks notice to arrange this. Where a property has been left empty for some time, services may have been disconnected. There may be a small reconnection charge.

Electricity

The electricity supply is 240 volts AC, 50 hertz (cycles), single phase. Standard plugs have three flat pins and are generally fitted with 3, 5 or 13 amp fuses depending on the wattage of the electrical equipment. Some equipment from Europe or the US may be usable with adapters, but generally it is probably safest to buy new equipment in the UK. Most light fittings use bulbs with push-in 'bayonet' fixings.

You will rarely encounter power cuts in urban areas of Scotland, but in rural areas, particularly during periods of bad weather, they are not infrequent. At times the power is cut off deliberately for a number of hours in order to allow maintenance work. In such cases you should be advised in advance of the interruption to supply. Because of the likelihood of loss of electricity, most Highland homes retain an open fire or some other form of back-up heating.

Electricity Supply Companies

British Energy plc: 3 Redwood Crescent, Peel Park, East Kilbride G74 5PR; ☎01355-262000; www.british-energy.com.

BNFL: Hinton House, Risley, Warrington, Cheshire WA3 6AS; ☎01925-832000; fax 01925-822711; www.bnfl.com.

EA Technology: Capenhurst Technology Park, Capenhurst, Chester CH1 6ES; ☎0151-339 4181; fax 0151-347 2404; www.eatechnology.com.

Electricity Association Ltd: 30 Millbank, London SW1P 4RD; ☎020-7963 5700; fax 020-7963 5959; www.electricity.org.uk.

Scottish and Southern Energy PLC: Inveralmond House, 200 Dunkeld Road, Perth PH1 3AQ; ☎01738-456000; www.scottish-southern.co.uk.

Scottish Power: Spean Street, Glasgow G44 4BE; ☎0845-270 6543; www. scottishpower.plc.uk.

Gas

Mains natural gas is available in all cities and most urban areas, but many rural areas do not have piped gas. Some gas appliances are adapted for use with bottled propane or butane gas (usually Calor Gas) which is available from local suppliers who will deliver to your door. In areas on the mains, most central heating is gas-fired.

Gas Supply Companies

Calor Gas: Customer Services ☎0800-626626; www.calorgas.co.uk. This website has a searchable database of UK suppliers. They also offer gas cylinder telephone ordering through Calor Gas Direct, ☎0800-662663.

Powergen: PO Box 7750, Nottingham NG1 6WR; www.powergen.co.uk.

Scottish Power: Cathcart Business Park, Spean Street, Glasgow G44 4BE; ☎0845-2700 700; www.scottishpower.co.uk.

Oil

In areas off the mains, the majority of central heating systems are oil-fired. Local suppliers will deliver oil which must be stored in approved tanks outside the property.

Oil Supply Companies

BP Oil: Witan Gate House, 500/600 Witan Gate, Milton Keynes MK9 1ES; ☎0845-303 3377; www.bp.com.

Highland Fuels: Affric House, Beechwood Park, Inverness IV2 3BW; ☎0800-224224; fax 01463-710899; www.highlandfuels.co.uk.

Gleaner Oils: Head Office, Milnfield, Elgin IV30 1UZ; ☎01343-557400; fax 01343-548534; www.shell.com.

Solid Fuel

Coal, smokeless fuel and logs for open fires and solid-fuel cooking and heating appliances are available from local suppliers. In the Highlands and Islands some people still dig and burn peat from their traditional peat cuttings. This is now dying out, but some local firms will supply ready bagged peat – worth trying at least once. The smell of peat-smoke is wonderful! Peat doesn't produce a great deal of heat on its own, so generally it is best augmented with coal.

See your local area Phone Book or Business Pages for local suppliers.

Water & Sewerage

In April 1996, the provision of water and sewerage services in Scotland was taken out of the hands of local authorities and became the responsibility of three public water authorities, covering the north, west and east of Scotland. In April 2002 the three water authorities merged to form Scottish Water.

Most domestic water and sewerage charges are based on the council tax banding of the property. There is a gradual move throughout the UK to introduce water metering where actual consumption, plus a standing charge, will be paid for. This is in its early days, and currently householders have the choice whether to have a meter installed or to continue with the existing arrangements.

In all urban areas and many rural areas, mains sewerage is available. However, in remote areas domestic waste is discharged via a septic tank. In such cases, there is no sewerage charge on the water rates, but a charge is made on each occasion the septic tank requires emptying.

Useful Address

Scottish Water: PO Box 8855, Edinburgh EH10 6YQ; ☎0845-601 8855; www.
scottishwater.co.uk

Refuse Collection

All residents have a weekly refuse collection. This is a local authority service and
is paid for through the council tax. This is free for domestic premises but there is
a charge made for business collections. In most areas, wheeled refuse containers
called 'wheelie bins' are supplied by the local authority.

Telephone

The telephone industry in Britain is dominated by British Telecom (BT), but
since their monopoly was ended in the 1980s many more telephone companies
have come into the market, introducing competition and consequently driving
down prices. mobile phone usage has grown exponentially over the past five years
and there is fierce competition between all the companies to secure their share of
the market.

Despite the competition causing the cost of telephone calls to come down,
no company has yet taken the step of making local calls free. All schools and
libraries and the majority of businesses and private homes are now connected to
the internet.

All telephones have Subscriber Trunk Dialling (STD) and International Direct
Dialling (IDD). All areas now have ISDN available, although remoter areas of the
Highlands and Islands still need their local exchanges upgraded to allow access to
high speed internet connections. BT aim to have completed this process by the
end of 2005, but it remains to be seen if they hit this target.

Nearly all telephone lines throughout Britain are owned and maintained by
British Telecom (BT). In some areas, telephone services are provided through
cable TV networks, but this is not an option in the many areas of Scotland where
cable is not available. If you move into a house or apartment which has been
previously occupied, there will probably be a phone line already installed. Reconnection is free. Where a new line has to be run into the property, a standard
charge of £174.99 is made, payable in 5 quarterly payments if desired.

In rural areas where houses are widely scattered, a phone line may need to be
run in from some hundreds of metres away, so the cost of connection may be
higher than average. BT have a consumer code of practice which states 'in most
cases residential telephone service will be provided within eight days, and business
service within six days'. If they do not install the line when they say they will,
customers can claim under the BT Customer Service Guarantee Scheme. Under
this scheme you can claim a daily rate of compensation for each day they are late,
up to a maximum of £1,000. Some customers in rural areas where there have
been particular difficulties in running a connection to their house because of its

location have actually done very well out of this scheme! Line rental is payable quarterly in advance but calls are charged as they are made, and will appear on the bill for the following quarter.

Since deregulation of the telephone industry, other companies have come into the market. They provide either 'direct access' or 'indirect access' telephone service. Direct access companies provide you with physical telephones lines which connect to the telephone network. Indirect access companies redirect your calls over their own network, but you will still have to pay line rental to your direct access company, such as BT.

There are numerous mobile phone companies operating in Scotland. Mobile phone coverage has improved greatly in recent years but is still not complete. Inevitably, it is the remote areas (where one might argue mobile phones are most useful) which are the last to get full coverage.

Useful Address

British Telecom (BT): BT Correspondence Centre, TVTE, Gateshead NE11 0ZZ; ☎0800 800 150 (from a BT line) These calls are free; fax 0141 220 2867; www.bt.com/customer services.

Regulatory Bodies

If you have complaints about services or charges in any of the utilities, you should contact the regulatory body for that industry. They exist to promote competition and protect customers' interests in relation to prices, security of supply and quality of services.

Useful Addresses

Office of Gas and Electricity Markets Scotland (Ofgem): Regents Court, 70 West Regent Street, Glasgow G2 2QZ; ☎0141-331 2678; fax 0141-331 2777; www.ofgem.gov.uk.

Water Industry Commissioner: Ochil House, Springkerse Business Park, Stirling FK7 7XE; ☎01786-430200; fax 01786-462018; www.watercommissioner. co.uk.

Office of Communications: Riverside House, 2A Southwark Bridge Road, London SE1 9HA; ☎020-7981 3000; fax 020-7981 3333; www.ofcom.org.uk.

REMOVALS

When choosing a removal company, it is wise to ensure that they are members of the International Federation of Furniture Removers (FIDI) www.fidi. com; the Overseas Moving Network International (OMNI) www.omnimoving. com; or of the British Association of Removers (BAR) www.bar.co.uk. You should then be covered by insurance and guarantees of safe delivery.

International Removals

It should take only a few days to have your belongings shipped from continental Europe, around four weeks from the east coast of the US, six weeks from the west coast. From Far Eastern countries it should take around six weeks, eight weeks or so from Australasia.

Make sure that you are adequately insured to the replacement cost in the UK of lost or damaged items. Your removal company will send you the UK Customs Form 3 for completion. A separate C3 must be completed for each shipment – for example if you are sending some by air and some by sea.

UK Removals

Most UK removal companies will move items anywhere on the mainland, but some smaller local companies may charge excessively for long distance moves. Large companies with branches throughout the UK, or Scottish companies, are likely to be best geared up for long distance removals to remote areas of the mainland or the islands.

Beware of special requirements for large or particularly heavy items e.g. pianos. They may insist, for safety reasons, that four men are available to move a piano, so in order to avoid paying for four men to travel all the way, you could arrange for two strong men to help out the basic team when they arrive.

If your new home is situated on a narrow, single-track road – common in many parts of the Highlands – you should inform the removal company as they may need to use a smaller van, or arrange to transfer your belongings to a smaller van at one of their northern depots.

Removal companies can be found in Yellow Pages or on www.yell.co.uk.

Storage Depots

If you are moving into rented accommodation temporarily you may need to arrange to have your belongings put into storage. If so, you must ensure your goods are properly insured. Storage is charged at a monthly rate depending on the size of the consignment. If you need to access any items during the storage period you will have to pay a fee to have the container opened, so it is as well to be sure you only put items you will not need for some time into storage. There are storage depots in most Scottish cities. If possible try to ensure your belongings will be stored as near as possible to your abode as this will be more convenient and also cut down on the cost when you finally have your belongings delivered to your permanent address.

The largest UK firm of removers is Allied Pickfords. They also do international removals and have storage depots throughout the UK.

Useful Addresses

Pickfords Ltd: Heritage House, 345 Southbury Road, Enfield EN1 1UP; ☎0800-

289229; www.pickfords.co.uk. Includes a branch locator listing over 100 branches throughout the UK.

British Association of Removers: 3 Churchill Court, 58 Station Road, North Harrow HA2 7SA; ☎020-8861 3331; fax 020-8861 3332; www.bar.co.uk. The website includes a searchable database of BAR members, national and international.

Britannia Greers of Elgin: The Depository, Edgar Road, Elgin, Moray IV30 6YQ; ☎01343-542229/545307; fax 01343-541426; www.greers.co.uk.

Customs Regulations

Used household goods and personal effects are allowed into the UK free of duty and value added tax (VAT), provided that they have been in your possession and used abroad at least six months prior to your arrival and that you have lived out of the EU for at least 12 months. All items less than six months old are subject to duty and VAT. Keep with you any receipts/invoices for new and dutiable items as they may be required by Customs and Excise.

Customs clearance for goods from Europe is usually made without delay, but International Customs clearance can take up to two weeks. If your belongings are sent unaccompanied, the receiving freight or removal company will send you a customs form for completion when your goods arrive in Britain.

IMPORTING YOUR CAR

You may bring your motor vehicle free of duty and tax provided you have used it in your home country for at least six months, you keep it for personal use and you do not sell or hire it out in the UK within 12 months.

Your removal company will supply you with a C104A customs form to complete. This should be supported by copies of your passport, utility bills to prove you have resided previously in another country, your car insurance policy and a purchase invoice.

If the motor vehicle is under six months old you will have to pay the full rate of duty and VAT, approximately 29 per cent of the car's value.

Upon clearance and payment of any duties, you will be given a clearance form and registration instruction. These should be taken, together with proof of car insurance, to the nearest Department of Transport Vehicle Registration Office to get the vehicle licensed. A road tax disc will be issued and car registration plates can be collected.

Even if your car is less than six months old, it may be cheaper to import it and pay duty rather than buy a car in the UK. Motor vehicles are expensive compared with most other countries, although UK prices have come down in recent years, largely as a result of the increasing numbers of UK residents buying vehicles in Europe, often via internet marketing sites. Even once import duties and tax are paid, you can save thousands of pounds compared with buying the same make and model of car from a UK outlet.

Useful Address

Advice on importing personal effects and goods into the UK may be obtained from *HM Customs and Excise* Portcullis House, 21 India Street, Glasgow G2 4PZ; ☎0845-010 9000; www.hmce.gov.uk.

IMPORTING PETS

On 28th February 2000, the Pet Travel Scheme (PETS) was introduced in the UK. This allows dogs, cats, ferrets, pet rabbits and rodents from specified countries which had undergone a certain procedure to ensure their health, into the UK without the need to go into quarantine. Prior to this, if you wished to bring your pet to the UK from anywhere other than the Republic of Ireland, it had to stay in quarantine at approved premises for a fixed period of six months.

Other pets may be imported as long as they meet either national import rules or the general rules for trade in the animal species. For further information see www. defra.gov.uk/animal/int-trde/default.htm.

Pet Travel Scheme

The PETS system allows animals resident in a qualifying country to enter or re-enter the UK if they satisfy the following requirements: Dogs, cats and ferrets are fitted with an electronic microchip so that they can be properly identified; they are vaccinated against rabies; their blood is tested to ensure that the vaccination has given a satisfactory level of protection, at least six months before entering the UK; they are issued with an EU pet passport or, in a non-EU listed country, an official third country veterinary certificate; they are treated against ticks and tapeworms between 24 and 48 before the journey to the UK. The owner must sign a declaration that the pet has not been outside any of the PETS qualifying countries in the previous six months. Animals not meeting all the rules must be licensed into quarantine.

There are slightly different systems for pets registered in France, Denmark and Sweden. For the latest information, see www.defra.gov.uk/animalh/qurantine/pets/procedures/Suppot-info/tattoos.htm.

The whole process of health checks and documentation can take up to six months, but at a cost of £200-£300 it is far less expensive, and less traumatic to owner and pet, than the previous quarantine regulations.

Pet rabbits and rodents are not subject to any requirement with regard to rabies when travelling between EU Member States or into the EU from Andorra, Iceland, Liechtenstein, Monaco, Norway, San Marino, Switzerland and the Vatican. When imported into the UK from other countries, animals must be licensed into quarantine for six months.

Qualifying Countries. Under the scheme, pets can travel between these countries as long as they are accompanied by the appropriate official certification.

EU MEMBER STATES AND TERRITORIES

Austria; Azores; Balearic Islands; Belgium; Canary Islands; Ceuta; Republic of Cyprus (Animals travelling from Northern (Turkish) Cyprus will have to be licensed into quarantine for 6 months on arrival in the UK); Czech Republic; Denmark; Estonia; Faroe Islands; Finland; France; French Guyana; Germany; Gibraltar; Greece; Greenland; Guadeloupe (French part); Hungary; Ireland (there are no requirements for pets travelling directly between the UK and the Republic of Ireland); Italy; Latvia; Lithuania; Luxembourg; Madeira; Malta; Martinique; Melilla; Netherlands; Poland; Portugal; Reunion; Slovakia; Slovenia; Spain; Sweden; United Kingdom.

NON-EU LISTED COUNTRIES

Andorra; Antigua & Barbuda; Aruba; Ascension Island; Australia; Bahrain; Barbados; Bermuda; Canada; Cayman Islands; Chile; Croatia; Falkland Islands; Fiji; French Polynesia; Grenadines; Hawaii; Hong Kong; Iceland; Jamaica; Japan; Liechtenstein; Mauritius; Mayotte; Monaco; Montserrat; Netherlands Antilles; New Caledonia; New Zealand; Norway; Russian federation; St Helena; St Kitts & Nevis; St Pierre & Miquelon; St Vincent; San Marino; Singapore; Switzerland; United Arab Emirates; USA (mainland); Vanuatu; Vatican; Wallis & Futuna.

PETS Routes. You can only bring your pet into the UK using approved routes and transport companies. For a full list see www.defra.gov.uk/animalh/quarantine/pets/territory.htm. These routes and transport companies are amended from time to time. You cannot bring a pet into the UK under PETS from a private boat or plane.

Quarantine

Cats and dogs which are not from the qualifying countries or which have not followed the required procedure for entry under PETS must be detained in quarantine for six months. The animal's owner must first choose suitable quarantine premises. There is a list of authorised premises on www.defra.gov.uk/quarantine/Quarantine/procedures/qprocs.htm.

You must complete Form ID1 'Application for a licence to import a dog or cat for detention in quarantine' produced by the Department for Environment, Food and Rural Affairs (DEFRA). This can be filled in by the quarantine premises on your behalf. Once completed, this form should be sent to one of the following addresses:

For animals which land and clear HM Customs in England or Wales: Defra, Quarantine Section, Area 211, 1A Page Street, London SW1P 4PQ; ☎020-7904

6222; fax 020-7904 6834.

For animals which land in England but are transhipped to Scotland for clearance by HM Customs, or which land directly into Scotland: SEERAD, Pentland House, 47 Robb's Loan, Edinburgh EH14 1TY; ☎0131-244 6181/6182; fax 0131-244 6616.

Form ID1 is available from these addresses, or may be downloaded from the DEFRA website www.defra.gov.uk.

The cost of keeping a pet in quarantine varies between about £900 and £1500 for cats and about £1500 and £2000 for dogs.

Authorised Quarantine Premises

A list of approved quarantine premises is available from Ministry of Agriculture, Fisheries and Food (MAFF)3 Whitehall Place, London SW1; ☎0645-335577; PETS helpline 0870-241 1710; www.maff.gov.uk.

Aquithie Boarding and Quarantine Kennels & Cattery: Kemnay, Inverurie, Aberdeenshire AB51 9PA; ☎01467-643456; fax 01467-642616.

Edinburgh & Lothians Kennels: Seton East House, Longniddry, Lothian; ☎0131-665 2124 or 01875-811478; fax 01875-814553.

Milton Quarantine Kennels: Milton, Dumbarton G82 2UA; ☎01389-761208; fax 01389-734648.

Dangerous Dogs

It is against the law in Great Britain to possess certain types of dogs, and these cannot be brought into the country either under PETS or via quarantine. The prohibited breeds are pit bull terriers, Japanese tosas, dogo Argentinos and fila Brazilieros. Any of these brought into Great Britain could be seized and destroyed.

USEFUL BOOKS & WEBSITES

Books

Buying a Home in Britain, David Hampshire (Survival Books 1999). How to find, choose, buy and pay for your own home.

Buying A House: A Step by Step Guide to Buying Your Ideal Home: Adam Walker (How To Books 1999).

The Legal System of Scotland, Derek Manson-Smith (The Stationery Office Books 2004)

Who Owns Scotland? Andy Wightman & James Hunter (Canongate Books 1996). A ground-breaking look at the land ownership question, proposing a radical system of land reform in Scotland.

Websites

The Comprehensive Guide to UK Property Relocation Services, Lettings Agents and Estate Agents is a handy and wide-ranging collection of links to relevant websites: www.latroba.co.uk/uk/ukpropty.php.

Conveyancing Solicitors and Licensed Conveyancers throughout the UK are listed on www.conveyancing-cms.co.uk.

Up My Street is a guide to various facts and figures regarding different areas of the UK, including property prices, top schools, crime figures and council performance: www.upmystreet.co.uk.

Houseweb is a comprehensive site including wide-ranging advice, guides and services relating to all aspects of house buying and selling, plus properties for sale: www.houseweb.co.uk.

UK-Mortgages gives advice about mortgages, free quotations and a directory of the UK's most competitive mortgage companies and brokers: www.uk-mortgages. uk.com.

Gordon Shields estate and letting agency for the Glasgow area: www.gordonshields. demon.co.uk.

Hannah Homes estate and letting agency covering the Highlands: www.hannah-homes.co.uk.

Your Moving Guide to Edinburgh with information about aspects of living in the capital city including services, shopping and transport: www.yourmovingguide. com.

DAILY LIFE

CHAPTER SUMMARY

o **Scotland's Main Cities.** Glasgow is the UK's coolest city, according to National Geographic magazine.
  o Edinburgh has three times been voted Best UK City by Condé Nast Traveller magazine.
o **Language.** English is the main language of Scotland, but efforts are being made to revive both Gaelic and Scots.
  o Primary school children can do all their classes in Gaelic if parents wish.
o **Education.** The school year runs from mid-August to the end of June.
  o Scottish students studying at Scottish Universities do not pay tuition fees, but they must pay into the Graduate Endowment fund once they are earning, which goes to help fund future generations of students.
o **Communications.** Britons send 21.3 billion text messages a year.
  o Britain is one of the fastest-growing markets for broadband.
o **Transport.** There are eight motorways in Scotland.
  o Many roads in rural parts of the country are single track.
o **Money.** Mortgages can be obtained from banks or building societies.
  o The standard rate of value added tax is 17.5%.
o **Health.** Scotland has imposed a total smoking ban in enclosed public spaces from 2006.
o **Religion.** Scotland is becoming more secular, but there are still many areas where shops do not open and transport services do not run on Sundays.

Although a part of the United Kingdom, and hence not really thought of as a 'different country' by many living south of the border, there are distinct cultural and legislative differences in Scotland which become apparent once one moves there. Devolution has already increased the differences, and will continue to do so, as more specifically Scottish legislation is introduced by the new Parliament.

If you move to the Highlands the differences are even more striking. Its remoteness and the sparsity of population require a certain 'frontiersman' attitude in those who are to make a successful transition to the wholesale change in lifestyle entailed. The prime quality required is a certain amount of non-conformism – not 'rebellion'; you'll just be someone who feels unsatisfied and unfulfilled working and living in an environment where your freedom of thoughts and actions are constrained by those around you. You have a desire for a greater amount of personal freedom and you recognise that the wide open spaces of the Highlands can give you much of what you want.

If you are not yet certain whether living and working in Scotland is for you, this chapter will help you to decide whether you have the courage, the energy and the temperament to actually make the move. It will also act as a day to day survival guide if you do take the plunge. Of course, even if you decide to move, it's not an irreversible decision. Many people move to Scotland and stay for five years, seven years, eleven years, before returning, or moving on, for a variety of reasons – advancing years, failing health, change of personal circumstances. Few of these people regret having come in the first place. So if you're concerned about whether it would suit you in the longer term, that's not necessarily a reason for not doing it at all. Don't forget, you can go back to where you came from at any time.

LANGUAGE

English is the main language of Scotland and is spoken by the vast majority of the population as their first language. Gaelic is a recognised minority language, spoken mainly in the Highlands and Islands. The various Scots dialects, collectively known as Lowland Scots, are widely spoken in the south, east and far north of the country.

Gaelic

The Gaelic language was originally introduced to Scotland from Ireland around the fifth century, when the Scots, a Gaelic-speaking people of Northern Ireland, colonised the area of Argyll and Bute, later expanding eastwards and northwards. It remained the main language in much of northern Scotland until the early seventeenth century, resisting the inexorable march of English northwards. Its death knell was sounded in 1616 when James VI of Scotland (James I of England), a cruel and ruthless man who deemed all Highlanders barbarians, passed an Act proscribing Gaelic. After the Jacobite rising of 1745, Highland culture generally was suppressed, leading to a further decline in the speaking of Gaelic, even behind closed doors. The nineteenth century Highland clearances, which depopulated Gaelic-speaking areas, brought the language to the brink of extinction.

A move to revive Gaelic began in the late nineteenth and early twentieth centuries. The 1918 Education Act specifically allowed Gaelic to be taught in

Gaelic-speaking areas, although not until 1958 did Inverness-shire lead the way by introducing the teaching of Gaelic in primary schools.

The movement to revive Gaelic has received a boost in recent years. Today, children have the option of taking their education in Gaelic, either at Gaelic medium units within mainstream primary schools or at free-standing Gaelic medium schools.

However, despite these efforts to boost the use of the language, at the 1991 census only 1.4 per cent of the Scottish population spoke it, and the majority of these were aged over 65. By the 2001 census there was a further 11 per cent drop in this figure. It is often those who are not indigenous to the country who see more value in the language. Many of the pupils to be found in the Gaelic medium schools and units are the children of incomers, while those whose grandparents or parents were brought up speaking the language are in the minority.

In 2004 the Scottish Parliament introduced the Gaelic Language Bill which aims to secure the status of Gaelic as an official language of Scotland. It is to set up the *Bòrd na Gàidhlig* which will prepare a national Gaelic language plan to promote the use and understanding of the Gaelic language and increasing the number of persons able to use and understand Gaelic.

Lowland Scottish

The various forms of 'Scots' include Lowland Scots, Lallans and Doric, which is a group of dialects with a strong Scandinavian influence, spoken in Aberdeen and the north-east. Although they are, strictly speaking, dialects rather than full-fledged languages, the European Charter for Minority and Regional Languages recognises Scots as a minority language. However, although the UK government ratified the European Charter in 1998, no official recognition or encouragement has yet been given to Scots. This may change in the future if a cross-party group of MSPs has its way: it is pressing the Scottish Executive to use the Scots tongue, as well as Gaelic, on public signs and official forms alongside English.

Although Gaelic language Bibles have been around for many years, only now is the Old Testament to be translated into the Scots language. The translation, being undertaken with the support of Queen's University, Belfast – interestingly in Ireland, not Scotland! – is expected to be published in 2006.

SCHOOLS & EDUCATION

Scottish education has long had a reputation for its quality and its breadth. There is a long history of Scotland being a well-educated country, with the university system being well-established by the fifteenth century. The Scottish Education Act of 1696 heralded the first national education system in the modern world. Until the 18th century, Scotland boasted the highest percentage of primary, secondary and tertiary educated citizens in Europe, while England had the lowest. In 1864, for example, 1 in 205 Scots were educated to secondary school level, while in Prussia it was 1 in 249, in France it was 1 in 570 and in England it was only 1 in 1300.

The excellence of the Scottish education system is one of the main reasons given by many parents for moving from England and Wales to Scotland. Unfortunately, with local authorities suffering cuts in the levels of their budgets overall and some of these cutbacks inevitably showing in the education departments, the Scottish reputation for high educational standards has suffered slightly in recent years. The Scottish Executive is resolved to put this right through increased spending on education in all areas from pre-school up to university level. After devolution, the first minister, Donald Dewar, pledged 'Our aim is nothing less than the return of Scotland to its rightful place as a world leader in education'.

The Structure of the Education System

Responsibility for education in Scotland lies with the Scottish Executive Education Department, which formulates policies and aims to maintain consistency in educational standards throughout the country. Most school education is locally administered, so although the Scottish Executive is responsible for the broad allocation of resources for education, local authorities make many of their own day to day expenditure decisions according to their local situations. Support for higher and further education and other specialised areas of education comes directly from central government.

Schooling in Scotland is compulsory for all children between five and 16 years. After this age they can take the option of staying on and pursuing further studies for one or two years, in order to gain either academic qualifications for entry to university, or vocational qualifications for specific careers.

The academic year runs from mid-August to the end of June, while the intake year for Scottish schools commences on 1st March. Children who are five after this date will start primary school in the following August. Primary education lasts for seven years, through classes Primary One to Primary Seven. Children move up to secondary school at the age of 12 and stay there for a minimum of four years, through classes Senior One to Senior Four. Pupils may undertake two further years at school, classes Senior Five and Senior Six, leaving at the age of 17 or 18.

The Scottish secondary system is comprehensive in nature. There is no system of selection at the end of primary school – secondary schools, usually called either high schools or academies, take pupils of all levels of attainment.

Although generally children will attend a school in whose geographical catchment area they live, parents may express a preference for a particular school by making a 'placing request' which must be satisfied if the school is not oversubscribed. There are around 26,000 placing requests made each year, of which around 85 per cent are granted. The scope for this in the Highlands is limited because of the low number of schools. Gairloch High School, for example, has a catchment area of 700 square miles. In these cases an arrangement for your child to attend another school would be likely to involve them living away from home, at least during the week.

Choosing A School: A Guide For Parents is available online via the Parentzone website: www.parentzonescotland.gov.uk. This website contains useful information about all aspects of Scottish education.

All schools are required to make specific information freely available, including such things as public examination results, truancy rates and destination of leavers. They are also required to establish school boards comprised of parents, teachers and co-opted members. School boards are responsible for many matters concerning the day to day running of the school including the appointment of staff.

Schools are regularly inspected by teams from HM Inspectors of Schools in Scotland, who also monitor and report on further education institutions. Higher Education establishments are inspected by the Scottish Higher Education Funding Council.

Private & State Schools

In Scotland, the majority of schools are provided by the state. These are called public (or state) schools and charge no fees to pupils, being financed by local government through a combination of central government grants and local taxation. Independent schools receive no government grants and charge fees to pupils. They are subject to government registration and HMI inspection. There are a few grant-aided schools, mainly providing education for those with special educational needs, which receive grants direct from the Scottish Executive Education Department. The total number of schools in Scotland in 1998 was 3,983, including about 70 independent schools. For a full list, contact the Scottish Council of Independent Schools.

The most famous private school in Scotland is Gordonstoun at Elgin, Morayshire, where Prince Charles took his secondary schooling. It prides itself on instilling international awareness and understanding in its pupils. It has a Junior School, Aberlour House, which takes pupils from 9-13, and a Senior School for pupils over 13. Up to 25 per cent of Gordonstoun pupils come from outside Great Britain, with around 40 nationalities represented in the school. The majority of pupils enter the school at third form level (age 14) and take a year's foundation course. The following year they follow a number of GCSE courses plus core subjects, the examinations taken in the fifth form. At sixth form level, they are joined by the substantial number of pupils who enter from other schools in order to study GCE A levels and in some cases the more advanced AS levels. The school is renowned for its high standard of education, but it does not come cheap, at around £14,000-£21,000 per year for boarders and £8,000-£14,000 for day pupils, depending on age. There are a number of scholarships and bursaries available per year, awarded to especially gifted children in various disciplines who are need of financial assistance. Sixth form scholarship exams and interviews take place in November and junior ones in February.

Useful Addresses

Scottish Council of Independent Schools (SCIS): 21 Melville Street, Edinburgh EH3
7PE; ☎0131-220 2106; fax 0131-225 8594; www.scis.org.uk.

Admissions Secretary, Gordonstoun School: Elgin, Moray IV30 5RF; ☎01343-
837829; fax 01343-837808; www.gordonstoun.org.uk.

Pre-school & Nursery Education

Education before the age of five is not compulsory, but many parents choose
to send their children to nurseries or pre-school play groups either part-time or
full-time. Local authorities have a duty to ensure there is a free, part-time nursery
place to all three and four-year old children whose parents want one. If you wish to
send your child to pre-school before they are three years old, your local authority
may be able to accommodate this, but you may be required to meet the costs. In
January 2004, 85 per cent of three year olds and 100 per cent of four year olds
attended pre-school education. Nursery schools and nursery classes in primary
schools take children from two to five years old. These are run by trained teachers.
Contact the relevant local authority for details of state run nursery classes.

In January 2004 1,236 children were receiving Gaelic medium pre-school
education.

There are also numerous mother and toddler groups run on a voluntary basis
in public and church halls throughout the country, where mothers can take their
young children for a couple of hours a week, to chat and drink tea while their
offspring play together.

Some businesses and universities run crèche facilities which take care of pre-
school age children while their parents are at work, but the provisions are patchy
and in many areas such places are in short supply and costly. There is a network
of private child-minders throughout the country, even in the most remote areas,
who look after children and babies in their own homes while their parents are at
work.

Useful Addresses

For private nurseries, contact *Scottish Independent Nurseries Association* SINA
Scotland Ltd, Hydepark Business Centre, 60 Mollinsburn Street, Springburn,
Glasgow G21 4SF; ☎0141-557 3040/3304; fax 0141-557 3040; www.
sinascotland.com.

Pre-school playgroups are run by parents and voluntary bodies, in particular the
Scottish Pre-School Play Association. They are preferred by some parents because
the emphasis is less on structured learning, more on learning through play. All
providers of pre-school education are subject to inspection. *Scottish Pre-School
Play Association,* 45 Finnieston Street, Glasgow G3 8JU; www.sppa.org.uk. See

the website for phone and fax numbers by local authority area.

For those who wish their children to become familiar with Gaelic from an early age, the Gaelic pre-school council, *Comhairle Nan Sgoiltean Araich (CNSA)*, runs Gaelic playgroups, mainly in the Highlands and Islands. CNSA, 53 Church Street, Inverness IV1 1DR; ☎01463-225469.

A comprehensive guide for parents on Gaelic education is available from the *Gaelic Development Agency (Comunn na Gàidhlig):* 5 Mitchells Lane, Inverness IV2 3HQ; ☎01463-234138; fax 01463-237470; www.cnag.org.uk. This is a bi-lingual Gaelic/English website.

The *Scottish Childminding Association* keeps a register of approved childminders. Suite 3, 7 Melville Terrace, Stirling FK8 2ND; ☎01786-449063; fax 01786-449062; www.childminding.org.

Primary Education

Primary education begins at the age of five and is usually conducted in mixed classes of boys and girls. Generally, primary schools are divided into infants' classes, for the five to sevens, and primary classes for the seven to twelves. Many schools also provide nursery classes for children under five.

National testing is carried out on core areas of the curriculum, to produce standardised results of achievement across the country's schools in various basic subject areas, such as English and mathematics.

Children may take their primary education totally in Gaelic, with English being one of the subject areas taught. These children are educated in 'Gaelic medium units' within mainstream primary schools. A great step forward for those campaigning for the higher status of the Gaelic language within Scotland was made in August 1999 when Scotland's first dedicated Gaelic medium primary school, with a capacity of 231 pupils, was opened in Glasgow where there is a significant number of Gaelic speakers. Gaelic medium education is provided in 58 primary schools, mainly in the Highlands and Islands. The number of pupils in Gaelic medium education has risen from 2,661 in 2002-3 to 2,879 in 2003-4. If parents wish their children to be taught in the Gaelic language, they should contact their education authority.

In rural areas where the population, and therefore the school intake, is small, the distinction between age groups is less clear cut. There are many schools in the Highlands and Islands, for instance, which have primary schools of fewer than 50 pupils, some with only a dozen or so. In these cases they will have just one or two teachers teaching mixed age classes.

A consideration for families moving from urban areas to the Highlands is how well their children will settle into a small school. When the author moved to Ross-shire with her two boys, aged eight and ten, she had some concerns. Having previously lived in a densely populated area of England, the boys had attended a primary school of 300 pupils. Their new school in the Highlands had just 23 pupils, infants and juniors, taught by two teachers. Any doubts about whether they would fit in easily and whether the teaching quality would be acceptable proved groundless. The boys settled in from day one, found no hostility from the other children and with the one-to-one attention the teachers could offer, they blossomed intellectually and socially.

> **Ruairdhri Wright aged 5, who moved with his family from Cambridgeshire, also loved his new school despite initially missing his friends in England**
>
> *I like my school because it has got lovely things in it like pictures on the wall and computers we can play games on. I like doing painting at school and I liked learning the Gaelic action song for the Mod.*

There have long been debates on optimum class sizes, many driven by local authority needs to cut costs, but overall the high teacher to pupil ratio in small schools is seen – by parents at least – as a good thing. Specialist subjects such as art, music and physical education (PE) are provided by peripatetic teachers who travel round all the schools in the region.

There are, of course, some drawbacks to a small school. The pupils get a lot of individual attention, certainly, but some activities are necessarily curtailed. They may have no school football or netball team: with only a handful of children per school year, it's just not practicable. If the school building is too small to boast a decent-sized gym, PE lessons are limited. School dinners may have to be brought in from a central point, so they are variable in quality. Lack of resources is a constant problem, although with computers available in even the smallest schools nowadays, there is greater access to learning materials and links between the schools in the region have been set up.

But the advantages outweigh these drawbacks. With less rigid divisions between age-groups, both the extra bright child and those with learning difficulties can be allowed to work at the appropriate level for their abilities. At break-times the children play together without regard to age-groups or sex, like one large family – with the same fallings-out as occur within families, of course. But, just as within a family, it's impossible in such a small community to stay fallen-out for long. There's no serious bullying – the school grounds aren't big enough for anti-social behaviour to pass unnoticed by the teachers for long.

Sadly, with pressures on local authorities to save money across the board, small rural schools can be seen as easy targets. This was starkly brought home to Highland parents in 1997. School rolls in the region's primaries had dropped, in line with the rest of the country – the normal fluctuations in population were in a phase of falling numbers of school age children. This coincided with the Highland Council facing a cash crisis, and the Education Committee making the short-sighted decision that the amalgamation of small schools with larger ones, ten or more miles away, necessitating daily bus journeys of up to an hour for very young children, was a sensible 'quick fix'. They proposed to close ten primary schools across the region, particularly in the western areas, those where services were already fewer and further between than on the more populous and urban east. After a vociferous campaign of opposition from parents and the wider community, eight of the threatened schools were reprieved. The remaining two were moribund anyway, so there was no opposition to their closure. This was a victory for the communities concerned, whose main argument without exception was that the school is in so many ways the heart of a community – lose the school and eventually you lose the children and their families. In time, these school-less areas end up being predominantly peopled by retired couples and second home-owners and tourists on holiday in the cottages which once housed families year-round. There were a number of primary schools closed in the western Highlands in the 1960s, and these areas now have tiny numbers of children living in them because the families have gravitated nearer to the school. This is bad both for the communities and for the children, who have fewer playmates to hand and further to travel to meet their friends.

Secondary Education

Children move up to secondary school at 11 or 12 and stay until they are at least 16. Those who wish to can stay on for one or two further years. Most Scottish secondary schools are co-educational – i.e. they take both boys and girls – although there are some single sex schools. They are comprehensive and provide a full range of courses appropriate to all levels of ability from first to sixth year. There may be some restrictions on the courses that can be followed in smaller schools where the smaller number of teachers can produce timetabling difficulties when it comes to providing the widest range of options.

Although there is no national curriculum, as such, in Scotland, with content and management of the curriculum being the responsibility of education authorities and individual headteachers, there are guidelines which give recommended hours of study for a selection of core subjects. There are separate guidelines regarding the curriculum from age 5-14 and that from 14-16.

Gaelic is taught as an individual subject at schools in Gaelic-speaking areas. Provision is made for those who wish to carry out all their learning in Gaelic, but it may not be available at the nearest secondary school. There are 34 secondary schools in Scotland which offer Gaelic language classes for fluent speakers, while 15 teach other subjects in Gaelic.

In December 2004, a Gaelic medium secondary school in Glasgow was approved, the first in the country. The school is due to open in 2006. It will share a campus with a Gaelic medium pre-school and primary school and will allow pupils to study all their education, from the age of three to 18, in Gaelic.

In May 2005 a new Scottish Survey of Achievement will be introduced which uses a representative sampling approach to assess the attainments of pupils aged 5-14 in the areas of English language, mathematics, science and social subjects. It will be based on teachers' assessments of their pupils, and will replace the previous system of national testing which was unpopular with the majority of Scottish teachers, and with many parents.

One thing to be considered in rural areas is whether problems might arise when the primary children move on to high school. To those who have moved from a school with as few as five pupils, a high school with 200 or more can appear dauntingly large, particularly where they only know one or two other pupils at the school. With large secondary school catchment areas this is unavoidable.

The general consensus, however, is that the majority of children have no problems of transition other than those all children experience in moving to secondary school, wherever they may be: the new subject areas, the need to do homework, to start studying for exams, the expectation that they have now 'grown up', and all these just at the time they are coping with puberty, are enough to put any child under a little stress for a while.

The author's experience in Ross-shire is that the children are, in general, far more articulate and easy in the company of adults than those in the urban area of England she moved from. This is partly due to the excellent Scottish education system, partly to the fact that they know everybody and everybody knows them.

Despite the legislation allowing parents the right to choose the schools their children attend, you are limited to what is available in the local area. Certainly, in sparsely populated areas there is no choice in practice, unless you want to send your children away for their schooling.

It is not so long ago that this occurred anyway in most west coast communities. Once the children reached secondary school age they were sent to larger schools on the east coast where they stayed in hostels for a week or a term at a time. Over the last twenty years this situation has changed. Government policy has been to build up a network of secondary schools so that no child has to travel more than an hour to reach the school.

As a result of this investment, most west coast secondary schools are new and up-to-date and the older ones are being redeveloped over the next few years. The importance of computers is recognised in remote communities as much as anywhere, and the technology available in the schools reflects this.

A plus point of the lack of choice of school is that all the children in the area go to the same secondary school. They all know each other, and there are no inter-school rivalries, so there really is a feeling of community about the place.

The author noticed before she left England that her eldest son was beginning to be infected by the prevalent 'anti-work' culture – he stopped trying so hard at his school work for fear of being called a 'swot'. She was very pleased to find that this culture was not in evidence in the Highlands. The children seem to be very competitive in all areas and this is reflected in their achievements both in and out of school.

> **Matthew Taylor, now at university, appreciates the benefits of his schooling in the Highlands**
>
> *When I started at Inverasdale Primary School, which had 21 pupils, after my school in England which had 300, there was initially a big culture shock, but I soon found it has massive advantages. In such a small school you mix with all the age groups and make lots of friends. It meant too that we all received far more individual attention from the teacher than I had been used to.*
>
> *The benefits continued when I moved to the brand new High School at Gairloch. There were plenty of resources to go round and class sizes were small. When I reached the sixth form, I was the only pupil taking the Certificate of Sixth Form Studies in English, so I had on- on-one teaching, and consequently achieved a good result.*

A beneficial 'knock-on' effect of the small west coast population is that the secondary schools are community facilities. Many High Schools share their libraries and sometimes their sports facilities with local residents and visitors.

Special Education

Children with special educational needs, as a result of physical or mental disabilities, are assessed and a 'statement of special needs' produced. On the basis of this, parents together with education authorities decide where the child should be schooled and arrange for any special requirements to be satisfied. Wherever possible, children with special needs are integrated into normal schools. In addition, there are special schools and special classes within mainstream schools for those children who require a different environment or specialised facilities.

Contact the relevant local authority education department for further information on provision for special education.

Independent Schools

There are a range of independent schools in Scotland, covering all ages and including day as well as boarding schools. Although many are traditional in outlook and approach, there are some experimental schools following different models of education from the norm. Some independent schools are established and run by religious or ethnic minorities. Around four per cent of children in Scotland attend independent schools.

Most independent schools offer a similar range of courses to state schools and enter pupils for the same examinations. At some it is also possible to take GCE A level examinations at 18, as in English schools. The majority are single sex schools, although an increasing number have mixed sixth forms. Some parents prefer to move their children from a state school to a private school for their pre-university courses and examinations.

Independent schools receive no public funds. They charge fees to pupils and are managed under special trusts. Profits are used for the benefit of the school.

Useful Address

The Scottish Council of Independent Schools: 21 Melville Street, Edinburgh EH3 7PE; ☎0131-220 2106; fax 0131-225 8594; www.scis.org.uk.

Home Education

In Scotland, parents have to apply for permission to educate their children at home. The local education authority will inspect the provision made before giving approval, to ensure that the child is receiving full-time education suited to his or her age, abilities and aptitudes. In 2003-2004 only 545 children were known to be educated at home due to parental choice.

Useful Addresses

Information and advice on educating a child at home is available from *Education Otherwise* PO Box 7420, London N9 9SG; ☎0870-730 0074; www.education-otherwise.org.

Homeschool Resource Guide: www.homeschool.com. Contains resources and links to information on all aspects of home schooling.

Eclectic Homeschool Online: www.eho.org. Describes itself as 'The Magazine for Creative Homeschoolers… Published from a Christian Perspective.'

Examinations

Scotland's system of public examinations is distinct from that in England, Wales and Northern Ireland. The Standard Grade of the Scottish Certificate of Education is taken at the end of the fourth year at secondary school, about the age of 16 (this is roughly equivalent to the GCSE taken in England, Wales and Northern Ireland). Most pupils take seven or eight Standard Grade examinations (Standards), but they will take them at different levels depending on their abilities. For most Standard Grade courses there are three separate examination papers at the end of the two year course. These are set at Credit, General and Foundation levels. Passes in Credit level are awarded at grade one or two, in General at grade three or four and in Foundation at grade five or six. Normally pupils take examinations covering two levels, either Credit and General, or General and Foundation. This allows a 'safety net' for those who do worse – or indeed, better – than anticipated.

Students who require more support with their learning can take Access courses. Access 1 is designed for those who have learning difficulties, while Access 2 meets the needs of students with more moderate support needs. Access 3 is comparable with Standard Grade Foundation level. Access courses are assessed by the school or college and do not involve sitting examinations. Groups of units in different subjects built up by a student can lead to 'Cluster Awards'.

Pupils aged 17 and over take the next level of examinations. Higher Grade examinations (Highers) are taken at the end of the fifth year after one year of study. Pupils take up to five Highers in this year.

In the sixth year, pupils may resit Highers they failed in the previous year; take further Highers in other subjects; or take Advanced Highers in any of the subjects they passed at Higher level. University entrance requires passes at Higher and/or Advanced Higher level.

Intermediate 1 & 2 are qualifications which can be used as a stepping stone towards Higher. They are aimed at students who may have passed subjects at Standard Grade Foundation level, or Access 3, and would find taking a Higher in just one year would be too demanding. It is, however, not necessary to study a Standard Grade before taking an Intermediate. Higher students who don't achieve the required standard in their examination will be awarded an Intermediate 1 or 2 instead.

Scottish Vocational Qualifications (SVQs) aim to teach students practical skills in a particular occupational field. They are based on National Standards drawn up by people from industry, commerce and education and are designed to meet the needs of potential employers. There are SVQs for nearly all occupations in Scotland and are available at five levels of difficulty, to suit people who are just starting to study it hat field as well as those who already have years of experience. They can be taken at schools or colleges, or they can be taken part-time while in employment.

All these awards are administered and awarded by the Scottish Qualifications Authority (SQA). Students' qualifications are recorded on their personal 'Scottish Qualifications certificate' which is a cumulative record of their achievements. It is updated each time the student achieves new qualifications. Details of all these courses can be found on the SQA website.

In the Scottish education system emphasis is laid on achievement in all areas, not just the academic. In addition to the academic and vocational qualifications described above, sporting, musical and drama achievements are also applauded.

Useful Address
Scottish Qualifications Authority (SQA): Hanover House, 24 Douglas Street, Glasgow G2 7NQ; ☎0845-279 1000; fax 0141-242 2244; www.sqa.org.uk.

International Schools
There are a number of international schools in Scotland, mainly in Aberdeen, a city which has a large population of foreign workers in the oil industry. The schools are open to both local and expatriate children. The International School of Aberdeen offers the International Baccalaureate, an internationally recognised two-year pre-university course and examination which is designed to facilitate

the mobility of students and to promote international understanding. Shawlands Academy in Glasgow, which was recently approved as an international school, offers Scottish national qualifications. There are other small, private schools which cater to foreign pupils. For further details contact the schools direct.

Useful Addresses

The International School of Aberdeen: 296 North Deeside Road, Aberdeen AB13 0AB; ☎01224-732267; fax 01224-735648; www.isa.aberdeen.sch.uk.

Ecole Total Oil Marine: 1-5 Whitehall Place, Aberdeen AB2 4RH; ☎01224-645545; fax 01224-645565.

Hamilton School: 80-84 Queen's Road, Aberdeen AB1 6YE; ☎01224-317295; fax 01224-317165.

Shawlands Academy International School: 31 Moss-side Road, Glasgow G41 3TR; ☎0141-582 0210; fax 0141-582 0211; www.shawlands.academy.glasgow.sch. uk.

Scottish Council of Independent Schools (SCIS): 21 Melville Street, Edinburgh EH3 7PE; ☎0131-220 2106; fax 0131-225 8594; www.scis.org.uk.

School Transport

There is an efficient school transport network in Scotland for primary and secondary pupils. If a child lives more than three miles from the nearest school, two and a half miles for the under eights, he or she is picked up and dropped off close to home.

School Meals

School meals at competitive prices are provided at lunchtimes within schools. Families with a low income may be eligible for free school meals. Alternatively, most schools allow children to take packed lunches from home which they eat in the school dining room.

Further Education

This refers to all education provided outside schools to people aged over 16, comprising courses leading to Higher Grade, GCE A level and their equivalent, as well as various work-based vocational qualifications. Courses are taught mainly at the 47 colleges of further education throughout Scotland.

The Scottish Qualifications Authority (SQA) awards qualifications for most occupations, which may be studied for on a full-time, part-time or work-based learning basis. These include the Higher National Certificate (HNC) and Higher National Diploma (HND) courses which are designed to meet the needs of employers and can also be a rout into degree level courses. The courses are made up of Higher National Unit credits where one credit represents about 40 hours of timetabled learning. HNCs are made up of 12 credits and usually take one year to complete, HNDs are made of 30 credits and usually take two years to complete. Some HNCs allow direct entry into the second year of a degree course and HNDs direct entry into the third year.

Scottish Vocational Qualifications (SVQs) can also be taken at Further Education institutions (see above).

Useful Address
There are 46 further education colleges in Scotland. Applications for further education courses are generally made direct to the colleges concerned. Details of all further education colleges in Scotland are available from the *Scottish Further Education Funding Council (SFEFC)*: Donaldson House, 97 Haymarket Terrace, Edinburgh EH12 5HD; ☎0131-313 6500; fax 0131-313 6636; www.sfefc. ac.uk.

HIGHER EDUCATION

This term is used to describe education above Advanced Higher level and is provided in universities and colleges of higher education. Over 50 per cent of young Scots enter higher education courses of one type or another.

In 1992, the distinction between universities and certain other classes of higher education institution was removed, since which time all the Scottish polytechnics and art colleges have adopted the title of university and now award their own taught course and research degrees. Despite this apparent equality between the institutions now, there is a perception that the quality of education at the longer-established universities is better. Certainly, the entry requirements for the 'ex-polytechnics' tend to be lower, so they are attracting the less able students. It is open to debate whether this is because the education they provide is actually of a lower standard, or whether the public perception that this is the case means that there is less demand for places at these institutions as a first choice. Employers are certainly more impressed by degrees from the older universities, so for the foreseeable future these are going to remain the elite of higher education establishments in Scotland.

The following list of the Scottish universities, with the date they were established as such, clearly shows that there have been three 'waves' of new universities: the original four, established in the Middle Ages, a further four during the 1960s when there was a great expansion in higher education across the UK with the construction of many new so-called 'red-brick' universities, and the remaining five which were upgraded to university status in the nineteen-nineties.

SCOTLAND'S UNIVERSITIES

The University of Aberdeen: (1495), King's College, Aberdeen AB24 3FX; ☎01224-272000; fax 01224-272086; www.abdn.ac.uk.

The University of Abertay Dundee: (1994), Bell Street, Dundee DD1 1HG; ☎01382-308000; www.abertay.ac.uk.

The University of Dundee: (1967), Dundee, DD1 4HN; ☎01382- 344000; fax 01382-201604; www.dundee.ac.uk.

The University of Edinburgh: (1583), Old College, South Bridge, Edinburgh EH8 9YL; ☎0131-650 1000; fax 0131-650 2147; www.ed.ac.uk.

The University of Glasgow: (1451), University Avenue, Glasgow G12 8QQ; ☎0141-330 8855; fax 0141-330 4808; e-mail admissions@gla.ac.uk; www.gla.ac.uk.

Glasgow Caledonian University: (1993), 70 Cowcaddens Road, Glasgow G4 0BA; ☎0141-331 3000; fax 0141-331 3005; www.gcal.ac.uk.

Heriot-Watt University: (1966), Edinburgh EH14 4AS; ☎0131-449 5111; fax 0131-449 5153; www.hw.ac.uk.

Napier University: (1992), 219 Colinton Road, Edinburgh EH14 1DJ; ☎0131-444 2266; fax 0131-455 6333; www.napier.ac.uk.

University of Paisley: (1992), Paisley PA1 2BE; ☎0141-848 3000; www.paisley.ac.uk.

The Robert Gordon University: (1992), Schoolhill, Aberdeen AB10 1FR; ☎01224-262000; fax 01224-263000; www.rgu.ac.uk.

The University of St Andrews: (1411), College Gate, St Andrews, Fife KY16 9AJ; ☎01334-476161; fax 01334-462570; www.st-and.ac.uk.

The University of Stirling: (1967), Stirling FK9 4LA; ☎01786-473171; fax 01786-463000 www.stir.ac.uk.

The University of Strathclyde: (1964), John Anderson Campus, Glasgow G1 1XQ; ☎0141-552 4400; fax 0141-552 0775; www.strath.ac.uk.

Brief details of all these universities, including student numbers, courses available, accommodation costs and so forth can be found on the UCAS website at www. ucas.ac.uk. It also has links to all UK university websites.

One of the most radical developments in further and higher education in the UK is the University of the Highlands and Islands (UHI). For decades a dream within the region, it is now becoming a reality thanks to modern technology and to large sums of money input by the National Lottery and other bodies. After years of work behind the scenes, the blueprint strategy for UHI was finally made public on 28th February 1998. Through a network of over 50 learning centres, colleges and research institutions across the Highlands and Islands, it aims to bring educational, social and economic benefits to the region. Courses are conducted both in the partnership institutions and through distance learning, students being linked and learning together through modern technology – video, internet and PC. It was designated a Higher Education Institution in 2001 and aims to achieve full university status in 2007.

In addition, there is the Open University (OU) which offers degrees by distance learning. It admitted its first students in 1971 and claims to be the UK's largest university with 200,000 students enrolled. This figure may be a little misleading because nearly all the students are part-time and degrees can be taken over a period of many years. Unlike other universities, undergraduate level courses do not require any entry qualifications, so it does provide access to degree courses for those who might otherwise not have the opportunity. The OU is Scotland's largest provider of part-time university education with 13,500 students.

Courses are conducted through correspondence, TV programmes and videos, summer schools at various universities throughout the UK, limited face to face seminars and interactive on-line studying.

Useful Addresses

UHI Millennium Institute: Caledonia House, 63 Academy Street, Inverness IV1 1LU; ☎01463-279000; fax 01463-279001; www.uhi.ac.uk.

The Open University in Scotland: 10 Drumsheugh Gardens, Edinburgh EH3 7QJ; ☎0131-2263851; fax 0131-220 6730; www.open.ac.uk/near-you/in-scotland/index.asp.

Courses

The main higher education courses available are: first degree and postgraduate degrees; Diploma in Higher Education (Dip.HE), which is designed to serve as a stepping stone to a degree course; Higher National Diploma (HND); Higher National Certificate (HNC); preparation for professional examinations; in-service training of teachers.

Most undergraduate courses lead to the title of Bachelor of Arts (BA) or Bachelor of Science (BSc), followed by graduate degrees of Master of Arts (MA) or Master of Science (MSc). (However, some Scottish universities use the title Master for a first degree in arts subjects, which is somewhat confusing.) Most undergraduate courses in Scotland run for four years, one year longer than their equivalent in the rest of the UK. Professional courses in subjects such as medicine, dentistry and veterinary science take longer, up to seven years.

Postgraduate courses vary in length depending on whether they are taught or research degrees. A taught MA, for example, may take just one year, whereas research projects leading to a Doctorate (PhD) have been known to take up to ten.

HIGHER EDUCATION RESOURCES

Details of undergraduate level courses and of predicted entry requirements for the following year's intake, throughout the UK, are provided in the annual University and College Entrance: Official Guide, published by the Universities and Colleges Admissions Service (UCAS). This is expensive, at £32.50, or £27.50 plus p&p when ordered direct from UCAS, but it is the only guide to include compete entry requirements for HE using the UCAS tariff. It contains university profiles and A level and Scottish Higher entry requirements, and comes with a CD-ROM containing all entry requirements. This information is all available on www.ucas.ac.uk.

UCAS/Universities Scotland Entrance Guide to Higher Education in Education lists course available in Scotland and gives advice on how to apply for them. It also provides information on Scottish universities and colleges, grades and offers. £9.95 from UCAS Distribution, PO Box 130, Cheltenham Gloucestershire GL52 3ZF; ☎01242-544610; fax 01242-544960; www.ucas.com.

For details of taught postgraduate courses and research degree opportunities contact the relevant universities – there will be details on their websites. www.prospects.ac.uk has a searchable directory of courses.

For information and advice on postgraduate study, contact the *Careers Research & Advisory Centre:* Sheraton House, Castle Park, Cambridge CB3 0AX; ☎01223-460277; fax 01223-311708; www.crac.org.uk.

Scottish Credit & Qualifications Framework (SCQF)

The SCQF brings together all Scottish mainstream qualifications into a single unified framework. This allows comparison of levels of achievement across different types of qualification. There are 12 levels, ranging from Access 1 to Doctorate, with level 1 representing outcomes designed for students with severe and profound learning difficulties, through to level 12 representing outcomes associated with doctoral studies.

LEVELS IN THE SCOTTISH CREDIT & QUALIFICATIONS FRAMEWORK			
SCQF level	**SQA National Qualifications**	**Higher Education**	**SVQs**
1	Access 1	–	–
2	Access 2	–	–
3	Access 3/Foundation Standard Grade	–	–
4	Intermediate 1/General Standard Grade	–	SVQ1
5	Intermediate 2/Credit Standard Grade	–	SVQ2
6	Higher	–	SVQ3

7	Advanced Higher	Higher National Certificate	–
8	–	Higher National Diploma/	
		Diploma in	
		Higher Education	SVQ4
9	–	Ordinary degree/Graduate	
		Diploma/Certificate	–
10	–	Honours degree/Graduate	
		Diploma/Certificate	–
11	–	Masters	SVQ5
12	–	Doctorate	–

Admissions

Applications for admission to courses of below postgraduate level at most universities and higher education courses are made through the *Universities and Colleges Admission Service (UCAS)*. This is a central clearing house which allows potential students to apply to a number of institutions simultaneously. The individual institutions then indicate whether they wish to make the student an unconditional offer of a place on their chosen course, an offer conditional on them achieving certain minimum grades in their Highers, or to refuse them. They may also call the potential student for interview. On the basis of this information, the student then decides which course at which institution to take up.

The Open University and a few higher education colleges conduct their own admissions. Applications should be made direct to these bodies.

Most applications for admission as postgraduate student are made to individual institutions, but there are central clearing houses for postgraduate courses in the fields of teacher training and social work.

Initial teacher training courses in Scotland are either taken in colleges of education or universities. Details of courses on offer can be obtained from UCAS.

Useful Addresses

UCAS, the *Graduate Teacher Training Registry (GTTR)*, and the *Social Work Admissions System (SWAS)* are all based at: Rosehill, New Barn Lane, Cheltenham, Glos. GL52 3LZ; UCAS ☎01242-222444; fax 01954-280200; www.ucas.com; GTTR ☎0870-112 2205; fax 01242-544962; www.gttr.ac.uk; SWAS ☎0870-112 2207; fax 01242544962; www.ucas.ac.uk/getting/before/swas.html.

Tuition Fees & Student Loans

Since the 1980s, a number of changes have been made to the arrangements regarding the payment of tuition fees and living expenses for students in higher education. Prior to this, UK students made no contribution towards the costs of their tuition, and means-tested local education authority grants were available to help with student living expenses. The system of non-repayable grants was first replaced by student loans, repayable by the student once he/she graduated and was earning above a certain level. In 1998, the UK Government announced that in future UK students would also pay around £1,000 per year towards their course tuition.

The introduction of tuition fees was a major issue in Scotland during the Scottish Parliament elections in 1999, and a proposal to abolish them was one of the first matters considered by the new parliament. After a process of consultation and the production of the 'Cubie Report' by an independent committee set up to report on the matter, it was decided that tuition fees for full-time Scottish domiciled undergraduate students studying at Scottish institutions would be paid for by the Student Awards Agency for Scotland (SAAS).

There is also a Mature Students Bursary available. It is run by colleges and universities, so students should apply directly to them to find out if they are eligible.

Students are eligible for a loan of up to £4,095 per annum for those living in halls of residence or lodgings, and up to £3,240 per annum for those living in the parental home. The amount of loan available is means tested on the basis of family income (parents, husband or wife), with contribution expected from those with higher earnings. Students from families with income of less than £18,260 do not have to make a contribution.

Scottish students from low-income families can apply for a non-repayable Young Students Bursary of up to £2,150, to assist with the living expenses of new students entering full time higher education. Those with family income under £10,740 are eligible to apply for the highest amount of £2,150 per year. The bursary goes down to £1,445 a year for a family income of £15,000 and tapers off on a sliding scale down to zero for a family income of £28,000 per year. The level of student loan available is reduced by the level of bursary assessed. Student Loans are paid through the Student Loans Company.

The student loan is repaid once you have finished or left your course. It is repaid to the Inland Revenue and payments begin automatically once your income reaches £10,000. The amount repaid each year is then 9 per cent of income over £10,000 gross.

Some graduates must pay a fixed amount of Graduate Endowment after they finish their degree, in recognition of the higher education benefits they have received. The funds go towards student support for future generations. It applies to Scottish domiciled students and EU students and is paid from the April following the time they complete their course. For students who began their degree course in session 2004-5 the amount payable is £2,154 and it can be paid in a lump sum, as a student loan, or as part loan, part lump sum. Various classes of student are exempt from payment of the Graduate Endowment, including independent students, lone parents and disabled students.

Different rules apply to mature and independent students. Mature students are those aged 25 or over, while independent students are those who have no parents living, or who have been married for at least two years, or have been self-supporting from earnings or benefits for at least three years.

Scottish students studying at institutions outside Scotland are eligible for income-assessed student loans. Tuition fees are also assessed, with the student or his/her parents paying part, the SAAS paying the rest. Those on lower incomes may not have to pay anything towards tuition fees. These students do not have to pay into the Graduate Endowment Fund.

Students domiciled in England, Wales or Northern Ireland have the same liability for personal contribution towards tuition fees and the same means tested students loans entitlement as if they were to study at universities or colleges elsewhere in the UK. These students, if they choose to undertake a four year programme in Scotland, will only be liable to pay tuition fees for three years. Final year fees will be met by the Scottish Executive. They do not have to pay the Graduate Endowment.

Useful Addresses

Student Awards Agency for Scotland (SAAS): Gyleview House, 3 Redheughs Rigg, Edinburgh EH12 9HH; ☎0845-11101777; fax 0131-244 5887; www.saas. gov.uk.

The Student Loans Company: 100 Bothwell Street, Glasgow G2 7JD; ☎0800-405010; www.slc.co.uk.

Top-up Fees

In 2003, the UK Government introduced top-up fees in England, which allowed English universities to charge undergraduate tuition fees of up to £3,000 per year. The Scottish Executive have said they will not introduce top-up fees in Scotland.

International Students

EU students applying to take a degree course in Scotland are entitled to free tuition of up to £1,150 per year.

FEES FOR FULL-TIME EU STUDENTS AT THE UNIVERSITY OF STRATHCLYDE FOR SESSION 2004/5		
Faculty	**Undergraduate courses**	**Postgraduate courses**
Faculty of Engineering	£1,150	£3,010-£4,695
Faculty of Science	£1,150	£3,010-£4,140

Faculty of Law, Arts and Social Sciences	£1,150	£3,010-£6,995
Faculty of Education	£1,150	£3,010-4,200
Strathclyde Business School	£1,150-	£3,010-£17,500

Non-EU students are required to pay full tuition fees. These vary depending on the course and the institution.

NON-EU FEES AT GLASGOW CALEDONIAN UNIVERSITY FOR SESSION 2004/5

Faculty	Undergraduate courses	Postgraduate courses
School of the Built & Natural Environment	£7,000	£8,100
Caledonian Business School	£7,000-£7,500	£7,800-£10,000
School of Computing & Mathematical Sciences	£7,000-£8,000	£8,800-£9,000
School of Engineering, Science & Design	£7,300	£8,800
School of Health & Social Care	£7,000	£10,000
School of Law & Social Sciences	£7,000	£7,400-£8,300
School of Life Sciences	£7,300	£8,000-£8,800
School of Nursing, Midwifery & Community Health	£7,000	£8,100

Scholarships to assist with fees may be available to domestic, EU and non-EU students on various courses at various levels. Enquire to institutions direct or see their websites for details.

International students, including those from the EU, are not eligible to apply for a student loan to assist with living costs. The University of Paisley estimates that living costs, including university accommodation, for the academic year 2004/5 would amount to between £6,700-£7,000.

For further details, contact relevant universities direct. Information for international students is contained in their prospectuses, and some have an International Office specifically to assist overseas students. See above for contact details of all Scottish universities.

Adult & Continuing Education

This covers a wide range of options including non-vocational general interest courses, vocational courses providing skills needed in industry and commerce and degree-level study at the Open University.

Most courses are part-time and are provided by a number of bodies including education authorities, further and higher education colleges, universities, residential colleges and several voluntary bodies.

Local adult education evening classes, both vocational and non-vocational, are provided by local education authorities via the Community Education Service and take place in a number of centres including schools and village halls across Scotland.

Useful Addresses

The largest voluntary education body in Scotland is the *Workers Educational Association (WEA)* which reaches around 150,000 students annually throughout the UK. *WEA Scotland:* Riddle's Court, 322 Lawnmarket, Edinburgh EH1 2PG; ☎0131-226 3456; fax 0131-220 0306; www.weascotland.org.uk.

Means-tested bursaries and grants are available for some adult education courses, from local education authorities and the *Scottish Executive Enterprise, Transport and Lifelong Learning Department:* Meridian Court, 5 Cadogan Street, Glasgow G2 6AT; ☎0141-248 5665; fax 0141-242 5665; www.scotland.gov. uk/About/Departments/ETLLD.

Advice on all aspects of adult and community education is available from *Community Learning Scotland:* Rosebery House, 9 Haymarket Terrace, Edinburgh EH12 5EZ; ☎0131-313 2488; fax 0131-313 6800; www.communitylearning. org.

For advice on Scottish secondary schools, university courses, and careers, See the *PlanIT Plus* website www.planitplus.net or phone their CareersLine ☎0800-442222.

Trans-national Education & Training Programmes

There are a number of schemes for those wishing to come to study in the UK. Within the EEA, the European Education programme SOCRATES includes a number of programmes allowing a period of study in another EU country. Under the ERASMUS programme, students in higher education may study on a full-time basis for a minimum of three months and a maximum of one academic year. Grants may be available.

The programme has 31 participating countries, including the 25 member states of the EU, plus Iceland, Liechtenstein, Norway, Romania, Bulgaria and Turkey.

For a full list of programmes available see the European Commission website: http://europa.eu.int/comm/education/programmes/socrates/socrates – en.html.

Useful Addresses

UK SOCRATES-ERASMUS: R and D Building, The University of Kent, Canterbury CT2 7PD; ☎01227-762712; fax 01227-762711; www.erasmus.

ac.uk.

For further details about these programmes, and other European Commission schemes introduced from time to time, there is lots of useful advice on http://europa.eu.int/index – en.htm.

A number of study programmes for students from different countries, within and outside the EU, are run by CIEE Council Exchanges. They have offices around the world including:

UK: Rosedale House, Rosedale Road, Richmond, Surrey TW9 2SZ; ☎020-8939 9057; fax 020-8939 9090.

Australia: 91 York Street, Level 3, Sydney NSW 2000; ☎+61 28235-7000; fax 61 28235-7001.

France: 39 Rue de l'Arbalète, Paris 75005.

Germany: Oranienburger Str. 13-14, 10178 Berlin; ☎4930-2848-590; fax 4930-2809-6180.

Italy: Via F. Pozzo 21/6Genova 16145; ☎+39 010-362 2489; fax +39 010-362 0805.

Spain: Nunez de Balboa, 49, 28001 Madrid; ☎+91 7819-910; fax +91 4319-050.

USA: 3 Copley Place, 2nd Floor, Boston 02116, MA; ☎+1 617-247 0350; fax +1 617-247 2911.

For further information of educational schemes available in the UK and a full list of CIEE offices world-wide, see www.councilexchanges.org.

Of particular relevance to intending students from the USA are the programmes run by the British Universities North America Club (BUNAC). Contact them at:

BUNAC USA: PO Box 430, Southbury CT 06488; ☎203-264-0901; fax 203-264-0251; www.bunac.org.uk/usa.

BUNAC Scottish Office: 60 The High Street, Edinburgh EH1 1TB; ☎0131-558 9313; fax 0131-558 9314; www.bunac.org.uk.

BUNAC also run programmes allowing students from other countries to study in the UK. In Canada this is done through SWAP (Student Work Abroad Programme) at www.swap.ca. BUNAC's partner in Australia and New Zealand is International Exchange Programs (IEP).

IEP (Australia): PO Box 13278, Law Courts Post Office, Melbourne, Vicoria 8010; www.iep.org.au.

IEP (NZ): PO Box 1786, Shortland Street, Auckland; www.iep.co.nz.

There are links to all relevant national websites from the main BUNAC website www.bunac.org.

Another comprehensive source of information on studying in the UK is the British Council, which has two offices in Scotland. *The British Council Scotland:* The Tun, 4 Jackson's Entry, Holyrood Road, Edinburgh EH8 8PJ; ☎0131-524 5700; fax 0131-524 5701. 25 High Street, Old Aberdeen AB2 3EE; ☎01224-486640; fax

01224-480371; www.britishcouncil.org. The British Council has offices around the world, details of which can be found on their website. US nationals should also look at www.britishcouncil.org/usa-education.

MEDIA

Britain is media mad! There are about 1,000 daily, Sunday and weekly newspapers published, around 8,000 general interest magazines and 4,000 trade and technical publications. In addition there are many specialist or local magazines and newspapers with a small but loyal readership. It is estimated that the British buy more newspapers than any other country in the world, around 14 million national newspapers and five million regional newspapers every weekday.

There is also a plethora of radio stations, national, regional and local. Until recent years, the number of TV stations was tiny in comparison, with just four terrestrial channels, with a fifth introduced in 1997. However, there are literally hundreds of TV stations now accessible via satellite and cable.

Newspapers

In Scotland there are around 160 national, regional and local daily and weekly newspapers, some 30 per cent of which are distributed free, making their income solely from advertising. Of the others, daily and weekly papers usually cost between 30 and 50 pence per issue, Sunday papers between 50 pence and £1. Their price is low partly because of intense competition between different newspapers, and partly because there is no value added tax (VAT) charged on newspapers, magazines or books in the UK. In addition, in sparsely populated areas of the Highlands, which the regional papers tend not to cover in depth, there are many small local papers, often produced on a voluntary basis, usually weekly, fortnightly or monthly. These provide a valuable service – they tell you everything you need to know, and nothing you don't need to know. Whichever area you move to, try to get hold of the local newspaper – it will give you a flavour of what life there is like.

Although national newspapers ostensibly deal with matters of interest nationwide, in practice, just as the national press in England tends to have a bias towards London and the south east, in Scotland they concentrate on Glasgow, Edinburgh and the Central Belt. Regional papers such as the Press & Journal, produced in Aberdeen, try to redress the balance by focussing on issues in their region of the country.

Scotland has both its own distinct newspapers and Scottish editions of some of the UK national newspapers. The 'big two' genuinely Scottish dailies are *The Scotsman* and *The Herald*, with head offices in Edinburgh and Glasgow respectively. They both have 'sister' Sunday papers, *Scotland on Sunday* and *The Sunday Herald* respectively. Their circulation is outstripped many times over, however, by the *Sunday Post*, based in Dundee, the best-selling newspaper of Scotland.

UK newspapers with Scottish editions include the *Daily Star of Scotland*, *Daily Telegraph*, *The Guardian*, *Scottish Daily Mail*, *Scottish Express* and *The Scottish Sun*.

The main UK Sunday newspapers with Scottish editions are *The Independent on Sunday*, *Mail on Sunday in Scotland*, *The Observer*, *Scottish Sunday Express*, *Sunday Mail*, and *Sunday Mirror*. Sunday newspapers are large and complex publications, most with a 'free' colour magazine together with numerous other supplements covering such diverse issues as leisure, business, property, the internet and so forth.

The 'big eight' Scottish regional daily newspapers are the *Courier and Advertiser* (Dundee), *Daily Record* (Glasgow), *Edinburgh Evening News*, *Evening Express* (Aberdeen), *Evening Times* (Glasgow), *Greenock Telegraph* (Dunfermline), *Paisley Daily Express* (Glasgow), *Press and Journal* (Aberdeen).

UK newspapers are usually financially independent of any political party, but most adopt a political stance in their editorial content. An exception to this is *The Independent* which claims no political bias.

In most parts of the country, other than the remotest areas, newsagents will usually deliver newspapers to your door for a small weekly charge. Most are not available by subscription, but your local newsagent will order and reserve a regular copy for you to either collect or have delivered.

Some local papers in the Highlands carry regular sections in Gaelic. The *West Highland Free Press*, produced on the Isle of Skye and distributed throughout the north west, in particular caters for Gaelic readers.

Many of the national newspapers now have websites where some or all of the content of the print version can be accessed:

The Scotsman Online www.scotsman.com, contains a Gaelic section.

The Electronic Herald www.theherald.co.uk.

The Sunday Herald www.sundayherald.com.

Press & Journal www.thisisnorthscotland.co.uk.

Magazines

There is no distinctively 'Scottish' magazine market as such, because most magazines, apart from those with a very local reference, are distributed across Britain. There are a number of magazines which take Scotland as their subject, but these are available via large newsagents in the rest of the UK and indeed, overseas by subscription. The most well-known of these are *Scottish Field*, *Scottish Memories* and *The Scots Magazine*. The latter is very popular around the world with expatriate Scots and those with Scottish ancestry.

Scottish Magazines

The Scots Magazine: D.C Thomson & Co Ltd, Albert Square, Dundee DD1 9QJ; ☎01382-223131; e-mail editor@scotsmagazine.com.

Scottish Field: Craigcrook Castle, Craigcrook Road, Edinburgh EH4 3PE;

☎0131-312 4550; fax 0131-312 4551; e-mail editor@scottishfield.org www. scottishfield.co.uk.

Scottish Memories: Lang Syne Publishers Ltd, Strathclyde Business Centre, 120 Carstairs Street, Glasgow G40 4DJ; ☎0141-554 9944; fax 0141-554 9955.

Although many magazines are available in newsagents, smaller circulation and specialist magazines tend to be available only by subscription. Most of them also have their own websites, some just as a medium for advertising and selling subscriptions, while others include at least part of their editorial content online.

UK magazines and newspapers, together with their contact details, are listed in two annual guides, *Writers' & Artists' Yearbook*, published by A&C Black (London) and *The Writer's Handbook*, Macmillan (London).

Books & Bookshops

Scotland has a long literary heritage. Names from the past such as Robert Burns, Sir Walter Scott and Robert Louis Stevenson are known worldwide, but among the new generation of Scottish writers are others who have achieved recognition beyond their home land. Irvine Welsh, in books such as the notorious *Trainspotting*, shows a completely different side of the country in his non-romanticised but vigorous pictures of modern Scottish city life.

Edinburgh was the birthplace of many famous publishing companies: Chambers, of dictionary fame, and the Encyclopaedia Britannica both started here. Companies such as Blackie and Son and Collins started elsewhere in Scotland as publishing expanded. It was only when world markets opened to English language publishers that publishers started to move south to London, which is now the centre of UK publishing. During the second half of the twentieth century, there was upheaval in the publishing industry, with a scramble by multinational organisations to buy up longstanding family-owned companies. The inevitable reaction to this was for new, small breakaway companies to form, to fight back against the perceived 'big bucks and boardroom' atmosphere which many saw as antithetical to the business of publishing good books. By the 1970s, Scottish independent publishing was growing again and the Scottish Publishers Association (SPA) was set up by a group of 12 publishers in 1973. It now has around 80 members, most of which publish books with a distinctively Scottish flavour.

However, these are but a small percentage of the total books sold in Scotland. The domestic book market is essentially UK wide – best sellers in England and Wales tend to be the best sellers in Scotland. There are around 125,000 new books published every year in the UK. The top selling books are almost exclusively a mix of popular 'genre' fiction by big name authors and non-fiction books such as cookery books, horoscopes, biographies and TV or cinema tie-ins. Around 50 per cent of these are written by British authors, 40 per cent by Americans, with fewer than ten per cent from elsewhere.

For many years the price of books in the UK was controlled by the Net Book

Agreement (NBA), which gave publishers the legal right to set minimum retail prices for books. Large booksellers campaigned against this, as it prevented them from discounting books and thereby competing effectively with others. Small independent bookshops argued for its retention: they could not afford to discount books to compete with the large chains. The scenario they painted was one where many small shops would go to the wall as book buyers deserted them for cheaper books elsewhere. As competition between the giant chains intensified, it was argued, academic, restricted interest and specialist books which could not expect huge mass market sales would suffer and publishers would stop putting money into producing them as the large booksellers refused to stock them. Despite this argument, the NBA was abolished in 1995. Although the price of mass market paperbacks may have fallen somewhat, and although some small bookshops may have failed – some of which would doubtless have failed anyway – the predictions of doom and gloom and a black day for the publishing industry do not appear to have come true. There are still independent booksellers about, while the large chains seem to spend much of their energies on taking each other over, rather than swallowing up the 'little people'.

This trend has been noticeable in Scottish High Streets: in recent years John Menzies, a long-established Scottish newsagent/bookstore chain has been taken over by the English W.H.Smiths, while Waterstones (which was previously taken over by W.H Smiths before regaining its own identity) has taken over Dillons, another large chain. Scotland had its own bookseller chain, James Thin Ltd, with branches in towns and cities throughout Scotland, but this was taken over by the Ottakers chain in 2002. The interests of Scottish booksellers are promoted by the Scottish Book Marketing Group, set up by the Scottish Publisher Association.

VAT is not charged on books in the UK, although the spectre of adding the tax to their cover price is regularly raised. So far, the threat has been fought off. Despite this, books are comparatively expensive in the UK. Traditionally, mass market books were produced in expensive hardback format first, with a cheaper paperback edition following a year or so later. However, today much popular fiction is produced directly in paperback, meaning potentially larger returns for the publishers and authors.

Despite all the wranglings about the price of books, the desirability or otherwise of the NBA and the thorny question of VAT on books, one suspects that the biggest change to the book industry will come from the internet. With online publishing and selling of books increasing at a phenomenal rate, the way the public buys and reads books is already changing.

Details of publishers, booksellers and other publishing services can be found in the annual *Directory of Publishing in Scotland*, published by the Scottish Publishers Association. Both the *Scottish Publishers Association* and the *Scottish Book Marketing Group* are based at Scottish Book Centre, 137 Dundee Street, Edinburgh EH11 1BG; ☎0131-228 6866; fax 0131-228 3220; www.scottishbooks.org.

Television

Television can now be received throughout Scotland and the Islands, although it is comparatively recently that the final pockets of the country have been able to receive TV pictures. In some areas, reception can still be patchy. Domestic 'boosters' attached to your home aerial are necessary in many mountainous areas to improve the sound and vision. In order to transmit to isolated areas, particularly in the Highlands, some TV masts are inevitably sited in very exposed areas. This means that during bad weather TV reception can be badly affected, or even non-existent. Many people have switched to satellite TV reception because overall the quality and reliability of the picture is improved.

In the UK as a whole, 99 per cent of homes have at least one TV set and over 60 per cent have two or more. Britain watches more television than any other European country, average viewing being estimated at around 25 hours a week. The number and variety of programmes available to watch has undergone massive expansion since the 1980s, due to the introduction of cable and satellite TV companies. Prior to this there had been just four terrestrial channels, two provided by the British Broadcasting Corporation (BBC), BBC1 and BBC2, and two by Independent Television (ITV), Channel 3 and Channel 4. In 1997 the ITV introduced a fifth channel, unsurprisingly called Channel 5.

The BBC is not allowed to show advertisements, making its income from the sale of television licences. At the time of writing these are £121 per year for colour receivers, £40.50 for black and white receivers. The licence generally increases a few pounds every year or so. Every owner of a TV set in Britain must have a TV licence, even if they only ever watch ITV or cable and satellite channels, so in effect it is a tax on TV viewing. TV licences are free for the over-75s.

In Scotland the BBC channels are designated BBC Scotland on 1 and BBC Scotland on 2. Although programming is broadly the same across Britain, there are regional variations. For instance, BBC Scotland has a commitment to show Gaelic programmes, regional news programmes and certain current affairs programmes which are specific to Scotland.

The ITV network – known collectively as commercial TV – is run on a franchise basis by a number of companies across Britain with their programmes shown on Channel 3. In Scotland there are three ITV companies: Border TV, covering the Borders region as well as Cumbria (in England) and the Isle of Man (in the Irish Sea); Scottish TV, covering central Scotland; and Grampian TV, covering northern Scotland and the Islands.

ITV Channel 4 is commercial television's answer to BBC 2, showing the more 'highbrow' and smaller audience programmes.

ITV Channel 5, showing a more populist mix of programmes, was launched on 30th March 1997, and is not yet available everywhere in Scotland. It can only be received in about 70 per cent of households across Britain, those in the more heavily populated areas. Large areas of the Highlands are not able to receive Channel 5, and are unlikely to be able to in the foreseeable future, unless they receive it via satellite. The main ITV channels make their income purely from advertising.

Satellite TV is received through an external satellite dish fixed to your house and a box connected to your TV. Boxes now come in standard and digital format – the digital ones allowing greater services including the ability to record and playback TV programmes at times of your own choosing. The standard box and installation is usually free if you take out a subscription to the provider, such as Sky, with a reduced cost for a digital box. You can, however, purchase a box and pay for it and installation without taking out a Sky subscription, in which case the box and installation is around £200.

The main provider of satellite TV in Britain is British Sky Broadcasting, generally known as Sky, or BSkyB. In addition to its own channels, it also broadcasts a number of joint-venture channels and distributes other channels for third parties. Subscribers pay a monthly charge for satellite reception, which varies depending on the number of channels they wish to access and whether they choose a standard or digital box and service. Sky digital subscription has packages from £13.50 to £60 per month.

There are also cable TV companies which provide programming via underground cables, often in conjunction with telephone services. Again, subscribers pay a monthly fee for cable services. Because it is not cost-effective to run cable to areas of low population, cable TV is not available in large regions of the Highlands and other rural areas of Scotland. Many cable TV channels can, however, be received via satellite, which is available by subscription throughout Scotland.

In October 1998, Sky introduced a digital satellite service alongside the existing analogue service. Sky digital provides up to 200 TV channels, which include the terrestrial channels as well as specialised film channels, sports channels, children's channels and music channels as well as other restricted interest channels, such as Gaelic programming and channels in other minority languages to cater for such groups as immigrants from India and Pakistan. In addition there are a growing number of interactive shopping channels. There are some 'pay per view' broadcasts, usually large sporting events or box-office movies, where the broadcast can be only received and decoded in return for a one-off payment. All radio stations can be received through Sky digital and e-mail may also be sent and received.

The provision of television has been further complicated since 1997, when the 'digital television revolution', as it was hailed in the media, hit Britain. The BBC and ITV provide free digital transmissions of their existing programming alongside the traditional analogue version. They also have a number of digital channels which can be received through digital TVs, cable or satellite. Both have a 24 hours news channel and additional entertainment and information channels, such as BBC3 and BBC4. Channel 4 has 'Film on Four', a subscription digital channel which shows movies. There are a number of other independent channels also available; some of these are available free, others are only available if you pay a monthly subscription.

There are concerns that this revolution in TV viewing may pass large parts of Scotland by. The terrestrial TV channels are currently available free in digital format, as long as one invests in a digital TV or buys a set-top 'black box' which plugs into a non-digital TV and decodes digital broadcasts. This service is available through normal TV aerials in most of England and Wales and the southern and central areas of Scotland. However, it is, allegedly, not cost-effective to install digital transmitting equipment in northern Scotland and the Islands. There are fears that this will cause a big problem in the future, when digital broadcasting replaces analogue. This process is scheduled to begin in 2007 and to be completed by 2012, when analogue broadcasting will finally be 'switched off'. The government has said there are two crucial tests which will have to be met before the switch is made: viewers must be able to receive digital coverage and be able to afford it. There is no commitment, as yet, as to how the digital service should be delivered, nor what the test of 'affordability' is likely to be in practice. The Highland Council's response is that 'no Highland resident should be discriminated against, either by extra costs to receive public service broadcasting, or a reduced level of service when digital television is finally introduced.'

The Government say they will provide free to view TV via satellite, cable or broadband but the question remains whether the householder will have to pay for the satellite dish or broadband installation. The situation at present is that there is a broadband monthly subscription payable, so it's hard to see whether such a service would be genuinely 'free-to-view'. An increasing number of households in the Highlands now receive their terrestrial TV services through satellite, because the reception is far more reliable in remote and mountainous areas than through an aerial. This also allows them to receive Channel 5 which otherwise is not available even through one's aerial. The cynical might wonder whether the Government is banking on the vast majority of households paying for satellite reception by the time of the analogue switch-off, so the problem will only affect a few people.

Television Information Services

Most new TV sets will receive 'teletext' or 'fastext' services. These allow you to see online information, accessible through your TV remote controller, including current TV listings, news, weather, sport, travel, financial, consumer and entertainment for the region in which you live. The BBC offers its Ceefax service while the ITV version is called Teletext. Satellite stations provide their own teletext services. Teletext is also available online at www.teletext.co.uk.

There are a large number of TV listings magazines available in newsagents, including the *Radio Times*, the *TV Times* and *What's On TV*. These include the main satellite and cable channels as well as all five terrestrial channels, with regional programme variations, and the radio stations accessible in your area. They also have background articles on programmes and their stars, plus some general interest articles. There are also satellite TV listing magazines which include a wider selection of channels; full listings are available on-screen if you subscribe to satellite.

Most daily and many weekly newspapers also carry TV listings within the body of the paper or as a free supplement.

Television Companies
BBC Television
BBC Scotland has centres at Glasgow, Aberdeen and Edinburgh; their addresses are:

BBC: Broadcasting House, Queen Margaret Drive, Glasgow G12 8DG; ☎0141-338 8844.

BBC: Broadcasting House, Beechgrove Terrace, Aberdeen AB15 5ZT; ☎01224-625233.

BBC: Broadcasting House, The Tun, 111 Holyrood Road, Edinburgh EH8 8PJ; ☎0131-557 5888.

The BBC Scotland website address is www.bbc.co.uk/scotland.

Independent Television
The ITV network companies in Scotland are:

Border Television PLC: The Television Centre, Carlisle CA1 3NT; ☎01228-525101; www.border-tv.com.

Scottish Television PLC: 200 Renfield Street, Glasgow G2 3PR; ☎0141-300 3000; www.scottishtv.co.uk.

Grampian TV has offices at Aberdeen, Dundee and Inverness. Website www.grampiantv.co.uk:

Grampian Television PLC: Craigshaw Business Park, West Tullos, Aberdeen AB12 3QH; ☎01224-848848; fax 01224-848800.

Grampian Television PLC: Harbour Chambers, Dock Street, Dundee DD1 3HW; ☎01382-591000; fax 01382-591010.

Grampian Television PLC: 23-25 Huntly Street, Inverness IV3 5PR; ☎01463-242624.

The other main independent TV companies whose output is accessible in Scotland are:

Channel 5 Broadcasting Ltd: 22 Long Acre, London WC2E 9LY; ☎020-7550 5555; www.channel5.co.uk.

Channel 4 Television Corporation: 124 Horseferry Road, London SW1P 2TX; ☎020-7396 4444; www.channel4.com.

GMTV LTD (Breakfast Television): London Television Centre, Upper Ground, London SE1 9TT; ☎020-7827 3000. GMTV's Scottish office is at Unit 5, 3 Q Court, Quality Street, Edinburgh EH4; www.gmtv.co.uk.

Independent Television News Ltd (ITN): 200 Gray's Inn Road, London WC1X 8XZ; ☎020-7833 3000; www.itn.co.uk.
Teletext Ltd: (Scottish Editor) 39 St Vincent, Glasgow G1 2QQ; ☎0141-221 4457; www.teletext.co.uk.

Satellite Television
BSkyB: Grant Way, Isleworth, Middx TW7 5QD; ☎020-7705 3000; fax 020-7705 3030/3113; www.sky.com.

Cable Television
ntl: ☎0800-052 1815; www.ntl.co.uk.

Quality of Programming
Despite perennial claims that standards are dropping, with the influx of dire American sitcoms and Australian soap operas, not to mention the home-grown varieties which are often worse, British television is still generally agreed to be the best in the world. Alongside the pap, both the BBC and ITV produce plenty of high quality documentaries, drama serials and films, current affairs programmes and sports coverage.

Although the satellite and cable channels have certainly increased the quantity, they have not improved the quality of TV available in the UK. There are any number of awful programmes which cater only to the lowest common denominator of television junkies and couch potatoes.

There are controls and restrictions on the content of TV programmes and advertisements broadcast in the UK. Programmes unsuitable for children may not be broadcast before 9pm (known as 'the watershed') and the amount of advertising on commercial TV is limited by a law to a maximum of 7.5 minutes per hour during peak viewing times (6 to 11pm).

Useful Address
Complaints about infringements of these rules and other matters can be made to the Office of Communications, Riverside House, 2A Southwark Bridge Road, London SE1 9HA; ☎020-7981 3000; fax 020-7981 3333; www.ofcom.org.uk.

Gaelic Television
There are a number of Gaelic programmes, including children's programmes, current affairs, music and culture, broadcast on BBC and commercial TV in Scotland, but this only amounts to a few hours per week. The Scottish Executive has announced its support for a dedicated Gaelic television channel as part of public service broadcasting. The BBC has been accused, however, of 'dragging its heels' and not making plans to produce enough Gaelic programming to merit a dedicated channel. The recently introduced Gaelic bill, with its commitment to

promoting and expanding the use of Gaelic should add impetus to the campaign for a Gaelic TV channel.

Useful Address

Seirbheis nam Meadhanan Gàidhlig/Gaelic Media Service: Seaforth House, Seaforth Road, Stornoway, Isle of Lewis HS1 2SD; ☎01851-705550; fax 01851 706432; www.ccg.org.uk.

Radio

UK domestic radio services are broadcast across three bands: FM (also called VHF); medium wave (or AM) and long wave. The FM waveband covers the range 87.5 MHz to 108 MHz and the medium waveband covers 531 kHz to 1602 kHz. Radio reception can be patchy in mountainous areas of Scotland. Car journeys in the Highlands can involve much twiddling of knobs to pick up the clearest radio signal at any point in your travels! Household reception can also be affected. Booster aerials can improve reception – again, a satellite dish may be the best solution.

Radio provision in Britain follows a similar pattern to TV provision, as described above. The BBC have five nationwide stations, Radio 1, 2, 3, 4 and 5. Each has a distinctive character, with Radio 1 broadcasting non-stop pop music for the younger age-group; Radio 2's output is a mix of pop music, 'golden oldies' and relaxed discussion; Radio 3 broadcasts mainly classical music and classic and serious drama; Radio 4 has a mix of documentaries, quiz shows, magazine programmes covering everything from arts to disabilities to financial advice, plus it is renowned for its new drama productions; while Radio 5 broadcasts live sport and news. In addition, Scotland receives BBC Radio Scotland, and several local BBC stations. Stornoway is the home of *Radio nan Gaidheal*, the BBC's Gaelic service, which is broadcast to the northern Highlands and Islands.

There are also independent (commercial) radio stations broadcasting nationally and locally. The three main national stations are Classic FM, TalkSport and Virgin 1215. There are numerous local independent stations covering a wide range of output. Some in the more populous regions are professionally run, well-funded businesses while, at the other end of the scale, are tiny stations in the Highlands and Islands run by voluntary organisations on a shoestring, reliant for funding on charitable organisations, local councils and local enterprise companies.

Altogether, there are around forty domestic radio stations which can be received in Scotland. Some European stations can also be picked up. Most radio stations can now be picked up via the internet.

Radio stations are now broadcasting digitally. It is necessary to have a radio (or TV) set with a digital decoder in order to receive digital radio broadcasts. Terrestrial digital radio broadcasts within the range 217.5 to 230 MHz.

The BBC World Service, true to its name, broadcasts across the world. Its output is over 1,000 hours of programmes a week in 44 languages, including English.

Listings of national and local radio programmes, plus details of broadcast wavelengths, can be found in the TV listings magazines and newspapers.

BBC Radio

BBC Radio Scotland can be contacted via the BBC Scotland addresses listed above. It broadcasts on the frequencies 810 AM and 92.4-94.7 FM. It broadcasts local programmes on the FM frequencies in Highlands, North-East, Borders, South-West (also 585 AM), Orkney, Shetland.

For the nationwide services, contact *BBC Radio* (Broadcasting House, Portland Place, London W1A 1AA; ☎020-7580 4468).

FREQUENCIES OF BBC RADIO STATIONS

Radio Scotland	92-95 FM
Radio 1	97.6-99.8 FM
Radio 2	88-90.2 FM
Radio 3	90.2-92.4 FM
Radio 4	94.6-96.1 FM, 103.5-105 FM, 1449 AM
Radio 5 Live	693/909 AM.

Independent National Radio Stations

Classic FM: 7 Swallow Place, London W1B 2AG; ☎020-7343 9000; fax 020-7344 2700; www.classicfm.com. Frequencies: FM 100-102 MHz.

TalkSPORT: 18 Hatfields, London SE1 8DJ; ☎020-7959 7800; fax 020-7959 7874; www.talksport.net. Frequencies: MW 1053 & 1089 kHz.

Virgin 1215: 1 Golden Square, London W1F 9DJ; ☎020-7434 1215; fax 020-7434 1197; www.virginradio.co.uk. Frequencies: 1215 AM.

There is one regional radio station, which covers central Scotland.

Real Radio Scotland: PO Box 101, Unit 1130, Parkway Court, Glasgow Business Park; ☎0141-781 1011; fax 0141-781 1112; www.realradiofm.com. Frequencies: 100-101 FM.

At last count, there were around 24 local independent stations, with new ones appearing (and disappearing) regularly. There is also a network of hospital radios stations, broadcasting to their patients and sometimes to the immediate locality.

COMMUNICATIONS

Post

The UK postal service is operated by two arms of the Post Office, the Royal Mail and ParcelForce. The Royal Mail delivers letters and small packages and parcels, while larger packages and parcels can be sent more economically by ParcelForce.

Throughout Scotland, postal deliveries are made to households and business premises at least once a day, Monday to Saturday. In larger towns there may be two deliveries a day, one in the morning, one in the afternoon.

Mail is posted in post boxes (usually red in colour) which are found outside post offices and by the side of roads throughout the country. Even the most remote communities should have a post box within a few minutes' walk or drive. Collections are made several times a day from large town centre post-boxes, while in rural communities one collection every day except Sunday is the norm.

Letters can be sent either first class or second class, which vary in their cost and speed of delivery. First class mail is usually delivered the next working day, as long as it is posted before stated times, while second class mail is usually delivered within three working days. Second class service is only applicable to items up to 750g in weight. Anything heavier must go first class (or by ParcelForce). Although these delivery times are what the Royal Mail aims at, and in most cases achieves, they are not guaranteed. In areas such as the Highlands and Islands, delivery times are often slower (and the stated posting times are earlier).

At the time of writing second class mail costs 21p for up to 60 grammes, 35p for up to 100g, then on a sliding scale up to £2.12 for a maximum of 750g. First class mail is 28p for up to 60g, 42p for up to 100g, then on a sliding scale up to £3.45 for 1,000g. Thereafter it is 86p for each additional 250g.

Enhanced services are available for important documents, date sensitive or valuable items. Recorded delivery requires a receipt from the post office on posting and a signature of the receiver on delivery. This costs 65p plus either first or second class postage. Compensation is paid for non-delivery of up to £28 or market value, whichever is lower. Special Delivery guarantees delivery the next working day by 9am or 1pm, or you get your money back. It is designed for financially valuable or urgent items and pays compensation at different levels, up to a maximum of £2,500 (registered delivery is not available to the USA). Later guaranteed times apply, however, to remote destinations in the Scottish Highlands and Islands. Consequential loss cover can also be added for a small additional charge.

Airmail letters should be delivered within three working days inside Western Europe, four days to eastern Europe and five working days to destinations outside Europe. Within Europe, all letters are sent airmail, but small packets and printed papers may be sent by surface mail, which should be delivered within two weeks in Western Europe, four weeks to eastern Europe and up to eight weeks outside Europe. Within Europe, airmail postcards and letters up to 20g cost 40p, letters up to 40g are 57p, then a sliding scale up to £2.704 for 300g. Thereafter it is 16p for each additional 20g. Outside Europe, airmail postage starts at 47p for 10g and 68p for 20g.

Postage stamps can be purchased from post offices, in a wide range of shops and in some places from vending machines – however, these are becoming a rarity. Bulk buys of stamps (minimum sheets of 100) can also be purchased through the Royal Mail website www.royalmail.co.uk.

Parcel Force rates vary on a sliding scale based on the weight and destination of the parcel. There is a special service of deliveries to British Forces Posted Overseas (BFPO). Further details on these can be found via the Royal Mail website.

Useful Address

Royal Mail: Customer Services, Freepost RM1 1AA; ☎08457-740740; www. royalmail.com.

Telephones

At the time of writing, the situation regarding the costs of using a telephone in the UK is in a state of flux. There is currently tremendous competition between British Telecom (BT), the main provider of services and lines, and newer companies on the scene. Since the deregulation of telephone services, new suppliers including various cable companies have emerged. In addition, 'resellers' are buying line capacity in bulk and passing it on to their customers at a discount. BT is now fighting back, by offering a variety of different packages aimed at both domestic and business customers. So it means very little to quote basic 'per minute' prices – these can vary widely depending on who you obtain your telephone service from and what particular package you pay for. The packages on offer are also apparently changing by the day. The only thing that can be said with certainty is that telephone charges have fallen over recent years.

Costs of installation of telephone lines are outlined above in Chapter 3, *Setting Up Home*. Regular monthly or quarterly telephone bills are made up of line rental plus the cost of telephone calls made from that line. Tariffs are based on a per minute charge which varies depending on the time of day at which the call is made – it is generally cheaper after 18:00 and at weekends – and whether the call is local, regional, national, international or has a non-geographical code. Local calls are those made within your own area or to neighbouring areas; regional calls are those out of your local call area but within 35 miles (56.4 km) of your own area; calls over this distance are charged as national. There are a variety of special codes used for non distance-related charges, such as mobile calls, personal numbering services or 'freefone' services. Calls to numbers prefixed by these codes may be free, cost the same as a local, regional or national call, or be charged at a special rate, which may be a one-off fee or reflect the length of the call or the time of day and day of the week on which it is made.

However, this basic picture has many variations. All sorts of incentives have been introduced by different companies in order to get your custom. Some charge a fixed monthly or quarterly payment which allows you discounts on the basic call charges, sometimes including a certain number of free local calls, or a reduction on national call charges, or a special low rate for numbers you call frequently. The BT 'Friends and Family' scheme, for example, allows you to nominate up to ten local, national or mobile numbers and a maximum of six international numbers which you phone frequently. One can be nominated as your 'best friend', and this attracts an even greater discount.

The number of mobile phones in use is growing by the day. With increasing mobile phone coverage of Scotland, the numbers bought here are now catching up with sales in England and Wales. At the time of writing it is estimated there are about 50 million mobile phones in Britain, a number which is rising by the day. It is estimated that the value of the mobile phone market will double to £1.6 billion by 2007, so there is fierce competition between mobile phone companies. They tempt customers from their rivals with offers of free phones, set numbers of free minutes and free text messages each month. Once the free minutes and messages are used up, the standard rate applies.

One of the most popular features of mobile phones is sending text messages – popularly known as 'texting'. The Short Messaging Service (SMS), to give it its official name, has taken off in a big way since it was introduced in 1995. Initially a hit mainly with young people, now texting is used on a daily basis as a business tool. 900 million text messages were sent in 2001, but around 21.3 billion were sent in 2004. For a light-hearted look at the phenomenon, see the BBC Joy of Text website www.bbc.co.uk/joyoftext.

The new generation of mobile phones with internet access and video-phone capability is now with us and will doubtless increase the total number of mobile phones in use in Britain, as well as give a boost to the market with people upgrading to more sophisticated models.

Telephone Numbers. Throughout the UK these are composed of an area code followed by a local number. If phoning a number in the same local area, the area code does not need to be dialled.

There has been a massive increase in the number of telephone lines in Britain over recent years, largely due to the explosion in internet use. In order to cater for this, BT introduced new telephone area codes throughout the UK in 1995. This meant that all telephone numbers were in the form of a four or five digit area code followed by a six or seven digit local number: e.g. 01234-567899 or 0161-234 5678. Although these changes allowed extra capacity for a few years, BT introduced further new numbers for certain cities from 22nd April 2000.

This did not affect any Scottish numbers, although there is no guarantee that this is not on the cards at some time in the future.

Public Telephones. These can be found on street corners, outside post offices and in places such as airports, railway stations and hotel reception areas. They generally take coins or phone cards which can be bought in shops and post offices. A knock-on effect of the growth in mobile phone usage is that BT are now removing phone boxes due to a drop in their use. This is affecting remote rural areas in particular where BT say the local public phone is not being used enough to justify its existence. Local communities are organising campaigns to ensure their local phone box is not a casualty.

BT offer various other services: if you need help making a call, you can contact an operator free of charge by dialling 100 for local and national calls, 155 for international calls. Dial 118 500 (local and national) or 118 505 (international) for directory enquiries – give the name and town of the person you wish to contact and they will give you the number if it is available. Since EU rules required that BT should no longer have a monopoly on directory enquiries, as had been the case previously, there are many other telephone number enquiry services, all six digit numbers prefaced 118. They can be found on the internet via a search engine such as www.google.com.

New computerised exchanges have allowed a number of new services to be made available to subscribers. Call return allows you to find out the last person who rang by dialling 1471 (although the caller has the option of withholding their number). This is a free service. For a charge, you can arrange 'caller display' which shows the numbers of up to 50 previous callers. Call minder, another service you pay for, is an automatic answering service which does not require you to have an answering machine in your home.

There are a whole range of other services, details of which can be found on the BT website or in the telephone directory, now called simply The Phone Book. The phone book for your area, together with the business and services directory Yellow Pages, are delivered free of charge to your house. Extra phone books for your area or another area cost £10 each. Electronic directories are available as a CD-ROM or online. If you choose to be 'ex-directory' your telephone number will not appear in any of these directories.

Emergency services. These can be contacted using 999 or 112 which will put you in contact with the fire service, police, ambulance, coastguard, mountain rescue or cave rescue.

Useful Addresses

British Telecom (BT): (Residential enquiries) BT Correspondence Centre, TVTE Gateshead NE11 0ZZ; ☎Freefone 0800-800150; www.bt.com.

British Telecom (BT): (Business enquiries) Business Customer Service Manager, PP RCAB, Receipting Centre, 5th Avenue Business Park, TVTE Gateshead NE82 6XX; ☎Freefone 0800-400400; www.bt.com.

O₂ Mobile Phone Service: Wellington Street, Slough, Berkshire SL1 1VP; ☎0870-5678 678; www.o2.co.uk.

Orange Mobile Phone Service: Customer Services; ☎150 (from an Orange phone) or 07973-100150 (from any other phone); www.orange.co.uk.

Vodafone Mobile Phone Service: PO Box 549, Banbury OX17 3ZJ; ☎08701-666777; fax 08701-616500; www.vodafone.co.uk.

Internet

At the time of writing, 52 per cent of households in the UK are connected to the internet. This is a figure which is growing by the day. There are numerous Internet Service Providers (ISPs) all with different connection packages and charges. These fall broadly into two groups: 'free' services which charge no monthly subscription, with telephone call charges applied for the time you are connected; and the others which charge a monthly subscription – typically around £12-£15 – with no call charges for certain levels of usage. So you may get 30 hours free calls per month, after which you pay. Some offer unlimited access with no call charges at all, however long you are connected to the internet. Virgin Net 247, for example, offers unlimited access for an all-in price of £12.49 per month.

'Traditional' internet connection over a standard telephone line is now being replaced by broadband connection. Broadband is the collective name given to a range of high speed internet connections that are (normally) always switched on – it has been likened to electricity or water supplies in this respect. At the end of 2004, more than one in five UK households had a broadband connection, with five million subscribers registered. Britain is one of the fastest growing markets for broadband internet access, and the market is expected to grow a further 64 per cent by 2006.

Broadband is a vast improvement on the previous generation of Internet connection, not just for business and personal web and email use, but also for other internet applications such as voice, video conferencing, e-business, radio, streaming video and digital TV. In business broadband will undoubtedly impact across almost every sector from education and healthcare to manufacturing and tourism. It offers speeds up to ten times faster (and sometimes even 40 times faster) than a standard internet connection, which makes it easy and cheap to transfer large quantities of data, images, graphics, video and high quality sound. As well as its advantages for businesses, it is also likely to revolutionise education, community life and home entertainment.

Broadband is delivered to homes and business using various technologies, including high speed ADSL telephone lines via telephone exchanges, wireless connections using radio repeater stations, and satellite systems. Now available in all large towns and cities across the UK, it is rapidly coming on stream in smaller communities. As always, the remoter less populated areas of Scotland are the last to be enabled to access this new technology. BT has a programme of upgrading small rural exchanges, aiming to have completed the work in a vast number of them by Summer 2005, but there are notable omissions from the list, with north-west highland communities not yet listed for upgrade. The Government has said all communities should be able to receive broadband by the end of 2005, but as always, there is likely to be some 'slippage' here. A concern is that they have not actually defined what is meant by a 'community' – some worry that they may not be classed as community if they have under a certain number of residents.

In some places local groups have been looking into the feasibility of installing their own community satellite broadband system, in case it turns out that they will not be part of the upgrade programme.

MAJOR INTERNET SERVICE PROVIDERS

BT Internet www.btyahoo.comconnect.com.

CompuServe www.compuserve.co.uk

Demon www.demon.net

Freeserve www.freeserve.com

Tiscali: www.tiscali.co.uk

Virgin Net www.virgin.net

Details of and links to a wide range of UK ISPs can be found at: www.egrindstone.co.uk/technoISP.asp.

CARS & MOTORING

In 2003, 62 per cent of households in Scotland had access to a car, compared with a figure of 73 per cent for the UK as a whole. Within this figure for Scotland as a whole, is hidden the fact that dependence on the car is greater in rural Scotland than in other rural parts of the UK with around 80 per cent of households in rural Scotland having access to a car, which was used for over three quarters of all journeys. Although normally high car ownership levels are a feature of high income levels, in remote rural areas of Scotland this is more to do with the lack of public transport provision and the distance people live from shops, employment and services. In these areas even low income families find a car a necessity rather than a luxury.

Roads

There are 32,999 miles (55,266 km) of roads in Scotland, of which 212 miles (344) are motorways and 1,807 miles (2,922 km) are other trunk roads. There are eight motorways, all in the southern half of the country. The terrain and level of population in the Highlands is such that it is doubtless not cost-effective to construct motorways in the area. The main trunk road in the Highlands is the A9 which runs from Falkirk, about midway between Glasgow and Edinburgh, to Thurso on the north coast. Although many roads in the Highlands and Island have been upgraded in recent years, there are still many single-track roads with 'passing places', small bays at regular intervals along the road used to allow oncoming traffic to pass.

Roads in Britain are classified using an alphabetical system. Motorways are high speed, multi-carriageway roads. They are indicated by M followed by a number: e.g. M8. They are marked on road maps in blue and the road signs on motorways have a blue background with white markings. Major roads are 'A' roads: e.g. A9. They are subdivided into 'Primary routes' which are marked in green on road maps and the road signs have green backgrounds with yellow markings. Other A roads are marked in red on maps and the road signs are generally red and/ or white with black markings. Smaller roads are indicated by B followed by a number: e.g. B778. They are marked on maps in yellow. Other minor roads are not numbered.

There are generally no charges for travelling on the network of motorways and trunk roads in the UK, but there are some road bridges in Scotland on which tolls are, controversially, payable. The Skye Bridge linking the Isle of Skye to the mainland at Kyle of Lochalsh is the most notorious in this respect. Since the bridge was completed in 1995 there has been a concerted campaign against firstly, the imposition of tolls, and secondly, the level of those tolls which are claimed to be some of the highest in the world, relative to the length of road. A pressure group called Skye and Kyle Against Tolls (SKAT) has been running an ongoing campaign of protests and challenges to the charging of tolls since the bridge was opened.

Tolls are also payable on the Erskine Bridge, the Tay Road Bridge and the Forth Road Bridge. A sliding scale of tolls operates on all these bridges, depending on size and type of vehicle and time of year. A look at the relative tolls charged on each of these roads explains SKAT's objections: in 2003 the car toll on the Forth Road Bridge and the Tay Bridge was 80p. These tolls need only be paid when crossing the bridge in one direction. Two-way tolls are payable on the Erskine Bridge and the Skye Bridge: the car toll here, for crossing in each direction, is just 60p on the Erskine – but 570p on the Skye Bridge! This, incredibly, is for a journey of only 6,156 feet (520 metres). The other bridges are all well over twice this length, the longest being the Tay Road Bridge which is over four times as long. The level of tolls has a significant effect on local residents who regularly have to cross the Skye Bridge.

In December 2004, the Scottish Executive gave the residents of Skye an early Christmas present when they paid off the outstanding debt on the Skye Bridge, eight years early, and completely scrapped the tolls. A victory for SKAT!

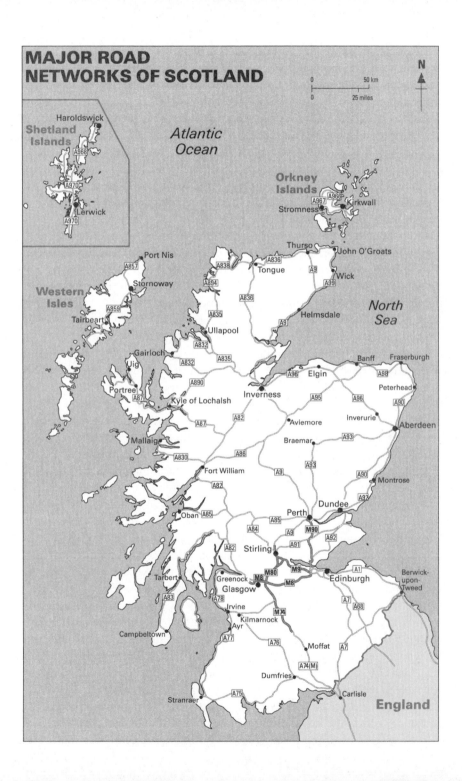

MAJOR ROAD
NETWORKS OF SCOTLAND

0   50 km

0   25 miles

N

Atlantic
Ocean

Shetland
Islands

Haroldswick

A968

A970

Lerwick

A970

Orkney
Islands

A966

A967

Kirkwall

Stromness

Thurso

Port Nis

A857

A838

A836

Tongue

A9

John O'Groats

Wick

A99

Stornoway

Western
Isles

A859

A894

A838

A835

Helmsdale

A9

North
Sea

Tairbeart

Ullapool

A832

Gairloch

A832

A835

Banff

Fraserburgh

A98

Uig

A890

A96

Elgin

Peterhead

Portree

A87

Kyle of Lochalsh

A82

Inverness

A95

A96

A90

Inverurie

Aberdeen

A87

Aviemore

Mallaig

A830

A86

Braemar

A93

A82

Fort William

A9

A93

A90

Montrose

A82

Perth

Dundee

A92

Oban

A85

A85

M90

A82

A84

A9

A82

A91

Stirling

M9

A1

M80

Berwick-
upon-
Tweed

Tarbert

Greenock

M8

M8

Edinburgh

A83

Glasgow

A78

A7

A68

Irvine

M74

A7

Kilmarnock

Ayr

A77

A76

Moffat

A7

Campbeltown

A74(M)

Dumfries

A75

Carlisle

England

Stranraer

When responsibility for Scotland's road network was devolved to the Scottish Parliament, a review of roads policy was begun. Following in England's footsteps, Scotland is now seeing the effects of mobility and the health risks of traffic congestion. Road transport is responsible for about 80 per cent of all transport emissions, with CO_2 emissions rising fastest. With traffic predicted to rise by 38 per cent over the next 20 years and by 53 per cent over the next 30 years, it is a problem that will become intolerable if measures are not taken to cut traffic levels in busy areas. With air pollution now a matter of international concern, the UK is committed to reducing CO_2 by 20 per cent from their 1990 levels by 2010, and is currently negotiating within the EU a legally binding target of reduction of six greenhouse gases, including CO_2.

Across the UK, councils in urban areas are examining schemes to discourage drivers from taking private cars into towns and cities. These include proposals such as 'road pricing' schemes, where drivers pay for the privilege of driving into towns; restricting access to certain vehicles on certain days of the week; and car-sharing schemes. Many towns and cities already have 'park and ride' schemes, where you park your car in a specific parking area outside the town, then continue your journey into the town centre on a free and frequent bus service.

Congestion charging in Edinburgh, in the form of a £2 a day toll, is planned to be introduced in 2007. During an enquiry into the proposal, there were, not surprisingly, many objections from individuals and businesses to the scheme, but the vast majority did agree that something had to be done to ease traffic congestion in the city. Doubtless, the debate will continue to rage over coming years – it remains to be seen what final plan is adopted and when.

Unless you are extremely fit, self-sufficient, or accustomed to making life very difficult for yourself, there is one thing you should bear in mind if moving to the rural north west of Scotland. You will need a car. Although there are local post buses and longer distance buses running to Inverness and other towns, these are few and far between and don't necessarily connect with each other. Once you are known in the community you will find there's always somebody to give you a lift if you need one in an emergency, but transport of your own is pretty imperative.

Single track roads with passing places are the norm in the coastal areas, although the main routes are gradually being upgraded to fast, double track roads. On the whole, the quality of the roads is good – even in the most remote areas, the council needs to keep them maintained to a reasonable standard in order to keep communities accessible. But however good the road surface, the mountains and lochs do mean that in many cases the roads are tortuously windy and hilly, so they are not fast to travel on. Of course, the plus side is that the slower journeys do give you time to really appreciate the landscape!

Expect to be slowed down by other factors than the state of the roads, and accept it as part of the slower, unhurried way of life in the Highlands. That's one of the reasons for moving there, after all. Two drivers stopping for a chat on a single track road is a common local pastime. And if it's not vehicles blocking the way, it's likely to be sheep or cows. Sheep can be a menace on the roads, especially at lambing time: if you come across a mother on one side of the road, drive very carefully, because the chances are that her lamb is on the other side and is likely to make a dash for Mum under the wheels of your car! The sheep have a tendency to settle down on the warm road surface in the evening – sometimes you need to be very persistent with the horn to make them move.

There is a certain etiquette to driving on single tracks. Stop on the left, in or opposite a passing place, to allow approaching traffic to pass. If you're being followed by faster traffic, follow the same procedure to let it overtake. You will find that local drivers will always acknowledge you as you pass each other, whether by a hearty wave or the merest twitch of a finger on the steering wheel – there's as much variety in the gestures used as can be seen in an auction room. You will soon develop your own style.

Driving Regulations

Throughout the UK, motorists drive on the left and vehicles are right-hand drive. This will make driving more difficult for you if you import a left-hand drive car. Overtaking is permissible only on the right.

Speed limits are 70 miles per hour (mph) (112kph) on dual carriageways, 60mph (96kph) on unrestricted single carriageways and generally 30mph (48kph) in built-up areas – in practice, any road with street lights unless signs indicate otherwise. Speed limits of 20mph (32kph) are enforced in some particularly dangerous areas such as near schools and in residential areas. Camper vans and caravans are restricted to a maximum of 50mph (80kph).

The maximum speed limit on motorways is 70mph (112kph) but in bad weather or where there has been a road traffic accident, electronic signs beside or over the road will advise of lower speed limits. Certain classes of vehicles and drivers, including bicycles, small motor cycles and learner drivers are not permitted on motorways.

Seat belts must be worn, with a few exceptions, by all drivers and passengers of cars. Crash helmets of approved design must be worn by drivers and passengers of motorcycles.

Traffic lights are used to control traffic in towns. A red light means stop. The amber light is an indication that the lights are about to change to green. You must not move when red and amber show together – do not pass through until the green light shows. Green means you may go on if the way is clear. Amber on its own means stop – you may only continue if the amber appears after you have crossed the stop line or if you are so close to it that to pull up might cause an accident.

It is illegal to drive on a public road without a current driving licence, vehicle excise duty, vehicle insurance cover or if the vehicle has not passed its annual

Ministry of Transport (MoT) test of roadworthiness. (See below for further details about these requirements.)

Driving Tests

Drivers of motorised vehicles must pass a driving test administered by the Driving Standards Agency (DSA). It is an executive agency of the Department of the Environment, Transport and the Regions and is responsible for approving driving instructors as well as carrying out driving tests.

The law states that you cannot learn to drive a car before you are 17, with the exception of disabled persons who are in receipt of mobility allowance, who can take their test at 16.

The car driving test consists of a theory test taken using a computer at a DSA Theory Test Centre and an in-car practical test of around half an hour with an approved DSA driving examiner. There are certain standard manoeuvres and procedures you will be required to perform satisfactorily before you can pass the test.

Your eyesight will be tested – you must be able (if necessary, with spectacles or contact lenses) to read a car number plate at a distance of 20.5 metres. It is illegal to drive if your eyesight does not meet the minimum standard. If you suffer from certain medical conditions you may be required to also have a medical test.

Additional driving tests must be taken for those wishing to drive large lorries or buses.

To drive a moped or motorcycle on a public road you must have completed and passed a Compulsory Basic Training (CBT) course provided by a DSA-approved training body.

There are fees payable for these various tests. They vary depending on the vehicle and when you take the test – there is a higher evening and Saturday rate. This ranged, in 2005, from £42 for cars to £80 for lorries and buses. The theory test costs £20.50. Tests for drivers of invalid carriages are free.

An extended driving test was introduced in 1992 for those convicted of dangerous driving (cars or motorcycles). The 1999 fee ranged from £84 to £102.

Driving Licences

Visitors to Great Britain who hold a valid licence issued in the following countries can drive any vehicle indicated on the licence for as long as it is valid: Austria, Belgium, Czech Republic, Denmark, Estonia, Finland, France, Germany, Greece, Hungary, Iceland, Ireland, Italy, Latvia, Liechtenstein, Lithuania, Luxembourg, Malta, Netherlands, Norway, Poland, Portugal, Republic of Cyprus, Slovakia, Slovenia, Spain, Sweden. Residents with a licence issued in the above countries must register their details with the Driver and Vehicle Licensing Agency (DVLA) but can continue to use their licences until the holder is aged 70 or for three years after becoming resident, whichever is the longer; vocational licence holders can use them until aged 45 or for five years after becoming resident. If you are aged over 45 (but under 65) you can use your licence until aged 66 or for five years after becoming resident. If you are aged 65 or over, you can use your licence for 12 months after becoming resident. To continue driving after these periods, a British driving licence must be obtained.

A full Northern Ireland driving licence can be exchanged for a GB licence or can be used until it expires, at which time you may apply for a GB licence.

Licences issued in Australia, Barbados, British Virgin Islands, Canada, Gibraltar, Hong Kong, Japan, Kenya, Malta, New Zealand, Cyprus, Singapore, South Africa, Switzerland and Zimbabwe are valid for 12 months from the time you become resident. After this time you must stop driving or exchange your licence for a GB licence. This can be done up to five years after becoming resident. The rules for licences issued in Jersey, Guernsey or the Isle of Man are the same except that you can exchange them for a GB licence for up to ten years after becoming resident.

Licences from all other countries entitle you to drive for up to 12 months, but you must obtain a provisional GB licence and pass your GB driving test before the 12 month period elapses.

The Driver and Vehicle Licensing Agency (DVLA) is responsible for issuing driving licences.

Before beginning driving lessons on a public road, you must have a provisional licence. The relevant forms are available from post offices and once completed should be sent to the DVLA. Learner drivers must be supervised by someone over 21 who has held a full licence for at least three years. A first provisional licence costs £38 up to 28ᵗʰ February 2005.

After you have passed your driving test, your licence is changed to a full licence. There is no additional fee payable. This covers you for a wide range of vehicles including provisional motorcycle entitlement, which is upgraded to full entitlement once you have passed your motorcycle test. Provisional motorcycle entitlement, where you do not hold a full car licence, lasts for two years and is then suspended for one year before you can apply for it again.

Driving licences stay valid for different periods for different categories of vehicle: for family cars and motorcycles, generally a driving licence stays valid until your 70th birthday while for larger vehicles, it is valid until your 45th birthday. After this it is renewable every five years until you are 65, when it is renewable annually.

If you need to apply for a renewal of licence for reasons of age or for medical reasons, the replacement is free. Failure to inform the DVLA of any medical condition which may affect your fitness to drive, or change in an existing condition, is a criminal offence with a fine of up to £1,000. There is a fee charged to replace a driving licence after disqualification or to replace a lost or stolen licence.

Useful Addresses

The full rules of the road can be found in *The Highway Code*, price £1.49 available from *The Stationery Office:* 71-73 Lothian Road, Edinburgh EH3 9AZ; ☎0870 6065566; www.tso.co.uk. It can be purchased online at www.highwaycode.gov. uk or from booksellers.

Driving Standards Agency: Stanley House, Talbot Street, Nottingham NG1 5GU; ☎0115-901 2500; fax 0115-901 2510; www.dsa.gov.uk.

British School of Motoring; 267-269 Argyle Street, Glasgow G2 8DL or 32 Morrison Street, Edinburgh EH3 8BJ; ☎; 0845-276276; www.bsm.co.uk. For other centres, phone or see the website.

DVLA: Customer Enquiries (Drivers) Unit, Sandringham Park, Swansea SA7 0EE; ☎0870-240 0009; fax 0870-850 1285; www.dvla.gov.uk.

Edinburgh Vehicle Registration Office: Saughton House, Broomhouse Drive, Edinburgh EH11 3XE; ☎0870-240 6281.

Endorsements & Disqualification

There are a whole range of traffic offences which may result in endorsements being added to your driving licence. These are in the form of 'penalty points', the number of which will be decided by a court on conviction for a specific offence. These points remain on a licence for eleven years from the date of conviction for offences relating to driving while under the influence of drink or drugs, and four years from the date of the offence or of conviction in other cases. If a total of 12 points is built up within three years, the driver is automatically disqualified (banned) from driving for a minimum of six months, or one year if the driver has been disqualified in the past three years. In addition, every offence for which you can be given penalty points carries a discretionary disqualification, decided by the court at the time of conviction, usually between a week and a few months. Serious offences such as dangerous driving and drink driving carry a mandatory disqualification of 12 months or more and can also result in a prison sentence if injury or death was caused. If you drive while disqualified you can receive a prison sentence and your car may be confiscated.

For details of the number of penalty points incurred for each offence, see www.dvla.gov.uk/drivers/endorsem.htm.

Motor Vehicle Licences

All motor vehicles are registered with the DVLA and a record kept of changing ownership during its life. When you change your vehicle, its registration documents must be sent to the DVLA for the new car to be registered to you.

Vehicles must display a vehicle licence disc, valid for six months or twelve months at a time. This disc, often called a 'tax disc' is available from post offices on payment of vehicle excise duty (VED). In order to encourage the use of cars which cause less pollution, there is a lower charge for smaller vehicles. Vehicle excise duty increases most years, the new rates announced in the UK Government's March Budget. From May 2003 the annual rate for cars with an engine size of 1549cc or less is £110, while those above 1549cc will pay the 'standard rate' of £165 per year. New cars registered after March 2001 attract discounts on their car tax levels depending on the levels of carbon dioxide emitted. The environmentally cleanest vehicles, including gas and electric-powered cars, have the biggest discounts while diesel cars are the most expensive. For example, for a low emission alternative fuel car VED is just £55 for 12 months.

Motorcycles are charged VED on a sliding scale depending on engine size. In 2004 this is £15 per year for those 150cc or lower, £30 for 151cc-400cc, £45 for 401cc-600cc and £60 for over 600cc.

Vehicles which are more than twenty-five years old are exempt from car tax.

Insurance

The law requires that vehicles using public and private roads in the UK must be covered by insurance. The minimum cover they must have is third party insurance, which includes cover for injury to other people. Some insurance companies may insist you take comprehensive insurance which covers all risks such as fire and theft or damage to your car and pays personal accident benefits and medical expenses where necessary.

The cost of car insurance varies greatly, because there are so many factors taken into account. These include the age and sex of the driver, the type of vehicle, its age and size of engine, in addition to the area in which you live. Insurance premiums tend to be lower in the Highlands because there is a lower rate of accidents due to the fewer cars on the road, and because car thefts are far less common than in urban areas.

Discounts are awarded on premiums payable if you have not previously claimed on your car insurance. This 'no claims bonus' is lost for succeeding years when you do make a claim. Drivers who have claimed more than once may have correspondingly heavier premiums to pay in future years.

A 'Green Card' providing western European cover for a maximum of three months a year is available at extra cost – it is not included in British motor insurance packages. The Green Card is, in effect, a certificate which gives proof that the driver has car insurance which complies with the minimum insurance requirements of the countries they drive through.

There is a lot of competition between insurance companies, so it is advisable to 'shop around' for the best quote. Motoring organisations such as the AA (Automobile Association) and the RAC (Royal Automobile Club) have their own insurance schemes, or you can get insurance from high street or internet insurance companies. If you don't want to do it yourself, insurance brokers will shop around to find a good deal for you. Ensure they are a member of the British Insurance Brokers' Association.

Useful Addresses & Websites

Direct Line: www.directline.com.

esure.com: www.esure.com.

J.C Roxburgh: (Insurance Brokers) 151 Glasgow Road, Clydebank, G81 1LQ; ☎0141-952 0371; fax 0141-952 0255; www.jcroxburgh.co.uk.

Royal & Sun Alliance: ☎01403-232323; www.royalsunalliance.com.

R.J. Shawcross: (Insurance Brokers) 139 Market Street, Atherton M46 0SH; ☎01942-883253.

Automobile Association: (insurance quotations) ☎0870-606 0483; www.theaa.com.

The AA Car Insurance Review UK: http://aa.car-insurance-online.uk.com. Contains comparisons of and links to a wide range of insurance providers.

British Insurance Brokers Association: 14 Bevis Marks, London EC3A 7NT; ☎020-7623 9043; fax 020-7626 9676; www.biba.org.uk.

MoT Tests

All cars, motor cycles, motor caravans, light goods and dual purpose vehicles over three years old must have an annual test of roadworthiness. This is called an 'MoT test' because it was originally administered by the Ministry of Transport. Nowadays the MoT testing scheme is administered by the Vehicle Inspectorate.

MoT tests are carried out at official test centres. Most large garages and many small ones are approved as test centres, and there are also local authority test centres. Some will test your car while you wait although you may need to book in advance. Smaller garages in the Highlands are more likely to ask you to collect your car later the same day. The test normally takes about 20 minutes and covers a specified list of checks which must be made of the condition and cleanliness of the car, including the state of the lights, brakes, suspension, tyres and wheels, seat belts and so forth. If any of the items tested are not up to standard, a test certificate will not be issued until the fault has been rectified. This will be done by the same garage, if you wish. If the test centre issues a 'warning' on any defect, you will only be allowed to drive the vehicle home, or to a garage for repair. It is an offence, otherwise, to drive a vehicle without a valid test certificate.

However, the police have the power to carry out roadworthiness spot checks on vehicles, and if your vehicle is found to be unroadworthy, the possession of a valid test certificate is no defence. The cost of the MoT test in 2004/5 is £42.10 for cars and £15.55 for motor cycles.

Useful Address

Vehicle & Operator Services Agency: Berkeley House, Croydon Street, Bristol BS5 0DA; ☎0117-954 3200; fax 0117-954 3212; www.vosa.gov.uk. For further information about MoT testing.

Motoring Organisations

The two main motoring organisations in the UK are the Automobile Association (AA) and the Royal Automobile Club (RAC). There are also smaller ones for specific groups of people, such as the Civil Service Motoring Association (CSMA). There are also organisations which provide breakdown services, wherever you may be in the country. Green Flag Motoring Assistance is one such.

These organisations offer all or some of the following services to members: vehicle insurance cover, breakdown services with recovery anywhere in the UK, free public transport or hire car, hotel charges, home start and legal advice and aid. These organisations charge from around £40 per year for the basic recovery service, up to around £150 for their full service which includes transport of the vehicle plus passengers to any destination in the UK if necessary.

Useful Addresses

Automobile Association (AA): Contact Centre, Carr Ellison House, William Armstrong Drive, Newcastle-upon-Tyne NE4 7YA; ☎0870-600 0371; fax 0191-235 5111; www.theaa.co.uk.

Civil Service Motoring Association (CSMA): 21 Station Street, Brighton BN1 4DE; ☎0845-345 7444; www.csma.uk.com.

Green Flag Motoring Assistance: Cote Lane, Pudsey, Leeds LS28 5GF; ☎0845-246 1557; fax 0113-257 3111; www.greenflag.co.uk.

Royal Automobile Club (RAC): RAC Motoring Services, Great Park Road, Bradley Stoke, Bristol BS32 4QN; ☎08705-722722; www.rac.co.uk.

Breakdowns, Theft & Accidents

If you have an accident in which a person or a horse, cow, ass, mule, sheep, pig, dog or goat is injured, you must call the police. You must also contact the police if the road is blocked or if damage is caused to the property of a person who cannot be contacted. You should, if possible, move your vehicle off the road. On a motorway, you should, if possible, pull on to the 'hard shoulder' along the left-hand side of the road and stay with your vehicle. It is best to wait on the embankment beyond the hard shoulder, or on nearby land, rather than sitting in the car – a surprising number of accidents occur where other vehicles run into cars on the hard shoulder. If you have a mobile phone or can reach an emergency phone beside the road, call the police and/or the emergency services on 999, or contact a breakdown service if there is only vehicle failure or damage. If you do not or cannot do this, wait until the police arrive, as they will do eventually. With most people now having a mobile phone, the police and emergency services are usually inundated with calls about every accident from passers-by, so you won't be ignored!

Take note that since December 2003 it has been an offence to use a hand held mobile phone while driving. There is a fixed penalty of £30 or a fine of up to

£1000 if the offender goes to court. It will eventually be an endorseable offence resulting in 3 penalty points on the driver's licence and a £60 fine. If you wish to use your phone while in the car, you must pull over and turn your engine off. For the time being, hands-free mobile phones are not subject to this law.

You should exchange your details and those of your insurance company with any other drivers or pedestrians involved; if not, you should inform the police within twenty-four hours. It is an offence punishable by a fine and penalty points on your licence to fail to stop after an accident, to fail to give your particulars or to report the accident to the police. You should inform your insurance company also of any accident, even if you don't intend to make a claim – this will allow you to make a claim later if you wish. Your own insurance company may handle a claim against another driver for you, or you may need to write to the other driver's insurers to make your claim.

If you are a member of a motoring organisation, you will have a contact number to ring if you break down. They will arrange to send a repair person or recovery vehicle from the locality. If you do not belong to an organisation, other breakdown services are available. Motorway breakdown services are notoriously expensive, so if your vehicle is less than reliable, or even if it is brand new, membership of the AA or similar might be a good investment.

If your vehicle is stolen, you may (but are not obliged to) report it to the police. If you intend to claim for it on your insurance, however, your insurer will require you to report the theft to the police. Car theft is a huge problem in the UK which has the highest per capita rate of stolen vehicles in Europe. This disease has not yet reached rural areas of the Highlands and Islands, where vehicle theft is rare. It is one of the reasons many people give for moving there.

Driving & Drink or Drugs

The police have the right to stop any vehicle whose driver they suspect of being under the influence of drink or drugs. A 'breathalyser test' may be taken at the roadside to measure the amount of alcohol in the driver's system. This is done by blowing into a small machine which analyses the breath. If the reading is above the legal maximum level, this will be followed by a blood or urine test at a police station. If a driver is involved in a road traffic accident, the driver may be breathalysed as a matter of course.

The legal limit is 35 micrograms of alcohol in 100 millilitres of breath which is equivalent to 80 milligrams in 100 millilitres of blood (80mg%) or 107 milligrams in 100 millilitres of urine . This translates to relates to around 2 1/2 pints of normal strength lager or beer. However, the alcohol level is dependent on matters such as body weight, so the only safe way is not to drink at all if you are to be driving.

To address concerns that driving under the influence of drugs other than alcohol was not a specific offence, in 1992 a new offence was introduced of 'causing death by dangerous driving under the influence of drink or drugs'.

To test for the presence of drugs, a suspected driver is asked to do the following tasks:

- Counting out 30 seconds - drug users either under-read or over-read time.
- Walking in a straight line nine paces forward and then back - the classic test to test co-ordination and balance.
- Raising a foot in the air - designed to test balance.
- Touching finger to nose with eyes closed - tests co-ordination.

Penalties for driving under the influence of drink or drugs are harsh, and cover all the options – penalty points, fines and imprisonment. These increase in severity depending on the quantity of drink or drugs the driver has ingested, whether an accident has occurred, and whether injury or death occurred as a result of the accident. For instance, causing death by dangerous driving under the influence of drink or drugs carries a maximum penalty of 14 years imprisonment.

Servicing Your Vehicle

Garages are generally open between 9am and 5.30pm, although in larger towns they may be open longer hours. They may close at lunchtime for an hour between the hours of 12 noon and 2pm. In remote areas of the Highlands there are local garages, although sadly many have closed down in recent years, due to uneconomic viability of such small businesses which require expensive machinery. It may mean a drive of some distance to reach the next garage, which of course can cause problems if you need to leave your vehicle there for a day or more, bearing in mind the scarcity of public transport in such areas. Neighbours, however, are usually happy to act as a taxi service – as long as you are prepared to return the favour when their car goes into the garage!

Costs of labour vary between main dealers in large towns and smaller garages which may be slightly cheaper, but labour costs are expensive, between £25 and £45 per hour. At a small rural garage, you will often find you have to leave your vehicle in overnight, to allow for even everyday spare parts to be delivered from a large town. These are often delivered on the local bus or postbus. Consequently, you might find you have to pay more for parts in rural areas. Large garages in town may be able to carry out the work 'while you wait'.

Addresses of garages can be found in local Phone Books and Yellow Pages.

Car Rental

Car hire firms can be found in all big towns and cities. There are a number of international companies such as Avis, Budget, Europcar and Hertz as well as some large independents such as Kenning, Swan National and Arnold Clark. There are also small local firms, some of which offer budget car hire using older vehicles. *Sharps Reliable Wrecks* at Inverness is one which always raises a smile!

They can be found in the BT Yellow Pages classified under 'Car Hire-Self Drive' or at Yellow Pages online www.yell.co.uk It is advisable to ring round for a selection of quotes, because prices can vary widely depending on the size and type of vehicle, the period you require it for and so forth. Hire charges are usually based on a daily or weekly rate. You will collect the car with a full tank of fuel and should fill it up before you return it.

There may be restrictions on the type of vehicle you can hire if you are below 21, and you may be required to take out a higher level of insurance. If you have endorsements on your licence for careless driving, you may be refused car hire. It is also very difficult to hire a car if you are over the age of 70, as hire car companies may not cover you with their insurance. You may be able to arrange hire car cover through your own car insurers but this is likely to be expensive.

Some car insurance policies include free car hire for the period you are without your vehicle as a result of an accident.

Car Hire Companies

Europcar: ☎0870-607 5000, www.europcar.co.uk.

Hertz Rent-A-Car: ☎0870-846 0013; www.hertz.co.uk.

National Car Rental: ☎0870191 0552; www.nationalcar-europe.com.

Sharps Reliable Wrecks: Railway Station, Station Square, Academy Street, Inverness IV1 1LE; ☎01463-236684 /236694; or Inverness Airport, Unit 14A, Dalcross Industrial Estate, Inverness IV1 7XB; ☎/fax 01667-461212; www.sharpsreliablewrecks.co.uk.

Fuel

Vehicle fuel is expensive throughout Britain, and the further north you travel, the more expensive it is, making petrol prices in the Highlands and Islands reputedly the highest in the world. This is brought about by a combination of the high level of tax imposed by the Government – over 76 per cent of the pump price – with increased unit costs associated with low volume sales in remote areas. In October 2004, the price of unleaded petrol averaged 83.8p per litre in Scotland as a whole, but 86.5p per litre in remote areas of Scotland.

Diesel used to be significantly cheaper than petrol, with many people in recent years switching to diesel-engined vehicles to take advantage of the savings. However, once scientists produced evidence that diesel was less environmentally-friendly than unleaded petrol, the Government increased the tax on diesel too, and it is now the most expensive form of fuel. In October 2004 the average price for diesel in Scotland was 86.3p per litre, and in remote areas it was 89.4p per litre.

Since 1999, due to environmental concerns, leaded petrol has been banned.

Those vehicles which could only run on leaded petrol now use 'lead replacement petrol' (LRP) or use unleaded petrol together with an additive. The price of this in October 2004 was 89.6p per litre in Scotland, and 91.6p per litre in remote areas.

The UK has belatedly begun moves to adopt liquefied petrol gas (LPG) as an alternative vehicle fuel. It is environmentally far cleaner than the existing options and is also far cheaper. In July 2000 the first Highlands petrol station began selling the fuel, known as 'autogas', at 39.9p per litre, less than half the price of unleaded petrol. This was the first move in the oil company Shell's plans to supply autogas from 23 outlets in the Highlands and Islands and rural parts of the north-east. Shell estimates the use of LPG could cut annual fuel bills in rural areas by up to 45 per cent. The Scottish Executive, through its Rural Petrol Station Scheme, provides grants for the installation of the autogas equipment at selected filling stations. In November 2004 the average price of LPG at the 1200 outlets throughout the UK was 38.98p per litre.

There are few cars in Britain capable of running on autogas, although many of the major car companies are introducing dual fuel models. It is possible to have other cars converted, which costs around £1,500. Grants are available for between 40 and 75 per cent of the cost of conversion, under the Government-backed 'Powershift' programme. Further information on the scheme is available at www.powershift.org.uk.

For details of LPG outlets throughout the UK, see www.go-lpg.co.uk and www.lpg-vehicles.co.uk.

Because of high overheads and low volume sales, many rural villages do not have a petrol station because it is not economically viable to run one. In some areas this can mean a round trip of twenty miles or more to fill up. If you run a business, even a very low-key bed and breakfast, you may be able to obtain a fuel 'agency card' which allows you to buy petrol and diesel discounted to the average UK price.

Useful Address
Highland Fuels: Affric House, Beechwood Park, Inverness IV2 3BW; ☎01463-245815; fax 01463-710899; www.highlandfuels.co.uk. Supply Esso and Shell agency cards.

Buying a Car

Most local newspapers have a motoring section at least once during the week. Here you will find both private sellers and car dealers advertising the vehicles they have for sale. There are also national magazines for car buyers and sellers, such as *Auto Trader*, available from newsagents, and also online at www.autotrader.co.uk. *Scot-ads*, a classified ads paper distributed in the north of Scotland, has a large car section. ☎08457-434343; www.scot-ads.com.

Car dealers in large towns tend to cluster together, usually on the outskirts of town. This makes finding a car a convenient, if tiring, business. Literally thousands of new and used vehicles are lined up on the forecourts of dozens of dealers. Some specialise in specific makes, others will buy and sell anything.

Many car dealers now have their own websites, which can easily be found through the major internet search engines. There are some car newsgroups which are a forum for advertising cars for sale. Try afn.marketplace.cars; uk.rec.cars. imports; alt.cars.

When you buy a new or used car you must ensure your insurance has been transferred to the new vehicle before you drive it away.

Selling a Car

If you have imported a car, you may not sell it within 12 months without paying import duty and other taxes.

If you wish to sell your car privately, you can advertise it in local newspapers, in local 'free-ads' papers or on local noticeboards. If it is an expensive or collectors' car, it might be worth advertising nationally in the motoring press. The internet is also a good place for advertising a car, whether via an appropriate website or on motoring newsgroups.

Most car dealers will sell you a new or used car on a part-exchange basis, where they give you a discount depending on the value they put on the car you wish to get rid of. It is illegal to sell a car in an unroadworthy condition unless you are selling it as a 'non-runner' without an MoT test certificate. A potential driver can only test drive your car if he/she is covered by your or his own insurance. When you have sold it, you must inform your insurance company and either cancel your insurance or transfer it to a new car. There is a portion of your vehicle registration papers which you must complete and send to the Driver and Vehicle Licensing Agency (DVLA). The new owner must also register his/her ownership with them.

PUBLIC TRANSPORT

Bus & Coach

There is an extensive network of road passenger services in Scotland. Local and regional bus services usually run several times a day in areas of higher population, and once a day or less in remote rural areas. National coach services cover longer routes, generally travelling between large towns and cities, with stops along the way at smaller places. In 2002 there were 445 million passenger bus journeys in Scotland. Bus and coach services throughout the UK are provided by the private sector, although local authorities can and do subsidise socially necessary routes which private companies could only otherwise run at a loss.

Stagecoach Holdings at Perth is one of the largest bus operators in Great

Britain. They cover short, medium and long distance routes. There are many smaller private operators throughout Scotland operating local services. National Express runs a national network of long distance coach routes, mainly operating through franchises, and Scottish Citylink run medium and long distance services throughout Scotland. Megabus.com was launched in 2004, the UK's first low cost inter-city bus service. The web-based service rapidly gained passengers, increasing its passenger numbers to 1 million by October 2004, after its first seven months of operation.

Information on local bus routes and timetables can be obtained from bus stations, local council 'one stop shops' and tourist offices, and telephone numbers can be found in local telephone directories.

The Royal Mail operates a postbus service in rural areas, where passengers literally travel with the post as it is collected and delivered. The existence and continuation of these services depend very heavily on how much they are used – 'use it or lose it', as the saying goes. The Royal Mail is always looking for ways of cutting costs and this is an area which is vulnerable. Some post bus services receive financial assistance from local councils, in order to keep an essential lifeline viable. At the time of writing there are more than 150 postbuses covering routes throughout mainland Scotland, the Western Isles, Orkney and Shetland.

Bus & Coach Companies

Highland Scottish Buses: ☎01463-233371.
National Express Coach Services: ☎08705-808080; www.nationalexpress.com.
Royal Mail Post Bus : ☎08457-740740; www.royalmail.com.
Scottish Citylink Express Coach Services: ☎08705-505050; www.citylink.co.uk.
Stagecoach : ☎0870-608 2608; www.stagecoachbus.com.
UK Public Transport Information: www.pti.org.uk.
Megabus.com: www.megabus.com.

Taxis

Taxis (or cabs) are easy to come by in large towns and cities. There will be a taxi stand at most railway stations and airports where you can hire a taxi to take you to your destination. Alternatively, local taxi firm numbers will be found at public telephones, or in your phone book, so you can ring to arrange for a taxi to collect you.

In rural areas, taxis are harder to come by. There may be one enterprising cab driver to cover a large area, which means that he may have to travel some miles to pick you up, which inevitably makes fares higher. Added to this is the fact that people are likely to want to travel longer distances. Taxi drivers in the western Highlands, for example, offer long distance round trips to Inverness which can be as much as £70 or £80. However, this is for a minicab taking up to eight passengers, so if you can arrange to fill the vehicle, the price per person is quite reasonable – in fact, it works out slightly cheaper than taking the bus!

Although taxis are a relatively expensive form of transport, they have the advantage over other public transport of delivering you to the door of your destination. Higher prices are charged after midnight. Most are licensed by local authorities and will have a meter, so you can be sure that the fare you are charged is fair. If not, you should always agree a fare before you start the journey, to avoid being asked for an exorbitant amount when you arrive.

In practice, rural areas have developed informal 'car-sharing' schemes. If you need a lift to Inverness or wherever, enquiries with friends and neighbours will soon find someone who is going across when you need to be there. Or somebody will go out of their way to take you – they know that you will return the favour either in kind or by some other means. This informal 'bartering' system works well, and is one of the factors that helps to keep such communities viable and full of neighbourly spirit.

Air

Scotland's largest airports are at Aberdeen, Edinburgh, Glasgow and Prestwick and are operated by the British Airports Authority (BAA). Highlands and Islands Airports Ltd (HIAL) operates ten airports, the largest being at Inverness. In addition there are a number of airports and small airfields controlled by local authorities, including Dundee, Orkney and Shetland, while others are owned by private companies or local airstrip trusts, which gain assistance from their local councils. Fair Isle airfield is owned by the National Trust for Scotland, which owns the whole island. All operate flights to various destinations within Scotland, and the larger ones to other UK destinations and internationally. For further details on international services, see the section *Getting There* in the *General Introduction*.

HIAL has airports at Barra, Benbecula, Campbeltown, Inverness, Islay, Kirkwall, Stornoway, Sumbrugh, Tiree and Wick. The company receives subsidies for providing air links to remote areas of Scotland. Routes to and from Tiree, Barra, Kirkwall, North Ronaldsay, Stornoway, Benbecula, Sumbrugh and Fair Isle are directly subsidised, because they would otherwise run at a loss. There are flights to and from these island destinations on one or more days a week. Timetables are available from HIAL or via their website.

Airports and airfields in the Highlands and Islands are constantly having to argue for their continued existence: the low population means that airlines often cannot guarantee flying full planes. This must be balanced against the remoteness of the area, which means that for speedy, reliable access to other parts of Scotland and the UK passenger air services are essential. Despite serving all the other major Scottish airports plus the islands, Inverness Airport has seen services cut in recent years, purely on an economic basis. In the late 1990s British Airways discontinued its flights to London Heathrow, franchising flights to British Regional Airlines between Inverness and London Gatwick, which charges lower prices to airlines using the airport.

After a campaign conducted by the Highland Council together with Highlands and Islands Enterprise and the Inverness Chamber of Commerce are, the low cost airline bmi introduced flights between Inverness and Heathrow in March 2004. Heathrow, the main London airport, is the preferred destination for business passengers because of its central location and links to all international destinations.

'Airport tax' is payable on flights within Britain. On domestic flights this is £5 for single journeys and £10 for return flights. In the March 2000 budget it was announced that, in recognition of the fact that flights from and between the Scottish Highlands and Islands are a necessity not a luxury, tax would be abolished or reduced on flights from 2001. The tax has been removed completely on flights from or within the region, while the £10 charge on flights going into the region has been halved.

There are limited Sunday flights in the Highlands and Islands for religious reasons.

Useful Addresses

British Airports Authority (BAA): Edinburgh Airport, EH12 9DN; ☎0870-040 0007; fax 0131-344 3470; www.baa.co.uk.

British Airways: Waterside, PO Box 365, Harmondsworth UB7 0GB; ☎0870-850 9850; www.britishairways.com.

easyJet: easyLand, London Luton Airport, Bedfordshire LU2 9LS; ☎0871-7500 100; www.easyjet.com.

Highlands and Islands Airports (HIAL): Inverness Airport, Inverness IV2 7JB; ☎01667-462445; fax 01667-464216; www.hial.co.uk.

Ryanair: Dublin Airport, Co. Dublin, Ireland; ☎+353-1-8121212; www.ryanair.com.

Rail

The railway infrastructure in Britain – tracks, signals, stations and so forth – is owned and managed by Network Rail, which is also responsible for devising and publishing a national timetable of services. Train services themselves, however, are operated by private sector train operators, of which there are 25 in total. Scotland is served by Great North Eastern Railway, FirstScotrail and Virgin Trains.

Despite the great national pastime of complaining about the railways, they are well used in Scotland. In 2002-2003 there were nearly 50 million passenger journeys within Scotland and over 54 million originating in Scotland. As part of their strategy to cut down congestion and traffic emissions, there is a commitment by the UK government and the Scottish Executive to improve services and to increase use of the railways for passengers and freight. To this end, a Strategic Rail Authority has been set up with responsibility for such matters. There are Rail

Users' Consultative Committees which monitor the policies and performances of train and station operators in their area. These have a legal right to make recommendations for changes.

The Scottish railway system covers most of the mainland, with a notable exception: it stops short of the north-west Highlands. Above Kyle of Lochalsh and to the west of Achnasheen there are no train services at all, one reason why a car is so important to those who live in this area.

The fare structure on the British railways is complex, with different packages and prices available depending on different conditions offered by the various operators. This reached such a state of complexity and confusion for passengers, that in early 2000 the industry announced that the whole system would be simplified, so that different operators were offering a range of equivalent tickets with similar names.

Train tickets on all services can be bought online through www.thetrainline. com. The website includes timetables, allowing you to find your preferred route and time and to buy tickets using a credit card. Timetable, ticket and fare information are also available on the National Rail Enquiry 24 hour service, ☎0845-7484950. Tickets may be booked by telephone with rail companies, by telephone or in person from railway stations.

Useful Addresses

Great North Eastern Railway: Station Road, York YO1 6HT ; ☎08457-225 333; fax 01904 524532; www.gner.co.uk.

FirstScotrail: First ScotRail, Caledonian Chambers, 87 Union Street, Glasgow G1 3TA; ☎0845-601 5929; www.firstgroup.com/scotrail.

Virgin Trains: Customer Relations, PO Box 713, Birmingham B5 4HH; ☎0870-789 1234; fax 0121-654 7500; www.virgintrains.co.uk.

Glasgow Underground Railway. The only underground railway system in Scotland, the Glasgow underground was originally opened in 1897, and was reopened following modernisation in 1980. It has fifteen stations and around 6.5 miles of track. The underground is operated by Strathclyde Passenger Transport (Consort House, 12 West George Street, Glasgow G2 1HN; www.spt.co.uk. subway) and it carries over 13 million passengers a year.

Ferries

Because of the topography of the country, sea transport, both of passengers and freight, is very important in Scotland. Ferry services run between the mainland and the islands, between the islands and also, in certain places, short hops across sea lochs on the mainland – for instance, from Gourock (Strathclyde) to Dunoon (Cowal). If you time your journey right, you can cut hours off the travelling time by taking advantage of these 'inland' crossings on the west coast.

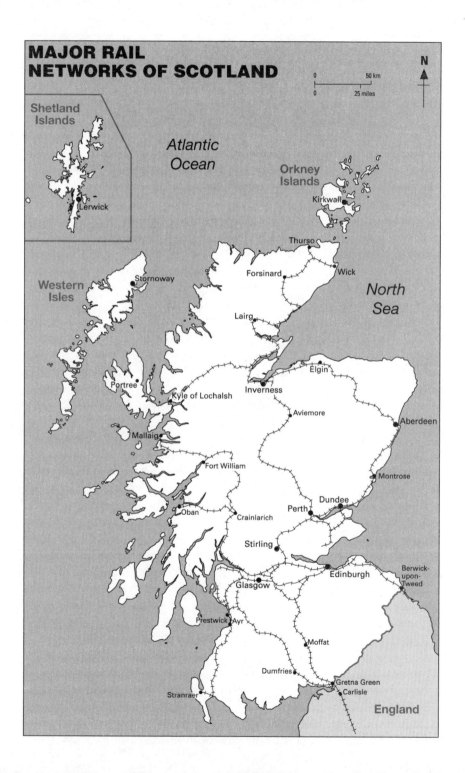

MAJOR RAIL
NETWORKS OF SCOTLAND

0   50 km

0   25 miles

N

Shetland
Islands

Lerwick

*Atlantic
Ocean*

Orkney
Islands

Kirkwall

Thurso

Western
Isles

Stornoway

Forsinard   Wick

*North
Sea*

Lairg

Portree

Kyle of Lochalsh

Elgin

Inverness

Aviemore

Aberdeen

Mallaig

Fort William

Montrose

Oban

Crainlarich

Perth

Dundee

Stirling

Glasgow

Edinburgh

Berwick-
upon-
Tweed

Prestwick Ayr

Moffat

Dumfries

Stranraer

Gretna Green
Carlisle

England

The main operators running ferry services within Scotland are Caledonian MacBrayne (usually known as CalMac) and P&O Scottish Ferries. For services between Scotland and other countries see *General Introduction*.

FERRY SERVICES WITHIN SCOTLAND

From	To
Aberdeen	Lerwick (Shetland) Stromness (Orkney)
Ardrossan	Brodick (Arran)
Claonaig (Kintyre)	Lochranza (Arran)
Colintraive (Argyll)	Rhubodach (Bute)
Colonsay	Port Askaig (Islay)
Fionnphort (Mull)	Iona
Gourock	Dunoon (Cowall)
	Kilcreggan
	Helensburgh
Kennacraig	Port Ellen (Islay)
	Port Askaig
Largs	Cumbrae
Lochaline (Lochaber)	Fishnish (Mull)
Mallaig	Armadale (Skye)
	Eigg, Muck, Rum, Canna
Oban	Castlebay (Barra)
	Colonsay
	Craignure (Mull)
	Lismore
	Lochboisdale (S.Uist)
	Tobermory (Mull)
	Coll, Tiree
Berneray (N.Uist)	Leverburgh (Harris)
Sconser (Skye)	Raasay
Scrabster	Stromness (Orkney)
Tarbert (Kintyre)	Portavadie (Cowal)
Tayinloan	Gigha
Tobermory	Kilchoan
Uig (Skye)	Tarbert (Harris)
	Lochmaddy (N.Uist)
Ullapool	Stornoway (Lewis)
Wemyss Bay	Rothesay (Bute)

In addition, the Shetland Islands Council operates an inter-island service in Shetland and Viking Sea Taxis runs services to several small Shetland islands.

Hebridean Cruises runs services to the small isles (Rum, Muck, Eigg and Canna) and Orkney Ferries operates an inter-island service in Orkney.

In many places there are no Sunday sailings for religious reasons. Recent debate on the subject suggests that change is inevitable, but it is likely to take several more years before it is seen to be politically or socially expedient.

Ferry Companies

Caledonian MacBrayne: ☎01475-650100 (general enquiries), 08705-650000 (car ferry reservations); fax 01475-637607; www.calmac.co.uk.

Hebridean Cruises: ☎01756-704704; fax 01756-704794; www.hebridean.co.uk.

Orkney Ferries Ltd: ☎01856-872044; fax 01856-872921; www.orkneyferries. co.uk.

P&O Scottish Ferries: ☎08705-202020; www.poferries.com.

Viking Sea Taxis: ☎01595-692463 or 859431.

UK Public Transport Information

The UK Public Transport Information website at www.pti.org.uk has details of all forms of transport in the UK, with links to relevant websites, online booking etc.

There are a number of national transport phone hotlines:

National Express Coach Enquiry Service: All National Express coach services in England, Scotland and Wales. National rate phone charges. ☎08705-808080 (from UK only).

National Rail Enquiry Service: For all rail in England, Scotland and Wales (except heritage railways). Local rate phone charges from anywhere in the UK, 24 hours daily. ☎0845-748 4950 (from UK); +44 20-7278 5240 (from outside UK).

Scottish Citylink Coach Enquiry Service: All Scottish Citylink coaches. National rate phone charges. 8am-9pm daily. ☎0870-505050 (from UK only).

Tripscope: Helpline for elderly and disabled people, giving advice and information about most aspects of transport for them, whatever their disability. ☎08457-585641.

BANKS & FINANCE

The British banking system comprises the Bank of England; the retail, clearing, or high street banks; the merchant banks; and the overseas banks. The Bank of England is the central bank which acts as banker to the Government and also issues bank notes, sets interest rates and oversees the national systems of payment and settlement.

The major retail banks are Abbey National, Alliance and Leicester, Bank of Scotland, Barclays, Clydesdale, Halifax, HSBC (formerly the Midland), Lloyds/ TSB, National Westminster (NatWest), Northern Rock, Royal Bank of Scotland and the Woolwich. Of these, the Clydesdale has branches only in Scotland. Between them, these banks have over 11,000 branches throughout the UK, although this is a number which is falling. For many years there has been an inexorable decline in the numbers of small rural branches throughout Britain, a decline which is set to continue with the increasing use of telephone and online banking. In areas of Scotland where there is only one bank for many miles, this has implications for the communities concerned. However, in such areas, travelling banks, which visit outlying areas on a weekly rota basis, provide a useful service.

Bank opening hours vary from place to place, with some city centre banks staying open late at night and at weekends. Core opening hours throughout Scotland are Monday to Friday 9am to 5pm. Smaller branches may close for an hour at lunchtime (between 12 noon and 2pm.)

Choosing a Bank

If you know whereabouts in Scotland you will be living, the most sensible course is to take out accounts with a bank which has a local branch. Many rural towns or villages will only have one bank, if they have one at all. In such areas, your best choice would be to join the Bank of Scotland or the Royal Bank of Scotland which serve these areas better than other banks. They also have 'mobile banks' which travel to rural areas on a weekly basis, when you can carry out most day to day transactions.

Most personal accounts carry no service or transaction charges, as long as you remain in credit, but if you need a business account, it is advisable to check charges made by different banks as they can vary widely. These details can be obtained from the banks or via their websites.

Most of the banks now have telephone banking services, and many have online banking, so the need to have a local branch is less important other than for the withdrawal of cash.

Bank Accounts

There is a great deal of competition between the retail banks, and they offer a wide range of services to both personal and business customers. Accounts offered vary from bank to bank, but there are basically two kinds of accounts, current accounts and savings, or deposit, accounts. For personal customers, there are usually no charges made on either current or deposit accounts as long as you keep your account in credit.

Current accounts generally pay a low rate of interest on credit balances, which varies depending on the type of account. Cheque books with a cheque guarantee card are available free. Cheque guarantee cards will, as their name suggests, guarantee funds to cover the value of the cheque, usually £50 or £100 for a normal account. If your bank deems your account to be healthy enough to deserve a gold card, this guarantees to a maximum of £250. In 99 per cent of cases, a cheque will not be accepted unless it is supported by a cheque guarantee card.

The card will also usually allow you to withdraw cash, request a balance or a statement, order a cheque or other services from 'cashpoints' (ATMs) situated outside banks or in other outlets such as supermarkets or garages. Most of the main banks belong to the Link system which means you can use your card in a cash machine provided by another bank. There will be a daily limit on the amount of cash you can withdraw, which will vary depending on the type of account you have and the funds you normally have available. However, cash can only be withdrawn if there are funds in your account to cover the amount.

Overdraft facilities are available on current accounts, at a variable interest rate set by the bank on the basis of current Bank of England rates. Overdrafts must first be agreed with the bank, although some accounts have a basic agreed overdraft limit of around £100, in case of accidentally or temporarily going into the red. Unauthorised overdrafts will be charged for, with service charges on transactions plus a high rate of interest, often equivalent to over thirty per cent per annum.

Standing Orders and Direct Debits can be arranged on current accounts for the automatic transfer of regular amounts of money for the payment of monthly bills and so forth.

Deposit accounts are savings accounts which pay a higher rate of interest, often on a sliding scale so that the larger your credit balance, the higher the rate of interest payable. A basic deposit account will allow withdrawals or money transfers on demand, and may offer a cheque book and cash card facility.

Other savings accounts require thirty or ninety days notice for withdrawal of funds without loss of interest. These pay a correspondingly higher rate of interest. Some accounts offer other facilities and may charge a maintenance fee. Individual banks will provide details of their range of accounts on request, or they are available in most cases online.

Business accounts for small to medium-size enterprises are similar in type and operation to personal accounts with the difference that fees are charged on each withdrawal or deposit, whether made by cheque or electronically. These charges vary from bank to bank so it is best to 'shop around' to find the best deal. Some banks will waive all charges for the first year of operation on the account, in order to attract your business. If you run a one-man or woman business – such as running a holiday cottage, or working as a freelance writer – it is best therefore just to have a personal current and/or deposit account and avoid bank charges, which can be punitive.

In March 2000 a report was published, at the behest of the Government, into banking practices. The conclusions were damning, with the 'big four' high street banks – Lloyds/TSB, HSBC, Barclays and NatWest – being accused of using their domination of the market to overcharge personal and small business customers by up to £5 billion a year. The report made around fifty recommendations for improving the situation, including setting up a new watchdog 'PayCom' to oversee charges on standing orders, direct debits and cheque clearing. It remains to be seen what difference this will make to the charges made by banks.

Banks issue quarterly or monthly bank statements which are posted to your address and itemise all transactions on the account in the period. You may also request a statement at other times.

Tax is generally payable on interest earned on savings. There are, however, special savings accounts, called ISAs (Individual Savings Accounts) which allow you to save a specified maximum amount tax-free. ISAs currently allow a maximum of £7000 per year to be saved, over a period of ten years. This will be cut to a £5000 limit in April 2006.

Opening An Account

Application forms for the various different accounts are available from branches or, increasingly, online. You will need to supply personal details of name, address, date of birth, occupation and so forth, together with proof of identity such as a driving licence or passport, and proof of address such as a utilities bill.

If you are planning to work in Scotland, you are most likely to be paid monthly and the money will be paid directly into your bank account with a payslip posted or handed to you separately by your employer. Some people are still paid weekly, and may be paid in cash, but this number is dwindling.

Plastic Money

Debit Cards. A cheque guarantee card will usually be combined with a debit card such as Switch/ Maestro, Solo or Delta. This allows money to be taken electronically from your card at point of sale as long as there are funds to cover it currently in the account. There is no cost for the service and no interest payable. Debit cards are beginning to replace cheques due to their ease of use and because they eliminate the need for cheque guarantee limits.

Most mail order companies, traditional and online, will take debit card payments. Many shops now allow customers to obtain up to £50 in cash, known as 'cash-back' when paying a bill with a Switch/Maestro card, which is a useful facility in areas where there is no bank cashpoint.

Switch debit cards are currently being replaced by Maestro cards, which allow all the facilties of Switch plus the ability to use the service internationally. From July 2005, new and replacement cards will no longer carry the Switch logo. Most cardholders will have Maestro-only cards issued by mid-2005.

Credit Cards. Credit cards are issued by most financial institutions including all banks and building societies and a range of other organisations such as car manufacturers, chain stores and charities. Charities find them a useful fund-raising tool as they pledge a certain percentage of their profits from their credit card services will go towards their charitable works.

The most widely accepted credit cards in Britain are Visa and Mastercard

(Eurocard). Most cards issued by banks, building societies and other institutions will have their name attached to a Visa or Mastercard or other credit card service, so although your card may be issued by a small institution, you can be assured that there is the guarantee of a safe financial backing to it.

Store cards, such as those issued by Marks & Spencer, are mainly intended for use against purchases in that store, and often incentives such as discounts on purchases are offered in order to encourage shoppers to use them.

Credit cards allow you to spread repayments over a period, with interest payable on the balance owing, unless you pay off all outstanding balances at the end of each month, in which case no interest is charged. There may be an annual fee charged in addition to the interest; while those cards with no annual fee may charge a higher rate of interest, so it is advisable to read the small print of any cards you are considering. Store cards tend to carry a higher than average rate of interest.

Most credit cards are issued as ordinary, gold or platinum cards with different credit levels. The gold and platinum cards may also have extra benefits included in the package.

Credit Card Websites
American Express: http://home3.americanexpress.com/uk.
Mastercard: www.mastercard.com/uk.
Visa: www.visaeurope.com.

Charge Cards. The main difference between credit cards and charge cards is that with a charge card you must pay the total outstanding balance when it is due, otherwise a penalty must be paid. These include American Express and Diners Club. They are far less popular in Britain, and to counteract this American Express introduced a credit card in 1995.

International charge cards, if lost or stolen, can usually be replaced at short notice, which may not be possible with a credit card. Gold and platinum cards may allow instant access to large amounts of cash or an unsecured overdraft facility at an advantageous interest rate.

Building Societies
In 1987, the regulations regarding financial institutions were changed, and now building societies offer much the same range of services as banks (and vice versa). Some building societies, in fact, have converted into banks. Of the main banks listed above, the Abbey National, Alliance and Leicester, Halifax, Northern Rock and Woolwich were all building societies up to a few years ago.

Many building societies now offer current accounts with a cheque book, cheque guarantee card and all the other 'add-ons' offered by the banks. Rather than issuing statements, building societies usually issue you with a 'pass book' in which all transactions on your accounts are recorded. You need to take or send the book to the building society for it to be updated.

Post Office

The post office has its own bank, called the Giro Bank, which offers a range of different accounts. Cash can be withdrawn through the post office or can be obtained from cashpoint machines.

The post office also operates the National Savings bank which has two main savings accounts, the ordinary account and the deposit account. These don't allow the use of cheques or cards, so are better for longer term savings. The deposit account pays a higher rate of interest, on a sliding scale depending on the balance, because it requires ninety days notice of withdrawals.

With banks closing rural branches, arrangements may be made in the near future for banking services to be accessible via post offices. However, with rural post offices also under threat – more than one-fifth of Scottish post offices have disappeared since the 1980s and the rate of closure is increasing – this may not help in those small communities most likely to be affected by bank closures.

Telephone & Online Banking

Most of the banks now have telephone banking facilities and online facilities. Both these allow you, either through your telephone, or your computer via a modem or the internet, to check recent transactions, make transfers of money between accounts, pay bills and so forth.

For security reasons, you must first set up accounts at your bank before you are eligible to use the telephone or online system. You can then sign up to the telephone banking service of your bank either in person at the bank or you can telephone and ask to have an application form sent to you. Online banking services are generally accessed via a downloadable form which you complete and sign, then post to the bank's Head Office. They will then send you either a software disk to input to your computer and configure your modem, or a password which will allow you to access your account via their internet website.

Loans

Personal and business loans are available through a variety of financial institutions, such as banks, building societies and credit card companies. With the relaxation of the law, other institutions such as mail order catalogue companies and high street shops such as Marks and Spencer offer their own financial services including loans. Interest rates can vary greatly, so you should always shop around carefully to find the best deal for your own circumstances.

Currency

The unit of currency is the pound sterling (£) of 100 pence (100p). Coins are in denominations of 1p, 2p, 5p, 10p, 20p, 50p, £1, £2. Notes are in denominations of £5, £10, £20, £50 and £100.

All these are acceptable in England, Scotland, Wales and Northern Ireland. All coins are issued by the Royal Mint and banknotes by the Bank of England, the main bank of issue. In addition, there are three banks of issue in Scotland, the Bank of Scotland, the Royal Bank of Scotland and the Clydesdale Bank, each of which issue their own banknotes. You may find that outside Scotland, shop assistants will look askance at Scottish notes and refuse to accept them. By a strange anomaly Scottish banknotes are not technically classed as legal tender, but they are an authorised currency and have a status comparable to that of Bank of England notes. If you do have problems using Scottish notes, when south of the border, ask a bank to exchange them for English notes – they are generally accepted by banks irrespective of their place of issue.

It is best to avoid taking Scottish notes abroad, because you may receive a lower exchange rate than for Bank of England notes.

The Euro

Britain has not yet 'signed up' to the Euro, the single European currency. At the time of writing the UK Government is biding its time to see how the Euro performs, before making the step to get rid of sterling. It was introduced on January 1 1999, and is now used for trade between Britain and Europe. The current UK government position is that a referendum on whether to change to the Euro will be held once certain 'economic tests' have been met – it is unlikely that a referendum would occur before 2006. If there was a 'yes' vote, the Euro would probably not be in use in the UK before 2009.The EU's official multi-lingual website contains information about the euro. http://europa.eu.int.

Foreign Currency

Britain has no currency restrictions, which means you may take out or bring in as much money as you wish in most currencies. The major banks will change most foreign bank notes, but will not exchange foreign coins. You will probably get a better rate of exchange for travellers' cheques than for bank notes.

When buying or selling currency, shop around for the best deal. Exchange rates are posted by banks and bureaux de change, and may vary from place to place. In addition, there will be a commission charged on top of that, typically of around one or two per cent with a minimum charge of £2.50. Building societies and larger post offices will also buy and sell foreign currency. You may need to order currency or travellers' cheques two or three days in advance. Take your passport if buying or selling foreign currency.

Transferring Funds

Money can be transferred to Britain by banker's draft or a letter of credit. It may take up to two weeks to be cleared. Money can also be sent via a post office by international money order, a cashier's cheque or telegraphic transfer such as Western Union. You will need your passport to collect money transferred from abroad or to cash a banker's draft or other credit note.

You can send money direct from your bank to another via an interbank transfer. Both the sending and receiving bank will charge a service charge or a percentage of the amount transferred, so it may be expensive for small sums.

Useful Addresses & Websites

Addresses and phone numbers of local bank and building society branches can be found in local Phone Books or Business Pages. Head offices of the main ones are:

Abbey National plc: Abbey National House, 2 Triton Square, Regent's Place, London NW1 3AN; ☎08459-724724; www.abbey.com.

Alliance & Leicester plc: Customer Service Centre, Carlton Park, Narborough, Leicester LE19 0AL; ☎0500-959595; www.alliance-leicester.co.uk.

Barclays Bank plc: 54 Lombard Street, FREEPOST LON13542, London EC3B 3PJ; www.barclays.co.uk.

Clydesdale Bank plc: 30 St Vincent Place, Glasgow G1 2HL; ☎0141-2487070; www.cbonline.co.uk.

Halifax Bank of Scotland: PO Box 5, The Mound, Edinburgh EH1 1YZ; ☎0870-600 5000; www.bankofscotlandhalifax.co.uk.

HSBC Bank plc: 8 Canada Square, London E14 5HQ; ☎020-7991 8888; www.hsbc.com.

Lloyds TSB Bank plc: Henry Duncan House, 120 George Street, Edinburgh EH2 4LH; ☎0845-3000 033; www.lloydstsb.com.

National Westminster Bank plc: 135 Bishopsgate, London EC2M 3UR; www.natwest.com.

Northern Rock plc: Northern Rock House, Gosforth, Newcastle Upon Tyne NE3 4PL; ☎0845-601 1581; www.northernrock.co.uk.

The Royal Bank of Scotland plc: 36 St Andrew Square, Edinburgh EH2 2YB; ☎0845-722 2345; www.royalbankscot.co.uk.

Woolwich plc: Watling Street, Bexleyheath, Kent DA6 7RR; ☎020-8298 5000; www.woolwich.co.uk.

Internet banks include *Egg* www.egg.com and *Smile* www.smile.co.uk.

TAXATION

Whether or not you are liable to pay taxes in the UK depends on whether you are classified as 'resident' or 'ordinarily resident' in the country. To be classified as resident in a particular year you must normally be physically present in the UK for 183 days (6 months) or more in the tax year, which runs from 6th April to 5th April. It does not matter whether you have been in the UK continuously for this period or whether you have come and gone in the meantime, as long as the total count of days is 183 or more. In certain cases, where you visit the UK regularly over a number of years, you may be classed as resident even if you have been in the UK for less than 183 days. The rules are laid out in the Inland Revenue leaflet IR20, 'Residents and non-residents – liability to tax in the United Kingdom'.

Ordinarily resident means that you are resident in the UK year after year. You may be resident but not ordinarily resident for a tax year if you normally live outside the UK but are in the country for more than 183 days in one particular year. On the other hand, you may be ordinarily resident but not resident for a tax year if you usually live in the UK and have gone abroad for a long holiday and do not set foot in the UK during that year.

In addition, the Inland Revenue use the concept of 'domicile' to determine tax liability. There are many factors which affect your domicile, but broadly speaking you are domiciled in the country where you have your permanent home. Domicile is distinct from nationality or residence and you can only have one domicile at a given time.

Income Tax

Residents of the UK are liable to pay income tax on earned income and, with a few exceptions, on unearned income. Income tax on investments is usually deducted at source, interest being paid net of tax, although those who are non-taxpayers due to their low earnings may fill out a tax exemption form which allows them to receive the gross interest on investments. If you are not ordinarily resident in the UK you can also apply to have the interest paid without deduction of tax. Ask your bank or building society for a declaration form R105. You are still liable to tax on the interest, but you may be exempted or qualify for tax relief during years or part years where you are not resident in the UK.

Income tax on earned income is paid in two ways: for employees, under a system called PAYE (Pay As You Earn), and for the self-employed by a system of self assessment. With PAYE, income tax is deducted at source from your gross pay, so the employer will pay your salary with the income tax already deducted. The amount of tax payable is determined by a tax code which you are assigned by the Inland Revenue based on your personal circumstances.

With self assessment, you are sent a tax form at the end of the tax year on which you itemise all your earned and unearned income for that year, and either send it to the tax office for the tax payable to be calculated, or calculate it yourself on the basis of rules given. Under self assessment tax is payable 'on account' in two lumps, due on 31st January in the tax year and 31 July following the tax year, each normally equal to one half of the previous year's tax liability. Any over or underpayments for the year are settled by 31st January in the following year.

In April 2000 the Inland Revenue introduced a system of filing self assessment tax returns over the internet. They offer various discounts on tax due for filing the return in this way and for paying tax due electronically.

All tax payers are allowed a 'personal allowance', an amount they are allowed to earn before starting to pay tax. Personal allowances and tax rates for the following year are announced in March each year in the UK Government budget.

TAX ALLOWANCES AND RATES IN THE 2004-05 TAX YEAR

Taxable income	Rate	
0-£2,020	10%	Starting rate
£2,021 - £31,400	22%	Basic rate
over £31,400	40%	Higher rate

Age	Personal Allowance
up to 65	£4,745
65 -74	£6,830*
75 and over	£6,950*

*Allowances reduced if total income over £18,900

National Insurance

National Insurance (NI), known as social security in other countries, is mandatory for most working people between 16 and 65. Paying NI contributions regularly entitles you to state benefits including the state retirement pension, unemployment benefit, sickness benefit, maternity allowance and so forth. The rules are complicated – you have to have paid the right number of contributions at the right rate at the right time to qualify for these benefits. If there is a 'gap' in your contributions at any time – due to unemployment, say, when you did not claim benefit – you may find that you are not entitled to a full pension. This is a position that many women in particular find themselves in if, for instance, they have taken a few years out of work to have a family.

Anybody who comes to Britain to work should apply for a National Insurance number from their local Department of Social Security (DSS) office. This personal NI number is stamped on a plastic card and stays the same for life, so must be kept safe.

Contributions paid depend on the level of earnings and whether you are employed or self-employed. Those who are self-employed pay their own contributions while employees have their contributions deducted at source, and their employers also have to pay a contribution for each of their employees. Basically, contributions are calculated as a percentage of salary and are paid on earnings between £91 and £610 per week. These are the figures for tax year 2004-2005 – they are usually adjusted in the March budget of each year, to take effect from 6th April following, i.e. the new tax year. In 2004-2005 the basic employee's contribution is 11 per cent of their income between £91.01 and £610 per week, and one per cent above £610 per week. The employer's contribution is 12.8 per cent on earnings above £91 per week. For the self-employed, the basic contribution is £2.05 per week (Class 2 contribution), although you can choose to pay a higher voluntary contribution of £7.15(Class 3) which will give enhanced benefits. In addition, the higher-earning self-employed must pay Class 4 contributions of eight per cent of any profits between £4,745 and £31,720 per year, and then one per cent of profits above £31,720 per year.

However, there are different categories of contribution where you may choose to pay reduced rates: married women, for instance have this option, and the self-employed with earnings below £4,215 are exempt.

If you are not working because you are in full time education, are on an approved training course, you have taken early retirement or are claiming unemployment, sickness, maternity or invalidity benefit, you will receive NI credits to ensure your contribution record is unbroken during that period. If you are at home looking after children or a sick, elderly or disabled person you may be eligible for Home Responsibilities Protection which helps to keep your pension rights although you are not working.

Value Added Tax

Value Added Tax (VAT) is payable on most goods and services, at a standard rate of 17.5 per cent. There are some exceptions to this: certain categories of goods and services carry VAT at a lower rate, some are zero-rated, others are exempt. Domestic fuels for heating and lighting carry a rate of five percent, while children's clothes and footwear, books, magazines and newspapers, and most foods, are zero-rated. Sales and lettings of land and buildings are completely exempt of VAT, as is insurance, the provision of credit, and the services of doctors, dentists and opticians.

A company or a self-employed person with an annual turnover of more than £58,000 must be registered for VAT. Those with a lower turnover can choose to be VAT registered. A business which makes only VAT exempt items cannot register for VAT, but one making zero-rated items can. The VAT charged on goods and services used in setting up or running your business can be reclaimed, subject to certain conditions. It is a person rather than a business which is registered for VAT, so registration covers all business activities of the registered person.

There are high penalties for failing to register for VAT or making a false declaration, and the Customs and Excise are renowned for making stringent checks. Publications and leaflets explaining the regulations regarding VAT are available from VAT offices or from the Customs and Excise website www.hmce.gov.uk.

Council Tax

All Scottish residents must pay council tax, which is based on the value of their dwelling house. For further details see the section on Council Tax in *Setting Up Home*. Businesses must pay non-domestic rates to pay for local services. Further details on these can be found in *Starting A Business*

Other Taxes

Corporation tax is payable on company profits, at varying rates depending on levels of profit. See *Starting A Business* for further details.

Capital gains tax is payable on profits made from selling land, property or businesses (other than one's own dwelling house). The tax is payable on any increase in an asset's value during the period while you have owned it. Any profit made on the transaction over the exempt allowance of £8,200 is added onto the top of income liable to income tax for individuals and is charged to CGT below the starting rate limit at 10%, between the starting rate and basic rate limits at 20%, and above the basic rate limit at 40%. (See above for income tax rates.) If profits made are invested in another business, however, capital gains tax may not be payable.

Inheritance tax (death duty) is payable at 40 per cent on estates with a value of above £263,000. This only affects, at current rates, around four per cent of all deaths of British residents.

For further information regarding taxation, see *Retirement*.

Scottish Parliament's Tax-Varying Powers

The Scottish Parliament does have limited tax varying powers, which means that it could introduce a higher (or indeed, lower) rate of income tax or other taxes. This proposal, dubbed 'the tartan tax', was one which the opponents of devolution tried to frighten the electorate with during their campaigns. However, despite this, in the referendum on 11 September 1997, almost two-thirds were in favour of the proposition 'that the Scottish Parliament should have tax-varying powers'. Whether the Scottish Executive would ever take this option remains to be seen – one suspects that, for political reasons, any attempt to raise taxes above those in England and Wales would be seen as very much a last resort by any party in power.

Further Information

The Inland Revenue produces a whole range of leaflets on UK tax matters, available free of charge on request. Contact the Orderline: ☎08459-000404; fax 08459-000604. Or write to PO Box 37, St Austell, Cornwall PL25 5YN. Most leaflets are also available at www.inlandrevenue.gov.uk.

If you have any queries on your tax position, you should contact your local Tax Office. The address will be listed in the phone book under 'Inland Revenue'. Alternatively, there is a national telephone helpline to deal with queries about National Insurance, tax or VAT, phone 0845-900 0444. They will ask for your NI number when you call.

VAT is dealt with by Customs and Excise, Portcullis House, 21 India Street, Glasgow G2 4PZ; ☎0845-010 9000; fax 0800-528 5000; www.hmce.gov.uk.

HEALTH

Public health policy is a devolved power and is now the responsibility of the Scottish Executive Health Department, as is the administration of the National Health Service in Scotland. There is currently a campaign in the country to improve the health of the population of Scotland, renowned for many years as one of the unhealthiest countries in Europe. There are high rates in particular of coronary heart disease, strokes and cancers. A government paper on public health in Scotland, 'Towards a Healthier Scotland' was published in February 1999. It announced initiatives to improve the health of people in Scotland and set targets to measure the effect of these by 2010. These include reductions in the death rates from cancers, heart disease and stroke; reducing levels of smoking; reducing teenage pregnancy rates and increasing levels of exercise taken by adults.

A significant decision in this area was taken in November 2004 when the Scottish Parliament introduced a total ban on smoking in enclosed public spaces, to take effect from the end of March 2006, their stated aim being to reduce deaths and other damage to the nation's health by both direct and passive smoking. Very large fines will be imposed on individuals caught smoking, and on owners allowing smoking on their premises. This was introduced after a public consultation where a large proportion or the Scottish population came out in favour of such a ban.

Targets to improve the Scottish diet have also been included in the programme, in recognition of the fact that many of the health problems of Scotland are diet related. These include increasing the average daily intakes of fruit, vegetables, cereals and oily fish; reducing intakes of sugar and salt and increasing the proportion of mothers breastfeeding their babies.

These measures are promoted mainly through advertising and advice from the Health Education Boards for Scotland (HEBS) whose role is to provide health information and advice to the public, health professionals and other organisations. They also advise the Government on health education needs and strategies.

Useful Address
Health Education Board for Scotland (HEBS): Woodburn House, Canaan Lane, Edinburgh EH10 4SG; ☎0131-536 5500; fax 0131-536 5501; www.hebs. scot.nhs.uk.

The National Health Service

The National Health Service (NHS) was set up in 1948 with the stated aim of providing medical treatment according to clinical need rather than ability to pay, and that it should be free at the point of delivery. Since that time charges for various aspects of the service, such as charges for prescriptions and some dental and ophthalmic treatments, have been introduced.

The NHS is Europe's biggest organisation, with a workforce of around one million people who treat and care for millions of people every year. Its budget of around seventy billion pounds in 2004 is the largest item of central government expenditure after social security. In 2004, the NHS budget in Scotland was around eight billion pounds. This works out at a higher per capita spend than in England and Wales, about £1,700 for every resident of Scotland, compared with £1,200 south of the border. The NHS is funded mainly through general taxation, with additional funds from National Insurance contributions and patient charges plus other sources of income.

Every person ordinarily resident in the UK is entitled to use any NHS services, which include hospitals, specialist treatments, general medical, dental, ophthalmic and pharmaceutical services, artificial limbs and appliances, the ambulance service and community health services.

Although the NHS provides a generally good standard of care across the country, with family doctors (called General Practitioners or GPs), dentists and opticians accessible in even the remotest areas of the Highlands and Islands, there are increasing pressures on the service as child mortality decreases, life expectancy increases, and more diseases become treatable. As a result, patients expect, quite rightly, higher standards of care and a wider range of services than in the past. In effect, the NHS has become a victim of its own success, requiring higher funding to provide the services which are now available, with consequent pressure on its sources of income. There are constant complaints about the length of waiting lists in hospitals for non-emergency, although serious, treatments and operations. In recent years targets to reduce waiting lists have been introduced, but in some areas hospitals find it difficult to meet these targets, for a variety of reasons which all stem from shortage of money. In order to address this problem, the UK government in early 2000 pledged an injection of extra funding to the NHS which included a substantial pay rise to nurses. They have been traditionally underpaid and undervalued and had finally started 'voting with their feet' and leaving the NHS in droves. Many hospitals found that, although they had bed space and theatre time to carry out operations, the problem lay in shortage of nursing staff to provide care before, during and after an operation.

Health Boards

The NHS in Scotland is administered through fifteen regional Health Boards, addresses below, which provide information and advice on all NHS services in

their area. There is a combined website for the health boards at www.show.scot.
nhs.uk.

Argyll and Clyde: Ross House, Hawkhead Road, Paisley PA2 7BN; ☎0141-842
7200; fax 0141-848 1414;www.show.scot.nhs.uk/achb.

Ayrshire and Arran: Boswell House, 7-10 Arthur Street, Ayr KA7 1QJ; ☎01292-
611040; fax 01292-610636; www.show.scot.nhs.uk/aahb.

Borders: Newstead, Melrose, Roxburghshire TD6 9BS; ☎01896-754333; fax
01896-823476; www.show.scot.nhs.uk/bhb.

Dumfries and Galloway: Grierson House, The Crichton Hospital, Bankend Road,
Dumfries DG1 4ZG; ☎01387-272700; fax 01387-252375; www.show.scot.
nhs.uk/dghb.

Fife: Springfield House, Cupar KY15 5UP; ☎01334-656200; fax 01334-652210;
www.show.scot.nhs.uk/fhb.

Forth Valley: 33 Spittal Street, Stirling FK8 1DX; ☎01786-463031; fax 01786-
471337; www.show.scot.nhs.uk/nhsfv.

Grampian: Summerfield House, 2 Eday Road, Aberdeen AB15 6RE; ☎01224-
663456; fax 01224-404014; www.show.scot.nhs.uk/ghb.

Greater Glasgow: Dalian House, PO Box 15329, 350 St Vincent Street, Glasgow
G3 8YZ; ☎0141-201 4444; fax 0141-201 4601; www.show.scot.nhs.uk/
gghb.

Highland: Assynt House, Beechwood Park, Inverness IV2 3HG; ☎01463-
717123; fax 01463-235189; www.show.scot.nhs.uk/hhb.

Lanarkshire: 14 Beckford Street, Hamilton, Lanarkshire ML3 0TA; ☎01698-
281313; fax 01698-423134; www.show.scot.nhs.uk/lhb.

Lothian: 148 Pleasance, Edinburgh EH8 9RS; ☎0131-536 9000; fax 0131-536
9164; www.nhslothian.scot.nhs.uk.

Orkney: Garden House, New Scapa Road, Kirkwall, Orkney KW15 1BQ;
☎01856-885400; fax 01856-885411; www.show.scot.nhs.uk/ohb.

Shetland: Brevik House, South Road, Lerwick ZE1 0TG; ☎01595-743060; fax
01595-696727; www.show.scot.nhs.uk/shb.

Tayside: King's Cross, Clepington Road, Dundee DD3 8EA; ☎01382-424000;
fax 01382-424003; www.show.scot.nhs.uk/thb.

Western Isles: 37 South Beach Street, Stornoway, Isle of Lewis HS1 2BN; ☎01851-
702997; fax 01851-704405; www.wihb.org.uk.

Private Health Care

In the UK, the NHS and private heath care overlap to some extent. Private patients
can choose to pay for treatment either within NHS hospitals or in private hospitals.
NHS consultants treat private patients alongside their NHS commitments. One
of the main reasons for patients choosing private medicine over the NHS is to
avoid long waiting lists for non-emergency operations – generally the quality of
medical treatment and care will be just as good on the NHS as that received

privately; it is the 'add-ons' such as private rooms with TV, telephone, en-suite bathrooms and room service which the private patient will benefit from.

Outside of hospitals, doctors in private practice may be consulted for specialist matters – Harley Street in London is the famous centre of private specialists in the UK. NHS GPs are not permitted to take private patients in addition to their NHS workload. In addition, many people go privately for second opinions, health checks or screening, and for complementary or alternative health therapies.

In recent years there has been an increase in the numbers of people taking private health insurance. At the end of 2002 there were nearly seven million people in the UK with private health insurance, sometimes paid for by employers as a benefit of the job. Most private health insurance schemes pay only for specialist and hospital treatment, and don't include routine visits to GPs and dentists which are covered by the NHS. If you wish, therefore, to have private GP or dental treatment, you will have to pay for this, rather than the insurance company.

Private Healthcare UK has a website listing private hospitals, nursing homes and the major private health insurance companies operating in the UK, with contact details and links to their websites. www.privatehealth.co.uk.

The highest profile health insurance company in the UK is BUPA.

Useful Address
British United Provident Association (BUPA): BUPA House, 15-19 Bloomsbury Way, London WC1A 2BA; ☎0800-001010; www.bupa.com.

General Practitioners
All areas in Scotland are well-served by local GP practices running daily surgeries, Monday to Friday, as well as carrying out house calls. GP practices deliver services to patients who live within a recognised practice boundary. They all have a practice leaflet providing information about the services and clinics available at the practice. These may help you decide where to register. In rural areas, however, you will usually find that there is only one practice for the area. You can obtain lists of GP practices from the health board dealing with the relevant area of the country.

Appointment systems are run by GPs, who will either work as individuals or as part of a practice with two or more doctors. If you have an urgent need to see a doctor, you should always be able to see a doctor the same day, even if this means sitting waiting until there is a break in his/her scheduled workload. In emergencies, it is best, therefore, to call an ambulance or to go to your nearest hospital accident and emergency department for treatment (see *Hospitals* below). In less urgent cases, you may be given an appointment in the next few days. Most surgeries operate between 9am and 5pm on weekdays, with a break for lunch, although this will vary from place to place depending on population levels. In addition, they will usually hold an evening surgery between 6pm and 8pm on at least one evening per week. There may also be a surgery on Saturday mornings for urgent cases only.

In most areas there is an alternative 'out of hours' and emergency service called NHS24. Your call to the surgery will be diverted to NHS24 and they will take your details and arrange for a nurse to call you back and give you advice or arrange for a doctor to visit. This system, introduced in 2004, has experienced some teething problems with the system finding itself overloaded, resulting in delays in treating patients, some with serious health problems. So if you have a severe medical emergency it is always advisable to phone the emergency services on 999 or 112.

GP practices may offer other services, such as 'well woman' clinics where preventive health checks are made, and baby clinics which offer advice and support for mothers with new babies. They will usually have a practice nurse who may assist with routine matters such as changing dressings, taking blood, giving inoculations and the like.

In rural areas, elderly people or those with transport difficulties are far more likely to be visited at home than if they lived in town. Because the doctors are part of the local community they understand the special problems of getting to the surgery for some, and act accordingly.

If you wish to see a GP under the NHS you must register with a practice. To register you must complete part of your NHS medical card and hand it to the practice receptionist. If you do not have a medical card, you will be given a form to complete. Your medical card will be sent to you within a few weeks of registration. Once you are registered, this entitles you to NHS treatment.

Useful Address
NHS24: Delta House, 50 West Nile Street, Glasgow G1 2NP; ☎08454-242424; www.nhs24.com.

Drugs & Medicines
If a GP decides you require drugs or medicines you will be given a prescription which you take to your local dispensing chemist (or pharmacist). In rural practices where there is no local chemist, drugs and medicines may be dispensed from the surgery.

Most drugs prescribed are available on the NHS, in which case you pay a set prescription charge per item prescribed. Prescription charges are set each year, usually on 1st April. From 1st April 2004 the charge was £6.40 per item. There are several groups of patients who are exempt from prescription charges, including children below 16 and those between 16 and 18 who are in full time education; those above state retirement age; pregnant women and those who have had a baby in the past year; those in receipt of certain social security benefits; and patients suffering from certain specified medical conditions. Full details are given in booklet HC11, 'Help With Health Costs', available from doctors' surgeries. Currently, four out of five prescriptions are dispensed free of charge.

In November 2004, a draft proposal for a bill to abolish all prescription charges in Scotland was introduced in the Scottish Parliament, so it may be that this will eventually come to pass. This follows on from a Welsh Assembly decision to abolish prescription charges there.

Some drugs and medicines are not available on the NHS, in which case the doctor will give you a private prescription and the full cost of the drugs must be paid. Contraceptives are free for all patients, whether you are normally exempt from charges or not.

Prepayment certificates are available for those who need a number of medicines regularly and are not exempt from prescription charges, in which case they may represent substantial savings. If you think you will have to pay for more than five prescription items in four months or 14 items in 12 months, you may find it cheaper to buy a pre-payment certificate (PPC). From 1st April 2004 a 4-month PPC cost £33.40 and a 12-month PPC £91.80. You can apply for prepayment certificates via your doctor or health board or ☎0845-850 0030.

Hospitals

Major hospitals with a range of departments providing diagnosis, treatment and care for in-patients, day patients and out-patients, are usually called General Hospitals. Typically they will have an accident and emergency (or casualty) department, maternity department, surgical, psychiatric, paediatric and geriatric departments as well as a range of outpatient clinics. Generally, a GP will refer you to a specialist clinic at your local hospital if deemed necessary.

The main hospital for the Highlands and Islands, Raigmore Hospital, is located in Inverness. Travel expenses are paid to those who have to travel a fair distance for appointments. For certain specialist operations and treatments, patients may be sent to hospitals at Aberdeen, Edinburgh or Glasgow, because Raigmore does not have the facilities or expensive equipment necessary to provide such treatment.

In smaller towns there may be a small 'cottage hospital' providing a limited range of services which may include convalescent care and care for the elderly and infirm.

Details of hospitals in various areas of Scotland can be obtained from the relevant Health Boards and are listed in the local Phone Book. There is a list of the main hospitals in Whitaker's Scottish Almanack, or go to www.show.scot.nhs. uk.

Dentists

Dentists can provide dental care either on the NHS or privately. Dentists have a quota of NHS patients they can take, so you may find that the dentist you choose has filled his quota and can only take you as a private patient. There is no 'catchment area' as such for dentists, so you can choose to go to any you wish as long as the practice will accept you as a patient. For NHS treatment you need to register using your medical card, as with a GP.

Dental treatment on the NHS is subsidised rather than free, although there are a number of exemption categories, generally in line with the exemptions from prescription charges. It is recommended that you visit your dentist once every six months for a check-up, in order to catch any problems at an early stage and prevent potential problems getting any worse. Most dentists, once you are on their books, will send you a six monthly reminder. A basic examination costs around £5.64, and a extensive examination £8.44 (in 2004) with additional charges if any treatment is needed. A patient who is not eligible for free treatment or help with payment will pay 80 per cent of the cost up to £378 per course of dental treatment.

In the Highlands and Islands, dentists' practices are generally located in the larger towns, holding surgeries in outlying areas on a weekly or fortnightly basis. Local practices can be found in the telephone directory or may advertise in local papers. Details of dentists can also be supplied by the local Health Board. Contact them if you have difficulty finding a dentist who can treat you on the NHS.

Useful Address

The UK dentists' governing body is the British Dental Association, based in London. BDA Scotland: Forsyth House, Lomond Court, Castle Business Park, Stirling FK9 4TU; ☎01786-433810; fax 01786-431810; www.bde-dentistry. org.uk.

Opticians

There is no need to register with an optician. Their addresses can be found in local papers or the telephone directory. In recent years, the regulations on prescribing and supplying ophthalmic services and goods have been relaxed, since when there has been a boom in 'high street' opticians' shops. At one time, only a registered ophthalmic optician (also known as an optometrist) could test your eyes, prescribe and supply spectacles or contact lenses. Today, you must have your eyes tested by a qualified practitioner, but you have the option of taking the lens prescription to have your glasses or lenses made up at another dispensing optician. This has had the effect of bringing the prices of spectacles down, with competition producing some 'bargain offers' – two pairs of glasses for the price of one, for example. The costs of frames and lenses vary widely, but generally you should expect to pay £120 upwards for a pair of spectacles and around £85 upwards for contact lenses.

It is also now possible to buy magnifying reading glasses 'off the peg' in chain stores such as Marks and Spencer and Boots the Chemist without an eyesight test. These are much cheaper, at around £20-£30.

However, it is recommended that if you have any difficulty with your sight, you should consult an ophthalmic optician, who will make a thorough examination of your eyes which may identify medical problems such as glaucoma and cataracts which might otherwise go unrecognised until the disease is well-advanced.

Eye tests are free if you are under 16, or under 19 and in full-time education; if you receive certain social security benefits or allowances; if you have diabetes or glaucoma; if you are aged 40 or over and have a close relative who has glaucoma; or if you are registered blind or partially sighted. If you are not entitled to free eye tests you will be seen as a private patient and the test will usually cost between £17 and £30. Where medical problems are found, the optician will refer you to your GP who can refer you on to an eye specialist.

Laser surgery to correct short-sightedness is available at laser surgery clinics. These are unregulated and the effectiveness of the process has mixed reports – many eye specialists warn against having it done because it can cause permanent eye damage. It is an expensive treatment, at between £600 and £1,200 per eye.

Useful Address

The UK governing body of optometrists and dispensing opticians is the *General Optical Council:* 41 Harley Street, London W1N 2DJ; ☎020-7580 3893; fax 020-7436 3525; www.optical.org.

Alternative Medicine

Alternative therapies and complementary medicine are booming in the UK. Many people swear by the results achieved by using such treatments as acupuncture, homeopathy, chiropractic or naturopathy. Although scorned by the medical profession for many years, recently there has been a noticeable increase in the numbers of doctors who admit, albeit grudgingly, that there might be something in some of these therapies. In an increasing number of cases, GPs may suggest patients try certain alternative therapies alongside the traditional medical approach – hence the term 'complementary'.

It is rare to find any of these therapies available on the NHS, so you would have to pay as a private patient, and some courses of treatment can be extensive, making this an expensive option. Most alternative therapies in the UK have some form of governing body, so it is always wise to go to a practitioner who has been approved by their professional association.

Addresses of practitioners of various therapies can be found in the telephone directory or Yellow Pages. A useful guide to the options available is the *Reader's Digest Family Guide to Alternative Medicine.*

Useful Addresses

Scottish College of Complementary Medicine: c/o The Complementary Medicine Centre, 11 Park Circus, Glasgow G3 6AX; ☎0141-332 4924; fax 0141-353

3783; www.complementarymedicinecentre.co.uk.

Scottish Chiropractic Association: Laigh Hatton Farm, Old Greenock Road, Bishopton, Renfrewshire PA7 5PB; ☎/fax 01505-863151; www.sca-chiropractic.org.

Scottish College of Homeopathy: 17 Edinburgh Road, Biggar S., Lanarkshire ML12 6AX; ☎01899- 222 0931; www.homeopathy-scotland.co.uk.

A wide-ranging collection of alternative and complementary therapy links can be found at www.scottishhealthdirectory.com.

SOCIAL SERVICES

Social work services are a devolved responsibility of the Scottish Parliament and are administered by sections of the Scottish Executive Health Department and, in the case of children's services functions, the Scottish Executive Education Department.

Social work services for elderly and disabled people, for families and children, and those with mental disorders, are administered by local authorities according to Scottish Executive policies. They assess the needs of the population and provide, or commission others to provide, care required. Contact the relevant local authority for details of provision in the area.

Services for the elderly, the disabled, the mentally ill and those with learning difficulties are designed to enable them to remain living in their own homes or in the community wherever possible. Local authorities provide support in the home, short term care, day centres and respite care in order to allow carers, usually close family, temporary breaks from their responsibilities.

Social workers can apply for a mentally disturbed person to be compulsorily detained in special hospitals or residential homes.

Where residential care is required, there is usually a choice between local authority and private provision available. If an elderly person is admitted to residential home they will be charged for residence on the basis of a means test. If they cannot afford to pay, the charges will be met by the local authority.

Children considered to be at risk of physical injury, neglect or sexual abuse may be placed on the local authority's child protection register. If it is decided to be in the best interests of the child, they will be put into the care of the local authority. They may then live at home, with friends or relatives, with foster carers or in residential care. The provision for each child is decided on a case by case basis by a group of professionals including social services staff, health visitors, school nurses and other agencies.

Further information regarding social services in each area is supplied by the relevant local council. See *General Introduction* for contact details.

SOCIAL SECURITY BENEFITS

State benefits are paid to residents of the UK via the Department of Social Security (DSS) Benefits Agency. There is a wide range of benefits to which recipients' entitlement is assessed depending on their situation, their income or the amount of National Insurance contributions they have made.

Income-related benefits take into account both income and savings and include Income Support, Family Credit, Housing Benefit and Council Tax Benefit.

Situation-related benefits depend on such things as your health, or whether you are caring for a child or a chronically ill or disabled person. They include Child Benefit, Disability Living Allowance, Invalid Care Allowance and Industrial Injury Compensation. Child benefit is paid weekly for each child in full time education, with a higher rate for the first child than for subsequent children.

National Insurance related benefits depend on the amount of National Insurance contributions made, and include Jobseeker's Allowance, Maternity Allowance, Statutory Sick Pay, Invalidity Allowance and the state Retirement Pension. Jobseeker's Allowance is in the form of a weekly cash payment for up to six months from the date you are unemployed, as long as you are actively looking for a job.

These benefits are governed by many rules and provisos, and are payable at different rates depending on personal circumstances, so it is not possible to give a definitive run-down here. Levels of benefit are set each year, usually in April, broadly in line with the retail Price Index. Full details of benefits available and current rates can be found on the comprehensive Benefits Agency website at www. dss.gov/uk/ba. The site has downloadable leaflets on all aspects of benefits, leaflets which are also available from local DSS offices. Addresses can be found in the local telephone directory. The Citizen's Advice Bureau can also give information and advice on these matters.

LOCAL GOVERNMENT

Local Government in Scotland is carried out by 29 unitary authorities on the mainland and three Islands councils. For a full list of contact details, see the General Introduction

The local authorities (also referred to as local councils) are made up of directly elected councillors. The geographical area covered by the council is divided into a number of wards and a councillor is elected for each ward. Elections take place every three years, normally on the first Thursday in May. All British subjects and citizens of the Republic of Ireland aged over eighteen who are resident in the area at the time of the election and whose names appear on the electoral register are entitled to vote in the elections.

The chairman of the council is usually known as a convenor. Some cities have a provost, which is the equivalent of a mayor. The chairmen of the city councils of

Aberdeen, Dundee, Edinburgh and Glasgow are called Lord Provosts.

Local government is financed from the council tax, non-domestic (business) rates, government grants and income from charges for services.

Areas of Responsibility

The Scottish Parliament has responsibility for legislation on local government and has established the Commission on Local Government to make recommendations on the relationship between local authorities and the Scottish Parliament.

Scottish local councils are responsible for the following functions within their areas: education; social work; strategic planning; roads provision and repair; consumer protection; flood prevention; coast protection; valuation and rating; the police and fire services; emergency planning; electoral registration; public transport; registration of births, deaths and marriage; housing; leisure and recreation; building control and planning; environmental health; licensing; public conveniences; the administration of district courts.

Overall policy is decided by the full council, while the administration of the services listed above is the responsibility of committees of councillors, who delegate day to day decisions to the council's officers.

Contacting Your Local Council

Scottish councils can be contacted in a number of ways. They issue their own local guides listing phone numbers and addresses of their various departments. They all now have their own websites, so e-mail is another way the different departments can be contacted.

They may also have local offices, or 'one-stop shops', which can provide services and deal with queries from the public. For instance, it may be possible for a tenant to pay their council tax bill over the counter, and also to report a repair that needs making on their council house. The staff of the local office will make sure the maintenance department is informed and arrange a visit. The Highland Council, because it covers such a large area serving many remote communities, has an extensive network of Service Points which is the first contact with the council many residents will have.

Alternatively, people may contact their own local councillor direct with any queries, comments, complaints or requests. If they are serving their ward properly, they should then ensure that the matter is dealt with.

Useful Address

All Scottish local councils belong to the *Convention of Scottish Local Authorities (COSLA)*. They can be contacted at Rosebery House, 9 Haymarket Terrace, Edinburgh EH12 5XZ; ☎0131-474 9200; fax 0131-474 9292; www.cosla.gov.uk.

Community Councils

There are over 1,000 community councils throughout Scotland. Their role is to ascertain and express the view of the communities which they represent on a range on matters pertaining to local government and other local services. Legally, they must be consulted on all local planning issues and on decentralisation schemes being set up by local councils at the behest of central government.

Local councils are committed to taking their representations seriously. They are constituted of locally elected community councillors, who are unpaid but may claim small expenses for council work they carry out.

Most community councils are members of the *Association of Scottish Community Councils* (21 Grosvenor Street, Edinburgh EH12 5ED; ☎0131-225 4033; fax 0131-225 4033; www.ascc.org.uk).

CRIME & THE POLICE

Levels of crime in Scotland vary widely depending on the area. As would be expected, levels tend to be highest in city areas, with Glasgow City council area topping the list (1,338 crimes per 10,000 population); followed by Aberdeen City (1,163 per 10,000); Edinburgh City (1144 per 10,000) and Dundee City (1,104 per 10,000). At the bottom are Aberdeenshire (415 per 10,000); and the three island council areas: Shetland (300 per 10,0000; Western Isles (293 per 10,000); Orkney (264 per 10,000).

Although the data should be treated with some caution, because recording methods adopted by different police areas and the profile of crimes committed, can have a distorting effect on the figures, this does give a broad indication of the patterns overall. In the main, urban areas appear in the top half of the list and the rural areas in the bottom half. Despite the high rate for Aberdeen City, it is interesting to note that Aberdeenshire Council area appears fourth from the bottom of the thirty-two council areas.

Even in today's security conscious world, there are large areas of the country, especially in the Highlands and Islands, where people routinely leave their houses and cars unlocked. The low crime rate is a factor which many incomers to the area cite as a strong reason for their move north.

The Police

There are eight police forces in Scotland, responsible for all day to day policing matters in their area. In total, there are around 15,500 officers, although there are wide variations in the strength of individual police forces (see *Police Forces* below).

The three main branches of the police force which most people will come across are the uniformed officers who investigate complaints of offences and misdemeanours and from whom the famous 'bobbies on the beat' are drawn. Today, however, their beats are far more likely to be patrolled in cars than on foot or bicycle, a custom many would like to see return. In rural areas, where a single police officer may be required to cover a vast area, that just isn't practicable anyway. The Criminal Investigation Department (CID), usually plain clothes, will take over ongoing crime investigations, while the traffic police, who do wear uniform, deal with all traffic emergencies, accidents and breakdowns where injuries, traffic obstruction or other difficulties are caused. They can be seen patrolling the motorways and major roads of the country, often in highly-visible Land Rovers.

Nearly every town throughout Scotland will have its own police station. In the Highlands and other rural areas, where communities are small and scattered, there will often be one police station to cover a large area.

Police Forces. The central Scottish police service website is at www.scottish. police.uk. It has links to all police force websites listed below (Figures in brackets are the strength of the force in 2004).

Central Scotland Police: HQ, Randolphfield, Stirling FK8 2HD; ☎01786-456000; fax 01786-451177; www.centralscotland. police.uk. (Strength 730).

Dumfries and Galloway Constabulary: HQ, Cornwall Mount, Dumfries DG1 1PZ; ☎01387-252112; fax 01387-262059; www.dumfriesandgalloway.police. uk. (Strength 462).

Fife Constabulary: HQ, Detroit Road, Glenrothes, Fife KY6 2RJ; ☎01592-418888; fax 01592-418444; www.fife.police.uk. (Strength 930).

Grampian Police: HQ, Queen Street, Aberdeen AB10 1ZA; ☎01224-386000; fax 01224-643366; www.grampian.police.uk. (Strength 1,271).

Lothian and Borders Police: HQ, Fettes Avenue, Edinburgh EH4 1RB; ☎0131-311 3131; fax 0131-311 3038; www.lbp.police.uk. (Strength 2,602).

Northern Constabulary: HQ, Old Perth Road, Inverness IV2 3SY; ☎01463-715555; fax 01463-230800; www.northern.police.uk. (Strength 664).

Strathclyde Police: HQ, 173 Pitt Street, Glasgow G2 4JS; ☎0141-532 2000; fax 0141-532 2475; www.strathclyde.police.uk. (Strength 7,188).

Tayside Police: HQ, PO Box 59, West Bell Street, Dundee DD1 9JU; ☎01382-223200; fax 01382-200449; www.tayside.police.uk. (Strength 1,170).

In addition, there are three specialist police forces in operation in Scotland: the British Transport Police who deal with incidents on public transport vehicles or premises, the Ministry of Defence Police, and the UK Energy Authority Constabulary.

British Transport Police: Scottish HQ, 90 Cowcaddens Road, Glasgow G4 0LU; ☎0141-332 3649; fax 0141-335 2155.

Ministry of Defence Police: Operational Command Unit HQ Scotland, HM Naval Base, Clyde, Helensburgh, Dunbartonshire G84 8HL; ☎01436-674321; fax 01436-677230.

UK Atomic Energy Authority Constabulary: UK HQ, Building E6, Culham Science
Centre, Abingdon, Oxfordshire OX14 3DB; ☎01235-463760; fax 01235-463764.

The Prison Service

There are 23 prison establishments in Scotland, all but one run by the Scottish
Prison Service under the supervision of the Scottish Executive Justice Department.
Kilmarnock Prison was built, financed and is run by private contractors.

Scottish Prison Service: Calton House, 5 Redheughs Rigg, Edinburgh EH12 9HW;
☎0131-556 8400.

All prisoners are classified according to the perceived security risk they pose
and are housed in conditions appropriate to that level of risk. Female prisoners,
who make up only 3 per cent of the prison population, are housed in women's
establishments or in female wings of mixed prisons.

The Scottish prison population has been steadily rising in recent years, currently
numbering more than six thousand.

The Scottish Judicature

Scotland's legal system is separate from the English system, and it differs widely
from it in many respects. The Lord Advocate is the head of the public prosecution
system which is independent of the police, who have no say in the decision to
prosecute.

Scotland is divided into six sheriffdoms which are themselves divided into
sheriff court districts. Sheriff courts are the lowest criminal courts, in which legally
qualified sheriffs may either sit with a jury of fifteen members to try more serious
cases or, sitting alone, may try less serious cases under summary procedure. Minor
summary offences are dealt with in district courts presided over by lay justices of
the peace or, in Glasgow, by stipendiary magistrates.

More serious matters will be heard at the High Court of Justiciary, which is also
where cases go on appeal. These cases are tried by a High Court judge sitting with
a jury of fifteen, in Edinburgh or on circuit in other towns.

Prosecutions in the High Court are prepared by the Crown Office and
conducted in court by a solicitor advocate while in the inferior courts the decision
to prosecute is made by lawyers called procurators fiscal, subject to the directions
of the Crown Office.

Useful Addresses

Crown Office: 25 Chambers Street, Edinburgh EH1 1LA; ☎0131-226 2626.
Sheriff Court of Chancery: 27 Chambers Street, Edinburgh EH1 1LB; ☎0131-225 2525.
Scottish Court Service: Hayweight House, 23 Lauriston Street, Edinburgh EH3
9DQ; ☎0131-229 9200.

Scottish Land Court: 1 Grosvenor Crescent, Edinburgh EH12 5ER; ☎0131-225 3595; fax 0131-226 4812.

Sheriffdoms

Glasgow and Strathkelvin: Sheriff Court House, PO Box 23, 1 Carlton Place, Glasgow G5 9DA; ☎0141-429 8888.

Grampian, Highlands and Islands: Sheriff Court House, Castle Street, Aberdeen AB10 1WP; ☎01224-657200.

Lothian and Borders: Sherriff Court House, 27 Chambers Street, Edinburgh EH1 1LB; ☎0131-225 2525.

North Strathclyde: Sheriff Court House, St Jame's Street, Paisley PA3 2HW; ☎0141-887 5291.

South Strathclyde, Dumfries and Galloway: Sheriff Court House, Graham Street, Airdrie ML6 6EE; ☎01236-751121.

Tayside, Central and Fife: Sheriff Court House, Tay Street, Perth PH2 8NL; ☎01738-620546.

EMERGENCY SERVICES

The number to call in a life-threatening emergency is 999. Alternatively, 112 may be used throughout the EU. People using 'typetalk', the UK National Telephone Relay Service run by the Royal National Institute for Deaf People, should call 0800-112 999 text. This number is to call assistance from the police, ambulance, fire, coastguard, mountain or cave rescue services.

In emergency you should lift the telephone handset and press or dial 999 or 112. Tell the operator who answers which emergency service you want and wait to be connected to that service. Tell the emergency service where the trouble is, what the trouble is, where you are and the number of the phone you are using. All emergency calls are free of charge.

If the emergency is not life-threatening, do not use the emergency number. Instead find the number of your local branch of the service you require in your Phone Book.

The fire brigade and ambulance services have vehicles and equipment available in remote areas, often manned by trained part-time volunteers, to respond to emergency calls as quickly as possible. Despite this, it is inevitable that you may have to wait longer for the emergency services to reach you if you live in such an area. It's as well to have your own emergency procedures to hand, such as fire extinguishers, first aid kits or even a pond in the garden!

In medical emergencies where time is of the essence, helicopters are used to airlift serious emergencies to hospital.

There will be one or more policemen permanently on duty in your area, with reinforcements from the larger force as and when necessary. But in the almost crime-free areas of the Highlands you shouldn't need to call on them very often.

Veterinary Services

Although not classed as an emergency service, in the agricultural areas of Scotland vets are very important. Although veterinary practices tend to be based in the larger towns or villages, they will have weekly or fortnightly surgeries in outlying places. They will visit farmers or crofters who need 'in the field' assistance, and are prepared to assist with transporting your pet or working animal to the surgery if it needs an operation or similar. For instance, the vet would take your pet back with him/her after the local visit, for you to pick up the following day from the main surgery, thus saving you one long trip.

Addresses of vets can be found in local Phone Books and Yellow Pages.

SOCIAL LIFE

It probably should not need saying here, but to lay to rest any preconceptions which may still exist, the red-haired kilt-wearing Scotsman living in a land of mountains, glens and lochs is a myth. True, you will see many red-haired people, and you may well see the occasional kilt-wearer, and large areas of the country have mountains, glens and lochs to spare, but like all other stereotypes, this falls far short of the truth. Modern Scotland is a multi-cultural society with a large proportion of the population living and working in towns and cities in modern industries, many of whom only see the mountains on their holidays.

The other preconception, that of the typical Scotsman being a whisky drinking, gregarious soul prepared to be friendly with anyone is also a mixture of fact and fiction. There is no doubt that the Scottish people as a whole are a friendly and polite nation, far less reserved and cold than the English are perceived to be. You will generally be treated courteously, warmly and helpfully in shops, hotels and the like, whether in the cities or the country. But you may find it a little harder to immediately feel part of the community, especially in the Highlands and Islands and other rural areas.

English people in particular are always apprehensive that they may come across some 'anti-English' feeling. Despite the occasional incident, which is sure to be well-publicised in the English (and Scottish) media, such cases are few and far between. More often than not, any conflict is likely to arise from the new arrivals upsetting their neighbours for one reason or another unconnected with their origins, and their Englishness being used as a stick to beat them with. The best approach, as in moving to any new place, is to treat the existing residents courteously, respect their traditions and not to overstep any social lines before you are really sure where those lines are drawn.

Nowadays, most parts of the Highlands are well used to incomers – there are plenty of people who have decided to make their homes here, both from other areas of Scotland and from south of the border. However, you may find it a little harder to get to know the indigenous locals than the incomers; they have a natural reserve and, although very polite and courteous, they tend to 'weigh you up' for a few months before becoming overtly friendly. The best approach is to be polite and courteous back, and open and helpful too. With few exceptions, they (and the incomers too) are tremendously helpful. If you need a lift anywhere, or someone to look after your pet while you are away, they would feel offended if you didn't ask. In an area where neighbourliness still means something, that's what being neighbours is all about.

Social Attitudes

There is little difference today between attitudes in Glasgow and Edinburgh to those in the other cities of the UK. Women work alongside men and, although there are still 'glass ceilings' in existence which mean they may have a harder time progressing to the top jobs, changing attitudes backed by strong anti-discrimination legislation mean this is changing year on year.

Marriage has shown a steady decline, with 30,755 marriages in Scotland in 2003, compared with over 40,000 per year in the 1960s. This equates to 6.1 per 1000 population, which is the third highest rate of all European countries apart from the Czech Republic and Denmark. There were 10,928 divorces in 2003, slightly higher than in 2002, but there has been an overall fall in levels since the 1980s, which is probably due to the increase in numbers of couples cohabiting – when their relationship breaks up no formal divorce is required. With more couples cohabiting, there is little stigma attached to it, nor to children born out of wedlock.

However, greater prejudice may well be encountered in the rural areas, particularly those where the church still retains a strong hold. Social attitudes in these areas are behind the times and, if you have moved from the south of England, say, to the Highlands, it can feel as if you have stepped back in time ten or twenty years. However, the natural courtesy of the local people would generally prevent them from showing disapproval to your face – although what they say behind your back might be a different matter!

Although gay and lesbian relationships are still looked at askance by many, social attitudes are changing in this area too. As self-defining unconventional people, such couples are often attracted to the Highlands. One of the many curious anomalies you will encounter in the Highlands and Islands is that such couples are more often than not treated with a tolerance by the population as a whole, and accepted into the social life of the community, in a way that you may not find in the middle of a city. On the other hand, when the Scottish Parliament voted to remove a clause from the education act which prevented teachers from discussing issues relating to homosexual relationships during the course of their lessons, it provoked a vociferous campaign of opposition from a vocal minority throughout the population, so there is still a strong underlying prejudice against homosexuality in the country.

With a comparatively low level of immigrants in Scotland compared with

England and Wales, racial intolerance does not appear to be rife. The Race Relations Act of 1976 made racism illegal, and the Commission for Racial Equality works towards the elimination of discrimination and promotes equality of opportunity and good relations between different racial groups.

It is a truism the world over that rural areas are more traditional in outlook and more resistant to and suspicious of change than urban areas. This is certainly true in large areas of the Highlands and Islands. Many of the older generation look on with disapproval at the increasing pace of change in their communities. However, without these changes there is little doubt that some of these communities would be moribund, with young people moving away, schools, shops and post offices closing, leaving these areas as isolated backwaters.

Generally, the combination of indigenous locals and those who have moved to the Highlands more recently makes for a good social mix and keeps these communities vibrant and looking to the future. Some communities used to the traditional pattern of agriculture with a little tourism as a sideline are finding it difficult to come to terms with current political interest in modernising the land management system, along with the loss of traditional industries and the growth in Information Technology which are changing working habits out of all recognition. As the future of agricultural subsidies comes under the microscope because of financial pressures from Europe, with the promise of a greater emphasis on incentives to use the land in more environmentally conscious ways, communities need to be in touch with current thinking in order to change with the times. The more forward-looking are happy to see new blood, with new areas of expertise, moving in.

Making Friends

If you are prepared to put yourself out to make the first move, it is not difficult to make friends. There are many opportunities for meeting and mixing with others, whether you are in a city or in a small rural community.

It is quite acceptable to go out with work colleagues for lunch or after work and close friendships often arise this way. Or if you are a parent, your children can be a way of meeting new people. The parents of your children's friends could become your friends. Acquaintances met in your local bar can also become friends.

The Scots are a very hospitable race, and you can be sure that if you call on your neighbours, particularly in more traditional rural areas, you will be offered – and expected to partake of – tea or coffee with biscuits, cakes (often home-made) and sometimes sandwiches. Try not to refuse the refreshment offered, for fear of offending.

Entertaining people in one's home in the evening, whether for a meal (a dinner party) or for drinks with maybe some light snacks, is a popular way of relaxing, although this is a relatively new phenomenon, which has only really caught on in the last twenty years or so. The older generation are less likely to take naturally to this sort of entertaining. The traditional Scottish way of getting together in the Highlands and Islands was to call on friends or neighbours, with maybe a bottle of whisky, and an impromptu *ceilidh* (pronounced 'kay-lee') would develop, involving chat and maybe singing, music and even dancing if space permitted.

If you prefer more organised ways of getting to know people, there are a wide range of clubs and other activities you can get involved in. Depending on the area in which you live and your own proclivities, you may find and decide to join a boat club, a golf club, other sports clubs and leisure centres, the Scottish Women's Rural Institute, a writers' circle, a drama group or any number of other organisations for enthusiasts of specialist activities and pastimes. If you are interested in the indigenous culture, there are local classes in Scottish dancing and traditional instruments such as the bagpipes or the *clarsach* (Celtic harp.) You may also wish to join a local church, which is another popular way of finding a group of people on your own wavelength.

Every school in Scotland has a school board which has a hand in running the school. They are made up of a mixture of teachers, parents and local people, which is a way of getting to know people while performing a useful function. You might even wish to serve your new community by standing as a community councillor.

All of these groups are keen to attract new members, especially those willing to take a seat on the committees that run them. Many of these are run on a shoestring and are always delighted to come across new people who are prepared to take a hand in fund-raising.

Probably the one thing that is likely to start you off on the wrong foot with the local community, especially in a small rural community, is if you move in to the area and immediately try to 'tell the locals how to run their lives' – however well-intentioned you may be. It appears inevitable that most of the committees in these areas end up having a number of incomers on them, very often because they have previous experience of working in a bureaucratic environment. The traditional Highland industries tend towards the manual, such as agriculture, construction trades and hotel work, so few are skilled in committee procedure and will not put themselves forward for such roles. This does not stop some of them showing resentment because they feel that certain incomers are trying to run everything. At the same time, things don't get done unless people – however recent to the area – put themselves forward for these committees, so anybody who is prepared to do this is likely to be welcomed with open arms by existing members.

On the whole, it's only a minority who do have these complaints – the more reasonable individuals are happy to make use of the administrative/executive skills of the incomer when it comes to writing business letters or taking on obstructive officials – just as you may have cause to be grateful for the manual skills of those around you when it comes to needing fences erected or leaking roofs repaired.

The Highlands, long recognised as a region of rural deprivation, offer some very worthwhile projects to get involved in if you feel the urge to do something significant. Over recent years the trend has been for local groups to be set up to help with the sustainable development of the region.

About six months after the author and her husband arrived in Wester Ross with their children, and the initial 'let's see what they're like' period had worn off, they were asked to get involved in a fledgling community group whose brief, at the behest of the local authority, was 'to devise and bring about a regeneration strategy for the area'. Over the months this group grew into a charitable company which succeeded in attracting funds to employ a local development worker. The group was committed to carrying out projects aimed at increasing jobs, houses, residents and visitors in the area. Once it was realised that this wasn't 'incomers telling us what to do' (the majority of the group's directors were local themselves) the community supported what they were trying to do and it soon had a strong and flourishing membership. Quite unforeseen when it was started, their greatest contribution to the community to date, was to spearhead the campaign to prevent the Highland Council from closing the local primary school. The community triumphed when the decision was reversed.

Children

If you are considering moving to a remote rural area with your children you have a whole extra set of factors to consider. The first is, will they have a good life? The answer to that is emphatically yes – they're likely to have an even better time than you do. In small Highland communities, where everybody knows everybody else, children still have the freedom to roam safely which is sadly fast-disappearing elsewhere. (On the other side of the coin, you'll soon be told if your child was spotted doing something or being somewhere he or she shouldn't have been – in the nicest possible way, of course, leaving you to sort it out in the way you think best). The roads are safe for cycling and there is constant coming and going between houses – often the most popular are those which have the latest computer game, just like anywhere else. Scratch games of football are popular, where all the local children, all ages and both sexes, play together. And of course there's access to the sea, rivers and lochs for fishing, swimming and sailing, miles of accessible country for walking and camping, easy access to skiing when conditions are right. Those children who love the outdoor life very quickly become hardy and well able to take care of themselves.

For those who are less confident, or more gregarious, there are also plenty more formal and organised activities for children available across Scotland in the town and the country. Courses in a whole range of sporting activities are available in leisure centres throughout the country. In the more remote communities, leisure centres often visit outlying areas and run courses in village halls and other community facilities. Other clubs and societies for children include church groups, youth clubs, music and drama groups.

One thing to bear in mind in this context is the lack of public transport in the

Highlands and Islands and the fact that children often need to travel, whether to visit their friends or to attend a club. Mum and Dad do need to be aware they will be required to act as a taxi service to run the children here and there. Having said that, the same often applies in towns. The advantage of a small close-knit community is that there will inevitably be several other children needing to be at the same place at the same time, so efficient rotas are arranged which prevent four cars travelling in convoy to pick up four children.

ENTERTAINMENT & CULTURE

Many members of the older generation may bewail the fact that people are not as sociable as they once were, a state of affairs for which television and computers are blamed. Although there is no doubt that a great deal of relaxing is done in front of the TV or computer screen, there are plenty of other ways of passing your time, whether you are in Glasgow or the Highlands – doubtless far more than was the case in the days before widespread access to TVs and computers.

Whether your preference is for traditional cultural pastimes or for modern entertainment, all groups are catered for. Eating and/or drinking out, going to the cinema or theatre, visiting museums or historical monuments, music and dancing or playing or watching sports are all popular pastimes.

Food & Drink

Eating out in restaurants has seen a boom in recent years. Renowned for many years as having a bad diet, and traditionally a conservative race as far as foreign food is concerned, the Scots are now becoming far more adventurous. In the large towns and cities restaurants serving a wide variety of foods can be found. Indian, Chinese and Italian restaurants in particular abound, as well as the ubiquitous burger chains, but you can now choose to eat in Japanese Sushi Bars, Spanish Tapas bars or French restaurants. Traditional British fish and chip shops are to be found throughout Scotland (often serving oddities such as the deep fried Mars bar, or pizza alongside the fish). Sadly, one of the hardest things to find is probably good quality traditional Scottish fare! The most likely place to find haggis, salmon and venison dishes is in hotels or good standard guest houses in the tourist areas. You'll also find the traditional Scottish breakfast of porridge and kippers here.

Take away meals are popular, from fish and chips to Chinese and Indian take-aways, to pizzas, kebabs and burgers. In Scotland though, remember the term for take away food or drink bought from a bar or off-licence to take home is a 'carry-out'.

The Scottish male is renowned for his liking for a 'wee dram' – which may indeed be whisky, but is just as likely to be Bacardi and Coke, surprisingly a favourite tipple of the Scottish working man in the Highlands! Beer too is consumed in copious quantities in bars. The traditional English style pub (public house), whether oak-beamed, sawdust floored or full of plastic and chrome, is somewhat of a rarity in Scotland. The local bar is quite likely to be in a hotel, or to be a serious drinking den without any pretence at being an attractive and comfortable place to spend a few hours. This is a throwback to the tradition of bars being a place women would rarely, if ever, be seen, a place where men would go to drink hard and return home drunk.

Things are changing now, and women are no longer a rarity in bars. Bar owners have cottoned on to the fact that if they make their premises more comfortable and attractive they are going to attract a wider range of people and therefore increase their profits, especially if they serve food as well. With women more independent than they were in the past, they now frequent bars and clubs, many of them consuming plenty of alcohol themselves.

Alcoholism and alcohol abuse has long been a problem in Scotland, particularly in the Highlands and Islands, a fact which is recognised in the government paper 'Towards A Healthier Scotland' published in February 1999. One of the targets set is, by 2010, to reduce alcohol consumption exceeding recommended weekly limits from 33 to 29 per cent for men and from 13 per cent to 11 per cent for women. Maximum recommended weekly limits are set at 21 units per week for men and 14 units per week for women, where a unit is equivalent to 1/2 a pint of beer or cider, a glass of wine or one measure of spirits.

Underage drinking is also seen as a problem, and targets have been set to reduce the frequency and level of drinking from 20 per cent of 12-15 years to 16 per cent by 2010.

At the time of writing, pubs and clubs are allowed to serve alcohol between 11am-11pm on Monday to Saturday, 12.30-2.30pm and 6.30-11pm on Sundays. There is currently consultation in progress on the pros and cons of relaxing licensing laws to allow 24 hour drinking, subject to local licensing decisions. There are arguments both for and against such a dramatic change, and in the end a political decision will doubtless be taken.

You must be 18 or over to buy and consume alcohol on licensed premises. Children aged 14 or over are allowed on licensed premises if they do not consume alcohol. If the establishment has a children's certificate, under 14s are allowed into specified parts of the establishment in order to consume a meal, as long as they are accompanied by an adult.

A total ban on smoking in enclosed public spaces, including pubs and clubs, will be introduced in Scotland in 2006. The issue is also being considered in England, but it appears unlikely that a total ban will be introduced there in the near future.

Cinema

Cinema is popular, with most reasonable size towns having their own cinema, and cities having large 'multi-plex' cinemas with half a dozen films or more showing on different screens.

For many years, a highlight of the Highland lifestyle would be the days when a screen would be set up in the village hall and the latest Hollywood film shown. Most of the community would gather to watch the film together. As people became more mobile through owning their own cars, and with some smaller towns getting their own cinemas, this custom died out. For many years, residents of large parts of the western Highlands had to travel to Inverness – a round trip of one hundred miles or more – to visit the cinema.

Later, the introduction of videos to buy or to rent and watch in your own home brought about a decrease in the numbers of people visiting the cinema. In recent years, however, the cinema industry has seen a rebirth in Scotland. With larger more attractive premises and a wider choice of films to view, visiting the cinema has again become popular.

In 1999, after years of planning and fund-raising, the cinema was finally brought back to the western Highlands and the Islands. A travelling cinema called 'The Screen Machine' now travels the area, showing the latest releases throughout the remotest areas of the country. It takes the form of a large pantechnicon which, when it reaches its destination, opens out into a comfortable eighty seater cinema. The wonders of modern technology have brought cinema in the Highlands and Islands full-circle!

Theatre, Opera & Ballet

There is a thriving arts scene throughout Scotland. The Scottish Arts Council funds arts organisations and artists with monies received from the Scottish Executive and the National Lottery Fund. Scotland has its own national ballet and opera companies. Both are based in Glasgow but make regular tours to other venues.

Even the smallest village halls in the Highlands pay host to high quality arts performances. There are many touring companies bringing drama, music and other events to remote communities. The Highland Festival runs during May and June each year and organises a wide range of art and cultural events throughout the Highlands.

The Scottish Youth Theatre is a lively and vibrant organisation which taps into the talent of young Scottish residents. As well as running classes and other events throughout the year, they run a summer festival during the school holidays in which hundreds of young people take part, producing and performing publicly in musical and dramatic productions in a number of centres.

Matthew Taylor first got involved with the Scottish Youth Theatre when he was 14

I spent several weeks during my summer holidays performing with SYT each year until I was 17. It was dead good fun and gave me my first taste of professional theatre. Each year we would rehearse and put on several performances at the

> *highly-regarded Citizens Theatre in Glasgow and at other venues. It also gave*
> *me the opportunity to try different types of drama, from improvisation to street*
> *theatre.*
>
> *I enjoyed the whole experience so much that now I am doing a BA degree in*
> *Theatre Studies and aim to set up a theatre company when I finish my course.*

The Edinburgh International Festival and Dance, started in 1947, has now reached
such a status that it is known worldwide simply as the Edinburgh Festival. Today,
both it and its alter ego, the Edinburgh Fringe, attract thousands of people to the
city every August.

Useful Addresses

Edinburgh Festival Fringe Society: The Fringe Office, 180 High Street, Edinburgh
    EH1 1QS; ☎0131-226 0026; www.edfringe.com.
Edinburgh International Festival: The Hub, Castlehill, Edinburgh EH1 2NE;
    ☎0131-473 2000; fax: 0131-473 2002; www.eif.co.uk.
Hi-Arts (Highlands and Islands Arts): Suites 4&5 Ballantyne House, 84 Academy
    Street, Inverness IV1 1LU; ☎01463-717091; fax 01463-720895; www.hi-arts.
    co.uk.
Scottish Arts Council: 12 Manor Place, Edinburgh EH3 7DD; ☎0131-226 6051;
    fax 0131-225 9833; www.scottisharts.org.uk.
Scottish Youth Theatre: 3rd Floor, Forsyth House, 111 Union Street, Glasgow, G1
    3TA; ☎0141-221 5127; fax 0141-221 9123; www.scottishyouththeatre.org.

Music & Dancing

From traditional Scottish country dancing to disco to line dancing, from bagpipes
to chamber music to rock and roll, the Scots love music and dancing. Village halls,
hotels and concert halls throughout the country offer a wealth of musical events.
Scotland is very proud of its musical heritage, particularly in the Highlands and
Islands.

The Mod is a Gaelic music festival where singers and musicians compete for
honours in various categories. It is held every year at local, regional and national
levels. It is run by *An Comunn Gàidhealach*, founded in Oban in 1891 to help
preserve and develop the Gaelic language.

The *fèisean* movement aims to keep traditional music and the Gaelic language
alive, by running classes and residential courses throughout the Highlands and
Islands where children and adults can learn and improve their skills in traditional
Celtic instruments and Gaelic singing.

**Adam Taylor found his move to Scotland, at the age of eight, musically
inspirational**
Music is an important part of the school curriculum in primary and secondary

school. We were all encouraged to develop our talents from an early age. I first went to the Junior Fèis when I was 12, and it was then that I started learning the guitar. I found I had a natural talent for the instrument, and my skills improved rapidly with the assistance of the professional musicians who take the time to tutor young people at the Fèis.

I have had some great opportunities through my involvement with the Fèis. I have played and written songs with Jim Hunter, a well-known traditional musician, and also have collaborated and performed with some of the top Celtic bands in Scotland, including Annie Grace from 'Iron Horse' and members of 'Capercaillie'.

The music scene in Scotland is thriving, from small village bands, such as the one I used to perform in, whch travel about the Highlands performing at local pubs and dances, to big names in Indy and Rock, such as Franz Ferdinand and Snow Patrol. There are excellent music venues in all the cities. 'T in the Park', an annual outdoor music festival in Kinross, is the highlight of the music year, featuring everything from pop to traditional Celtic music to opera.

I am sure I would never have had such opportunities if I had not moved to Scotland. My musical experience has now led to me being accepted, against massive competition, to do a degree in Sound Technology at the elite Liverpool Institute of Performing Arts.

Useful Addresses

An Comunn Gàidhealach: 109 Church Street, Inverness IV1 1EY; ☎01463-231226; fax 01463-715557; www.ancomunn.co.uk.

Celtic Music website: www.musicscotland.com.

Fèisean Nan Gàidheal: Nicholson Buildings, Wentworth Street, Portree, Isle of Skye IV51 9EJ; ☎01478-613355; www.feisean.org.

Scottish Music Information Centre: 1 Bowmont Gardens, Glasgow G12 9LR; ☎0141-334 6393; fax 0141-337 1161; www.smic.org.uk.

Traditional Music and Song Association: 95-97 St Leonard's Street, Edinburgh EH8 9QY; ☎0131-667 5587; fax 0131-441 3189; www.tmsa.info.

For a fuller list of arts organisations in Scotland contact the Scottish Arts Council or see Whitaker's Scottish Almanack published by A&C Black Ltd.

Museums, Galleries & Historical Monuments

One thing Scotland is not short of is history. Aberdeen, Stirling and Perth received their charters as Royal Burghs as early as the 12th century, and there are buildings and monuments of interest dating from this time and earlier throughout the country. Each town of any size and many villages have their own museums, displaying historical and social artefacts from the area. There are castles around practically every corner – the history fan has no shortage of places to visit.

There are many historic buildings and monuments open to the public. Opening hours vary, many being closed in winter and some being closed in the mornings. Admission fees also vary, but most fall in the range of £2.50 to £5 per person.

There are nearly three hundred museums and galleries in Scotland. National collections are held at the National Galleries of Scotland and the National Museums of Scotland in Edinburgh. An online art museum has also been awarded national collection status. www.24hourmuseum.org.uk

Admission to many museums and galleries is free, but where there is a fee charged it is rarely more than £4 per person.

Gambling

The Scots as much as the rest of the UK love a flutter. Bookmakers, found in high streets throughout the country and now on the internet, will take bets on just about anything from horse races to whether snow will fall at Christmas. Bingo is popular, particularly among women, and the National Lottery is a national obsession. There are several national draws each week, and the jackpot prize is generally between five and eight million pounds. If the jackpot is not won, the prize rolls over to succeeding weeks with the jackpot accumulating until it is won, sometimes reaching over twenty million pounds, causing a ticket-buying flurry!

Scratch cards, on sale in newsagents at £1 each, promise instant cash prizes ranging from a few pounds to a fortune – and people spend a small fortune on them.

Gambling for large stakes can only take place in a casino licensed for the purpose by the Gaming Board. Gambling in public houses and bars is not permitted other than for small stakes. Bets cannot be taken in such premises.

Sport

A wide variety of sport is played in Scotland. Around 62 per cent of the population regularly participate in some form of sport. The highest rates are found, not surprisingly, in the 16 to 24 age group, with 80 per cent taking part, but even among the over 55s, nearly forty per cent take part in sport. There are many more armchair sportsmen and women who watch sport, whether on the TV in the comfort of their own home or by visiting sporting events in person.

The Scottish Parliament, via Sportscotland (formerly the Scottish Sports Council), aims to increase participation in sport and sporting success at the highest levels. The Scottish national sports centres at Cumbrae, Aviemore and Largs provide professionally coached training courses and a training base for several national squads.

Football (soccer and rugby) are among the most popular sports, both as regards numbers of participators and spectators. Golf too is popular and attracts tourists who wish to play on the many superb courses throughout the country, from the high status historical courses such as St Andrews to small courses in beautiful settings on the west coast of the Highlands.

The ancient games of shinty and curling are still popular, with curling being one of the few sports at which the Scots are among the world leaders in international competition.

Highland Games, including such esoteric pursuits as caber-tossing and other tests of strength as well as Highland dancing and piping, take place in many venues every summer.

Outdoor pursuits such as walking, climbing, cycling and skiing are popular in the Highlands, attracting people from all over the world to face the challenges of the terrain.

Leisure Centres run by local authorities provide a range of facilities for different sporting activities.

Useful Address

Sportscotland: Caledonia House, South Gyle, Edinburgh EH12 9DQ; ☎0131-317 7200; fax 0131-317 7202; www.sportscotland.org.uk.

Details of other sports organisations can be obtained from Sportscotland or Whitaker's Scottish Almanack.

CLANS & NATIONAL DRESS

The word 'clan' is derived from the Gaelic word clann, meaning children. It once referred to an extended family or tribe occupying a certain area of land. As these territories became established, most by the 16th century, the clan came to signify all the people, including those not related by blood, living on the lands owned by a clan chieftain. These clan names became used as surnames. As a result, there are relatively few original Scottish surnames – the vast majority of which begin 'Mac' or 'Mc', signifying 'son of'. Even today, in some areas of the Highlands and Islands it is easy to identify who were the clans in the area centuries ago, because the same surnames crop up time and again.

The problem with this is that you are likely to find several Donald MacKenzies or Roddy MacDonalds in an area. To differentiate between them, a nickname will have been assigned to them in the past. For example, the original Donald MacKenzies might have been designated 'Donnie Botlan' and 'Donnie Caol'. Their children would then have been tagged with their father's nickname: Hector Botlan and Annie Caol, say, which would be used locally in preference to their surname name. The original nickname was sometimes purely descriptive of the person – *caol* means thin; at other times, the reason for it is lost in the mists of time.

In another version of this, when a man takes a wife, very often his wife will be named with reference to her husband. So Hector's wife might be known locally as 'Maggie Hector', say. The consequence of this is that someone who is introduced to you as Donald MacKenzie is referred to by others as Donnie Ocko. This can be confusing when you first arrive in an area, before you have cracked the code!

It is well to be aware that the Highlands and Islands are very small worlds. Family and kinship networks and relationships are very complex, but because of the small, relatively isolated populations, which are only now widening, you may find your neighbour on the west coast or one of the Islands turns out to be related to a great number of other people in the area – or even to people in Inverness. So the rule is, don't speak ill of anybody unless you are sure they are not related to the person you are sounding off to!

The famous Scottish tartans are clan-based. To be entitled to wear certain tartans you must be a member of the clan somewhere back in your ancestry. If you wish to research this, there are many books and an increasing number of websites which will help you. Most if not all of the clans have their own societies, to which any clan member is entitled to belong. Many now have their own websites, which can be accessed through www.scotlandsclans.com.

On a day to day basis you will not see many people wearing the kilt – Scottish national dress – but it is normal and accepted wear at celebratory occasions. Nearly all the menfolk will wear their kilts to weddings, and many to ceilidhs or other light-hearted occasions – hence the prevalence of them at Scottish national football matches. They are not, however, worn to funerals. On such sombre occasions a subdued dark suit will be worn.

Useful Book
For historical information on the clans and their tartans, see *Scottish Clans and Tartans*, Neil Grant (Hamlyn 2000).

RELIGION

Around a quarter of the population professes active membership of a religious faith. Of these, over 90 per cent are Christian. 14 per cent of the adult population regularly attends a Christian church.

The four largest churches in Scotland are the Church of Scotland, the Free Presbyterian Church (also known as the 'wee free') and the Associated Presbyterian Church (flippantly known as the 'split p's' from the time they split from the Free Presbyterians). They are attended by 65 per cent of Scottish Christians.

Of the rest, 22 per cent are Roman Catholics while just under five per cent attend the Scottish Episcopal Church (attended largely by the 'expat' Church of England congregation). The remainder belong to various Christian denominations including Methodists, Baptists, Pentecostal churches, Congregational churches, assemblies of Brethren, Quakers, and the Salvation Army.

The Christian churches in the UK come under the umbrella organisation of the Council of Churches for Britain and Ireland. In Scotland, most of the main Christian denominations belong to Action of Churches Together in Scotland (ACTS) and the Churches Agency for Inter-Faith Relations in Scotland.

Although as a whole the UK is becoming a more secular society, with membership of Christian churches falling steadily, it is an important element of life in the Highlands and Islands. Just how important is illustrated by ongoing disagreements and schisms appearing within the different denominations. As recently as January 2000, more than 20 hard-line Free Church ministers left the church, walking out of a General Assembly meeting before they were suspended due to repeatedly refusing to comply with church court decisions. They have now set up a schismatic group calling itself the Free Church (Continuing).

The Christian Church, of whichever complexion, still holds a stronger influence on the community in the Highlands and Islands than is generally the case elsewhere in the UK. You need to be aware of local sensibilities in this regard. Although most children are now allowed to play out on Sunday, rather than being required to stay in and read the Bible, there are still many activities which are frowned upon on the Sabbath. The one which is quoted by many people is 'Don't hang your washing out,' but it's tactful to avoid any noticeable pastimes which smack of 'work'. Even if nobody says anything, it's politic not to get the lawn-mower out or to wash the car in full view of the road as your neighbours return from church.

Of course, you can work as hard as you like inside the house! However, a day of enforced rest every week does have its advantages – it might cure some of the stress that seems endemic among the working population today.

It follows that there are few shops open on a Sunday in many rural areas, although things are changing slowly, particularly on the main tourist routes: in the holiday season you may find some shops open on the Sabbath, you can play golf, visit a leisure centre, have a drink or a meal. But don't assume that you can buy petrol if your tank runs dry on a Sunday; many service stations will be closed. There are now some Sunday ferry and air services to the islands, but always check well in advance of your trip because these are very limited and not available to all destinations.

Adherents of other religions make up less than 2 per cent of the population. These include Buddhism, Hinduism, Islam, Judaism and Sikhism. There are fairly large Islamic communities in Glasgow and Edinburgh, and a significant Jewish community in Glasgow.

Churches of Scotland

Associated Presbyterian Churches of Scotland: Clerk of the Scottish Presbytery, Revd Dr M. McInnes, Drumalin, 16 Drummond Road, Inverness IV2 4NB; ☎01463-223983; www.apchurches.org.uk.

Baptist Union of Scotland: 14 Aytoun Road, Glasgow G41 5RT; ☎0141-423 6169; fax 0141-424 1422; www.scottishbaptist.org.uk.

The Church of Scotland: Church Office, 121 George Street, Edinburgh EH2 4YN; ☎0131-225 5722.

The Free Church of Scotland: General Treasurer, I.D. Gill, The Mound, Edinburgh

EH1 2LS; ☎0131-226 5286; www.freechurchcontinuing.co.uk.

The Free Presbyterian Church of Scotland: Napier House, 8 Colinton Road, Edinburgh EH10 5DS.

Methodist Church: 20 Inglewood Crescent, East Kilbride, Glasgow G75 8QD.

Reformed Presbyterian Church of Scotland: Clerk of Synod, Revd A. Sinclair Horne, 17 George IV Bridge, Edinburgh EH1 1EE; ☎0131-220 1450.

The Roman Catholic Church: Secretariat of the Bishops' Conference of Scotland, 64 Aitken Street, Airdrie ML6 6LT; ☎01236-764061; fax 01236-762489.

Scottish Congregational Church: PO Box 189, Glasgow G1 2BX; ☎0141-332 7667.

The Scottish Episcopal Church: General Synod, 21 Grosvenor Crescent, Edinburgh EH12 5EE; ☎0131-225 6357; fax 0131-346 7247; www.scotland.anglican. org.

United Free Church of Scotland: General Secretary, Revd J.O. Fulton, 11 Newton Place, Glasgow G3 7PR; ☎0141-332 3435; www.ufcos.org.uk.

SHOPS & SHOPPING

Since the 1980s, the American fashion for having out-of-town shopping centres has caught on in Scotland as much as in the rest of the UK. This has caused the decline of many a once-vibrant town centre, with many of the big chain stores moving out to new, pristine premises on the outskirts of town, leaving the smaller independent stores to struggle to attract custom, in many cases having to close down.

Although the out-of-town centre with ample parking conveniently close to the stores is now an accepted feature of the Scottish way of life, there have been signs of a backlash against them since the late nineties. Large supermarket chains such as Tesco have introduced smaller city centre branches – coming back full circle to the position several decades ago. Other companies have followed suit, once again bringing some life, economic and social, to areas which appeared moribund not many years ago.

Town and city centres, as well as the out-of-town shopping centres, are dominated by the huge, sometimes multinational, chain stores which make every town seem much like the last. There are still independent shops around, but you have to look carefully to find them. Often smaller tourist towns and the quieter areas of Glasgow and Edinburgh are the best places to track them down.

One city which is noticeably thriving, and has grown enormously over recent years, is Inverness, often called 'the capital of the Highlands'. It attracts shoppers from the entire Highlands and Islands area and is prospering as a result of greater spending power in these areas.

In the small communities of the western Highlands and the Islands, often there is only one general store, so the monthly trip to Inverness to stock up on those things unavailable locally is essential. The town is ringed by a large 'Retail and Business Park' which stocks everything you are likely to need, from cars to concrete, furniture to farm supplies, either retail or wholesale. If you have a business of some kind, even if just doing a small amount of bed and breakfast in the summer, this entitles you to a card for a Cash and Carry which can save you pounds on groceries.

But there's certainly no need to go to Inverness for everything. Remote rural areas often have better local supplies than suburban-dwellers. Here, the shops come to your door. Butchers, fishmongers, banks, libraries – their vans can be seen travelling around the Highlands stopping at their regular ports of call week in, week out. Local residents and tourists are encouraged to use their local shops, even if some of their shopping comes from further afield, because without regular custom many cannot survive. The slogan 'Use It or Lose It' can be seen on many shop doors. Companies selling clothes, pots and pans, soft furnishings and the like regularly set up in village halls for an all-day sale.

If there's anything you need from Inverness or elsewhere that you can't transport yourself, there's a network of local carriers transporting goods throughout the country and to the Islands everyday.

The growth of computer technology has been a boon to remote areas – nowadays mail order is so easy. Clothes, office and computer supplies, books, CDs, boat parts – all these can be bought through mail order. Just pick up your phone, or log on to the Internet, and your goods are delivered to your door in a matter of days.

PUBLIC HOLIDAYS

National Holidays

Statutory public holidays are called 'bank holidays' – because, obviously, the banks are closed on these days. So are many other shops and services, although increasingly the retail trade has realised this is an excellent opportunity to attract all those customers who would normally be at work, and in many shopping centres it is difficult to see any difference between a public holiday and working days.

Apart from holidays related to stated religious or secular dates (such as Christmas and New Year), public holidays are normally on a Monday. If the holiday would otherwise fall on a Saturday or Sunday, the official holiday is on the Monday following. The annual Scottish statutory public holidays are New Year (two days); Good Friday, Easter Monday, May Day, Spring Bank Holiday, Summer Bank Holiday, Christmas Day and Boxing Day.

New Year, known as Hogmanay, is traditionally the most important Scottish holiday. It is only a matter of thirty years or so since it was normal for many people to work at Christmas, taking their holiday at Hogmanay instead. Christmas is now as much of a holiday as in the rest of the UK, while Hogmanay is just as important, with celebrations countrywide. The annual Edinburgh Hogmanay street party is the largest New Year celebration in the world. Many companies close down for two full weeks to take in the whole Christmas and New Year period.

The May Day holiday is officially known as 'Early Spring Bank Holiday' and falls on the first Monday after 1st May; Spring Bank Holiday falls on the last Monday in May; and the Summer Bank Holiday falls on the last Monday in August.

Late in 2004 there is a campaign underway to make 30th November – St Andrew's Day – a national holiday. Many people think that the day which commemorates the patron saint of Scotland should be officially deemed a day off work to allow people to celebrate all things Scottish. Retailers also have in mind that it would be an ideal time for people to start their Christmas shopping, so wouldn't be averse to seeing more people in their shops! The First Minister is reported to be against the idea, but it may be that public opinion will sway his mind.

Local Holidays

Despite the official bank holidays, however, in Scotland the picture is less clear-cut than in England. In most parts of Scotland there are local and fair holidays, dates varying according to the locality. One town may have a holiday on the first Monday in every month, say, while the next closes on every second Monday. To compensate for this, you may find that your local Post Office is open as normal on an official Bank Holiday. Or, because Inverness has a holiday when Gairloch doesn't, you may find that although your mail is collected, there won't be a delivery until the following day.

Dates of local holidays should be obtainable from the local authority. The Glasgow Chamber of Commerce publishes a diary of national Public Holiday dates and local Glasgow holiday dates on their website, with links to other local authority sites which publish their own local holiday dates.

Useful Address

Glasgow Chamber of Commerce and Manufactures: 30 George Square, Glasgow G2 1EQ; ☎0141-204 2121; fax 0141-221 2336; www.glasgowchamberonline.org.

TIME

The standard time throughout the UK is Greenwich Mean Time (GMT). This operates between Autumn and Spring. In late March, British Summer Time (BST) is imposed, and all clocks are 'put forward' one hour. They are 'put back' one hour in October, thus reverting to GMT.

Most of Europe is one hour ahead of the UK during GMT. The USA is between 5 hours and 12 hours behind the UK, depending on the state. Australia is between 7½ and 11 hours ahead. The telephone directory lists time differences for all countries in the world in the International Dialling Codes section.

METRICATION

Allegedly, metrication of weights and measures was introduced many years ago, and schoolchildren are no longer taught in, or about, feet and inches or stones, pounds and ounces. However, anybody who left school more than twenty years ago will almost certainly still use such measurements, and profess not to be able to work in the metric version. This has produced a gulf between parent and child where help with Maths homework becomes fraught with difficulty!

In an attempt to bring the UK into step with Europe, because voluntary codes have not had much effect, in early 2000 shops were legally obliged to display the price per kilogram on their products; whether the price was also shown in pounds and ounces (avoirdupois) was optional. Fabric has been sold by the metre for decades, but still many shops will sell you fabric by the yard, and quote prices for both measurements.

Distances on road signs are in miles and speed limits are given in miles per hour. Road maps, however, do now show both miles and kilometres.

USEFUL BOOKS & WEBSITES

Books

The Complete Guide to Celtic Music, Jane Skinner Sawyers (Birch Lane Press 2000).

The Crofter and the Laird, John McPhee (House of Lochar 1998) The author, a staff writer on the New Yorker, writes about his experience of living with his family on Colonsay, island of his ancestors.

The Crofting Way, Katherine Stewart (Mercat press 2000) A collection of columns about her life as a crofter written for The Scotsman.

Heritage of Scotland, Nathaniel Harris (Hamlyn 2000) Culture and traditions of the Scottish people.

Websites

City News: free classified ads sites for buying and selling in a number of Scottish towns and cities. www.citynews.com/uk.htm.l

Education UK: www.educationukscotland.org. Information on all aspects of studying in Scotland plus links to websites of education establishments.

Electric Scotland: www.electricscotland.com. Scottish community site for Scots and their descendants world-wide.

Gaelic Scotland: www.gaelic-scotland.co.uk. Online resources on all aspects of Gaelic and Celtic culture.

Scottish Search: www.scottishsearch.com. Scottish links directory.

Scottish Quality: ww.scottishquality.com. Buy a range of Scottish products online, including art, whisky, tartan and bagpipes.

RETIREMENT

CHAPTER SUMMARY

- Scotland has an ageing population. By 2041, it is estimated, more than 60 per cent of the population will be over 65.
- To relocate to the UK as a retired person of independent means, you must be at least 60 years of age and must be able to show that you have an annual income of at least £25,000.
- State retirement pensions are paid to men aged 65 or over and to women aged 60 or over.
- If you are resident in the UK you will normally pay UK tax on all your investment income, wherever in the world it arises.
- The problem of isolation is one that is likely to be more acute the further north you move, especially if you choose a remote rural area.
- Prescriptions, eye tests and dental treatment on the National Health Service are free for those over retirement age.
- Services for elderly people are designed to enable them to remain living in their own homes for as long as possible.
- Most entertainment events and educational facilities offer discounts on admission or enrolment fees for retired people.
- The law relating to the disposal of an estate is different in Scotland from that in England and Wales.

Rural areas of Scotland, particularly the Highlands, are a popular destination for retired people from elsewhere in the UK. Very often they will have spent holidays in Scotland for decades and, on retirement, decide to move there permanently. Some have planned this for many years, buying a second home in Scotland for their holidays while they are still working, then retiring there when they leave work.

Another significant group of people who retire to Scotland are those who were born there, but moved away elsewhere in the world for work. As they grow older, they find the call of their home country gets stronger, and they finally return to their roots.

A sub-group of these people are those with Scottish ancestry who feel an affinity with the country. Once they retire, they have the opportunity to express their essential Scottishness by moving to the country. This feeling of an affinity with the country by those who have only a distant connection, or may have no blood connection at all but have discovered it during holidays, has been called 'Celtic soul' by some. There is certainly something about Scotland which gets into the blood of many people, and they spend much time and effort trying to find a way to relocate permanently. In so many cases, this only proves possible or practicable at the time of retirement from work. With modern work patterns giving the possibility of taking early retirement, and with life expectancy increasing, this can mean people still have several decades in which to satisfy their Celtic souls.

In many ways, rural Scotland, although peaceful, restful and unhurried, the very things which many retired people come for, is not a sensible place for elderly people to end their days in. It means distancing oneself from friends and family networks, often built up over many years; it means moving to a place where the shops may be a long distance away, and where social and health services are less easy to access because of geographical remoteness; it means subjecting oneself to a climate which is often cold, wet and windy. And it can mean finding oneself somewhat isolated. This is perhaps potentially worse where a couple moves together and one then dies – a single person moving is likely either to be used to being alone or will set out to build up a circle of friends and acquaintances for company.

But despite these shortcomings, there is a significant number of people who choose to retire to Scotland above anywhere else. For them, the pleasures outweigh the disadvantages and inconveniences.

Background Information

There is a bit of a crisis in Scotland currently, as the nation faces the prospect of dramatic falls in population over the coming years. The population is declining at a faster rate than anywhere else in Europe, due to a falling birth rate and younger people moving away. The only group on the increase for the foreseeable future is the elderly who are living longer. In the last 30 years, a quarter of a million Scots have moved away and not been replaced either by inward migration or by births. It is predicted that Scotland's population will have fallen to 4.84 million by 2027, and it will lose ten per cent of its population – 500,000 people – in the next four decades. In the worst case scenario of zero net migration and a decline in fertility rates consistent with the decline over the last 20 years, the population could fall to 3.47 million by 2101.

It is estimated that by 2041, more than 60 per cent of the population of Scotland will be over 65, with huge knock-on effects: it will inevitably mean increased demand for such services as pension provision and health care, at the same time as a reduction in tax revenues as the labour market contracts and there is a reduction in demand for teachers and schools.

RESIDENCE & ENTRY REGULATIONS

Retired persons with the right of abode, as described in the chapter Residence & Entry Regulations, have no restrictions on moving to Scotland, and can claim all social security benefits they are entitled to (See Daily Life).

Non-economically active nationals of EEA countries have a right to live in the UK only if they have sufficient funds to support themselves during their stay without needing financial assistance from UK public funds. Dependent parents or grandparents of EEA nationals may also live here, as long as they do not need recourse to public funds.

In order to relocate to the UK as a retired person of independent means, you must be at least 60 years of age and must be able to show that you have an annual income of at least £25,000, disposable in the UK. You must be able to support and accommodate yourself and any dependants indefinitely without working, without assistance from anyone else and without recourse to public funds. In addition to the financial requirements you will also need to show that you have a close connection with the UK.

For full details of these regulations, see *Residence and Entry Regulations.*

PENSIONS

In the UK, state retirement pensions are currently paid, as long as the requisite National Insurance contributions have been made, to men aged 65 or over and to women aged 60 or over. Women may be eligible for a pension in their own right, if they have the required level of insurance contributions, or may be entitled to a pension on the basis of their husband's insurance. Widows may be entitled to a widow's pension on the basis of the insurance paid by their late husband.

To bring pension ages into line, in the interests of avoiding sex discrimination, the pension age for women is changing to 65 over a ten year period from 6th April 2010. Women born before 6th April 1950 will reach retirement age at 60, while women born on or after 6th April 1955 will not be eligible for a state pension until they are 65. Women born between 6th April 1950 and 6th April 1955 will reach pension age at 60 plus one month for every month that their date of birth falls after 5th April 1950. They will be entitled to their pension starting from the 6th of that month.

UK state pensions are paid at a standard weekly rate, which in April 2004 was £79.60 per person. Increases on the basic amount may be payable if you have adult or child dependants. There is an enhanced pension for those aged 80 or over – in 2004 this was just 25p per week. There is also a non-contributory pension available for the over-80s who do not have enough contributions to be eligible for a full state pension. Claimants may be eligible to additional pension through the State Earnings-Related Scheme (SERPS) which pays amounts over and above the basic pension depending on your earnings sine April 1978. Some employees will have been 'contracted out' of SERPS by their employers or a personal pension plan, in which case additional pension will be paid in the form of a company or private pension.

Most pensioners will receive more than the basic pension, through the addition of SERPS, occupational pensions, a range of benefits and allowances, plus other sources of income. In 2002-2003 average UK pensioner incomes were £177 net a week for single persons, £327 net a week for pensioner couples. Younger pensioners tend to have higher incomes than older pensioners because they are likely to receive more occupational pension and earnings income than older pensioners. The largest source of income for pensioners is state benefits (which include the state retirement pension). In 2002-2003 the average pensioner unit received 51 per cent of its income from state benefits. This proportion rose to 60 per cent for single pensioners over the age of 75. Occupational pensions accounted for 27 per cent and investment income for 9 per cent.

UK residents more than four months from retirement age can receive a personal pension forecast from the Benefits Agency. Either contact your nearest office for an application form or download it from the Department for Work and Pensions (DWP) website (see below).

The UK has social security agreements with a number of countries whereby state retirement and widows pensions for residents from other countries are payable at the level they would receive in their home country. These countries currently include Barbados, Bermuda, Canada, European Community, Jamaica, Jersey & Guernsey, Gibraltar, Iceland, Israel, Liechtenstein, Mauritius, New Zealand, Norway, Philippines, Switzerland, Turkey, USA, Republics of the former Yugoslavia. The Department for Work and Pensions (DWP) website at www.dwp.gov.uk has downloadable leaflets explaining the arrangements for all these countries.

The general principle is that, where old age or widows pensions are payable to a person from their home country, on the basis of insurance paid, this will be paid to them in the UK when they arrive here, or when they become eligible, at the same level as they would receive if they were in their home country.

Where a person has paid insurance both in the UK and another country, he or she may be eligible to a pension from both countries. If, on the other hand, his or her insurance contributions are not at a high enough level in either country to entitle them to a pension in either country, the two sets of contributions may be combined, treating the foreign insurance as UK insurance, which may entitle them to a UK pension

Because pension payments are dependent on individual circumstances, it is important to contact the relevant authorities in the UK or in your home country in order to determine your entitlements.

Payments from company or private pension plans will depend on the details of the plan, but generally will continue to be payable directly to you while in the UK.

Useful Address

For further information, contact The Pension Service at *International Pension Centre*: Tyneview Park, Newcastle Upon Tyne NE98 1BA: ☎0191-218 7777; fax 0191-218 7293. Opening hours are 8.00 am-8.00 pm.

TAXATION

Tax liability in the UK is determined on the basis of whether you are classed as resident, ordinarily resident or non-resident, domiciled or non-domiciled. For an explanation of these terms, see Taxation in Daily Life.

As a retired person, the main considerations regarding your tax position are likely to be those pertaining to your pensions, investments in the UK or overseas, and property owned or rented in the UK or overseas. The rules are fairly complicated, taking into account how long you intend to stay in the UK; whether you regard it as your main home; the lengths of time you spend in the UK and abroad; whether you own a property in the UK or have 'available accommodation' there (i.e. it is available for you to use as and when you wish) and so forth. You are advised to get the advice of a tax consultant regarding your own particular circumstances. You may find that by making adjustments to your lifestyle – e.g. by dividing your time strategically between the UK and your home country – you can limit your tax liability. However, if you are classed as not liable to UK tax in a particular area, you will doubtless find you are liable to tax in your home country, so it's a question of working out which country's taxes are least onerous!

Liability to tax in a particular tax year can become complicated by the fact that the UK tax year runs from April to April and it may cover a different period in your home country. Again, advice should be sought from a professional on how this may affect you personally.

Double Taxation Agreements

The UK has double taxation agreements with a long list of countries, designed to prevent an individual being taxed in both countries for the same income or gains.

COUNTRIES WITH DOUBLE TAXATION AGREEMENTS WITH THE UK
Antigua & Barbuda; Argentina; Australia; Austria; Azerbaijan; Bangladesh; Barbados; Belarus; Belgium; Belize; Bolivia; Botswana; Brunei; Bulgaria; Canada; China; Croatia; Cyprus; Czech Republic; Denmark; Egypt; Estonia; Falkland Islands; Fiji; Finland; France; Gambia; Germany; Ghana; Greece; Grenada; Guernsey; Guyana; Hungary; Iceland; India; Indonesia; Republic of Ireland; Isle of Man; Israel; Italy; Ivory Coast; Jamaica; Japan; Jersey; Kazakhstan; Kenya; Kiribati; Republic of Korea; Latvia; Lesotho; Luxembourg; Macedonia; Malawi; Malaysia; Malta; Mauritius; Mexico; Mongolia;

Montserrat; Morocco; Myanmar (formerly Burma); Namibia; Netherlands; New Zealand; Nigeria; Norway; Oman; Pakistan; Papua New Guinea; Philippines; Poland; Portugal; Romania; Russian Federation; St Kitts & Nevis; Sierra Leone; Singapore; Slovakia; Slovenia; Solomon Islands; South Africa; Spain; Sri Lanka; Sudan; Swaziland; Sweden; Switzerland; Thailand; Trinidad & Tobago; Tunisia; Turkey; Tuvalu; Uganda; Ukraine; USA; Uzbekistan; Venezuela; Vietnam; Federal Republic of Yugoslavia; Zambia; Zimbabwe.

Pensions

Income tax is not charged, or is charged at a reduced amount in certain circumstances, on lump sum retirement benefits relating to employment overseas, under an overseas pension scheme or provident sum.

Regular pension payments are liable to tax in the UK if you are classed as resident, but there may be a certain amount of tax relief allowed (i.e. a discount on normal rates) in certain circumstances. Tax relief is allowed on payments into private pension plans.

Investment Income

This refers to any income which is not a pension and is not earned by you as an employee, from carrying on your profession or from running your own business. This includes interest from bank and building society accounts, dividends on shares, interest on stocks and rental income (unless your business amounts to a trade).

If you are resident in the UK you will normally pay UK tax on all your investment income, wherever in the world it arises.

However, if you are resident but not domiciled in the UK, or resident but not ordinarily resident in the UK and a British or Commonwealth citizen, or a citizen of the Republic of Ireland, you are liable to UK tax only on the amount of your overseas investment income which is 'remitted' to the UK: this means if it is paid in the UK or brought to the UK in any way.

If you are not resident in the UK, you are only charged UK tax on investment income arising in the UK. If you are a resident of a country with which the UK has a double taxation agreement you may be able to claim exemption or partial relief from UK tax on investment income.

Any profits you make from letting property in the UK are taxable there, even if you cease to be resident in the UK.

Useful Address

There are certain UK Government securities known as 'Free of Tax to Residents Abroad' (FOTRA) securities which are free of UK tax to people who are not ordinarily resident in the UK. For a list of eligible FOTRA securities, write to *Financial Intermediaries & Claims Office:* Fitz Roy House, PO Box 46, Nottingham,

NG2 1BD; ☎0115-974 2000.

Capital Gains Tax

For an explanation of the basic rules on capital gains tax, please see *Taxation* in *Daily Life*. If you are resident or ordinarily resident in the UK, you may be liable to capital gains tax on disposing of assets situated anywhere in the world. However, where you are a resident of a country which has a double taxation agreement with the UK you may be exempt from capital gains tax in the UK.

Sources of Information

Information on all these matters, in more detail, is given in the Inland Revenue booklet IR20 'Residents and non-residents - Liability to tax in the United Kingdom'. Other useful leaflets are IR90 'Tax allowances and reliefs' and IR139 'Income from abroad? A guide to UK tax on overseas income'. There is also a number of other leaflets available free of charge on request, most of which can be downloaded from the Inland Revenue website.

Inland Revenue: PO Box 37, St Austell, Cornwall PL25 5YN; Leaflet Orderline
   ☎08459-000404; fax 08459-000604; www.inlandrevenue.gov.uk

Inland Revenue (Scotland): Clarendon House; 114-116 George Street, Edinburgh
   EH2 4LH; ☎0131-473 4000.

If you have any queries on your tax position, you can contact your local Tax Office. The address will be listed in the phone book under 'Inland Revenue'. However, it is sensible to consult a tax advisor or accountant first who can work out the most tax efficient way of managing your affairs. Any advisor you consult should be a member of the Chartered Institute of Taxation (CIOT).

Anderson, Anderson & Brown: Chartered Accountants, 6 Carden Place, Aberdeen
   AB10 1UR; ☎01224-625111; fax 01224-626007; www.aab.co.uk.

Chartered Institute of Taxation (CIOT): 12 Belgrave Street, London SW1X 8BB;
   ☎020-7235 9381; fax 020-7235 2562; www.tax.org.uk.

Chiene & Tait: 61 Dublin Street, Edinburgh EH3 6NL; ☎0131-558 5800; fax
   0131-558 5899; www.chiene.co.uk.

LEAVING ONE'S FAMILY

One reason people do not make the move north once they have retired is because they are not happy being so far away from their family. For other people, who are prepared to make regular visits 'home' – probably long and tiring journeys – to keep contact with family, what is acceptable when they are still active and healthy at 60, becomes far more of a problem as they get older and less vigorous. It is almost inevitable that you will see your family less frequently once you have moved to Scotland, so you must be sure that this will suit you. On the other hand, it is probable that when they do visit you, they will stay for longer. Many people who have retired to Scotland find that their children and grandchildren like to combine a holiday in Scotland with an extended family visit.

Of course, you may not find yourself living away from family and friends for long; one feature of moving to the Highlands is that, once they come to visit you and realise what a beautiful place it is, and what a pleasing way of life, some of them will be inspired to make the move themselves. In this way, clusters of family and friendship groups, particularly from the north of England, not infrequently find themselves neighbours in the Highlands. So if you are moving to get away from them, you might be disappointed!

The problem of isolation is one that is likely to be more acute the further north you move, especially if you choose a remote rural area. You need to appreciate that, however many committees you get involved in, however many rounds of golf you play or hills you walk, the long winter evenings are very long, the 'big city' of Inverness is a long drive away, and the weather does conspire to keep you indoors for long stretches. The result is that you are almost certain to find yourself spending more time in close proximity to your partner or alone. So it is essential that you are totally happy in their – or your own – company. With modern communications and transport it is no longer necessary to be as self-sufficient as was once the case. But you do need to be emotionally self-sufficient. If you're used to having a strong family support network close to hand, the chances are when you move they won't be coming with you. It's not so easy to take a few hours out to visit daughter, son, sister or brother when things get on top of you. Be very sure that this suits your temperament.

HEALTH CONSIDERATIONS

The state of one's health, both now and potentially in the future, is an important thing to bear in mind when deciding to relocate on retirement. Thanks to the National Health Service, wherever you settle in Scotland there will be free health services available. Prescriptions, eye tests and dental treatment on the NHS are all free for those over retirement age. However, if you are planning a move to the more remote areas of the country, these may entail travelling some distance, especially if you are likely to need hospital care at any time. By and large, if you wish to avail yourself of a private doctor, you will need to be nearer to the centres of population as this is where they tend to set up their practices.

Having said that, even in the most remote areas, you should have reasonably easy access to medical, dental and ophthalmic care. GPs, dentists and opticians, even where they are based in larger towns, visit outlying areas on a regular basis, usually weekly in the case of GPs, and weekly, fortnightly or monthly in the case of dentists and opticians. In the case of emergencies, GPs will visit you at home, wherever that may be, or will call an ambulance – land or air – to take you to hospital in serious cases. Dentists will undertake emergency work, but this may entail a journey of some distance to their home surgery.

Patients in need of a serious or specialised operation may be unable to have the operation locally. Raigmore Hospital in Inverness, for example, although the main hospital for a huge area of the Highlands, lacks some specialist equipment. In these cases, patients are sent to Aberdeen or to Edinburgh for such procedures as specialised scans or heart bypass operations. After a heart operation at Edinburgh, once the patient's condition has stabilised, he/she will be brought back to Raigmore for recuperation.

BUYING A RETIREMENT HOME

Access to health care and other services is just one thing to bear in mind when buying a home for your retirement. The other aspects of social infrastructure, such as distance from shops, garages, public transport and your nearest neighbours are also important. If you are the sociable type, you may find it important that there are clubs to join and social events to attend. Ask local residents about these things, or failing that, get hold of the local paper and see what events are coming up in the area.

The climate too is important. If you suffer from the aches and pains of old age which are exacerbated by cold and damp conditions, Scotland may not be the best place to retire to. On the other hand, of course, if you suffer from breathing difficulties which are exacerbated by a polluted atmosphere, the clean air of the Highlands and Islands could improve your health no end.

If you choose to settle in an area of Scotland on the basis of having spent many summer holidays there, it is wise to make sure that you find it as amenable at other times of the year. It is a good idea, before you take the big step of buying a house, that you arrange to take an extended holiday of three to six months during the winter months in your chosen area. It is not unknown for it to rain almost every day for six months in Highland areas of Scotland, and for the sun to be rarely seen during this period. Even the most stoical of individuals can find this depressing. So if you find you need regular doses of sunshine, you might find you just cannot live with that.

This is also an opportunity to identify those places which are almost deserted in the winter months. Some villages, particularly in tourist areas, have a high proportion of holiday and second homes which are not occupied all year round. If you want to be part of a community, look for a place with a year-round population, and where second and holiday homes are not in the majority.

On the other hand, many regular visitors to the Highlands avoid the months of June to August because this is when the dreaded midge is most active. If this is you, take a holiday here at the height of the midge season; you may find they are not as bad as you fear – alternatively you may vow never to return in summer again! More seriously than the irritation aspect, some people do prove to be allergic to midge bites, so it is an important consideration for them. Midges are less common on the east and in the south of Scotland, so this may be a deciding factor when choosing the area in which you will live.

Many people buy a holiday home in Scotland long before they retire, with the intention of living there permanently when the time comes. In this case, it is well to consider whether what suits you now is going to be as amenable when you are in your sixties and seventies. When young and vigorous, living at the end of a rutted cart track, or where you have to park your vehicle a mile or more from your home, can be a good holiday adventure. But when you're older and less nimble, bouncing through pot holes or clambering up a hillside can be less appealing, especially in the middle of winter when it's cold and wet. So choose your house with the future in mind.

SOCIAL SERVICES

Services for elderly people in Scotland are designed to enable them to remain living in their own homes for as long as possible. There are a range of services available from local authorities, to assist elderly people and their carers, usually close family members. These include advice, domestic help, meals delivered to the elderly person's home (usually called 'meals on wheels'), house alterations to aid mobility, emergency alarm systems, day and/or night attendants and laundry services. Day centres and recreational facilities are also provided by local authorities. Respite care may be provided to give carers temporary relief from their responsibilities. Charges may be made for these services, based on the ability of the person to pay.

There are a wide range of social security benefits and allowances to which elderly people may be entitled, depending on their circumstances and state of health and mobility. These include Attendance Allowance, Disability Living Allowance, Invalid Care allowance, Council Tax Benefit, Housing Benefit, Income Support, War Disablement Pension, Widow's Pension and War Widow's Pension.

Sheltered Housing

Local authorities and the private sector provide 'sheltered housing' for elderly people. These are houses, available either to buy or rent, especially designed for elderly people who are capable of living alone but may need some day to day help. Usually built in small complexes, they often have a resident warden always on hand for emergencies. These house usually include alarm system for the elderly person to summon emergency help if needed.

Residential & Nursing Homes

Elderly people unable to care for themselves may be admitted to a residential home, run by the local authority or private sector. Charges are made according to a means test. If a resident cannot afford to pay the costs are met by the local authority.

Generally a distinction is made between residential care homes and nursing homes. Where ongoing medical care is required, there may be a requirement for the person to move to a nursing home as they have medically qualified staff always available.

Details of residential and nursing homes in Scotland can be found in the Yellow Pages or can be obtained from the local council. A number can also be found online at www.bettercaring.co.uk/nursinghomes/scotland.

DAILY LIFE, HOBBIES & INTERESTS

There is no need for the socially inclined to become reclusive when they move to Scotland. Even in remote rural communities there will be clubs and groups which meet regularly. The Scottish Women's Rural Institute (SWRI) is an affiliate of the Women's Institute, and there are numerous groups throughout Scotland meeting usually on a monthly basis, as well as organising trips and shows of various kinds. Another nationwide group for older people is The Association of Retired and Persons Over 50 (ARP/050). www.arp050.org.uk. They offer a range of facilities to members, including local friendship groups, holidays, educational courses and advice on a range of matters. There are also a number of charities working specifically on behalf of older people, in particular Help the Aged and Age Concern, who may also offer social and educational facilities of various kinds.

Sports facilities of all kinds are available throughout Scotland and private or local authority leisure centres offer a range of courses, some specifically aimed at older people. Golf and swimming are popular too and can be enjoyed even when other physical pursuits become too onerous.

Local groups meet all over the country to enjoy all manner of pastimes, from carpet bowls to Scottish country dancing, writing to yoga. They are all friendly – and always overjoyed to boost their numbers with new members.

For people who are less keen on organised activities, retirement is an ideal time to take up pastimes such as painting, photography or walking – Scotland offers unbeatable scenery for all three!

If you enjoy travelling and sightseeing, Scotland is a country of such varied terrain and so much historical heritage that you could spend many years exploring its rural, urban and historical treasures. Many historical monuments and museums have discounts for retired persons. You may also be eligible for discounts on public transport.

Most entertainment events and educational facilities also offer discounts on admission or enrolment fees for retired people. From large theatres in city centres to the smallest village halls in the Highlands and Islands, there is a great variety of entertainment on offer. Adult education courses, both vocational and just for fun, are provided by the community education service throughout Scotland.

If you wish to do something useful for the community with your spare time, you could do voluntary work for a charity, sit on the committee of a local group, or even become a community councillor.

Of course, there's no reason why you should just concentrate on voluntary work or hobbies. You could do part-time work or set up your own home business. It is wise, however, to check how this might affect your tax and benefits or whether it is precluded by the regulations under which you are staying in the UK.

See local newspapers and telephone directories for the groups active in your area, or contact head offices as below.

Useful Addresses

Age Concern Scotland: 113 Rose Street, Edinburgh EH2 3DT; ☎0131-220 3345; fax 0131-220 2779; www.ageconcernscotland.org.uk.

ARP/050: Greencoat House, Francis Street, London SW1P 1D2; ☎020-7828 0500; fax 020-7233 7132; www.arp.org.uk.

Help The Aged: 11 Granton Square, Edinburgh EH5 1HX; ☎0131-556 6331 fax 0131-557 5415; www.helptheaged.co.uk.

Scottish Women's Rural Institutes: 42 Heriot Row, Edinburgh EH3 6ES; ☎0131-225 1724.

WILLS & LEGAL CONSIDERATIONS

If you move to Scotland from elsewhere in Britain, it may be wise to make a new will, because the law relating to the disposal of an estate is different in Scotland from that in England and Wales. The rules relating to Scottish wills and bequests are detailed in Setting Up Home. It is advised that every adult should make a will, despite the fact that around 70 per cent of people in Britain die without doing so. Getting legal help to draw up a will should ensure that your assets are passed on to your nearest and dearest in the most tax-efficient manner.

If you are a foreign national and do not wish your estate to be subject to Scottish law you may be eligible to state in your will that it should be interpreted under the law of another country. If you do not specify this in your will then Scottish law will apply. If you establish your country of domicile in another country you will not be subject to UK death duty and inheritance laws. A solicitor familiar with the law in both countries would be useful to advise you on the most tax efficient way of arranging your affairs.

Banks or solicitors will draw up a will for you at a cost of between £50-£120. Alternatively you can purchase a simple will form from stationers and post offices for around £4.00 and do it yourself. Make sure this is a will 'according to Scottish Law'. It is only really suitable for very simple and straightforward disposal instructions. Anything complex is best drawn up by a solicitor.

The Scots Wills website allows interactive forms to be completed online, and once completed a fully valid Scottish Will is displayed to be printed out on the customer's printer and signed by them there and then. This service costs £35 and the site is accessible at www.scotwills.co.uk.

You will need to appoint an executor for your estate; although your bank, building society or solicitor will act as executor, this can prove costly. A preferred approach may be to make your beneficiaries the executors – they can then consult a solicitor after your death if they need legal assistance.

Your will and insurance policies should be kept in a safe place, such as your bank, and a copy left with your solicitor or your executors.

DEATH

If a death occurs at home, the family doctor must be contacted. If the death occurs at night and it is sudden and unexpected the doctor should be notified at once, otherwise he/she can be called in the morning. The doctor will issue a medical certificate of cause of death ('death certificate') if there are no unusual circumstances surrounding the death. If there are, the death may be reported to the Procurator Fiscal.

If the death was violent, accidental, if there are unusual circumstances or if the cause death is not known for certain, the police should also be called. In such cases the death may be reported to the Procurator Fiscal by the police, a doctor or a Registrar of Birth, Deaths and Marriages.

The Procurator Fiscal will investigate any deaths which are unexpected, violent, suspicious or not obviously explained, caused by industrial disease or associated in any way with medical or surgical care. In such cases, relatives and other witnesses may be interviewed by the police and a further medical report, a post-mortem examination or a fatal accident inquiry may be ordered.

If the death occurs in hospital, they will contact the nearest relative, the police if death was accidental, and will either issue a death certificate or report the death to the Procurator Fiscal. The staff may ask you for permission to use organs for transplant purposes. It is useful therefore to know the person's wishes in this respect. They may have discussed it with you or may have carried an organ donor card (freely available at doctor's surgeries). In most cases where death occurs at home only the corneas may be used for transplant purposes. However, the body may be donated for medical research as long as no organs have been removed or a post-mortem taken place.

The death must be registered by any relative, person present at the death, legal representative, executor or the occupier of the premises where the death took place. It must be registered as soon as possible, or at any event within eight days, by the local Registrar of Births, Deaths and Marriages, whose address will be given you by the undertaker, the hospital or the doctor. The address will also be listed in the telephone directory or can be given you by the Post Office. Documents required by the registrar are the death certificate, and any pension or benefits book, NHS medical card, birth and marriage certificates of the dead person, if available. The registrar will issue a Certificate of Registration of Death to be given to the undertaker so that the funeral can go ahead.

Final funeral arrangements should not be made until you are sure that the death does not have to be reported to the Procurator Fiscal because this may affect the date when the funeral can take place. You can make funeral arrangements yourself but most people go to a funeral director (or undertaker) who can make all the arrangements. A funeral director who is a member of the National Association of Funeral Directors must give a full estimate of funeral costs when you enquire. As funerals can be expensive it is as well to get at least two estimates. Check whether the deceased has an insurance policy or a pre-paid funeral plan or funeral bond to pay for the funeral. If they do not, the cost will be taken from their estate. If this does not cover it, you may be required to pay from your own pocket. If you or your partner are in receipt of certain benefits you may be able to get assistance with funeral costs.

The body may be either buried or cremated. It can only be cremated once the cause of death is definitely known, and only once two cremation certificates have been signed by the family doctor and another doctor. There will be a charge for this.

If you wish to have a religious funeral service the minister of religion should be contacted as soon as possible. If you do not know of a minister in the area, the funeral director should be able to advise you or arrange for a minister to officiate at the service. If you prefer to have a non-religious service at the funeral, you may contact the Humanist Society of Scotland who can advise and assist you.

If you prefer an environmentally-friendly approach, the Natural Death Centre is a non-profit-making charitable group who can advise on and arrange woodland burials, and provide biodegradable cardboard or regular coffins by mail order. Contact them at www.naturaldeath.org.uk.

USEFUL ADDRESSES & BOOKS

The Natural Death Centre: 6 Blackstock Mews, Blackstock Road, London N4 2BT; ☎0871-288 2098; fax 020-7354 3831; www.naturaldeath.org.uk.

Humanist Society of Scotland: Registered officiants: Pam MacDonald (North of Scotland), ☎07010-714775;Robin Wood (West of Scotland), ; ☎07010-714776; Ivan Middleton (East of Scotland) ☎07010-714778.

National Association of Funeral Directors: 618 Warwick Road, Solihull, West Midlands B91 1AA; ☎0845-230 1343; fax 0121-711 1351; www.nafd.org. uk.

A leaflet telling you everything you need to know about 'What to do after a Death in Scotland' can be downloaded from the Scottish Executive website at www. scotland.gov.uk/library5/social/waad-00.asp.

Leaflets and advice are also available from the Citizens' Advice Bureau. See the telephone directory for the local branch or contact *Citizens' Advice Scotland:* 1st Floor, Spectrum House, 2 Powderhall Road, Edinburgh EH7 4GB; ☎0131-550 100; fax 0131-550 1001; www.cas.org.uk.

The Which? Guide to an Active Retirement, ed. Jane Vass (Which? 2000).

Managing Your Money in Retirement, John Whiteley (How To Books 2000).

SECTION II

WORKING IN SCOTLAND

EMPLOYMENT

PERMANENT AND TEMPORARY WORK

BUSINESS AND INDUSTRY REPORT

STARTING A BUSINESS

EMPLOYMENT

CHAPTER SUMMARY

○ **Levels of Employment.** Employment levels vary significantly between areas in Scotland.
  ○ The average unemployment rate in Scotland is slightly higher than in the UK.
○ **Industry.** The structure of the economy has changed significantly in recent years, with heavy industry now far less important to the economy than the service industry and IT.
  ○ Many residents in rural areas run small businesses.
○ **Foreign Workers.** If you enter the UK as an employee, you may need a work permit in addition to your entry clearance or visa.
  ○ EEA nationals do not require any formal permission to enter the UK and there is no time limit put on their stay.
○ **Earning Levels.** Average earnings are highest in Aberdeen and Edinburgh, lowest in rural areas.
  ○ The UK has a national minimum wage of £4.85 for workers aged 22 and over.
○ **Employment Opportunities.** The biggest employers in Scotland are in the Public Sector.
  ○ There is plenty of temporary work available in tourism.
  ○ There is a growth in employment in new technology companies, including computer software and hardware, optoelectronics and telecommunications.
  ○ The biggest three companies in Scotland are in the financial services sector.

THE EMPLOYMENT SCENE

Unemployment rates in Scotland tend to be slightly higher than those for the UK as a whole. The fluctuations in Scottish employment levels, however, do tend to mirror those for the UK. Throughout the UK, unemployment has been falling steadily over recent years. In the first quarter of 1999, the overall rate of unemployment for Scotland was 7.6 per cent, compared with 6.3 per cent for the UK. By the fourth quarter of 2003 it was 5.8 per cent, compared with 5.1 per cent for the whole of the UK.

This 'headline' rate of Scottish unemployment disguises differences between regions and between the sexes. For example, unemployment rates for men are consistently higher than those for women – in 2003 the rates were around 5 per cent for women, and 6 per cent for men. There are also wide differences between regions: in March 2003, unemployment in Edinburgh was 3.8 per cent; Highland 5.5 per cent; Aberdeen 6 per cent; Fife 8.4 per cent; and Glasgow 11.1 per cent.

There has been a significant change in the structure of the Scottish economy during recent decades. Heavy industry and manufacturing, in particular shipbuilding, once the mainstay of Scotland's economy, now account for less than 20 per cent of GDP. Construction and agriculture are also both in decline. Service industries including tourism and financial services now account for over 70 per cent of output and heavy engineering and manufacturing is being replaced by hi-tech electronics and IT industries. With the current expansion in the internet and e-commerce this is a trend which is likely to continue for some time. For an overview of the make-up of the Scottish economy, see the *General Introduction*.

At root, there are two reasons for moving to Scotland to work: it may be a way of developing yourself and furthering your career with valuable experience, at the same time as getting to know a new country; or it may simply be a means of earning money to enable you to fulfill your ambition to live in Scotland. If you are attracted to the Highlands and Islands rather than southern Scotland, you are far more likely to fall into the second category. You want to move because you love the Highlands. It's the environment and way of life that you're after. In these circumstances, your approach must be different, because the relationship between where you live and the job you do is different. For most people of working age, the choice of where you live depends on your place of work: whether due to promotion, change of career, redundancy, whatever, the work you do determines where you live.

Working in the Highlands

If you're contemplating moving to the Highlands, it is unlikely to be because your job is taking you there, it will be first and foremost because you want to live there. In that case, where you live determines the work you do. The general belief is that there isn't much work in remote Highland communities. There are two questions asked of many incomers by their friends and family: what are you going to do with yourselves? And what are you going to live on? The truth of the matter, as they quickly discover, is that the opportunities for work are numerous. But don't necessarily expect a 'career' – 9am to 5pm and weekends off for the rest of your life until you collect your pension. That isn't an option; to be honest, nowadays it doesn't happen so much in urban areas either. The nature of work has changed everywhere.

Outside the bigger towns, few Highlanders have one full-time job. Most have a number of different means of earning money which together bring them a living wage, sometimes a mixture of employment and self-employment. It's a noticeable feature of the way of work there that it's a fairly common practice to switch jobs completely for a change or a rest – from car mechanic to tanker driver, insurance salesman to car salesman, plumber to fisherman.

Few crofters can survive on the income from their croft alone. A common pattern is for the crofter to augment it by working for a local builder, for instance, while his wife works part-time in a shop and offers bed and breakfast during the holiday season. Their neighbour rents out a holiday cottage and produces paintings which she sells through craft shops across the Highlands.

A similar pattern is evident in the working practices of the non-crofters. Clare O'Brien is a freelance writer who sells articles and short stories to a wide range of magazines and newspapers, and who also teaches creative writing on a correspondence course. The company that runs the course is based in Manchester, she works in Wester Ross, her students (over a thousand at the last count) come from as far away as Kenya, Australia and Singapore as well as many nearer home. A few miles down the road lives Anne Solomito, a freelance indexer who also classifies academic journal articles for an internet database, produces organic vegetables and is looking into converting her steading to a bunkhouse for tourists. Across the loch Tom Lister the postman runs a vital sideline as a computer supplier and fixer, providing a lifeline service for those working from home – advice at the end of a phone when your computer's crashed and there's a deadline round the corner is essential. Come the summer season all the hotels in the area are advertising for staff, and whenever the tide's low enough, there are always a few people down on the shore collecting whelks for sale to the continental markets which can't get enough of them.

This is just a sample of the variety of ways you can make money. You may have a business that's readily transferable to the area, like Ric Holmes, who moved his sailing school from Lancashire in England to Wester Ross in the Highlands. Or you may have a skill that could be the basis of a business, such as Jill Holmes, his partner, a talented artist who sells her work locally and internationally.

Clare O'Brien found that this way of life suited exactly what she was searching for when she moved to the Highlands
My main reason for moving was my wish to find a more integrated lifestyle where our family could live and work together rather than on different, sharply delineated careers. I now describe myself as a jack of all trades: journalist, editor, teacher, crofter, horticulturist, craft-worker, mother. Not necessarily in that order.

But even if you've worked all your life in administration in a multi-national company, feel seasick if you look at a boat and don't have an artistic bone in your body, don't immediately think 'there's nothing I could do'. With a little lateral thinking, you too can come up with a cracking business idea – which may end up creating employment for other people.

Janis MacLean did just that, setting up practically overnight a highly successful business called 'Highland Wedding Belles'. Through the use of the internet and a home computer she began to organise Highland weddings for clients across the world, arranging weddings large and small, formal and informal, in venues as diverse as castles and lighthouses. Less than a year on it was a phenomenal success and she 'gave up her day job' to concentrate on the weddings full time, soon finding the need to employ part time help. All this was sparked off by being asked to witness the wedding of a German couple at a Highland registry office.

Alternatively, you can train to do something new, from the comfort of your own home (either before or after you move). There are correspondence courses in all sorts of fields – maybe you could tutor on one? The University of the Highlands and Islands is both a potential source of employment for those with the right background and a means of acquiring new areas of knowledge needed to bring your brilliant business idea to pass. Linking students and centres of learning throughout the Highlands and Islands, it makes use of computer and video technology to deliver education to the remotest parts.

Tourism is one of the main industries of the Highlands. When you look at the scenery, it's easy to see why. Visitors come from around the world to stay there. There are few Highlanders who are not connected with or affected by tourism in one way or another. Whether they work in the hotels or the shops, run a B&B or a self-catering cottage, take visitors on boat trips or guided walks, a proportion of their income between April and October is likely to come from the tourists.

RESIDENCE & WORK REGULATIONS

If you enter the UK as an employee, you may need a work permit in addition to your entry clearance or visa. There are, however a number of groups of people who do not need a permit to work in the UK.

Permit-Free Employment

EEA nationals have the right to travel for the purposes of work between all member countries. They do not require any formal permission to enter the UK and there is no time limit put on their stay. Once here, they are free to stay to work or set up in business and do not need to apply for permission to do so at any time. However, if they wish, they may obtain a 'residence permit' from the Home Office as confirmation of their right of residence in the UK. It is not compulsory, but it is an official document which will prove the individual's identity and immigration status in the UK.

This is particularly useful if you wish to apply for permanent settlement in the UK. After four years, during which the applicant has been working or doing business for most of that time, an EU national may apply for permanent settlement. A residence permit can be useful proof that they are entitled to apply, but proof of continuous employment in the UK for four years may be sufficient to obtain settlement status.

Commonwealth citizens over 17 and with a grandparent born in the UK, are granted entry for a period of four years on arrival in the UK and do not need a work permit. This means that they can seek employment once they arrive.

In addition, there is no requirement for a work permit for those whose employment falls into one of the following categories: a working holidaymaker or au pair; a Minister of religion, a missionary or a member of a religious order; the representative of an overseas firm with no branch or subsidiary in the UK; a representative of an overseas newspaper, news agency or broadcasting organisation on long term assignment to the UK; a teacher or language assistant coming to a UK school under an exchange scheme; a member of the operational ground staff of an overseas airline; a postgraduate doctor or dentist coming for training; a seasonal worker at an agricultural camp; writers, composers and artists; an overseas government employee; a science or engineering graduate; dependants of the above.

Working Holidaymakers

The working holidaymaker scheme allows Commonwealth citizens between 17 and 27 to come to the UK for up to two years. This is classed as an extended holiday, and they may help to fund it by working. To qualify you must either be unmarried, or married to a working holidaymaker who is taking the holiday with you. Eligible employment is classed as that which is 'incidental to a holiday'.

A working holidaymaker may engage in some part-time study and short periods of full-time study while in the UK, but not engage in business or pursue a career.

Au Pairs

Au pairs may stay up to two years, living and working with a resident family. They must be aged between 17 and 27, be unmarried and have no dependants, be taking up a pre-arranged placement and be a national of one of the following countries: Andorra, Bosnia-Herzegovina, Bulgaria, Croatia, Faroe Islands, Greenland, Macedonia, Monaco, Romania, San Marino, Turkey. Although European Economic Area nationals are not included in the au pair scheme, they are free to come to the UK to take au pair placements. Further details regarding the immigration rules and regulations can be found in *Residence & Entry Regulations*.

Work Permits

Work permits are issued by Work Permits (UK), part of the Immigration & Nationality Directorate, in relation to a specific individual and a particular job.

Generally, work permits are only issued for jobs involving a high level of skill and experience for which no resident labour is available in the UK or elsewhere in the European Union. An exception may be made to enable overseas nationals to come to the UK for training or work experience.

Work permits are normally issued for a limited period of between six months and four years. The permit may be extended after this time if the employment continues. Permit holders may be allowed to settle in the UK once they have completed four years' continuous employment.

An individual cannot apply for a work permit on their own behalf. This has to be done by an employer in the UK who wants to employ you. Application forms are available from Immigration & Nationality Directorate, Lunar House, 40 Wellesley Road, Croydon CR9 2BY; ☎0870-606 7766. They can also be downloaded from www.workingintheuk.gov.uk.

Alternatively, you can apply via www.workpermit.com. They make an additional charge for this service, but they will advise and guide you through the application process. You cannot travel to the UK to start work before you have received the permits, so your intended employer should apply for a permit at least eight weeks before you are to start work – it normally takes between one and two months for an application to be processed. You will be refused admission to the country if you arrive to take up your employment without a valid work permit. If you are a 'visa national', as described in *Residence & Entry Regulations*, you will need a visa in addition to your work permit, and the visa will not be issued until you have your work permit.

Those people who are admitted as work permit holders are normally allowed to settle in the UK on completion of four years' continuous employment in that capacity.

There are other conditions a work permit holder must satisfy in order to be allowed to enter the UK. These include being able to maintain and accommodate themselves without recourse to public funds. Where a work permit is valid for twelve months or less the holder must demonstrate that they intend to leave at the end of the period of employment. As a work permit is only valid for one specific job, the holder must also show they have no intention to take any other job than that for which the permit has been issued.

Full Work Permit. This is usually granted to employ high level executives and managers, or those with scarce technical skills, which are not readily available in the UK or EU. The job would normally be one that requires at least two years' post-qualification work experience in addition to a degree or a degree-level professional or technical qualification.

A work permit will only be granted if the employer is intending to pay the normal rate for the job in the UK. They are seldom granted for positions paying an annual salary of less than £20,000 (about US$30,000).

Usually the spouse of a work permit holder will be automatically granted leave to take up employment. This leave is not job-specific so the spouse may change jobs without an application to the Department for Education and Employment.

Permits for Entertainers, Sports People and Models. These have their own less stringent category of work permit because most people in this category work on an international level, and they therefore do not normally wish to make their permanent home in the UK. In some circumstances, particularly where they are entering the UK for six months or less, it may not be necessary to apply for a permit.

Keyworker Permits. These are granted to those who have language, cultural or culinary knowledge which is rare in the UK. They are often used for hotel or restaurant managers, head chefs, highly skilled waiting staff and senior hotel receptionists. Keyworker permits will not generally be granted nor extended for more than three years so they do not lead to permanent residence status.

Training Permits

These enable people from abroad to enter the UK for up to three years to receive on-the-job training which is not readily available to them in their own country and which will be of use there. Such training should normally lead to a recognised professional qualification or, in exceptional circumstances, to a valuable occupational skill.

Candidates for training permits must be between 18 and 54 years old and have the necessary educational or professional experience to benefit from the training. The training must be provided by the employer who applies for the training permit, it must be for a minimum of 30 hours per week and the wages must be at the normal rate for such training.

After the training is completed the individual must spend at least two years outside the UK before they are eligible for a full work permit.

Work Experience Scheme This is similar to the training permit, but a permit under this scheme is normally granted for a maximum of one year. The candidate must be between 18 and 35 and have the necessary educational, professional or job experience to benefit from the work experience given. The employment must be surplus to the normal needs of the employer and only pocket money or a maintenance allowance can be paid.

Useful Addresses

Further information and personalised advice regarding work permits can be obtained from *Work Permit.com,* 11 Bolt Court, Fleet Street, London EC4A 3DQ; ☎020-7842 0800; fax 020-7353 0100; www.workpermit.com. Their website is full of useful information including online assessments which will help you and your prospective employer decide whether you are likely to obtain a visa and/or a work permit in your circumstances.

UK Visaswebsite gives useful summaries of the immigration regulations. www. ukvisas.gov.uk.

Accommodation

Any entrant to the UK, under any category, must be able to demonstrate they have adequate accommodation when they arrive and, in many cases, that they can support themselves without recourse to public funds. The exception to this latter condition is EEA nationals, who under a pan-European agreement are usually eligible to claim state benefits if they are 'habitually resident' in the UK.

It should also be remembered, when applying for most jobs in the UK, a permanent residence address is a prerequisite, so this must be a priority when considering a move to Scotland.

SKILLS & QUALIFICATIONS

When moving to the UK to take up a job with a work permit, you must have proof that you have the skills and qualifications appropriate for that job. Although your qualifications may be recognised for that kind of job in your home country, it cannot necessarily be assumed that they will be recognised in the UK, so you and your potential employer need to ascertain whether they are acceptable or whether further examinations or training periods need to be taken. Because there exists such a wide range of courses and diplomas, academic, professional and vocational, each qualification obtained in another country will be looked at on a case by case basis to see how it compares with those in the UK.

EU/EEA Nationals

Within Europe, academic qualifications will be assessed through the auspices of the National Academic Recognition Information Centres (NARICs) which have been set up in all member states to co-ordinate the drawing up of certificates for the academic recognition of diplomas.

As far as professional and vocational training are concerned, the EU has passed directives to ensure that these qualifications, plus practical experience, gained in one member country are considered valid throughout the EEA. This is achieved through a system of compensatory measures to take into account the differences in length and content of the courses. As a general rule, this means that if your training was much shorter or the content of your course was very different to that required in the UK, you would be asked to pass an aptitude test or to undergo a period of supervised practice.

For a number of professions, training requirements in all member states have been harmonised, which means that your national qualifications should be recognised automatically in any other EU country, allowing you to practice there.

These professions are doctors, general practitioners, dental practitioners, nurses, midwives, veterinary surgeons, architects, pharmacists and lawyers.

Mutual recognition of other professional qualifications within the EU is also made in respect of 'regulated' professions (i.e. those whose practice is regulated by law, Government regulations, private chartered bodies or professional associations) which require the completion of a higher education course of at least three years, or the equivalent part-time duration, at a university or other higher education establishment. Any professional training required in addition to the education course should also have been completed.

In the UK, regulated professions include lawyers, accountants, engineers, teachers, surveyors, physiotherapists, chemists, technologists, geologists, psychologists and shipbrokers. Where the education and training in the home country is at least one year shorter than that required in the UK, the professional organisation or authority regulating the profession may require additional practical experience of up to four years as a fully-qualified professional. Where the content of the course was very different you may be required to take an aptitude test covering the main subjects not covered by your training. Alternatively, you may be required to follow a period of supervised practice of up to three years.

In the case of other qualifications and diplomas obtained in regulated professions, all member states must recognise these, together with professional experience in the home country, although aptitude tests and periods of supervised practice may be required.

A number of jobs and trades are also recognised by EU member states, if the candidate can demonstrate professional experience elsewhere in the EU. In such cases, a Certificate of Experience can be issued by the home country showing that the individual has practical experience of between three and six years. These include self-employed work in the wholesale trade, in the manufacturing, processing, repair and construction industries, in providing food, drink or accommodation, in the wholesale coal trade, and in services relating to transport, travel agencies, storage and warehousing. Itinerant traders, insurance agents and brokers, hairdressers and those involved in various fishing, transport, post and telecommunications, recreational and community services can also be issued a Certificate of Experience.

Useful Resources

A series of guides is available from 'Citizens First', a programme established by the European Commission. They can be viewed on the Citizens First website at http://europa.eu.int/citizensrights. This is an excellent resource, containing a wide range of information in many European languages on all aspects of living, working and studying in other EU countries.

For further details about professional qualifications, contact the relevant professional body in your own country or in the UK. For a list of regulated professions and details of the relevant regulatory authority contact the *Department of Trade & Industry* DTI Enquiry Unit, 1 Victoria Street, London SW1H OET; ☎020-7215 4648; www.dti.gov.uk.

To apply for a Certificate of Experience, contact the Chamber of Commerce in your home country. There may be a processing fee. In the UK, this is around £80.

Scottish Chambers of Commerce: 30 George Square, Glasgow G2 1EQ; ☎0141-204 8316; fax 0141-221 2336; www.scottishchambers.org.uk.

Nationals of Other Countries

There are no international standard agreements between the UK and countries outside Europe, so each case will be looked at and advice given on an individual basis. This service is provided to international students inquiring on their own behalf by the UK NARIC (National Academic Recognition Information Centre). Independent enquirers should forward a photocopy of their qualification certificate(s) together with transcript(s), a translation in English if necessary and a covering letter to NARIC.

Advice on the comparability of qualifications is normally given free of charge, but if an additional certificate of comparability is required it will cost £35.25. There is lots of free information on their website www.naric.org.uk.

This free service does not extend to universities or business organisations. These bodies should apply to join the UK NARIC Subscription Service.

Useful Address

UK NARIC: Oriel House, Oriel Road, Cheltenham, Gloucestershire, GL50 1XP; ☎0870-9904088; fax 0870-990 1560; www.naric.org.uk.

Further details on the requirements for certain professions and occupations in Scotland can be found below in the section *Permanent Work*.

PROFESSIONAL AND TRADE BODIES IN SCOTLAND

Advice on the requirements of specific professions may also be obtained from their Professional Associations. This is a selection of the professional and trade bodies for Scotland. A fuller list can be found in *Whitaker's Scottish Almanack* published by A&C Black Ltd.

Professional Bodies

Association of Chartered Certified Accountants: 83 Princes Street, Edinburgh EH2 2ER; ☎0131-247 7510; fax 0131-247 7514; www.accaglobal.com.

Association for Management Education and Training in Scotland (AMETS): c/o Cottrell Building, University of Stirling, Stirling FK9 4LA; ☎01786-467364.

Booksellers Association: Milngavie Bookshop, 37 Douglas Street, Milngavie, Glasgow G62 6PE; ☎0141-956 4752; www.booksellers.org.uk.

British Hospitality Association (Scottish Office): Saltire Court, 20 Castle Terrace, Edinburgh EH1 2EN; ☎0131-200 7484; fax 0131-228 8888; www.bha.online.org.uk.

British Medical Association (Scottish Office): 14 Queen Street, Edinburgh EH8 1LL; ☎0131-662 4820; fax 0131-247 3001; www.bma.org.uk.

British Veterinary Association: SAC Veterinary Science Division, Mill of Crabstone, Aberdeen AB21 9TB; ☎01224-711177; fax 01224-711184; www.bva.co.uk.

Chartered Institute of Bankers in Scotland: Drumsheugh House, 38B Drumsheugh Gardens, Edinburgh EH3 7SW; ☎0131-473 7777; fax 0131-473 7788; www.ciobs.org.uk.

Chartered Institute of Marketing: 3rd Floor, 100 Wellington Street, Glasgow G2 6DH; ☎0141-221 7700; fax 0141-221 7766; www.cim.co.uk.

Chartered Society of Designers (Scottish Branch): Randal Design, 90 Mitchell Street, Glasgow G1 3NQ; ☎0141-221 2142; www.csd.org.uk.

Confederation of British Industry Scotland: 16 Robertson Street, Glasgow G2 8DS; ☎0141-332 8661; fax 0141-333 9135; www.cbi.org.uk.

Faculty of Advocates: Advocates Library, Parliament House, Edinburgh EH1 1RF; ☎0131-226 5071.

Federation of Civil Engineering Contractors: CECA (Scotland), Enterprise House, Springkerse Business Park, Stirling FK7 7UF; ☎01786 430007; fax 01786 461479; www.ceca.co.uk/regions/scots/asp.

Federation of Master Builders: 11 Mentone Gardens, Edinburgh EH9 2DJ; ☎0131-667 5888; fax 0131-667 5488; www.fmb.org.uk.

Federation of Small Businesses: 74 Berkeley Street, Glasgow G3 7DS; ☎0141-221 0775; fax 0141-221 5954; www.fsb.org.uk.

Freight Transport Association: Hermes House, Melville Terrace, Stirling FK8 2ND; ☎01786-457500; fax 01786-450412; www.fta.co.uk.

General Teaching Council for Scotland: Clerwood House, 96 Clermiston Road, Edinburgh EH12 6UT; ☎0131-314 6000; fax 0131-314 6001; www.gtcs.org.uk.

Institute of Chartered Accountants of Scotland: CA House, 21 Haymarket Yards, Edinburgh EH12 5BH; ☎0131-3470100; fax 0131-347 0105; www.icas.org.uk.

Institute of Chartered Foresters: 7A Colme Street, Edinburgh EH3 6AA; ☎0131-225 2705; fax 0131-220 6125; www.charteredforesters.org.

Institution of Engineers and Shipbuilders in Scotland: Clydeport Building, 16 Robertson Street, Glasgow G2 8DS; ☎0141-248 3721; fax 0141-221 2698; www.iesis.org.

Law Society of Scotland: 26 Drumsheugh Gardens, Edinburgh EH3 7YR; ☎0131-226 7411; fax 0131-225 2934; www.lawscot.org.uk.

National Farmers Union of Scotland: The Rural Centre, West Mains, Ingliston, Newbridge, Midlothian EH28 8LT; ☎0131-472 4000; fax 0131-472 4010; www.nfus.org.uk.

Offshore Contractors' Association: 58

Queens Road, Aberdeen AB15 4YE; ☎01224-326070; fax 01224-326071; www.oca-online.co.uk.

Professional Association of Teachers (Scotland): 4-6 Oak Lane, Edinburgh EH12 6XH; ☎0131-317 8282; fax 0131-317 8111; www.pat.org.uk.

Royal College of General Practitioners Scotland: 25 Queen Street, Edinburgh EH2 1JX; ☎0131-260 6800 fax 0131-260 6836; www.rcgp-scotland.org.uk.

Royal College of Nursing: 42 South Oswald Road, Edinburgh EH9 2HH; ☎0131-662 1010; fax 0131-662 1032; www.rcn.org.uk/scotland.

Royal Incorporation of Architects in Scotland: 15 Rutland Square, Edinburgh EH1 2BE; ☎0131-229 7545; fax 0131-228 2188; www.rias.org.uk.

Royal Institution of Chartered Surveyors in Scotland: 9 Manor Place, Edinburgh EH3 7DN; ☎0131-225 7078; fax 0131-240 0830; www.rics-scotland.org.uk.

Royal Pharmaceutical Society: 36 York Place, Edinburgh EH1 3HU; ☎0131-556 4386; fax 0131-558 8850; www.rpsgb.org.uk.

Scottish Committee of Optometrists: 7 Queens Buildings, Queensferry Road, Rosyth, Fife KY11 2RA; ☎01383-419444; fax 01383-416778.

Scottish Fishermen's Organisation: 601 Queensferry Road, Edinburgh EH4 6EA; ☎0131-339 7972; fax 0131-339 6662; www.scottishfishermen.co.uk.

Scottish Grocers Federation: 222-224 Queensferry Road, Edinburgh EH4 2BN; ☎0131-343 3300; fax 0131-343 6147; www.scottish-grocers-federation.co.uk.

Scottish Print Employers' Association: 48 Palmerston Place, Edinburgh EH12 5DE; ☎0131-220 4353; fax 0131-220 4344; www.spef.org.uk.

Scottish Publishers Association: Scottish Book Centre, 137 Dundee Street, Edinburgh EH11 1BG; ☎0131-228 6866; fax 0131-228 3220; www.scottishbooks.org.

Society of Indexers (Scottish Group): Bentfield, 3 Marine Terrace, Gullane, E. Lothian EH31 2AY; ☎/fax 01620-842247; www.socind.demon.co.uk.

Society of Law Accountants in Scotland: Johnstone House, 52-54 Rose Street, Aberdeen AB10 1HA; www.solas.co.uk.

Society of Scottish Artists: 4 Barony Street, Edinburgh EH3 6PE; ☎0131-557 2354; www.s-s-a.org.

Trade Unions

Trade Unions may also be able to provide useful information. Again, a full list may be found in Whitaker's Scottish Almanack or from the Scottish Trades Union Congress (STUC).

Scottish Trades Union Congress: 333 Woodlands Road, Glasgow G3 6NG; ☎0141-337 8100; fax 0141-337 8101; www.stuc.org.uk.

AMICUS: John Smith House, 145-146 West Regent Street, Glasgow G2 4RZ; ☎0141-248 7131; fax 0141-221 3898; www.amicustheunion.org.

Associated Society of Locomotive Engineers and Firemen (ASLEF): 70 Tantallon Garden, Muireston, Livingston

EH54 9AT; ☎01506-419641; fax 01506-412239; www.aslef.org.uk.

Association of University Teachers (Scotland): 6 Castle Street, Edinburgh EH2 3AT; ☎0131-226 6694; fax 0131-226 2066; www.aut.org.uk.

British Actors' Equity Association: 114 Union Street, Glasgow G1 3QQ; ☎0141-248 2472; fax 0141-248 2472; www.equity.org.uk.

Communication Workers Union: 2b Craigpark, Dennistoun, Glasgow G31 2NP; ☎0141-556 0159; fax 0141-554 8736; www.cwu.org.

Community and District Nursing Association: Westel House, 32-38 Uxbridge Road, London W5 2BS; ☎020-8280 5342; fax 020-8280 5341.

Educational Institute of Scotland (EIS): 46 Moray Place, Edinburgh EH3 6BH; ☎0131-225 6244; fax 0131-220 3151; www.eis.org.uk.

GMB: (Britain's General Union), Fountain House, 1-3 Woodside Crescent, Glasgow G3 7YJ; ☎0141-332 8641; fax 0141-332 4491; www.gmb.org.uk.

Prospect: (Union of Engineers, Scientists. Managers and Specialists), 18 Melville Terrace, Stirling FK8 2NQ; ☎01786-465999; fax 01786-465516; www.prospect.org.uk.

Musicians' Union: 11 Sandyford Place, Sauchiehall Street, Glasgow G3 7NB; ☎0141-248 3723; fax 0141-204 3510; www.musiciansunion.org.uk.

National Association of Schoolmasters/ Union of Women Teachers (NASUWT): 6 Waterloo Place, Edinburg EH1 3BG; ☎0131-523 110; fax 0131-523 1119; www.teachersunion.org.uk.

National Union of Journalists (NUJ): 3rd Floor, 114 Union Street, Glasgow G1 3QQ; ☎0141-248 6648; fax 0141-248 2473; www.nuj.org.uk.

Transport and General Workers' Union (TGWU): 290 Bath Street, Glasgow G2 4LD; ☎0845-345 0141 fax 0141-332 6157; www.tgwu.org.uk.

Union of Construction, Allied Trades and Technicians (UCATT): 53 Morrison Street, Glasgow G5 8LB; ☎0141-420 2880; fax 0141-420 2881; www.ucatt.org.uk.

Union of Shop, Distributive and Allied Workers (USDAW): Muirfield, 342 Albert Drive, Glasgow G41 5PG; ☎0141-427 6561; fax 0141-419 1029; www.usdaw.org.uk.

UNISON: Unison House, 14 West Campbell Street, Glasgow G2 6RX; ☎0870-777 7006; fax 0141-331 1203; www.unison-scotland.org.uk.

SOURCES OF JOBS

Employment Service

The UK Employment Service runs Jobcentres which can be found in most towns in Scotland. Here you will find advertisements for a wide range of job vacancies in that area. You can also register your details with the Jobcentre, who should then ensure that you are sent details of any relevant new vacancies as they arise. Employers may advertise jobs for free in Jobcentres, so it is a good place to start job-hunting if you are already in Scotland.

Useful Addresses

The address of your local Jobcentre will be in the local Phone Book or Yellow Pages, or contact *The Employment Service:* Argyll House, 3 Lady Lawson Street, Edinburgh EH3 9SD; ☎0131 221 4000; fax 0131 221 4004; www.jobcentreplus. gov.uk.

Job hunters from outside the country can contact the **Overseas Placing Unit** with their requirements and again you will be informed of any suitable vacancies as they arise. *European Employment Services (EURES), Overseas Placing Unit:* Rockingham House, 123 West Street, Sheffield S1 4ER.

Newspapers

Job vacancies are advertised in local and national newspapers. There are also some specific 'jobs newspapers'. One of the biggest is *Scottish Recruitment,* a weekly newspaper on sale throughout Scotland. It is a division of Scottish & Universal Newspapers Ltd, 38 Tay Street, Perth PH1 5TT; ☎01738-626211; fax 01738-643344.

Local and national newspapers often have a specific jobs supplement once a week, in some cases related to specific professions. The Times Educational Supplement (TES), for example lists teaching and academic vacancies, while the currently ubiquitous Internet supplements, to be found in many national newspapers, list IT vacancies.

Professional & Trade Publications

There are over 4,000 UK trade, technical and professional publications, which are a good place to look for job vacancies in specific fields. Names and addresses of these publications can be found in *Willings Press Guide* and *Benn's Media Directory,* which are available in libraries. There are also many so-called 'news-stand' magazines aimed at a more general readership, some of which include job advertisements. If your experience lies in the IT field, for example, take a look at the plethora of computer and internet publications; while photographers and videographers will find plenty of magazines dealing with their specialism. The main ones are listed in *Writers' & Artists' Yearbook* and *The Writers Handbook*. These can be purchased online through Amazon (www.amazon.com, or www. amazon.co.uk).

UK professional and trade bodies (see details above) should also be able to point you in the direction of publications carrying job vacancies.

The Internet

The newest, and a very effective, way of finding UK vacancies from abroad is, of course, the internet. There is a burgeoning number of websites including job databases searchable by type of job and/or geographical area. Some of them also allow you to input your own details, so you can be e-mailed about suitable vacancies as they arise, and so that potential employers may even come direct to you.

Here is just a selection of sites dealing specifically with Scottish vacancies. Not surprisingly, the vast majority of the jobs are in Glasgow, Edinburgh and the Central Belt. Jobs in the Highlands and Islands are few and far between on these websites:

www.edinburghguide.com. From the home page, go to 'Business' then to 'Recruitment'.
www.scottish-recruitment.co.uk.
www.s1jobs.com.

There are a number of employment newsgroups which are also worth checking regularly for suitable opportunities:

scot.jobs
alt.jobs.uk.jobsearch
uk.jobs
uk.jobs.contract
uk.jobs.offered

Employment Agencies

Private employment agencies take on the job of matching job vacancies to applicants. Some deal with general vacancies, some specialising in temporary workers to cover for holiday, sickness and maternity vacancies at short notice, (generally known as Temp Agencies) and others deal with recruitment in specific areas, such as IT, professional and executive posts.

One of the biggest UK employment agencies is Manpower Employment Services, which has branches throughout the country (website www.manpower. co.uk):

Aberdeen: Langstane House, 1-4 Dee Street, Aberdeen AB11 6DR; ☎01224-210320.
Dundee: 45 Reform Street, Dundee DD1 4ER; ☎01382-227491.
East Kilbride: 109 Strathmore House, East Kilbride G74 1LF; ☎01355-

237656.

Edinburgh: 38 George Street, Edinburgh EH2 2LE; ☎0131-226 5591.

Glasgow: 46 Gordon Street, Glasgow G1 3PU; ☎0141-226 4291.

Grangemouth: Manpower House, Station Road, Grangemouth FK3 8DG; ☎01324-485088.

There are many employment agencies which only advertise jobs in the local area, others which specialise in specific types of job. This is a selection from around the country:

Best International Group: Capital Buildings, St Andrew Square, Edinburgh EH2 2AD; ☎0131-5557 4477; fax 0131-524 9090; www.best-international.com. Information Technology recruitment specialists.

Chefs in Scotland: 2 Wentworth Street, Portree, Skye IV51 9EJ; ☎01478-613527; fax 01478-612291; www.chefsinscotland.co.uk.

Global Highland Recruitment: 19 Academy Street, Inverness IV1 1JN; ☎01463 725400; fax 01463 235246; www.globalhighland.com.

Medic Recruitment Ltd: Banchory Business Centre, Burn O'Bennie Road, Banchory AB31 5ZU; ☎01330-826508; fax 01330-820670.

Morson Human Resources Ltd: 17 Rose Street, Thurso; ☎01847-892888.

Orion Engineering Services Ltd: Castleheather, Inverness; ☎01463-230860.

Quality Link Recruitment: 133-135 Morrison Street, Edinburgh EH3 8AJ; ☎0131-229 4208/9; fax 0131-229 2580; and The Pentagon Centre, 36 Washington Street, Glasgow G3 8AZ; ☎0141-229 4208/2580; fax 0141-229 2580; www.quality-link.co.uk. Hospitality and catering, sales and secretarial recruitment specialists.

Select Training & Recruitment: 93 Irish Street, Dumfries; ☎01387-266755.

Techni-Pro (Scotland) Ltd: 64a Union Street, Broughty Ferry, Dundee; ☎01382-730033.

Vital Resources: 35a Union Street, Aberdeen AB11 5BN; ☎01224-588889; www.vitalresources.co.uk. Engineering, construction and rail recruitment specialists.

Details of local and national agencies can be found in the Yellow Pages or on the internet – most of them now have websites. You can search Yellow Pages at www.yell.com.

Talking Pages is a telephone service which will give lists of specific services by geographical area. Freefone 0800-600 900.

Business Pages is a specialist regional business to business directory – but as the region in question covers the whole of Scotland it is well worth obtaining. To order a copy ☎0800-671444.

Company Transfers

Although companies seldom recruit with the idea of international transfer in mind, it may be worth applying for a job in your home country which has branches or subsidiaries in Scotland. If the idea of working in Scotland is one you hope to pursue via the company it may be worth discussing at the initial interview. Then at least both sides know where they stand. Multinational companies with offices or subsidiaries in Scotland can be found in directories of companies such as *Who Owns Whom*, available in libraries. Some are listed at the end of this chapter in the *Directory of Major Employers*.

Job Wanted Ads

Another approach to try is to place advertisements in the Scottish press, ideally in the area(s) in which you would prefer to eventually live, detailing your qualifications and experience and the sort of job you are looking for. This gives employers the opportunity to approach you instead of vice versa.

The internet is becoming an effective alternative means of letting employers know you are in the job market. You can place your details on one of a number of databases, which can be searched by potential employers on the lookout for new talent.

APPLYING FOR A JOB

Application Forms & Letters

Generally, job advertisements will invite you to send for further details, which should include a fuller description of the job and the duties the jobholder will be expected to perform, together with details of the payment on offer, any additional benefits, such as a free car or the payment of travelling expenses, and any requirements (such as the need to hold a clean driving licence, for example).

It should also include instructions regarding how to submit your application and stating the last date applications can be accepted. You may be sent a printed application which you should fill in exactly as requested: block capitals in black ink may be specified for example, or they may state it should be typed. Alternatively, you may be asked for your curriculum vitae (usually abbreviated c.v.) together with a letter explaining why you want and/or are suited to the job on offer.

It is very important to follow the instructions to the letter – prospective employers are not impressed by candidates who cannot follow simple instructions precisely. One area in which individual quirks of the employers often display themselves is the covering letter: some insist on a hand-written letter while others will only look at a typed letter. Actually, where it is specified, that is easier than when you are left to guess which is going to go down better. In this case it is probably safest to type it as that is the normal procedure for a business letter in the modern age.

Until recently, applications were only acceptable if sent by post, but new technology is changing this. In some cases, applications may be faxed through, although you should only use this option if it is specified, because a long c.v. together with a covering letter can tie up a fax machine for an unacceptably long time. Small businesses in particular may not be pleased if this occurs. If for the sake of time – for example if it is close to the closing date for applications – it is best to check first whether a faxed application is acceptable to the company.

E-mail applications are becoming more widely encouraged, particularly within the IT sector, not surprisingly. Small businesses especially find that accepting applications by e-mail saves time and money. This applies equally to the applicants. Just as with paper applications, however, it is essential to follow instructions exactly.

If asked for a c.v. and supporting letter, you may be instructed to insert these into the body of an e-mail. Alternatively, you may be asked to send them as an attachment in a specified format. Ensure that you comply to the letter, because otherwise your documents may be unreadable on the receiving computer.

Curriculum Vitae

A c.v. is the equivalent of a résumé, but where a résumé is generally no more than couple of pages long, a c.v. may be much longer and contain a greater range of information. As well as your personal details such as name, address, date of birth, marital status, you should include your educational and employment history with dates. The more recent and most relevant jobs and/or qualifications should be described in more detail than the others. They should be listed chronologically, but there are two schools of thought as to whether the most recent should come first or last. If it is not stated on the application form, it really is down to personal preference.

In addition, a c.v. can include such things as your hobbies and interests, any volunteer or community work you have done, whether you are a member of a professional or other association, and anything else you have taken part in or achieved. What you include and what you leave out depends very much on the job applied for, so although the basic biographical details remain the same for most applications, to make your c.v. most effective you should reconsider the content for any particular application.

Make sure everything it includes is relevant and stated concisely while going into enough detail to impress the reader with your experience or skills. Personnel officers or interviewers with a large number of applications to assess are not prepared to wade through a lot of waffle, but equally the ones in which the applicant's personality and talents come through are going to stick in their minds.

It is perfectly acceptable to produce your own c.v., and computer software packages such as Microsoft Word make it easy with c.v. templates which lead you through the process step by step. There are also books which will give you step by step advice on how to write a sure-fire c.v. If you prefer to have yours professionally produced, c.v. writing services can be found in the classified adverts of newspapers and magazines and on the internet. However, some employers may not be impressed by this – it is, in the end, a fairly simple administrative task, so if you are reluctant to produce your own they may query this. If you do use a professional service, it is wise to ensure that the finished product does not betray its origin.

References

You will usually be asked to supply the names and contact details of a number of referees who can comment on your character in the work or social sphere. It could be a former employer, a teacher or professor, or a person with some status in the community such as your doctor or priest.

Generally, the referee(s) would only be contacted as a final double-check before offering you the job. They will be asked to either write a letter or fill in a form giving their opinion of your ability to do the job successfully.

Interview Procedure

Once your application has been received and processed, you may be invited for an interview. This invitation will probably come in the form of a letter, or possibly an e-mail, although it may be a phone call, which allows a mutually convenient time to be fixed for the interview. At the application stage, you may have been informed when the interviews would be taking place, so you could ensure you were available at that time.

If you are not to be invited for interview, you may be informed of that fact. However, very often, particularly where there have been a large number of applicants, you will hear nothing further.

Interview procedure varies from job to job, but usually it is a fairly formal situation with one or more interviewers asking questions of the interviewee across a desk. Although the dress code in some industries is becoming less strict, it is always wisest to dress formally for an interview, in suit and tie for men, suit for women, ideally with a skirt rather than trousers – this may not be politically correct, but it is expedient in case the interviewer is a traditionalist. Even if the general ethos of the company is to dress casually, you may not find this out until later and nobody can fault you for dressing 'up' for the interview – you can always dress down once you get the job.

Find out as much as you can about the company you will be working for in advance. It is important to show good knowledge of their activities in the interview.

Favourite questions at interview are those along the lines of 'why do you want this job?'; 'what are your key strengths and weaknesses?'; 'why should I employ you rather than another candidate?'; 'where do you see yourself in five years time?' It is as well to prepare answers for these sort of questions, as you can come across as tongue-tied, too modest or conceited if you have to answer them off the cuff.

You will generally be asked at the end of the interview if you have any questions you wish to ask – again, it can create a good impression if you've thought of some beforehand, so if you aren't asked, make sure you tell the interviewer you have some questions. Ask things like 'do you have any company information I can take away?', or 'could you describe a typical day in this position?' The danger of this can be that they've already told you these things during the course of the interview, or sent you information previously and you might come across as not paying attention – so it's as well to have more than one question prepared.

Often a decision will be made on the basis of your application and one interview. Where interviews of all candidates take place on the same day, you may be asked to wait for the successful candidate to be announced soon after the last interview. Or you may be free to leave after the interview, and will be informed later by telephone or letter if you've been successful. You should be informed also if you are not successful.

If you performed well at the first interview, you may be invited back for a second interview. This may take a similar form to the first one, but is more likely to be quite different in format. It is often used as an occasion to show the candidates still under consideration around the work premises. You may find that the employer wants to narrow the field more by seeing how the potential new employees interact with others and to find out more about their strengths and weaknesses. This can be done using a number of selection methods. Some favourite ones are as follows.

Group Discussion or Group Task. The candidates are asked to take part in a discussion, or perform a task or a problem-solving exercise, while being observed by a member of the selection panel. You may have a discussion topic given to you, or be able to choose from a number of topics – the way the individuals and the group as a whole interact during the process of decision and discussion will give an insight into their interpersonal skills.

Alternatively, the group may be asked to carry out a task, such as to build a model using material supplied, or to solve a problem by analysing information and deciding on a course of action. Whether you succeed or fail in the task is less important than the way you interact with the others. As so many jobs today stress 'working as a team', recruiters are interested in finding team players and identifying those who would be good as supportive team members and those who have leadership qualities within a group.

Oral Presentations. Each candidate is asked to prepare a talk to deliver to the other candidates and/or members of staff. You may be asked to prepare it in advance, or be given a period of time to prepare it on the day; it may be given to you or be on a subject of your own choice; it can vary in length from a few minutes to a quarter of an hour or more.

Written Presentations. The candidate is given a number of facts and statistics and asked to produce a written report with conclusions and a plan of action if appropriate. Again, this may be given to you to prepare and write in advance or on the day.

Psychometric Testing. Psychological tests designed to indicate the candidate's character, aptitudes and preferences have become very popular with personnel departments. They generally take the form of written tests, where the candidate is required to tick multiple choice answers to a series of questions.

If asked to sit a psychometric test as part of a selection process you should be briefed about the purpose of the test before you take it, be given some sample questions to do first, have the results of the test given to you in a private feedback session and be informed of company policy regarding distribution and storage of the results.

This sort of testing should never be used as the sole criterion on which a person's competence for a job is assessed. It should be just one of a number of different means of assessing the individual.

Useful Books & Websites
Writing a CV That Works, Paul McGee (How To Books 1997).
The Ultimate CV for Managers and Professionals, Rachel Bishop-Firth (How To Books 2000).
Passing That Interview, Judith Johnstone (How To Books 1999).
Resume Writing Services: www.free-resume-tips.com. Includes c.v. writing tips.
http://content.monster.com/ace/: Interview tips.
www.job-interview.net/: Information and advice.

ASPECTS OF EMPLOYMENT

WORKING PRACTICES

It is impossible to generalise about working practices throughout Scotland because they vary from place to place and industry to industry. However, the reputation of the British as somewhat work-shy, whether justified or unjustified in the past, is now far from the truth. There is a very strong work ethic, particularly within white collar occupations, and long working hours, above and beyond contractual obligations, are the norm in many areas. So much so that work-place stress seems to be endemic, with a high incidence of stress-related illness being reported. In occupations such as teaching and the police, there are record numbers of people applying for early retirement on the grounds of stress-related illnesses.

Connected with this, habitual lateness is frowned on, as is leaving work early, and is a justifiable reason for dismissal if carried to extremes. Long lunch hours too are generally disapproved of – although business lunches stretching long into the afternoon are part and parcel of certain executive positions. Flexi-time systems give workers control over when they work, within broad parameters, as long as they satisfy their contractual obligations of overall hours worked.

Factory and shift workers generally have far less leeway as regards arriving late for work and leaving early. Many of them will have to 'clock on' and 'clock off' at the beginning and end of the shift, so their hours of work are electronically recorded.

Tradespeople, such as plumbers and builders, have long had the reputation of being unreliable, not turning up when they say they will and charging high prices for minimal work. This is something which sadly doesn't seem to have changed. Consequently, the good, reliable tradesman who charges reasonably, is never short of work. It is a standing joke in the Highlands that builders in particular are harder to pin down than a will o' the wisp. Starting dates for construction work are notoriously fluid. On the whole, the reason for this is not that they are work-shy, but that they are extremely busy. They are reluctant to let any job go, so will agree to take on a project even at a time when they are busy on other jobs. They will get round to it eventually, but this is small comfort if you have a deadline to meet. However, on the plus side, if you have an emergency, they will deal with it quickly.

Traditionally, conservative formal dress – collar and tie for men, skirt or smart trousers for women – is expected in offices, although some companies, particularly within new industries such as IT, have loosened up in recent years, some following the US trend of having 'dress down Fridays'. Amongst the older age groups, however, such informality would tend to be frowned on. You are unlikely to be censured for dressing too smartly, whereas overly casual attire could affect your promotion prospects, even if your work is exemplary in other respects.

Generally, it is fine to address colleagues by their first names within the workplace, even where they are superior in position to yourself. However, in some offices you may find that the boss is addressed more formally, so be guided by what others in the office say and do.

Many workplaces now operate a no-smoking policy, because the law says that workers should be protected from discomfort caused by tobacco smoke. Smoking breaks may be allowed, with a special room set aside for those who need their dose of nicotine.

Friendships between work colleagues which spill over into social friendships are common, and sexual relationships between colleagues are acceptable as long as they do not affect the employees' work. The days when one half of a partnership would be moved elsewhere as a matter of course, are now gone. If such practices were to occur, an Employment Tribunal would almost certainly rule they were unlawful.

SALARIES

Most wages and salaries in Scotland are paid monthly (12 times a year), or sometimes four weekly (13 times a year), with payments generally being paid directly into bank accounts. The main exception to this will be at the lower end of the market, where manual labourers, shop and hotel workers and the like, as well as part-time workers, may be paid weekly, by cash. Casual labour may be paid cash in hand, which is a way some employers avoid certain aspects of employment legislation, so if you are offered this, make sure exactly what your safeguards are.

Average wages and salaries in Scotland are lower than the average for the UK as a whole. In 2003, average gross weekly adult earnings, before deductions for tax and National Insurance, were around £427 for Scotland, compared with £462 for the UK. Within the figures for Scotland there was quite a variation between the regions with Aberdeen, thanks to high paid offshore oil workers, heading the table at £504 per week with Edinburgh workers next, averaging £480. Lowest pay was in the Borders, at £346, while Highland region averaged £411. Because the Highland Council area is so large, covering rural, sparsely populated areas as well as the booming town of Inverness, there will be great variation within this last figure, with highest earnings doubtless being in Inverness.

These figures are averaged out over the whole range of full-time employment, so again there will be wide variation between the upper and lower rates paid within each area depending on the job. In 2004, graduate starting salaries averaged £18,500 across the UK.

Where a salary range is indicated in a job advertisement, it is negotiable on the basis of the applicant's previous experience. This is more commonly seen in jobs in the private sector. Public sector jobs, such as teaching, police, civil service and so forth, have set pay scales, with salaries paid at a set rate for a particular ranking of job with specified annual increments payable within that ranking. These pay scales are regularly renegotiated, and may be linked to the annual rate of inflation.

Salaries in the UK tend to be lower than those for equivalent jobs elsewhere in Europe and in the USA.

A **National Minimum Wage** came into force in the UK on 1st April 1999. In 2004, this was set at £4.85 per hour for workers aged 22 or over; £4.10 per hour for workers aged 18-21; and £3.00 per hour for those aged 16 & 17.

Benefits & Perks

The value of employment packages, especially in the higher paid and executive sectors, is often augmented by additional benefits, often called 'perks (perquisites) of the job'. These include such things as the provision of a company car for the sole use of the employee, or where this is not available, the payment of car allowance against travel made in one's own car; other expenses incurred in connection with the job may also be payable; private health insurance is sometimes offered as part of a salary and benefits package; where appropriate, a mobile phone or laptop may be provided; annual bonuses may be paid, either as a matter of course or on the basis of performance; commission is commonly payable in sales jobs depending on the numbers of new customers secured; in recent years, companies have begun offering share options to employees as part of a benefits package; occupations such as nursing and hotel work may include live-in accommodation, either free or at a subsidised rent.

These benefits and perks are usually taxable, although lump sum bonuses may be payable tax-free.

A SAMPLE OF JOBS ADVERTISED ON S1JOBS.COM DECEMBER 2004

Location	Job title	Salary
Edinburgh	Retail Branch Manager	£13,350
Perth & Kinross	Audit Supervisor	£30,000
Glasgow	Bank Financial Advisor	£24,000-£35,000
Stirlingshire	Social Worker	£19,632-£24,880
Borders	Engineer	£25,000-£27,000
Aberdeen	Chef de Partie	£14,000
Highlands	Chief Buyer – Construction	£30,000-£33,000
Orkney	Airport Manager	£38,000

Public Sector Salaries. In Scotland, teachers are paid on a six-point salary scale, with the entry point for individual teachers depending on their qualifications. Additional allowances are payable under certain circumstances. In 2003, teachers earned £18,000-£28,707, with school heads earning £36,414-£67,449.

In the same year, academic staff in universities were earning from £18,362 for an entry level lecturer, up to £43,968 for a senior lecturer. Head of Department salaries were £47,631-£53,761.

Basic rates of pay for police officers in 2003 were £18,666-£29,307 for a constable, rising to £58,242-£61,617 for a chief superintendent. Chief Constables received between £80,835 and £125,622 depending on the population of the police force area.

General Practitioners, dentists, optometrists and pharmacists are self-employed and work for the NHS under contract.

AVERAGE NHS SALARIES 2002

Consultant	£52,640-£68,505
Registrar	£25,920-£37,775
House Officer	£18,585-£32,520
GP	£66,280 (average intended net remuneration)
Nursing staff	£9,735-£32,760 (depending on grade)

WORKING HOURS, OVERTIME & HOLIDAYS

The hours worked by employees is regulated by the Working Time Regulations which came into force in October 1998 to implement the Working Time Directive of the European Parliament.

There is a limit of an average of 48 hours per week a worker can be required to work (although they can work longer if they wish to). Nightworkers can only be required to work up to an average of eight hours in every 24, and should receive free health assessments to ensue night working is not affecting their well-being. Workers also have rights to 11 hours rest each day, a day off each week, an in-work rest break if the working day is longer than six hours, and four weeks paid leave per year.

Young workers (those above the minimum school leaving age but below 18) have enhanced rights, including the right to two days off each week and longer statutory periods of rest.

Of course, employers can provide better conditions than these if they wish, and in many cases they do. Working hours vary depending on the type of industry as well as on individual employers and one's position in the company. In manufacturing industries the average working week is around 37.5 to 40 hours per week, while office workers are more likely to work between 35 to 38 hours per week. Traditionally, some employees in hospitals, security, catering and hotels have worked far longer hours, sometimes as many as 100 hours per week, but the recent working time regulations should have improved the conditions under which such people work.

Employees may find that their contract entitles them to five weeks' annual leave or more, although four weeks is the norm. During annual leave, the employee should be paid at their normal rate; where their normal hours include a regular amount of overtime, it may be that there is a requirement on the employer to pay them during holidays at their normal pay, which takes account of their average earnings where these generally include overtime.

The rules regarding overtime should be laid out in the contract of employment (see below). In general, working hours are a matter of agreement between employers and employees and their representatives, such as trade unions. Anything worked over these hours by blue-collar (e.g. factory or manual) workers would be paid as overtime, usually higher than the normal hourly rate, typically at time and a half or double time. In white collar jobs (e.g. office or executive) overtime may be compensated for by time off in lieu of the extra hours worked. This extra time off may be saved up and taken as a period of a day or more, depending on local agreements.

Many companies operate a flexi-time system, particularly in offices. This allows employees to vary their hours of work, as long as they are present between certain hours, known as 'core time'. They may prefer to start earlier and finish earlier, and to take a shorter lunch break than normal (although a minimum 30 minute lunch break is usually specified for legal reasons).

EMPLOYMENT CONTRACTS

Employers are required by law to give all employees taken on for periods of longer than one month a written statement of their main terms and conditions of employment. This must include the names of employee and employer, job title or brief job description, the date the employment begins, and the date it will end if it is for a fixed term. It must specify the amount of wages or salary plus the interval at which they are paid. It should also list the hours of work, amount of holiday entitlement and pensions entitlement. It should also include details of the employer's disciplinary rules and grievance procedures.

The written statement must be given to the employee within two months of starting work. If you think you are entitled to a written statement and have not been given one, you can refer the matter to an Employment Tribunal. These are legal bodies which deal with matters of employment law, redundancy, dismissal, contract disputes, sexual, racial and disability discrimination and related areas of dispute which may arise in the workplace.

Useful Address
Employment Tribunals: Central Office (Scotland), Eagle Building, 215 Bothwell Street, Glasgow G2 7TS; ☎0845-795 9775; www.employmenttribunals.gov. uk.

TERMINATION OF EMPLOYMENT

The written statement must state the entitlement of the employer and the employee to notice of termination of employment. The length of notice an employer must give depends on the length of time the employee has been continuously working for them. Normally, one month to two years' service requires one week's notice of dismissal; two years to 12 years' service requires 1 week's notice for each complete year; more than 12 year's service requires 12 weeks' notice. Sometimes a longer period may have been agreed in the contact of employment, in which case the longer period applies.

However, the employer needs to give a good reason for terminating the employment, it cannot just be on a whim. If the sacked employee feels they have been treated unjustly, they can take the matter to an employment tribunal who will make investigations and decide whether it is a case of unfair dismissal. For a dismissal to be fair, it must be because the employee is unable or unqualified to do the job, or that their conduct is unacceptable (such as a poor attendance record, for example) or that a legal requirement prevents them continuing to do the job (such as where a driver loses his/her licence) or because of redundancy (see below).

There are certain types of dismissal that are deemed to be automatically unfair. These include dismissal on the grounds of being – or not being – a trade union member, being pregnant or taking maternity leave, or for reasons relating to the national minimum wage or relating to the working time regulations.

Where an employment tribunal decides that an unfair dismissal has taken place, they may order the employer to re-employ the person, but more usually will order the employer to pay compensation to the individual.

Where notice of termination of employment has been given, the employee should be paid at their normal rate during the notice period, even if they are away on sick, holiday or maternity leave, or if they are willing to work but none is provided. If the correct notice is not given, the employee may seek damage from an employment tribunal or a civil court.

Redundancy

Where employees lose their jobs because the employer needs to cut jobs, move the place of work, or close down completely, they may be entitled to a lump sum payment called redundancy pay. Normally, the worker should have been continuously employed by that employer for two years or more to be entitled to redundancy pay. The amount payable is calculated on the worker's age, period of employment and weekly pay. If an employee does not receive redundancy pay to which they think they are entitled, the matter may be referred to an employment tribunal.

Rights of Part-time, Temporary & Seasonal Workers

In July 2000, the UK Government introduced new rights for part-time workers. The new regulations were designed to ensure that part-time workers are not treated less favourably than their full-time counterparts. Part-timers are entitled to the same hourly rate of pay, the same access to company pension schemes, the same entitlements to annual, maternity and parental leave on a pro rata basis, the same entitlement to sick pay and equal access to training as full-time workers in comparable jobs.

The Working Time Regulations and National Minimum Wage relate also to temporary and seasonal workers, and employers are also legally required to deduct tax and National Insurance from their wages, as well as making their part of the NI contribution. However, because of the administration and costs involved, many employers who want casual workers will avoid this legislation by paying strictly 'cash in hand'. In this case, the workers' employment rights are unlikely to be protected and there will probably not be any redress to an employment tribunal.

Short term casual work is just one form of temporary work. Jobs are often advertised on fixed term contracts, maybe because it is genuinely a project which will only last six months, or two years, or whatever. Sometimes jobs will be advertised in the form of 'six month contract in the first instance' which implies there is the likelihood of extending the contract at the end of that period. This gives both employer and employee the option of withdrawing easily after the first 'trial period'. In such cases, it is almost certain that the full letter of the employment laws will be complied with.

There is also a constant need for temporary staff to cover for staff absences caused by holidays, long term sickness or maternity leave. Many workers prefer to 'temp' in this way, moving from company to company for a few days or weeks at a time. Depending on their experience, temp rates can be good. There are employment agencies which specialise in finding and supplying temporary workers at short notice.

TRADE UNIONS & PROFESSIONAL ASSOCIATIONS

Workers in Scotland have the right to belong to a trade union relevant to their particular line of work, and it is unlawful for employers to penalise individuals for being – or, indeed, for not being – trade union members. Trade unions exist to represent the rights of employees, to ensure they have the most favourable conditions of work and levels of pay, and that they are not treated unreasonably or unfairly by their employers. Trade union members may ask to be represented by their trade union in any grievance with their employers.

The umbrella organisation for trade unions in Scotland is the Scottish Trades Union Congress (STUC), which in 2003 consisted of 46 unions with a combined membership of 630,000 together with 34 directly affiliated Trade Councils. The STUC helps its member unions to promote membership in new areas and industries and campaigns for rights at work for all employees, including part-time and temporary workers.

See *Professional and Trade Bodies in Scotland* for a selection of Scottish Trades Unions. For an exhaustive list contact STUC.

Those who have completed the required training and examinations will be entitled to join the association representing their trade or profession. Such associations will act, in a similar way to trade unions, to represent the rights and conditions of service of their members, as well as representing the profession as a whole at government level.

Many employers' associations are affiliated to the Confederation Of British Industry (CBI) which represents around 250,000 companies in Britain, and works to bring the problems of British business to the attention of the Government, which in turn consults it on relevant matters.

Near the beginning of this chapter is a selection of some of the main professional associations, employers' associations and trade associations in Scotland. For a full list contact CBI (Scotland).

TELEWORKING

Computers and the internet now allow employees to perform many of their duties from home or elsewhere, away from the central workplace, a process called teleworking. In 1994, the European Commission set a target of ten million teleworkers in Europe by 2000. By October 2002 there were 20 million, with one in ten people working from home more than once a week. Only two per cent worked from home on a full time basis.

There is wide variation between the take up of teleworking in different member states, with the UK coming low down the scale. In 2004, an estimated eight million people in the UK were working from home. Although there are no separate figures for Scotland, one would expect the majority of teleworkers to be based around London and the South East, so the Scottish percentage will be lower. The general pattern across Europe is similar, in that most teleworkers are male, and tend to be highly qualified, the majority qualified professionals.

It tends to be the larger companies with 250 employees or more which use teleworkers, with uptake figures significantly lower in small to medium companies. It is an interesting feature that teleworkers work longer hours than other workers. Almost half of regular teleworkers report an actual working week of more than ten hours longer than that specified in their contract of work, compared to only ten per cent of other workers.

The picture will vary throughout Scotland with, paradoxically, the biggest opportunities for teleworking as an employee in the main centres of population – rather than in the remote areas of the Highlands and Islands. However, there are significantly higher numbers of self-employed teleworkers, often one-man businesses, working from home offices in remote rural areas. (For more on this see *Starting A Business*).

There are some opportunities for employees to work from home, but despite claims of the 'teleworking revolution' being on the way, there is still little evidence of companies encouraging their staff to set up a computer at home and do most or all of their company work from there. There are signs of small steps in that direction – the Highland Council have indicated that they might look at the possibilities of having workers based away from their central offices – but it is likely to be some years before this comes to pass. At present, public administration ranks low for numbers of teleworking staff.

Scotland is a favourite place for company 'telephone call centres' due to the lower costs of property and wages compared with those in the south east of England, where so many companies are based. In Scotland as a whole, there are around 290 call centres, employing about 56,000 people, of which 30 per cent are in the finance sector. In the Glasgow area alone there are around 100 call centres at the time of writing, providing over 18,000 jobs. In the Highlands and Islands, around 400 jobs have been created in Call Centres in recent years.

Teleworking Websites
For further information on teleworking, see the following websites:
TCA (Telecottage Association): www.tca.org.uk.
Highland Telematics: www.teleworking.co.uk.
Gil Gordon Telecommuting: www.gilgordon.com.
Homeworking Information: www.homeworking.com.

INCOME TAX & NATIONAL INSURANCE

Employees are liable to pay income tax and National Insurance contributions, which are deducted at source so salaries and wages are paid net of these items. Low paid workers whose earnings are below the lower earnings limit are exempt from both income tax and NI. For full details of rates, see Daily Life.

Social Security and Unemployment Benefits
Low paid workers and those with family commitments and the like may be entitled to social security benefits in addition to their earnings from employment. The unemployed are entitled to 'Jobseeker's allowance' as long as they are actively looking for work. Entitlement to these may depend on the number of National Insurance contributions one has made. For full details see *Daily Life*.

WOMEN IN WORK

In Scotland in 2004, 67 per cent of women under 65 were working, compared to 79 per cent of men. Despite a growth in numbers of women in work every year, and although equal pay legislation was introduced in 1970, women in Scotland earn only 77 per cent of men's average weekly earnings. This is partly due to differences in types of work undertaken and working patterns of women and men. The majority of part-time workers are women, and generally in low paid jobs. 43 per cent of women and only 10 per cent of men worked part-time, while 236,000 women worked in administrative and secretarial jobs, compared with 61,000 men. But it cannot all be explained by type of work performed – female full-time employees earn on average only 84 per cent of the hourly earnings of male full-time employees. It may be that some of this difference is due to sex discrimination, which persuades women to apply for different types of work than they might otherwise if they could expect to be treated genuinely in the same way as men.

The Sex Discrimination Act, introduced in 1975, makes sex discrimination in employment unlawful, but there is still notable segregation in occupational areas between men and women. This, of course, is partly due to women's aspirations and proclivities, plus social attitudes about the 'right' sort of jobs for women. However, there is evidence that sexual discrimination occurs, with the Equal Opportunities Commission, Scotland, dealing with over 1,300 enquiries about sex discrimination annually, 30 per cent of these being treated as official complaints. In Scotland perhaps more than elsewhere in the UK, attitudes about 'women's work' and 'men's work' are still strong. Women predominate in the public administration and health sectors, distribution, hotels and catering, banking and finance. Men still dominate as managers in all sectors and in traditional industries such as construction, transport, motor trade, energy and water supply.

Maternity Benefits & Parental Leave

Expectant mothers may take 26 weeks' paid maternity leave, regardless of their length of service with their current employer. Those with one year of service or more may take additional unpaid leave of another 26 weeks. Some women may be entitled to pay during this period, depending on their employment contracts. Maternity leave can be taken from any time after the 11th week before the baby is due.

Fathers are entitled to one or two consecutive weeks' paid paternity leave after the birth of their child. The leave must be completed within 56 days of the birth of the child.

Mothers or fathers with children born or adopted after 15th December 1999 are entitled to 13 weeks' unpaid parental leave to care for the child up to its fifth birthday, or up to five years after the date of adoption, or the child's 18th birthday, whichever is the sooner. Parents of disabled children may take up to 18 weeks' leave up until the child's 18th birthday. Leave may be taken in individual days, weeks, one long block, as reduced working hours, or a mixture of these. Parents are also entitled to work flexibly if they have children under six or disabled children up to age 18.

Childcare

One of the biggest factors in preventing women working, or limiting the hours they can work, is the cost or lack of availability of childcare. As a result, women with children are less likely to be economically active than those without. In 2004, 69 per cent of women with dependent children were working, a figure which falls to 57 per cent of women with pre-school age children. Although some mothers make the choice not to work, as many as four out of five non-working mothers say they would work if they could afford and access the childcare of their choice.

The childcare problem is exacerbated in the case of lone parents, which overwhelmingly means single mothers – 24.5 per cent of families in Scotland are headed by lone parents, of which 93 per cent are single mothers. With no partner to share the childcare burden, and with low incomes, single mothers are often prevented from taking up employment or training which would give them the chance to increase their income level in the shorter or longer term; thus many single mothers are caught in the so-called 'poverty trap'. The position of lone mothers in Scotland is particularly bad compared with other parts of Europe; in France, 82 per cent of lone mothers are in work while in Sweden 70 per cent are employed. In Scotland, only 56 per cent of lone parents are in employment, a figure which leaps to 80 per cent for those with a baby. The Government has set a target of 70 per cent of lone parents in paid work by 2010.

Since the UK Government acknowledged that childcare provision in Scotland was inadequate and pledged to improve the situation by injecting an extra £30 million pounds into childcare between 1998 and 2003, there have been increases in provision. Now, every three and four year old is guaranteed a free nursery place. In 2004, 28 percent of children aged 0-14 were in formal childcare, a rise of seven per cent over the year before.

Many parents make informal arrangements for the care of their children, by asking a relative or neighbour to look after them while they work. This is usually the cheapest, and sometimes the most convenient, option.

For those who do not have family living nearby or who cannot call on friends or neighbours, there are a variety of options. Workplace nurseries are provided by some large employers, often with rates varying depending on the individual's salary level. For school-age children, after-school clubs take care of children after school and in the holidays. Younger children, from birth to five years of age, may be sent to private nurseries either full or part time. These must be registered with the local authority. This can be an expensive option, but some offer lower rates for a second child or for lone parents. Some parents prefer to send their children to a childminder who looks after children in their own home. Childminders must register with their local authority, which will check that their home meets safety standards and has good facilities for the care of children.

The average cost of a full-time nursery place is £136 per week, and after school care averages £26 for 5 sessions. An average playgroup session is £3.10 and a crèche place is £4.30.

Alternatively, parents choose to employ people to look after their children in their own home. Au pairs are young people from abroad who learn English while living in a family home and help with childcare and housework in exchange for their board and lodging. Another option is to employ a nanny who may live in the family home or not. The best nannies have childcare qualifications and are likely to be the most expensive option. The cost of a nanny can be lessened by sharing with another family.

As well as increasing the childcare provision available, the government has introduced a childcare tax credit which will help to pay for childcare costs for low and middle income families. Lone parents working at least 16 hours a week, or couples where both partners work at least 16 hours a week, are eligible for tax credits to cover up to 70 per cent on eligible costs of approved families up to a maximum of £94.50 per week for families with one child and £140 for families with two or more children.

Useful Addresses & Websites

Learning & Teaching Scotland: 74 Victoria Crescent Road, Glasgow G12 9JN; ☎08700-100297; www.ltscotland.org.uk. Lots of weblinks and educational resources.

Gaelic Playgroups Association, Comhairle nan Sgoiltean Araich (CNSA): 53 Church Street, Inverness IV1 1DR; ☎01463-225469; fax 01463 716 943.

Global Au Pairs and Nannies: Moorlands House, Oldfield Road, Bromley, Kent, BR1 2LE; ☎020-8467 6092; fax 020-8467 6121; www.au-pairs.co.uk.

Scottish Childminding Association: Suite 3, 7 Melville Terrace, Stirling FK8 2ND; ☎01786-445377; fax 01786 449062; www.childminding.org.

Scottish Out of School Care Network: Level 2, 100 Wellington Street, Glasgow G2 6DH; ☎0141-564 1284; fax 0141-564 1286; www.soscn.org.

Scottish Pre-school Play Association: Glasgow Office: ☎0141-227 3922; fax 0141-227 3923; www.sppa.org.uk. Has contact numbers for playgroups by local authority area.

PENSIONS

Many companies operate employee pension schemes. There is no obligation on employees to belong to such schemes, although generally they offer a better deal than a personal pension plan especially for an employee who stays with the same company until retirement. Where you change jobs, it may be possible to transfer the contributions made so far to another company scheme, or to a personal pension. In some cases, only the employer pays contributions to the pension fund in respect of employees, in which case it is termed a non-contributory scheme. More often both employer and employee make contributions, with on average employees paying around four per cent of their gross salary into a company pension fund, while employers make contributions of around eight or nine per cent.

Where employers do not provide an employee pension scheme, they may be legally obliged to provide access to a government-approved 'stakeholder pension'. Using their own money, together with tax relief and investment returns, employees can buy a pension which will give them a regular income for life when they retire. Stakeholder pension schemes are low-charge pensions meant for people who do not have access to an occupational pension or a good-value personal pension. There are a few exceptions to the requirement on employers to provide access to stakeholder pensions, mainly where very small companies are concerned.

Stakeholder Pension schemes have been designed to offer low charges, flexibility and security. They must also offer low minimum contributions of £20 or less and no transfer costs. They require tax approval from the Inland Revenue and have to be registered with the Occupational Pensions Regulatory Authority (Opra).

For further details see The Pension Service website. www.pensionguide.gov.uk. For more details on pensions, see *Daily Life*.

PERMANENT WORK

PROFESSIONAL & EXECUTIVE

There is a wide range of opportunities available for those professionally qualified. As well as positions which arise within professional practices, large companies such as those in the oil industry, for instance, need their own professionals to work 'in-house'. Local authorities also have their own departments dealing with legal matters, planning departments need qualified surveyors and architects, and so forth.

These jobs are advertised in a variety of places: professional associations have their own journals; local authorities advertise vacancies in the local press and on their websites; there are agencies dealing specifically with executive recruitment; recruitment newspapers and websites also carry advertisements for such positions. Most high prestige and high salary jobs are advertised in *The Scotsman* and *The Herald*, although job vacancies do not appear on the electronic versions of the newspapers.

Professional qualifications are not always transferable across the border. Because of the different legal systems in Scotland and England and Wales, lawyers have to retrain to work under the Scottish system. Salaries for executive and professional posts tend to be lower in the UK than elsewhere in Europe and in the US. Posts in Edinburgh and Glasgow are likely to attract higher remuneration than those in less central areas of the country.

Civil Service

The Civil Service is one of the largest employers in the UK, employing around 542,000 people in over 60 departments and 100 executive agencies. Civil Servants work for the Crown and perform their functions through the elected Government of the day, while remaining politically impartial. All posts in the Civil Service carry nationality requirements. The three-quarters of posts classed as 'non-reserved' are open to Commonwealth and EEA nationals. 'Reserved' posts are only open for applications from UK nationals, a category which includes British citizens, some Irish and Indian citizens with dual nationality, and British Dependent Territories citizens acquiring their citizenship from connection with Gibraltar. The Diplomatic Service only takes entrants who are British citizens.

Graduates can enter the Civil Service through the 'Fast Stream Development

Programme': contact either the Centre Manager, Fast Stream Assessment Centre, 67 Tufton Street, London SW1P 3QS or Parity (Civil Service Fast Stream), Parity House, Fleet Mill, Minley Road, Fleet, Hants GU7 9LY; ☎01252-776923. Alternatively, you can apply online at www.faststream.gov.uk.

Entry as Junior Managers can also be made through Departmental Recruitment schemes. In addition there are short term placements for graduates through sandwich course placements, vacation employment and vacation visits. For more on these, see *Temporary Work*. Non-graduates with suitable qualifications may apply to enter Departmental and Agency recruitment schemes. Vacancies are advertised on the Civil Service website, as well as in the press, relevant professional journals and Jobcentres. See www.careers.civil-service.gov.uk.

Experienced professionals are also welcomed in Civil Service roles at various levels. Again, application would be made for specific advertised vacancies.

Most recruitment is carried out by individual Departments and Agencies Advertisements for posts in Scotland are placed in The Scotsman and The Herald as well as local and/or specialist press. University careers services and Jobcentres may also hold details of recruitment schemes. For government departments in specific geographical areas, see the Yellow Pages or the local Phone Book.

Financial & Business Services

Insurance, banking and finance have traditionally been an important sector in the Scottish economy, especially in Edinburgh. Many large finance companies have their head offices in Edinburgh, most notably Royal Bank of Scotland and HBOS (Halifax Bank of Scotland) which are now ranked 5th and 12th largest financial services companies in the world respectively. In The Scotsman's 2004 list of Scotland's top 250 companies, the top three were Royal Bank of Scotland, Standard Life Assurance Company, and HBOS.

There are also dozens of smaller investment trusts, insurance companies and others supplying business services based in Edinburgh, Glasgow and other cities. Major global companies such as Morgan Stanley and State-Street have opted for Scotland as a UK base for supporting their international operations. In a knock-on effect, many small independent companies have been drawn by the 'cluster halo' and cost and lifestyle advantages of Scotland.

In the last decade there has been a significant increase in the number of businesses operating in this sector in Scotland. Asset management too is prospering. The sector is small in terms of numbers employed, but jobs are highly paid. Overall, the outlook for financial services is positive and the sector is predicted to increase its share of Scottish GDP.

Administrative

Those with good secretarial and clerical skills, and to a lesser extent those with administrative experience, should have no difficulty finding a job in Scotland.

The local authorities are among the biggest employers in the country and have a high demand for such skills.

Jobs can be found in the local and national press, in recruitment newspapers, in Jobcentres, on local authority websites, and the websites of other organisations. For instance the National Health Service has a need for administrators, and posts may be advertised on their websites. General recruitment websites also have sections listing administrative opportunities.

MEDICAL

The 21st century is a good time to get into the National Health Service in Britain. After years of under-funding leading to an inevitable decline in standards and conditions of work, with many health professionals leaving the NHS in favour of work with better pay and conditions, the Labour Government announced in July 2000 that it would be spending an extra six per cent per year on the health service, promising a massive increase in doctors, nurses and other staff. Although this 'national plan' applied only to England and Wales, its principles were broadly accepted by the Scottish administration, who indicated a commitment to improving the Health Service north of the border.

As part of this commitment, in 2004 an average increase in funding of 7.5 per cent, almost £6 billion in total, was given to regional Health Boards in Scotland. The investment is intended to increase numbers of doctors and nurses, reduce waiting times for patients and improve the quality of NHS services across the board.

Vacancies within the NHS are generally advertised on an area by area basis, so the best way to find out about what is currently available is to contact the local health board or NHS Trust.

Useful Resources

Nursing jobs countrywide are advertised in the *Nursing Times* EMAP Healthcare, Greater London House, Hampstead Road, London NW1 7EJ; ☎020-7874 0500; fax 020-7874 0505; www.nursingtimes.net.

The Doctors, Nurses and Health Practitioners webring on: http://r.webring. com/hub?ringdoctorsnursesand is a collection of websites with material of interest to those in the medical profession.

Other medical publications are:

British Journal of General Practice: 14 Princes Gate, Hyde Park, London SW7 1PU; ☎020-7581 3232; fax 020-7584 6716; www.rcgp.org.uk.

British Medical Journal: BMA House, Tavistock Square, London WC1H 9JR; ☎020-7383 6006; fax 020-7383 6418; www.bmj.com.

Hospital Doctor: Reed Healthcare Publishing, Quadrant House, the Quadrant, Sutton SM2 5AS; ☎020-8652 8745; www.hospital-doctor.net.

The Practising Midwife: 54 Siward Road, Bromley BR2 9JZ; ☎020-8466 1037; www.midwives online.com.

There are also jobs websites with specific healthcare listings, advertising job opportunities within the NHS and the private sector. One with a comprehensive selection regularly advertised is www.medic8.com/MedicalJobs.htm.

Scottish Health Boards

Information about job vacancies in particular areas may be available from the 15 Scottish health boards. For a full list of addresses go to Scottish Health at www. show.scot.nhs.uk.

NHS Trusts in Scotland

Aberdeen Royal Hospitals NHS Trust: Foresterhill House, Ashgrove Road West, Aberdeen AB9 8AQ; ☎01224-681818.

Angus NHS Trust: Whitehills Hospital, Forfar, Angus DD8 3DY; ☎01307-464551.

Argyll and Bute NHS Trust: Aros, Lochgilphead, Argyll PA31 8LB; ☎01546-606600.

Ayrshire and Arran Community Healthcare NHS Trust: 1A Hunter's Avenue, Ayr KA8 9DW; ☎01292-281821.

Borders Community Health Services NHS Trust: Huntlyburn House, Melrose, Roxburghshire TD6 9BP; ☎01896-662300.

Borders General Hospital NHS Trust: Melrose TD6 9BS; ☎01896-754333.

Caithness and Sutherland NHS Trust: Caithness General Hospital, Bankhead Road, Wick, Caithness KW1 5NS.

Central Scotland Healthcare NHS Trust: Royal Scottish National Hospital, Old Denny Road, Larbert, Stirlingshire FK5 4SD; ☎01324-570700.

Dumfries and Galloway Community Health NHS Trust: Crichton Hall, Crichton Royal Hospital, Bankend Road, Dumfries DG1 4TG; ☎01387-255301.

Dundee Healthcare NHS Trust: Royal Dundee Liff Hospital, Dundee DD2 5NF; ☎01382-580441.

Dundee Teaching Hospitals NHS Trust: Ninewells Hospital and Medical School, Dundee DD1 9S; ☎01382-660111.

East and Midlothian NHS Trust: Edenhall Hospital, Pinkieburn, Musselburgh, Midlothian EH21 7TZ; ☎0131-536 8000.

Edinburgh Healthcare NHS Trust: Astley Ainslie Hospital, 133 Grange Loan, Edinburgh EH9 2HL; ☎0131-537 9525.

Edinburgh Sick Children's NHS Trust: Royal Hospital for Sick Children, Sciennes Road, Edinburgh EH9 1LF; ☎0131-536 0000.

Falkirk and District Royal Infirmary NHS Trust: Major's Loan, Falkirk FK1 5QE; ☎01324-624000.

Fife Healthcare NHS Trust: Cameron House, Cameron Bridge, Leven, Fife KY8 5RG; ☎01592-712812.

Glasgow Dental Hospital and School NHS Trust: 37 Sauchiehall Street, Glasgow

G2 3JZ; ☎0141-211 9600.

Glasgow Royal Infirmary University NHS Trust: Glasgow Royal Infirmary, 84 Castle Street, Glasgow G4 0SF; ☎0141-552 4000.

Grampian Healthcare NHS Trust: Westholme, Woodend Hospital, Eday Road, Aberdeen AB2 6LS; ☎01224-663131.

Greater Glasgow Community and Mental Health Services NHS Trust: Gartnavel Royal Hospital, 1055 Great Western Road, Glasgow G12 0XH; ☎0141-211 3600.

Hairmyres and Stonehouse Hospital NHS Trust: Hairmyres Hospital, Eaglesham Road, East Kilbride, South Lanarkshire G75 8RG; ☎01355-220292.

Highland Communities NHS Trust: Royal Northern Infirmary, Inverness IV3 5SF; ☎01463-242860.

Inverclyde Royal NHS Trust: Larkfield Road, Greenock, Renfrewshire PA16 0XN; ☎01475-633777.

Kirkcaldy Acute Hospitals NHS Trust: Hayfield House, Hayfield Road, Kirkcaldy, Fife KY2 5AH; ☎01592-643355.

Lanarkshire Healthcare NHS Trust: Strathclyde Hospital, Airbles Road, Motherwell ML1 3BW; ☎01698-230500.

Law Hospital NHS Trust: Carluke ML8 5ER; ☎01698-361100.

Lomond Heathcare NHS Trust: Vale of Leven District Hospital, Main Street, Alexandria, Dunbartonshire G38 0UA; ☎01389-754121.

Monklands and Bellshill Hospitals NHS Trust: Monkscourt Avenue, Airdrie ML6 0JS; ☎01236-748748.

Moray Health Services: Maryhill House, 317 High Street, Elgin, Morayshire IV30 1AJ; ☎01343-543131.

North Ayrshire and Arran NHS Trust: Crosshouse Hospital, Kilmarnock, Ayrshire KA2 0BE; ☎01563-521133.

Perth and Kinross Healthcare NHS Trust: Perth Royal Infirmary, Perth PH1 1NX; ☎01738-623311.

Queen Margaret Hospital NHS Trust: Whitefield Road, Dunfermline, Fife KY12 0SU; ☎01383-623623.

Raigmore Hospital NHS Trust: Old Perth Road, Inverness IV2 3UJ; ☎01463-704000.

Renfrewshire Healthcare NHS Trust: Dykebar Hospital, Grahamston Road, Paisley PA2 7DE; ☎0141-884 5122.

Royal Alexandra Hospital NHS Trust: Corsebar Road, Paisley PA2 9PN; ☎0141-887 5122.

Royal Infirmary of Edinburgh NHS Trust: 1 Lauriston Place, Edinburgh H3 9YW; ☎0131-536 1000.

Scottish Ambulance Service NHS Trust: National Headquarters, Tipperlinn Road, Edinburgh EH10 5UU; ☎0131-447 7711.

South Ayrshire Hospitals NHS Trust: Ayr Hospital, Dalmellington Road, Ayr KA6 6DX; ☎01292-610555.

Southern General Hospital NHS Trust: Management Office, 1345 Govan Road, Glasgow G51 4TF; ☎0141-201 1100.

Stirling Royal Infirmary NHS Trust: Livilands, Stirling FK8 2AU; ☎01786-434000.

Stobhill NHS Trust: 133 Balornock Road, Glasgow G21 3UW; ☎0141-201 3000.

Victoria Infirmary NHS Trust: Queens Park House, Langside Road, Glasgow G42 9TY; ☎0141-201 6000.

West Glasgow Hospitals University NHS Trust: Western Infirmary, Dumbarton Road, Glasgow G11 6NT; ☎0141-211 2000.

West Lothian NHS Trust: St John's Hospital at Howden, Howden Road West, Livingston, West Lothian EH54 6PP; ☎01506-419666.

Western General Hospitals NHS Trust: Western General Hospital, Crewe Road, Edinburgh EH4 2XU; ☎0131-537 1000.

Yorkhill NHS Trust: Royal Hospital for Sick Children, Dalnier Street, Yorkhill, Glasgow G3 8SJ; ☎0141-201 4000.

TEACHING

There are around 46,000 teachers employed in the public sector in Scotland. Although the private education sector in Scotland is comparatively small, there are also job opportunities within that sector.

All teachers in publicly maintained schools (i.e. those run by local authorities) must be registered with the General Teaching Council for Scotland (GTCS). Teachers from elsewhere in the UK cannot, therefore, automatically transfer to a Scottish school. Registration is a requirement for teaching in all local authority nursery, primary, secondary and special schools in Scotland. There are three categories of registration, depending on qualifications and experience. 'Provisional Registration' is for new entrants to the profession and includes a period of probation, normally two years, where the teacher's performance in the school is monitored. Other candidates may be offered 'Conditional Registration', where their registration depends upon completing a period of supplementary study and/or monitored school experience. 'Full Registration' is awarded after successful completion of the probationary period.

Only graduates are accepted as entrants to the teaching profession. They are eligible for registration as primary teachers if they have gained an ordinary or honours degree at any UK university plus a one-year full-time postgraduate course (or equivalent) at a teacher education institution, provided their training related to the primary curriculum (3-12 age range.)

Secondary teachers must attain the four year Bachelor of Education (B.Ed) degree course, or a combined degree including subject study, study of education and school experience, or the one year Postgraduate Certificate in Education (PGCE) course following upon a degree. Further information on requirements can be found in the 'Memorandum on Entry Requirements to Courses of Teacher Education' issued annually by the Scottish Executive Education department,

available on line at http://www.scotland.gov.uk/library5/education/erct-00.asp.
It is published by The Stationery Office and may be bought from their website at
www.tso.co.uk. They also have a bookshop in Edinburgh. ☎0870-606 5566; fax
0870-606 5588; email edinburgh.bookshop@tso.co.uk.

EU Nationals who are recognised as teachers in any European Member State
are eligible for registration in Scotland provided that the course of teacher
education leading to such recognition was of not less than three years' duration.
Such teachers may initially be registered conditional on completing an aptitude
test or period of adaptation.

Teachers qualified outside the EU should either have qualifications which would
have entitled them to university entry in their own country, or have successfully
completed an access course approved by the GTCS. They should also have
completed a period of higher education at a university or equivalent institution of
at least three years' duration leading to an acceptable degree, as determined by the
UK National Academic Recognition Centre (NARIC). To be eligible for teaching
in the secondary sector, applicants must have studied at least one academic
subject in considerable depth over a substantial period of time. Those whose first
language is not English must satisfy the GTCS as to their proficiency in English.
For further details of GTCS regulations see their website at www.gtcs.org.uk.

Teachers who qualified outside Scotland must apply for 'exceptional Admission
to the Register' if they wish to teach in Scotland. There is an application form
available on the GTCS website. It must be submitted together with the following
documents: Copies of Birth Certificate; Marriage Certificate (only if a change
of name is involved); Documents confirming qualifications as described in
the covering letter issued with the application form; English translations of
documents in a foreign language; Completed Disclosure Scotland Form. This
requires an international police check to confirm you have no criminal convictions
or proceedings pending. There is an initial assessment fee of £40 to pay, and a
further registration fee of £40 if you are approved for registration.

Useful Addresses & Websites

Teaching vacancies in Scotland are advertised in the *Times Educational Supplement
Scotland (TES)*, Scott House, 10 South St Andrews Street, Edinburgh EH2 2AZ;
☎0131-557 1133; fax 0131-5581155; www.tes.co.uk/Scotland.

They are also advertised in local newspapers and can be obtained directly from
local authority education departments. They may be accessible through local
authority websites. For a full list of addresses, see *General Introduction*.

For jobs in the private sector, contact the schools direct, or see TES Scotland.
Online, http://www.jobsword.co.uk/teaching.html has listings of teaching vacancies.

Academia

Academics in the UK are generally lower paid than their counterparts in other

European countries and, particularly, in the USA and Canada. Lecturers earn between £18,362 and £36,626 per year, while senior lecturers earn between £30,223 and £43,968. Professors earn £45,000 upwards.

As a consequence of comparatively poor pay and benefits packages, the UK has seen a 'brain drain' of academics going abroad to take up better rewarded posts in overseas academic institutions. In an attempt to persuade top scientists back to Britain, and to persuade others not to leave, a fund has been created to top up the salaries of leading academics. This means they could be paid up to £100,000 per year, with the fund paying £50,000 on top of a salary of £50,000. The incentive package also includes provision to make payments to research assistants, as well as new equipment and improved working conditions.

Academic posts are advertised in *TES*, Scotland; in local newspapers and in *The Scotsman* and *The Herald*. They can also be obtained by applying directly to the institutions or through their websites. (See list of university addresses in *Daily Life*).

COMPUTERS & IT

There has been a massive expansion in the opportunities for employment within the computing and information technology sectors. With the rapid growth in company and domestic access to the internet since the late 1990s, there seems to be an insatiable demand for those with expertise in the area. Jobs are available for those with computer knowledge and qualifications to work on the computer infrastructure within traditional companies; to work within hi-tech companies; to join website design companies; and to work in the computer hardware and software development, production and supply sectors. Of the dozens of internet access providers, and the many computer hardware and software producers and suppliers, the vast majority have telephone and online 'Help Centres' which need technically qualified operatives to assist with the constant queries from those less computer literate.

IT job vacancies can be found in all the usual sources of information. For obvious reasons, there are thousands of IT jobs advertised on the internet, in online recruitment agencies and newsletters as well on the websites of large companies who need in-house staff.

Because of the nature of computer and internet work, allowing remote working, there may be relatively more jobs outside the central belt than will be found in other industries. In remote areas, computers and the internet are becoming increasingly essential for domestic users and small businesses. These people have difficulty accessing expert assistance when their computer crashes, so those with such skills in rural areas are much in demand. Local Enterprise Companies (LECs) may employ their own IT advisors and consultants who travel around their area advising on the IT requirements of those wishing to set up new businesses. For more on LECs see *Starting A Business*.

POLICE

Applicants to Scottish police forces must generally be of British nationality, although Commonwealth citizens and citizens of the Irish republic may also be eligible. They must be not less than 18 1/2 and not more than 39 years of age, must have a good standard of physical fitness and have good unaided vision. There is now no minimum height requirement, although there was in the past.

Applicants must show they have attained a good standard of education, and must then sit the Scottish Police Standard Entrance Examination which is based on four main themes: Listening Comprehension, Calculation and Number-work, Data Interpretation and Reading Comprehension. Applicants who perform well at this stage and at an initial interview will be subject to a Background Report which examines in depth their personal and family background and includes security checks on members of their family and associates.

If the Background Report is favourable they then go through an Extended Testing phase including an observation test, an essay on a given topic, a public speaking exercise, dictation exercise, learning skills exercise, debating session and a fitness test. After satisfactory completion of these tests they will have an extended interview, followed by a medical examination, and a final interview with the Assistant or Deputy Chief Constable. Only after successfully negotiating all these stages will any offer of appointment be made.

New recruits are taken on as uniformed constables who serve a two-year probationary period which includes training courses and basic duties at a Divisional Station.

Selection for promotion depends on ability and merit, and officers will not be considered for promotion until they have passed the appropriate qualifying examination which they may sit after completing their probationary period satisfactorily.

Graduate entrants and serving officers who display high potential for high rank may access the Accelerated Promotion Scheme. Further details are available from the recruiting departments of the various forces.

Because of the different legal system in Scotland, police officers serving elsewhere in the UK may not transfer directly to a Scottish Force. Generally, the officer would have to resign from his/her current force and re-apply to a Scottish Force, going through the selection and training process with other new recruits, although presumably their policing background and experience would be taken into account during the selection process. Senior officers may, however, be able to transfer to a Scottish Force.

Vacancies for police officers vary from force to force: at any one time some will have no vacancies while others may be having a recruitment drive. From time to time a force may run a Recruitment Fair in their area, with the aim of publicising the police as a career and attracting new entrants.

Applications should be made to the Recruiting Department of a specific force. There is a central website for the Scottish Police Service which has links to all the individual force sites, www.scottish.police.uk. Contact details of all police forces in Scotland are listed in *Daily Life*.

OIL & GAS INDUSTRY

The discovery in the early 1970s of vast energy resources under the North Sea had a substantial impact on the Scottish economy. By 1990, employment directly and indirectly related to the industry was almost five per cent of total employees in employment at the time. Although North Sea oil and gas production is now past its peak, it still makes a substantial contribution to the Scottish economy, creating many thousands of jobs both directly and indirectly, and will continue to do so well into the new century. The impact of oil on Scottish manufacturing industry has had far-reaching effects, with new technical developments enabling engineering companies to supply other offshore markets throughout the world. Over 100,000 Scottish jobs, 6 per cent of the workforce, depend directly or indirectly on the offshore oil and gas industry. Over 2000 companies in Scotland are involved in the oil and gas industry.

Useful Addresses & Websites

The Scottish Enterprise Energy Group: 10 Queens Road, Aberdeen AB15 4ZT; ☎01224-626310; fax 01224-627006; www.se.energy.co.uk. Encourages and supports increased competitiveness in the industry and fosters trade development, nationally and internationally.

The Grampian Oil and Gas Directory: www.oilandgas.co.uk. Online information about Scottish-based providers of products and services to the industry, and links to their websites.

Association of British Offshore Industries: 4th Floor, 30 Great Guildford Street, London SE1 0HS; ☎0171-9289199; fax 0171-9286599.

The majority of oil-connected jobs are in the Aberdeen area, this being the centre of the oil industry in Scotland. The Jobcentre there should be a good source of current vacancies. There is a comprehensive directory of online job sites at www.jobsword.co.uk/scotland.html. There are also oil and gas vacancies listed at www.s1.jobs.com.

TOURISM

Tourism is an important sector in the Scottish economy, providing around 200,000 jobs, 9 per cent of the workforce, directly or indirectly related to providing services for the millions of visitors to the country each year. In addition, another 17,000 people are self-employed in tourism related activities. This is forecast to grow as visitor numbers increase. People now have more disposable income to spend on leisure activities, and the annual world spend on all leisure and business travel is expected to double over the next ten years.

VisitScotland, the agency responsible for promoting tourism to Scotland, employs a substantial number of staff, while hotels, bars and restaurants need staff year round. Efforts have been made over recent years to increase the length of the holiday season, and spring, autumn and winter breaks are now more popular than they were in the past. This means that visitor attractions and other services are busier for longer periods during the year, with implications for employment.

Tourism Addresses and Websites

VisitScotland (Scottish Tourist Board): 23 Ravelston Terrace, Edinburgh EH4 3TP; ☎0131-332 2433; fax 0131-332 1513; www.visitscotland.com.

At the time of writing, VisitScotland is undergoing a wholesale review, and the new organisational structure will not be fully operational until April 2005. The main changes will be that membership fees will be scrapped, allowing tourism operators to buy into any services they require without also having to pay an up-front membership fee. The 14 Area Tourist Boards will also disappear as autonomous organisation, to become 'hubs' of VisitScotland, administered centrally.

VisitScotland Area Hubs:

Aberdeen & Grampian: Exchange House, 26-28 Exchange Street, Aberdeen AB10 1YL; ☎01224-288828; fax 01224-581367; www.agtb.org.

Angus & Dundee: 21 Castle Street, Dundee DD1 3AA; ☎01382-527527; fax 01382-527551; www.angusanddundee.co.uk.

Argyll, the Isles, Loch Lomond, Stirling & the Trossachs: 41 Dumbarton Road, Stirling FK8 2QQ; ☎08707-200620; fax 01786-450039; www.visitscotlandheartlands. com.

Ayrshire & Arran: Unit 2, 15 Skye Road, Prestwick, Ayrshire KA9 2TA; ☎01292-678100; fax 01292-471832; www.ayrshire-arran.com.

Dumfries & Galloway: 64 Whitesands, Dumfries DG1 2RS; ☎01387-253862; fax 01387-245551; www.visit-dumfries-and-galloway.co.uk.

Edinburgh & Lothians: 4 Rothesay Terrace, Edinburgh EH3 7RY; ☎0845-225121; fax 01506-832222; www.edinburgh.org.

Fife: Haig Business Park, Balgonie Road, Markinch KY7 6AQ; ☎01592-611180; fax 01334-472021; www.standrews.com.

Greater Glasgow & Clyde Valley: 11 George Square, Glasgow G2 1DY; ☎0141-204 4480; fax 0141-204 4074; www.seeglasgow.com.

Highlands of Scotland: Castle Wynd, Inverness IV2 3BJ; ☎01463-234353; fax 01463-710609; www.extranet.host.co.uk.

Orkney: 6 Broad Street, Kirkwell, Orkney KW15 1NX; ☎01856-872856; fax 01856-875056; www.visitorkney.com.

Perthshire Tourist Board: Lower City Mills, West Mill Street, Perth PH3 1LQ; ☎01783-450600; fax 01783-444863; www.perthshire co.uk.

Scottish Borders: Shepherds Mill, Whinfield Road, Selkirk TD7 5DT; 0870-608 0404; www.scot-borders.co.uk.

Shetland Islands: Market Cross, Lerwick, Shetland ZE1 0LU; ☎01595-693434; fax 01595-695807; www.shetland-tourism.co.uk.

Western Isles: 26 Cromwell Street, Stornoway, Isle of Lewis HS1 2DD; ☎01851-703088; fax 01851-705244; www.witb.co.uk.

OUTDOOR ACTIVITIES

Outdoor recreation in Scotland supports about 29,000 full-time equivalent (fte) jobs, while tourists participating in hiking and walking generate another 9,400 (fte) jobs and nature study activities contribute another 2,600 (fte) jobs.

The skiing areas of Aviemore, Glencoe, Glenshee and Lecht attract tourists in winter and summer, providing employment year round.

Many tourists head to Scotland for the salmon and trout fishing, while others prefer sea-fishing in the sea lochs. All these need knowledgeable and well-trained ghillies and guides.

Useful Addresses

Mountain Leader Training Scotland: Glenmore, Aviemore, Inverness-shire PH22 1QU; ☎01479-861248; fax 01479-861249.

Ramblers Association Scotland: Kingfisher House, Auld Mart Business Park, Milnathort, Kinross KY13 9DA; ☎01577-861222; fax 01577-861333; www.ramblers.org.uk.

Scottish Anglers National Association: The National Game Angling Academy, The Pier, Loch Leven KY13 8UF; ☎01577-861116; fax 01577-864769; www.sana.org.uk.

British Association of Snowsport Instructors: BASI, Glenmore, Aviemore, Inverness-shire PH22 1QJ; ☎01479-861717; fax 01479-861718; www.basi.org.uk.

Scottish School Ski Association: Dollar Academy, Dollar FK14 7DU; ☎01259-742511; fax 01259-742867.

Snowsport Scotland: Hillend, Biggar Road, Midlothian EH10 7EF; ☎0131-445 4151; fax 0131-317 7734; www.snowsportscotland.org.

AGRICULTURE & FISHING

The agriculture sector is shrinking in Scotland as a whole, and with European subsidies increasingly aimed at environmental activities rather than production activities, there are fewer opportunities for farm work. The sector is also characterised by lack of job security, with the vast majority of jobs being short-term contracts.

Fish farming, particularly of salmon, provides many jobs in Scotland, but the industry is contracting from its peak, due to competition from elsewhere in Europe, Norway in particular. During the late 1990s the industry was badly affected by outbreaks of the disease infectious salmon anaemia, which meant some farms had to be closed down completely to allow the area to recover. Fish farms do provide an important source of jobs in the Highlands and Island, but they tend to employ local people, so there are not many openings for those who have just moved to the area.

Sea fishing is in decline throughout the country, with many life-long fishermen leaving the industry. Declining fish stocks, together with stringent European fish quotas designed to protect stocks of some species and allow others to recover to previous levels, have had a serious effect on the numbers employed.

CONSTRUCTION

The construction industry in Scotland provides employment to a large workforce of skilled and unskilled workers. Again, they suffer from lack of job security and wages are generally low. Most workers are on short term contracts, liable to be laid off by their employer at the end of a project, to be re-hired when a new construction project comes along. However, there appears to be plenty of work around at present. High profile projects such as the new Scottish Parliament building have given a boost to the industry in the Edinburgh area, while new houses are being built on the outskirts of towns and cities throughout Scotland. Run-down city centre areas are also being transformed with prestigious new developments.

Recent efforts to repopulate rural areas, made possible by new technology which allows more people to work in remote areas and transact business across the internet, have brought about a growth in new housing. Councils are also putting money into renovating semi-derelict traditional houses in rural communities. Architects, planners, builders and other tradespeople all benefit from the increased workload. In a small Highland community, a contract to build just one house can provide valuable work for a number of local people for a period of months.

European funds together with the National Lottery have funded many community projects across Scotland in recent years, involving the construction of new facilities. These include a number of new high school buildings in the Highlands, new village halls and the improvement of existing halls under the '21st Century Halls for Scotland' scheme, and the construction of new jetties and slipways in a number of west coast communities.

ENVIRONMENT

With over two million hectares – more than 25 per cent – of Scotland protected under various environmental designations, the environment sector is a large provider of employment. There are over 8,000 jobs – 6,700 full-time equivalent – in natural heritage-related activities in Scotland. 40 per cent of these are based in rural areas, with 25 per cent in the Highlands and Islands. In total they account for two per cent of all jobs in rural Scotland.

The vast majority of these jobs are in the public sector, many working either directly or indirectly with Scottish Natural Heritage (SNH) the main environmental body in the country. There is also a significant number in the voluntary sector. Many are temporary jobs, created during the period of short-term projects. For further details on these opportunities, see *Temporary Work*.

Useful Addresses

Scottish Council for Voluntary Organisations (SCVO): Mansfield Traquair Centre, 15 Mansfield Place, Edinburgh EH3 6BB; ☎0131-556 3882; fax 0131-556 0279; www.scvo.org.uk.

Scottish Environment Protection Agency (SEPA): Erskine Court, The Castle Business Park, Stirling FK9 4TR; ☎01786-457700; fax 01786-446885; www.sepa.org. uk.

Scottish Natural Heritage: 12 Hope Terrace, Edinburgh EH9 2AS; ☎0131-447 4784; fax 0131-446 2277; www.snh.org.uk.

TEMPORARY WORK

Tourism

Tourism is a sector providing many temporary jobs. Hotels, bars and restaurants need temporary workers during the summer season, particularly in tourist areas. Holiday camps, activity centres and theme parks are also fruitful areas for short-term work. Board and lodging may be included as an element of the wage.

Outdoor activities, including hiking, skiing, nature study and various sporting activities, fishing and golf in particular, are popular with tourists, and there are opportunities for temporary employment in all these fields. See *Permanent Work* above for useful addresses and websites.

Working as an Au Pair

There are numerous agencies arranging to put au pairs in touch with those who wish to employ them. They can be found very easily on the internet, by searching for 'au pairs'. Two which provide jobs in Scotland are www.au-pairs.co.uk and www.100s-aupairs.co.uk.

Useful Address

Details of commercial agencies which place nannies and au pairs with families can be obtained from *The Federation of Recruitment & Employment Services* 36 Mortimer Street, London W1N 7RB; ☎020-7462 3260; fax 020-7255 2878; www.rec.uk.com.

Agriculture & Fishing

During the summer months, fruit and vegetable pickers are required on farms. The best area to find work of this kind is Perthshire.

Fish farms may take on extra workers at various times of year, particularly when the fish are being harvested.

Secretarial & Clerical

Temporary clerical and secretarial work can be found throughout the year. It generally requires you to be available at short notice, in order to cover for permanent employees on leave of various kinds. It is a good idea to register with private 'temping' or job agencies. Addresses can be found in the local phone book or at the Jobcentre. Good word-processing skills are much in demand for such jobs.

Supply Teaching

Qualified teachers who do not wish to work full-time can sign on with their local authority as supply teachers to cover for absent staff. This may involve you in the odd few days here and there, or in full-time cover for a number of months while a permanent teacher is absent on long-term sickness or maternity leave. Supply teachers must be registered with the General Teaching Council for Scotland. See *Permanent Work* for further details.

Shop Work

Temporary shop work is often available in tourist areas during the summer months which are their busiest periods. In the towns, supermarkets and other high street stores see their peak sales during the run up to Christmas, and often take on temporary staff during this busy period.

Factory Work

There may be seasonal demand for temporary labour in food processing factories. They tend to be busiest during the summer when freshly picked foods need to be canned or frozen quickly. Confectionery firms take on extra staff in the late summer, when they start increased production in the time for Christmas. Approach the personnel departments of factories to enquire about such opportunities.

TRAINING, WORK EXPERIENCE & EXCHANGE SCHEMES

There are a number of training and work experience schemes open to foreign nationals with positions available within Scotland. These are some of the major ones.

The **British Universities North American Club (BUNAC)** runs schemes for students to work temporarily in other countries. *BUNAC Scottish Office* is at Basement Level, 60 High Street, (The Royal Mile), Edinburgh EH1 1TB; ☎0131-558 9313; fax 0131-558 9314; www.bunac.org.uk. There are links to all relevant national websites from here.

The **British Council** runs similar schemes. *The British Council Scotland:* The Tun, 4 Jackson's Entry, Holyrood Road, Edinburgh EH8 8PJ; ☎0131-524 5700; fax 0131-524 5701. 25 High Street, Old Aberdeen AB2 3EE; ☎01224-486640; fax 01224-480371; www.britishcouncil.org. The British Council has offices around the world, details of which can be found on their website. US nationals should also look at www.britishcouncil.org/usa-education.

For further information on both of the above, see *Education* in *Daily Life*.

The **Central Bureau** is a division of the British Council which offers opportunities for pupils, students, teachers, trainers, lecturers and administrators in the UK education and training sectors, including short term posts for language assistants to work in schools in the UK. Contact *The British Council Scotland* at the Edinburgh address above or see the website at www.britishcouncil.org/cbiet/index.htm.

The **National Youth Agency** provides opportunities to work with young people and runs training courses in Scotland. Eastgate House, 19-23 Humberstone Road, Leicester LE5 3GJ; ☎0116-242 7350; fax 0116-242 7444; www.nya.org.uk.

The **Civil Service** offers vacation work for students in a number of its departments and agencies. Details of current opportunities are listed at www.careers.civil-service.gov.uk.

Research

Research assistants in all disciplines are required from time to time at educational institutions, for those suitably qualified. Current requirements are advertised in the TES, Scotland, local and national newspapers and can also be accessed direct from universities or via their websites. See *Daily Life* for contact details.

Useful Books & Websites

Details of sources of temporary work and volunteer posts in the UK can be found in the following Vacation Work publications:

Taking A Gap Year, Susan Griffith.

Gap Years for Growns Ups, Susan Griffith.

Green Volunteers, Fabio Ausenda.

Summer Jobs in Britain, ed. David Woodworth & Guy Hobbs.

The International Directory of Voluntary Work, Victoria Pybus.

Working in Tourism - The UK, Europe and Beyond, Verite Reily Collins.

The Au Pair & Nanny's Guide to Working Abroad, Susan Griffith.

Some temporary work can also be found listed on their website (www.vacationwork.co.uk).

Other resources include:

About Jobs: www.AboutJobs.com. Includes sections offering summer jobs, overseas jobs and resort jobs throughout the world, including Scotland.

Careers Europe: www.careerseurope.co.uk. Provides plenty of advice about working in the UK. Can also be contacted at Careers Europe, Onward House, Baptist Place, Bradford BD1 2PS; ☎01274-829600; fax 01274-829610.

Hotel Jobs and Seasonal Vacancies: www.livein-jobs.co.uk.

Hotel Jobs and Vacancies in the UK: www.hotel-jobs.co.uk.

BUSINESS & INDUSTRY REPORT

There has been a steady growth in the Scottish economy since the 1960s, gross domestic product (GDP) averaging 2.1 per cent growth. This compares with a growth rate of 2.3 per cent for the UK as a whole over the same period. Between 1963 and 1998 the Scottish economy doubled in size. This improvement has been less volatile in Scotland than elsewhere in UK – growth remained positive in the early 1990s, at a time when UK output contracted in both 1991 and 1992.

In 2003, GDP in Scotland rose 2.1 per cent overall, compared with a 1.6 per cent growth in the UK as a whole. Best performance was seen in Scottish construction (4.4 per cent growth) and services (3.5 per cent growth) while there was a drop of 3.1 per cent in the production sector.

Since the 1960s there has been a significant transformation of the Scottish economy. There have been two main strands to this change: new industries based on modern technologies have been created, with the traditional heavy industries declining in importance; and, following the trend of other western industrialised nations, the service sector has become an increasingly dominant part of the economy.

Financial and business services in particular have shown rapid expansion with this sector making a significant contribution to the wealth of the country. Scotland is the fifth largest equity management centre in the EU after London, Paris, the Netherlands and Frankfurt.

The big success story of recent years has been the electronics industry, which has captured a substantial proportion of the world market for its products, particularly in the field of information technology. At the turn of the new century, Scotland was producing 28 per cent of personal computers in Europe and more than seven per cent in the world; nearly 65 per cent of automated teller machines in Europe; and 29 per cent of electronic notebooks in Europe. Not bad for a country of only five million people.

The **electronics industry** employs over 43,000 directly and around 30,000 indirectly in the electronics supply infrastructure. The importance of the sector has attracted many overseas companies to the country, they in turn contributing to its growth. In 1996, overseas owned plants accounted for 58 per cent of employment in the electronics industry. Scotland's rapidly growing optoelectronics industry is valued at around £800 million and employs around 4,200 people.

Between 2001 and 2003 there was a downturn in the Electrical and Instrument Engineering sector, part of the general global economic slowdown and the global restructuring of this sector. The markets for many electrical goods, such as PCs and mobile phones, have also been approaching maturity, making cost an increasingly important deciding factor in assembly operations. The importance of the sector to the Scottish economy meant that these developments had a significant effect on total manufacturing output.

The entertainment side of technology is very important to the Scottish economy, with digital media and creative industries, including multimedia and computer games producers, estimated to account for four per cent of Scottish GDP and employing over 100,000 people.

Scotland's **telecommunications** industry employs more than 12,000 people, with many international companies involved in telecommunications equipment manufacturing. The expertise in telecommunications technology has encouraged the growth of call centres in Scotland. There are currently around 290 call centres countrywide, employing about 56,000 people, of which 30 per cent are in the finance sector. There has been a trend to move call centres to the third world, India in particular, where costs are far lower, but this has proved very unpopular with customers of these companies, and some businesses are now re-thinking this approach, and moving their customer services back to the UK.

Although its relative importance has declined since its peak in the 1980s, the **oil and gas** industry is still one of the largest industries in Scotland, employing directly and indirectly over 100,000 people, equivalent to six per cent of all Scottish employment.

The high calibre of **bio-technology research** in Scotland's universities has attracted several world class bio-sector companies. It was collaboration between PPL Therapeutics and the Roslin Institute which created the first clone from an adult cell, producing Dolly the Sheep, famous around the world.

The **food industry** has long been an important sector of the Scottish economy, with **whisky** sales a large element of this. Total annual sales in the industry are around £7.3 billion which include £2.6 billion from whisky alone. It employs over 48,000 people, 17 per cent of all manufacturing employees in over 1,500 businesses.

Around 900 enterprises undertake significant research and development in Scotland, half of them in manufacturing. The majority of the expenditure is from 55 large firms. Around 11,000 people work in research and development, 6,500 of them scientists and engineers.

The total number of enterprises in Scotland, excluding the public sector (i.e.

local and central government), increased by 4 per cent between 2002 and 2003, to 262,750, with a combined turnover of £168 billion. Together they employed 2,375,110 people, an increase of 17,920 over the year.

The vast majority of these enterprises are small. 64 per cent of the enterprises have no employees other than the proprietor, while 93 per cent are classified as 'micro-businesses' with 0-9 employees. Although there are only a small number of enterprises with over 500 employees, they accounted for 42 per cent of employment.

Unemployment has been falling steadily from a peak in December 1992 when nine per cent of the workforce were unemployed. By 2003 that had fallen to 5.8 per cent. Job creation was greatest in the construction industry, while the service industry is still buoyant. Traditional manufacturing and agriculture lost jobs in the same period, another trend set to continue as the restructuring of the economy continues.

REGIONAL EMPLOYMENT GUIDE

The best opportunities for employment are, obviously, clustered in and around the larger towns and cities of Scotland. In the outlying rural areas, where businesses are inevitably small, permanent vacancies are likely to be few and far between, although temporary work is usually available, particularly during the summer months. In these areas, a more viable option may be to start one's own business – this will be explored in detail in the next chapter.

In this section, the major cities of the mainland and the main towns of the islands are listed, with brief details of their main industries and some local sources of employment information.

EDINBURGH

Local Authority: City of Edinburgh Council, Wellington Court, 10 Waterloo Place, Edinburgh EH1 3EG; ☎0131-200 2000; fax 0131-529 7477; www.edinburgh.gov.uk.

Local Enterprise Company: Scottish Enterprise Edinburgh & Lothian, Apex House, 99 Haymarket Terrace, Edinburgh EH12 5HD; ☎0131-313 4000; fax 0131-313 4231; www.scottish-enterprise.com.

Chamber of Commerce: Edinburgh Chamber of Commerce & Enterprise, Conference House, 152 Morrison Street, EH3 8EB; ☎0131-477 7000; fax 0131 477 7002; www.ecce.org.

Jobcentre: 11-13 South St. Andrew Street, EH2 2BT; ☎0131-456 3300.

Employment Agency: Manpower UK Ltd, 11, South Charlotte St, Edinburgh, Midlothian EH2 4AS; ☎0131-226 5591; www.manpower.co.uk.

Local Newspaper: Edinburgh Evening News, Barclay House, 108 Holyrood

Road, Edinburgh EH8 8AS;www.edinburghnews.com.

Key sectors: Financial services, biotechnology, optoelectronics, microelectronics, software, creative industries (TV, Film)

Major employers: Agilent, Sun Microsystems, Quintiles, Sky.

Industry: Edinburgh is the capital city and seat of government of Scotland. Service industries, in particular those in the professional, scientific and financial sectors, have long dominated the economy, with less than one fifth of the population now employed in manufacturing industry. The surviving manufacturing sector is still important, however, especially in the areas of electrical and electronics engineering; paper, printing and publishing; and food and drink. These three provide over 75 per cent of manufacturing employment in the city.

Edinburgh's economy is underpinned by electronics, information technology, tourism and financial services. It is the second largest financial and administrative centre in the UK after London, a position unlikely to be challenged since the establishment of the Scottish Parliament in the city. The financial service sector continues to grow, at the time of writing taking up about a third of all office space in the city. It is now the fourth largest financial services centre in Europe.

Since 1990 a concentration of hi-tech companies has grown up around Livingston and along the 50 mile corridor between Edinburgh and Glasgow, earning the area the sobriquet 'Silicon Glen'. Home to one of the biggest clusters of hi-tech companies in Europe, the region is characterised by big, hi-tech businesses rather than small start-up companies At the forefront of new technology, Silicon Glen companies develop and supply computer chips, lasers and circuits to the world. The presence of these big employers has encouraged Heriot-Watt, Glasgow and Strathclyde universities to become centres of excellence in electronics and engineering.

Although it is best known for financial services, biotechnology, software and creative industries such as TV and film make a major contribution to the region's considerable economic wealth.

Edinburgh has a young, highly qualified workforce with a higher proportion of university graduates living in the area than anywhere else in the country.

Quotes from local employers

I believe that Scotland could be the electronics gateway to Europe. It's got fabulous infrastructure in the electronics industry within a 20 to 40 mile radius, and we've fed from that infrastructure well over the past five or 10 years. **Sun Microsystems**

Innovative software development is a key component of the knowledge economy and Scottish Enterprise Edinburgh and Lothian aim to ensure businesses are equipped with the infrastructure, skilled work force and resources to allow them to be globally competitive. **Scottish Enterprise Edinburgh and Lothian**

GLASGOW

Local Authority: Glasgow City Council, City Chambers, George Square, Glasgow G2 1DU; ☎0141-287 2000; fax 0141-287 5666; www.glasgow.gov.uk.

Local Enterprise Company: Scottish Enterprise Glasgow, 50 Waterloo Street, Glasgow G2 6HQ; ☎0141-204 1111; fax 0141-248 1600; www.scottish-enterprise.com.

Chamber of Commerce: Glasgow Chamber of Commerce & Manufactures, 30 George Square, Glasgow G2 1EQ; ☎0141-204 2121; www.glasgowchamberonline.org.

Jobcentre: 87-97 Bath Street, G2 2EE; ☎0141-800 3200.

Employment Agency: Manpower Employment Services, 46 Gordon Street, G1 3PU; ☎0141-226 4291; www.manpower.co.uk.

Local Newspaper: Evening Times, 200 Renfield Street, Glasgow G2 3PR; ☎0141-302 7000; www.eveningtimes.co.uk.

Key sectors: Bio sciences, Optoelectronics, contact centre management, software development, retail.

Major employers: National Australia Group, British Telecom, Lloyds TSB, Tasco, BBC, Direct Line, RAC.

Industry: Although not the capital, Glasgow is Scotland's largest city. Its economy is dominated by the service sector, which accounts for about 80 per cent of employment in the city, particularly in the areas of finance and banking, public administration, education, healthcare, hotels and tourism, and business services. There is still a significant manufacturing sector, covering quite a range of products within the areas of engineering, food and drink, printing and publishing, clothing, software and biotechnology.

The knowledge-based industries such as e-commerce technology, computing and science are a growth area in the city, which has probably seen the greatest change in its industrial make-up over recent years. Its traditional reliance on heavy engineering has been replaced by a modern mixed economy brought about by plenty of public and private investment.

Once an important shipbuilding centre, the Clyde has seen massive contraction in the scale of the industry over recent years. Shipbuilding yards have closed and others exist under constant threats of lay-offs or closure.

Glasgow has a large, highly qualified and technologically knowledgeable workforce with over 500,000 employees in the metropolitan area.

Quotes from local businesses

The decision to locate our first European Sales centre in Glasgow has unquestionably been a successful one. It is a pleasure to work in Glasgow, and this location has enabled us to grow our people and our business very quickly. **Monster.com**
Glasgow has met all our expectations....and more. **Scottish Amicable**

STIRLING

Local Authority: Stirling Council, Viewforth, Stirling FK8 2ET; ☎0845-277700; fax 01786-443078; www.stirling.gov.uk.

Local Enterprise Company: Scottish Enterprise Forth Valley, Laurel House, Laurelhill Business Park, Stirling FK7 9JQ; ☎01786-451919; fax 01786-478123; www.scottish-enterprise.com.

Jobcentre: Wallace House, Maxwell Place, Stirling FK8 1JU; ☎01786-424200.

Employment Agency: Top Staff Employment Ltd, The Centre Springfield House, Stirling, FK7 9JQ; ☎01786-451550.

Local Newspaper: Stirling Observer, 40 Upper Craigs, Stirling FK8 2DW; ☎01786-451110.

Key sectors: Distribution, tourism, pharmaceuticals, financial and business services, contact centre management.

Major employers: Thomas Cook Direct, Thorn EMI, Bank of Bermuda, Scotia Pharmaceuticals.

Industry: Four in ten of Stirling's jobs are in the public sector, retailing and tourist industries, these three industries together accounting for 70 per cent of the city's total gross domestic product (GDP). Financial and business services are also important sources of employment, with traditional industries such as mining and engineering accounting for a very small amount of Stirling's GDP. Despite being in a fairly rural area, agriculture and related industries account for only slightly over four per cent of Stirling's wealth.

A characteristic of employment in the area is that the city is heavily dependent on a few large employers, with just ten companies and organisations employing one third of Stirling's workforce. Public sector businesses are particularly important, with Stirling Council, Stirling Royal Infirmary and Stirling University being major employers. The other two-thirds of jobs are concentrated in firms with under 50 employees, with nearly half of these being in firms with 24 or less. The deep sea container port and oil refinery at Grangemouth are a profitable part of the local economy.

There are strong links in the region between industry, commerce and the academic sector. Stirling University is renowned for its high calibre graduates.

Stirling has excellent motorway links which allow for high mobility of the workforce. There is a potential workforce, within 30 minutes commuting time of the city, of 1.5 million.

Quotes from local businesses

We have chosen the Scotland area as our European IT hub as it has a strong IT infrastructure and has an excellent track-record of providing an associated pool of highly qualified IT professionals. We believe the Stirling area will offer access to a broad labour pool and an excellent quality of life for our staff. **Bank of Bermuda**

> *It is gratifying that our global partners have significantly backed what we believe is ground-breaking technology. We should keep in mind that, while we created the original software here in Scotland, the 130 new jobs that will develop and support it could have been established anywhere.* **Strategic Software Solutions**

PERTH

Local Authority: Perth and Kinross Council, 2 High Street, Perth PH1 5PH; ☎01738-475000; fax 01738-475710; www.pkc.gov.uk.

Local Enterprise Company: Scottish Enterprise Tayside, Enterprise House, 45 North Lindsay Street, Dundee DD1 1HT; ☎01382-223100; fax 01382-201319; www.scottish-enterprise.com.

Chamber of Commerce: Perthshire Chamber of Commerce, The Atrium, 137 Glover Street, Perth PH2 0JB; ☎01738-637626; www.perth.org.uk.

Jobcentre: 60-62 High Street, Perth, PH1 5TH; ☎01738-412900.

Employment Agency: Travail Employment Group, 7 Charlotte Street, Perth, PH1 5LW; ☎01738-637331.

Local Newspaper: Perthshire Advertiser, 38 Tay Street, Perth, PH1 5TT; ☎01738-626211.

Key sectors: Agriculture, food and drink, technology, crafts.

Major employers: Scottish & Southern Energy, Norwich Union, Bank of Scotland, Caithness Glass.

Industry: Perth is centrally located and, amazingly, has over 90 per cent of Scotland's population within a 90 minute drive. The Perth and Kinross area has a growing economy, which is mirrored by the growth in population. It was one of the fastest growing areas of Scotland during the 1990s.

The service industries are as important here as in other Scottish cities, with two thirds of employees within the Perth and Kinross area employed in the sector, particularly in tourism, insurance and finance.

Perth is renowned as one of the most fertile areas of Scotland, hence agriculture, food and drink are also important to the local economy. Famous Grouse whisky and Highland Spring mineral water are both produced locally.

> **Quote from a local business**
> *Since moving into our Perth location in 1998 we have found it to be ideally situated to cover our Scottish branch network. In addition the area provides an exceptional quality of life for our staff.* **Bank of Scotland Business Banking**

DUNDEE

Local Authority: Dundee City Council, 21 City Square, Dundee DD1 3BY; ☎01382-434000; fax 01382-434666; www.dundeecity.gov.uk.

Local Enterprise Company: Scottish Enterprise Tayside, Enterprise House, 45 North Lindsay Street, Dundee DD1 1HT; ☎01382-223100; fax 01382-

201319; www.scottish-enterprise.com.

Chamber of Commerce: Dundee & Tayside Chamber of Commerce & Industry, Chamber of Commerce Buildings, Panmure Street, Dundee; ☎01382-228545.

Jobcentre: 3 Gellatly Street, Dundee DD1 3DX; ☎01382-373000.

Employment Agency: Manpower Employment Services, 45 Reform Street, Dundee, DD1 1SL; ☎01382-227491; www.manpower.co.uk.

Local Newspapers: Courier & Advertiser, 80 Kingsway East, Dundee DD4 8SL; ☎01382-223131; www.thecourier.co.uk.

Key sectors: Biotechnology, digital media, biomedical, manufacturing, contact centre management.

Major employers: NCR, D.C.Thomson.

Industry: For many years, Dundee's economy was summed up glibly in the phrase 'jute, jam and journalism'. Today, although the textile industry has declined, the main industries in the city still include textiles, printing and food processing, together with computers and other electronic industries, lasers, tyre manufacture, carpets, engineering, clothing manufacture and tourism. Hi-tech industries are booming: Dundee is building on its claim to be 'Europe's computer-games capital' with Britain's first degree course in computer games running at Abertay University.

Dundee University has a proven track record in Life Sciences, and is renowned as one of the great cancer-research centres of the world, attracting biotechnology companies to the city. Another topical area which impinges on Dundee is the genetic modification of foods, because the Scottish Crop Research Institute has its home on the outskirts of the city.

In recent years its traditional industries, such as fishing and textiles, have thus been superseded by biotechnology and a creative sector that includes media and computer-gaming. Further wealth is generated by supplying the offshore oil and gas industry in the North Sea.

There is a higher than average proportion of female workers in Dundee, with the result that the city has lower than average wage levels.

Quote from a local business

Our ability to recruit a high standard of employees in Dundee has been instrumental in our strategic direction. The traditional customer service skill set formerly required in call centres is being overtaken by technical skill to support the fast moving e-commerce initiative. A multi skilled team in the centre underpins the business. **Tesco Customer Services**

ABERDEEN

Local Authority: Aberdeen City Council, Town House, Broad Street, Aberdeen AB10 1FY; ☎01224-522000; fax 01224-644346; www.aberdeencity.gov.uk.

Local Enterprise Company: Scottish Enterprise Grampian, 27 Albyn Place, Aberdeen AB10 1DB; ☎01224-252000; fax 01224-213417; www.scottish-enterprise.com.

Chamber of Commerce: Aberdeen & Grampian Chamber of Commerce, 213 George Street, Aberdeen AB25 1XA; ☎01224-620621; fax 01224-213221; www.agcc.co.uk.

Jobcentre: 11 Chapel Street, Aberdeen AB10 1SQ; ☎01224-618000 .

Employment Agency: Manpower Employment Services, Langstane House, 1-4 Dee Street, Aberdeen AB11 6DD; ☎01224-210320.

Local Newspaper: Press & Journal, Lang Stracht, Mastrick, Aberdeen AB15 6DF; ☎01224-690222; www.pressandjournal.co.uk.

Key Sectors: oil and gas extraction and associated industries, fishing, agriculture.

Major employers: Shell, Talisman.

Industry: Aberdeen is Scotland's third largest city. Widely known as the 'oil capital of Europe' it owes its prosperity to North Sea oil and gas, being the country's main centre for offshore oil exploration and production. This has attracted many international companies to the city, directly and indirectly linked with the oil industry. Aberdeen's universities and companies have made great advances in offshore technology which is now in use around the globe.

Alongside the modern industries, traditional activities including fishing, agriculture, textiles and papermaking are still an important part of the city's economy. In addition, new high technology businesses, like software development, are growing.

Aberdeen boasts an international workforce attracted by the oil industry, with highly technical skills as well as international management experience. Robert Gordon University has an excellent reputation for research, resulting in no fewer than four Nobel prizes, while the Aberdeen Science and Technology Park (ASTP) has attracted high calibre international companies.

Quotes from local businesses

The campus atmosphere at Aberdeen Science and Technology Park promotes open thinking and a good working environment for our employees. The university and campus atmosphere is attractive to our customers and reflects the fact that we are leaders in the development of drilling products, solutions and services. **Baker Hughes INTEQ**

Amenities such as excellent business development support, shared services and availability of skilled staff were the primary reasons for our move to the ASTP. The Park also provides excellent networking opportunities and the training support from Grampian Enterprise has been invaluable in the development of our business. **Biocure Limited**

INVERNESS

Local Authority: Highland Council, Glenurquhart Road, Inverness IV3 5NX; ☎01463-702000; fax 01463-702111; www.highland.gov.uk.

Local Enterprise Company: The Green House, Beechwood Park North, Inverness IV2 3BL; ☎01463-713504; fax 01463-702002; www.ine.co.uk.

Chamber of Commerce: Inverness & District Chamber of Commerce, PO Box 5512, Inverness IV2 3RQ; ☎01463-718131; www.inverness-chamber.co.uk.

Jobcentre: River House, Young Street, Inverness IV3 5BP; ☎01463-888100.

Employment Agency: Highland Recruitment Services, 1st Floor, Highland Rail House, Station Square, Academy Street, Inverness IV1 1LE; ☎01463-725400.

Local Newspaper: Inverness Courier, New Century House, Stadium Road, Inverness IV1 1FF; ☎01463-233059; fax 01463-238223; www.inverness-courier.co.uk.

Key Sectors: Retail services, public administration, healthcare, business services, technical support operations, tourism.

Major employers: Inverness Medical Limited, Westminster Health Care, Strathaird Salmon Ltd, Morrison Construction, Cap Gemini, The Highland Council, Highlands and Islands Enterprise.

Industry: Inverness is regarded as the 'capital as the Highlands' and as such is a very important retail, business and medical centre for those living in the Highland region – an area the size of Wales or Belgium. Of the 320,000 Highland population, 50,000 live in Inverness, and a further 75,000 live in its immediate surroundings. Inverness was granted city status in 2000 as one of the four 'millennium cities' created in the UK. Increasingly the quality of life in the Highlands has attracted many individuals and businesses to move to the area and in 2004 Inverness overtook Edinburgh as the fastest growing city in Scotland.

The biggest employers in Inverness are public sector administration and services, light engineering, technology and electronics, oil platform construction, food processing, timber, printing and tourism. In the Highland region as a whole, over one quarter of employment in Highland is in distribution, hotels and catering with a further quarter in public administration, education and health.

Fishing and agriculture also account for much employment. Over a quarter of the total Scottish catch is landed in Highland, while agriculture provides nearly 7,000 jobs. However, because of difficulties of distribution and poor yields in the remote hilly areas, Highland accounts for only nine per cent of the total agricultural output in Scotland.

Inverness benefits from a workforce that is well educated, skilled and adaptable. Loyalty, high productivity and low turnover are noticeable amongst the Highlands workforce.

Quotes from local businesses

Cap Gemini is committed to providing e-commerce solutions which will change the way businesses will operate in the next century. In 1993 we made the decision to make a long term investment in the Inner Moray Firth area. This is bearing fruit. We now employ over 500 people in the area and plan further expansion. This has been made possible by the quality of our local workforce and the strength of the business support infrastructure. **Cap Gemini Call Centres**

Inverness and Nairn is amongst the best areas in the country to establish a food and drink business. The area is renowned for its environmental cleanliness and it produces quality raw materials. It has a supply of high calibre labour supported by excellent training facilities and it is also well serviced in terms of transport links. **Claymore Dairies Limited**

PORTREE

Local Authority: Highland Council, Glenurquhart Road, Inverness IV3 5NX; ☎01463-702000; fax 01463-702111; www.highland.gov.uk.

Local Enterprise Company: Skye & Lochalsh Enterprise, Kings House, The Green, Portree, Isle of Skye IV51 9BS; ☎01478-612841; fax 01478-612164; www.sale.hie.co.uk.

Jobcentre: Bayfield Road, Portree, Isle of Skye IV51 9EN; 01478 633000.

Employment Agency: Highland Careers Services Ltd, Elgin Hostel, Dunvegan Road, Portree IV51 9EE; ☎01486-612328.

Local Newspaper: West Highland Free Press, Pairc nan Craobh, Industrial Estate, Broadford, Isle of Skye IV49 9AP; ☎01471-822464; fax 01471-822694; www. whfp.com.

Key Sectors: Tourism, IT, Gaelic education.

Major Employers: BUTEC – British Underwater Trials Evaluating Centre, Sabhal Mor Ostaig – Gaelic college.

Industry:Tourism dominates the local economy, but recently there has been growth in the IT and education sectors. The food and drink sector and its links with tourism and local produce are also important. Other industries include agriculture, fishing, aquaculture, crafts and teleworking.

The Gaelic College, *Sabhal Mor Ostaig*, part of the University of the Highlands and Islands, offers degree level courses in various aspects of Gaelic culture, including music and broadcasting. With the recent passing of the Gaelic Bill, the importance of this establishment is destined togrow.

Skye and Lochalsh Enterprise (SALE) has helped the development of many new businesses, and helped support essential services without which Skye would be less economically viable.

Quotes from local businesses
The funding has been great. Without it, it would be impossible to provide this essential service. **Uig Filling Station**
SALE has been more than helpful with their invaluable business advice and their financial assistance, without which I wouldn't be able to do this now – I would be looking at a few more years down the line. **The Skyak Sea Kayak School**

STORNOWAY

Local Authority: Comhairle nan Eilean Siar/Western Isles Council, Council Offices, Sandwick Road, Stornoway, Isle of Lewis HS1 2BW; ☎01851-703773; fax 01851-705349; www.cne-siar.gov.uk.

Local Enterprise Company: Western Isles Enterprise, James Square, 9 James Street, Stornoway, Isle of Lewis HS1 2QN; ☎01851-703703; fax 01851-704130; www.hie.co.uk.

Chamber of Commerce: Western Isles Chamber of Commerce, 30 Francis Street, Stornoway, Isle of Lewis HS1 2ND; ☎: 01851-700055; fax 01851-700066.

Jobcentre: 2 Castle Street, Stornoway, Isle of Lewis, HS1 2BA; ☎01851-763000.

Local Newspaper: Stornoway Gazette, 10 Francis Street, Stornoway, Isle of Lewis, HS1 2XE; ☎01851-702687; www.stornowaygazette.co.uk.

*Key Sectors:*Harris Tweed production, fishing, crofting, fish processing, construction/extraction.

Major employers: Stolt Sea Farms, Centrica plc, Quantanova (Singapore Technologies), Marine Harvest McConnell, Young's Bluecrest Seafoods, WISCO.

Industry: The population of the Western Isles is around 27,000, and the unemployment rate slightly higher than that in Scotland as a whole. In January 2003, the rate was 5.2 per cent.

The most important sectors of the Western Isles economy are fishing, fish farming and processing, agriculture, and the construction/extraction industry, particularly the oil-related elements of the latter. The other main sources of employment are local government and other services, distribution, transport and communications. Tourism too is important, although it is a vulnerable and somewhat unstable sector, with large annual variations in visitor numbers.

New sectors of potential growth are emerging, which include wind farming, renewable energies, fish farming diversification, teleworking, environment & niche tourism markets (e.g. activities, genealogy), Gaelic broadcasting.

Quotes from local businesses
The team we were able to recruit locally have exceeded all of our expectations in terms of their commitment and achievements. **CRITICALL**

> *Living and working in mainland Europe had lost its appeal and we decided that we needed to make a change. The infrastructure in the islands is world class, and the local skill register helped us find the right people for the company. On the islands you regain a sense of community – it's the quality of life that's made the biggest impression.* **IOMART plc**

KIRKWALL

Local Authority: Orkney Islands Council, Council Offices, School Place, Kirkwall, Orkney KW15 1NY; ☎01856-873535; fax 01856-874615; www.orkney.com.

Local Enterprise Company: Orkney Enterprise, 14 Queen Street, Kirkwall, Orkney KW15 1JE; ☎01856-874638; fax 01856-872915; www.scottish-enterprise.com.

Chamber of Commerce: Orkney Chamber of Commerce, PO Box 6202, Kirkwall, Orkney KW15 1YG; ☎01856-888791; fax 01856-876084.

Jobcentre: Tankerness Lane, Kirkwall, Orkney KW15 1AQ; ☎01856-875113.

Local Newspaper: The Orcadian, Hell's Half Acre, Hatston, Kirkwood, Orkney KW15 1HQ; ☎01856-879000.

Key Sectors: Farming, fishing, tourism, food processing.

Major employers: Orkney Islands Council, NHS Orkney, Talisman (UK) Ltd, Ortak.

Industry: Orkney has a population of 20,000. The unemployment rate in Orkney is favourable compared with the Western Isles and with Scotland as a whole: in January 2003 it stood at 2.4 per cent, below the national average.

The economy of the islands has traditionally been based on farming and fishing, but competition from elsewhere and the high costs of distribution and transport have affected their viability in recent years. The tourism and food processing industries are now increasing in importance. The food industry in particular is competing strongly in international markets.

As in the other islands, local government and other services are important employers in Orkney.

Orkney tops the list for school level educational attainment in Scotland – nearly 98 per cent of 19 year olds have level 2 qualifications, ie 5 standard grades or level 2 SVQs. Orkney College, based in Kirkwall, is an official partner of the University of the Highlands and Islands. The college offers state-of-the-art facilities and a range of learning opportunities.

Quotes from local businesses
Far from being a disadvantage, having an Orkney base has been instrumental in Aquatera's success. The work ethic is more sensitive, contacts are more personal, and clients pick up on the differences, compared to larger, anonymous companies with stereotypical business methods. **Aquatera**

> *Everyone involved is very excited about this development. It's great to see the new creamery being built – the future is looking good for us.* **Orkney Cheese Company**

LERWICK

Local Authority: Shetland Islands Council, Town Hall, Hillhead, Lerwick, Shetland ZE1 0HB; ☎01595-693535; fax 01595-744509; www.shetland.gov. uk.

Local Enterprise Company: Shetland Enterprise, Toll Clock Shopping Centre, 26 North Road, Lerwick, Shetland ZE1 0DE; ☎01595-693177; fax 01595-693208; www.shetland.hie.co.uk.

Jobcentre: Charlotte House, Commercial Road, Lerwick, Shetland ZE1 0LT; ☎01595-732050.

Local Newspaper: Shetland Times, Prince Alfred Street, Lerwick, Shetland ZE1 0EP; ☎01595-693622.

Key Sectors: Agriculture, knitwear, farming, seafood processing.

Major employers: BP, Shetland Islands Council.

Industry: The most northerly region of the British Isles, an area which seems to be added to maps almost as an afterthought (where it is not omitted altogether), Shetland is situated as far from Aberdeen as from Bergen in Norway – around 200 miles. It has a population of nearly 22,500. Because of the islands' situation in relation to fertile fishing grounds and major oil reserves, Shetland has favourable unemployment rates when compared with the rest of Scotland. At 2.1 per cent in 2003, it has the lowest unemployment rate of the three island groups.

Fisheries and oil production are far and away the biggest sectors of the Shetland economy. The relative value of the oil industry is declining since its peak in the 1980s, but it still contributes a significant input. To offset the loss in employment and revenue from oil production, efforts are being made to stimulate traditional industries such as agriculture and knitwear. Tourism, the knowledge based industries, including e-commerce and IT, and small scale manufacturing are growth areas.

Quote from a local business
SBIC is a first for Shetland and is part of an overall strategy to create new businesses and employment outwith the traditional fishing and oil industries. **Shetland Business Innovation Centre**

DIRECTORY OF MAJOR EMPLOYERS

20 LARGEST COMPANIES IN SCOTLAND 2003

Rank	Company	Activity
1	Royal Bank of Scotland Group	Banking/financial
2	Standard Life Assurance	Insurance
3	HBOS	Banking/financial
4	Scottish Power	Energy supply
5	Scottish & Newcastle	Brewing
6	Scottish & Southern Energy	Energy supply
7	FirstGroup	Public transport
8	British Energy	Energy supply
9	Stagecoach group	Public transport
10	Grampian Country Food Group	Food production & processing
11	Arnold Clark Automobiles	Vehicle retail
12	John Wood Group	Oil and gas exploration
13	John Menzies	Stationery & books retail
14	Weir Group	Engineering
15	Miller Group	Construction
16	Asco	Support operations, oil and gas industry
17	Johnston Press	Newspaper Publishing
18	Robert Wiseman Dairies	Milk products
19	Abbot Group	Oil and gas industry services
20	British Polythene Industries	Plastics manufacture

Source: the *Scotsman 250* annual list. For the full list of Scotland's 250 largest companies, see www.scotsman.com.

Public Services

The largest employers throughout Scotland are found in the public service sector. Relevant addresses have not been repeated if they are listed elsewhere in this book, as indicated.

Local councils – see *General Introduction* p. 35.

National Health Service – see *Daily Life* (Health Boards p.186) and *Employment* (NHS Trusts p. 271).

Universities – see *Daily Life* p. 126.

Police – see *Daily Life* p. 197.

Judicial system – see *Daily Life* p. 198.

Tourist Boards – see *Employment* p. 278.

Civil Service: The Scottish Executive Recruitment Unit, T Spur, Saughton House, Broomhouse Drive, Edinburgh EH11 3XD; ☎0131-244 3981; www.scotland.gov.uk; www.civil-service.gov.uk.

Scottish Water: PO Box 8855, Edinburgh EH10 6YQ; ☎0845-601 8855; www.scottishwater.co.uk.

*Highlands and Islands Enterprise:*Cowan House, Inverness Retail and Business Park, Inverness IV1 7GF; ☎01463-234171; fax 01463-244469; www.hie.co.uk.

The Post Office: Royal Mail Group plc, 148 Old Street, London EC1V 9HQ; ☎08457-223344; www.postoffice.co.uk.

Scottish Enterprise: Atlantic Quay, 150 Broomielaw, Glasgow G2 8LU; ☎0141-248 2700; fax 0141-221 3217; www.scotent.co.uk.

Scottish Executive: St. Andrew's House, Regent Road, Edinburgh EH1 3DG; ☎0131-556 8400; fax 0131-244 8240; www.scotland.gov.uk.

Retail

Arnold Clark Automobiles: 134 Nithsdale Drive, Glasgow G412PP; ☎0141-422 2700; www.arnoldclark.co.uk. Vehicle retail.

Booker plc: Equity House, Irthlington Road, Wellingborough, Northamptonshire NN8 1LT; ☎01933-371000; fax 01933-371010; www.booker-plc.com. Cash and carry wholesalers.

Dixons Group plc: Marylands Avenue, Hemel Hempstead, Herts HP2 7TG; ☎0870-850 3333; www.dixons-group-plc.co.uk. Electrical goods.

John Menzies: 108 Princes Street, Edinburgh EH2 3AA; ☎0131-225 8555; www.johnmenziesplc.com. Books and newspaper distribution and sales.

Kingfisher plc: 3 Sheldon Square, Paddington, London W2 6PX; ☎020-7372 8008; fax 020-7644 1001; www.kingfisher.co.uk. Owns the DIY retailer B&Q.

Kwik-Fit Ltd: 17 Costorphine Road, Edinburgh EH12 6DD; ☎0131-337 9200; fax 0131-337 0062; www.kwik-fit.co.uk. Motor parts.

Marks & Spencer plc: Marks and Spencer Group plc, Waterside House, 35 North Wharf Rd, London W2 1NW; ☎020-7935 4422; www.marks-and-spencer.com. Clothes, foods and household.

Robert Wiseman Dairies: 159 Glasgow Road, East Kilbride, Glasgow G74 4PA; ☎01355-244261; fax 01355-230352; www.wiseman-dairies.co.uk. Milk products sales.

J. Sainsbury plc: 33 Holborn, London EC1N 2HT; ☎020-7695 6000; fax 020-7695 7610; www.j-sainsbury.co.uk. Supermarkets.

W.H. Smith: Greenbridge Road, Swindon, Wiltshire SN3 3RX; ☎0870-444 6444; www.whsmith.co.uk. Stationery and books.

Somerfield plc: Somerfield House, Whitchurch Lane, Bristol BS14 0TJ; www.somerfield.plc.uk. Supermarkets.

Tesco plc: Tesco House, PO Box 44, Delamare Road, Cheshunt, Herts EN8 9SL; ☎0800-505555; www.tesco.com. Supermarkets.

Hotel, Bar & Restaurant Chains

Hilton Group plc: Maple Court, Reeds Crescent, Watford, Herts WD24 4QQ; ☎020-7856 8107; www.hiltongroup.com. Owns the famous hotels, as well as the Ladbrokes chain of betting shops.

Scottish and Newcastle plc: 33 Ellersly Road, Edinburgh EH12 6HX; ☎0131-528 2000; www.scottish-newcastle.com. Hotels, motel, bars and restaurants.

Whitbread plc: CityPoint, One Ropemaker Street, London EC2Y 9HX; ☎020-7606 4455; www.whitbread.co.uk. Pubs and restaurants.

Manufacturing

British Polythene Industries: 96 Port Glasgow Road, Greenock PA15 2UL; ☎01475-501000; fax 01475-743143; www.bpipoly.com. Plastics manufacture.

Norbord: Station Road, Cowie, Stirling FK7 7BQ; ☎01786-812921; fax 01786-815622; www.norbord.com. Wood-based laminates, veneers, flooring etc.

Ethicon Ltd: PO Box 408, Bankhead Avenue, Edinburgh EH11 4HE; ☎0131-453 5555; fax 0131-453 6011; www.ethicon.com. Medical and pharmaceutical products.

Grampian Country Food Group: New Grampian House, 3 The Boulevard, City West Business Park, Gelderd Road, Leeds LS12 6NX; ☎0113-386 5000; fax 0113-386 5133; www.gcfg.com. Meat and poultry production and processing.

Scottish and Newcastle plc: 33 Ellersly Road, Edinburgh EH12 6HX; ☎0131-528 2000; www.scottish-newcastle.com . Brewers.

Weir Group: 149 Newlands Road, Cathcart, Glasgow G44 4EX; ☎0141-637 7111; fax 0141-637 2221; www.weir.co.uk. Engineering.

Synetix Services: Unit 4, The Technology Centre, Offshore Technology Park, Bridge of Don, Aberdeen AB23 8GD; ☎01224-826628; fax 01224-827095; www.ici.com. Catalysts.

United Closures and Plastics: 1 Stuart Road, Bridge of Allan, Stirling FK9 4JG; ☎01786-833613; fax 01786-834233. Plastic bottles, caps and closures.

United Distillers & Vintners: Edinburgh Park, 5 Lochside Way, Edinburgh EH12 9DT; ☎0131-519 2000; fax 0131-519 2001. Alcoholic drinks.

Computers, IT & Electronics

Cisco Systems: Bothwell House, Pochard Way, Strathclyde Business Park, Bellshill ML4 3HB; ☎01698-847000; fax 01698-847070; www.cisco.com/uk. Networking for the internet.

GEC-Marconi Avionics: 6 South Gyle Street, Edinburgh EH5 2XS; ☎0131-343 4409; fax 0131-314 2839; www.gec.co.uk. Electronics.

*THUS:*1/2 Berkeley Square, 99 Berkeley Street, Glasgow G3 7HR; ☎0141-567 1234; www.thus.co.uk. Telecommunicarions, contact centres.

Motorola: Kelvin Industrial Estate, Colvilles Road, East Kilbride, Glasgow G75 0TG; ☎01355-355000; fax 01355-271959; www.

motorola.com. Computer hardware and electronics.

Finance & Banking

HBOS (Halifax/Bank of Scotland): The Mound, Edinburgh EH1 1YZ; ☎0131-470 2000; www.bankofscotland.co.uk. Banking and financial products.

The Royal Bank of Scotland: Customer Relations Manager, Freepost, PO Box 1727, Edinburgh EH12 9JN; www.royalbankscot.co.uk. Banking and financial products.

Scottish Building Society: 23 Manor Place, Edinburgh EH3 7XE; ☎0131-220 1111; fax 0131-220 2888; www.scottishbldgsoc.co.uk. Mortgages and savings.

Scottish Equitable: Head Office, Edinburgh Park, Edinburgh EH12 9SE; ☎08456 01 20 67; fax 0870 242 6788; www.scottishequitable.co.uk. Pensions and investments.

Scottish Life Assurance Company: 19 St Andrew Square, Edinburgh EH2 1YE; ☎0870-606 2000; fax 0131-456 7880; www.scottishlife.co.uk. Insurance, pensions and investments.

Scottish Widows: 69 Morrison Street, Edinburgh EH3 8BW; ☎0845 608 0371 0345-678910; www.scottishwidows.co.uk. Insurance, pensions and investments.

Standard Life Assurance: Standard Life House, 30 Lothian Road, Edinburgh EH1 2DH; ☎0131-225 2552; www.standardlife.co.uk. Insurance.

Construction

Barratt Construction: Golf Road, Ellon, AB41 9AT; ☎01358-724174; fax 01358- 724043; www.barratthomes.co.uk. House-building.

Bett Homes: Argyle House, The Castle Business Park, Stirling FK9 4TT; ☎01786-477777; fax 01786-477666; www.betthomes.co.uk. House-building.

Ferguson Shipbuilders Ltd: Castle Road, Port Glasgow, PA14 5NH; ☎01475742300. Ship-building and repair.

The Miller Group Ltd: 18 South Groathill Avenue, Edinburgh EH4 2LW; ☎0131-315 6000; fax 0131-315 6002; www.mining.miller.co.uk. General construction and civil engineering.

Morrison plc: Atholl House, 51 Melville Street, Edinburgh EH3 7HL; ☎0131-228 4188. General construction and civil engineering.

Redrow Homes: Redrow House, 3 Central Park Avenue, Larbert, Falkirk FK5 4RX; ☎01324-555536; fax 01324-574890; www.redrow.co.uk. House-building.

Fuel & Energy

AEA Technology plc: Exploration House, Offshore Technology Park, Bridge of Don, Aberdeen AB23 8GX; ☎01224-822535; fax 01224-822520; www.aeat.co.uk. Reservoir, process and pipeline engineering services.

Abbot Group: Minto Drive, Altens, Aberdeen AB12 3LW; ☎01224-279600; fax 01224-230400; www.abbotgroup.com. Oil and gas industry drilling services.

Asco UK: Aberdeen Offshore Supply

Base, South Esplanade East, Aberdeen AB11 9PB; ☎01224-241017. Oil and gas industry services/supplies.

BP Oil: Witan Gate House, 500/600 Witan Gate, Milton Keynes MK9 1ES; ☎0845-303 3377; www.bp.com. Oil exploration and supply.

Balmoral Group Ltd: Balmoral Park, Loirston, Aberdeen AB12 3GY; ☎01224-859000; www.balmoral-group.com. Surface and subsurface buoyancy design and manufacture.

British Energy plc: 3 Redwood Crescent, Peel Park, East Kilbride G74 5PR; ☎01355-262000; www.british-energy.co.uk. Electricity supply.

Gleaner Oils: Head Office, Milnfield, Elgin IV30 1UZ; ☎01343-557400; fax 01343-548534; www.shell.com. Vehicle and heating fuels.

John Wood Group: John Wood House, Greenwell Road, East Tullos, Aberdeen AB12 3AX; ☎01224-851000; fax 01224-851474; http://portal.woodgroup.com. Oil and gas exploration.

Scottish Power: Cathcart Business Park, Spean Street, Glasgow G44 4BE; ☎0845-2700 700; www.scottishpower.co.uk. Electricity supply.

Scottish & Southern Energy: Inveralmond House, 200 Dunkeld Road, Perth PH1 3AQ; ☎01738-456660; www.scottish-southern.co.uk. Energy supply.

Shell UK Exploration & Production: Shell Expro, 1 Altens Farm Road, Nigg, Aberdeen AB12 3FY; ☎01224-882000; www.shell.com. Oil exploration and supply.

Communications

British Telecom (BT): BT Correspondence Centre, TVTE Gateshead NE11 0ZZ; ☎Freefone 0800-800150; www.bt.com. National telephone network.

Vodafone: PO Box 549, Banbury OX17 3ZJ; ☎08701-666777; fax 08701-616500; www.vodafone.co.uk. Mobile phone network.

Media

BBC Scotland: Broadcasting House, The Tun, 111 Holyrood Road, Edinburgh EH8 8PJ; ☎0131-557 5888; www.bbc.co.uk/scotland. National and regional, non-commercial television and radio.

Border Television PLC: The Television Centre, Carlisle CA1 3NT; ☎01228-25101; www.border-tv.com. Regional commercial television.

British Sky Broadcasting Ltd: Grant Way, Isleworth, Middx TW7 5QD; ☎020-7705 3000; fax 020-7705 3030; www.sky.com. Satellite television.

Channel Four Television Corporation: 124 Horseferry Road, London SW1P 2TX; ☎020-7396 4444; www.channel4.com; www.channel4.com. National commercial television.

Grampian Television PLC: Craigshaw Business Park, West Tullos, Aberdeen AB12 3QH; ☎01224-848848; fax 01224-848800; www.grampiantv.co.uk. Regional commercial television.

ITN Scottish Bureau: 200 Gray's Inn Road, London WC1X 8XZ; ☎020-7833 3000; www.itn.co.uk. Television news.

Johnston Press: Oundle Rd, Woodston, Peterborough PE2 9QR; ☎01733-427184; www. johnstonpress.co.uk. Local newspaper publishing.

The Scotsman Publications Ltd: Barclay House, 108 Holyrood Road, Edinburgh EH8 8AS; ☎0131-620 8620; fax 0131-523 8615; www.scotsman.com. Newspaper publishing.

Scottish Television PLC: 200 Renfield Street, Glasgow G2 3PR; ☎0141-300 3000; www.scottishtv.co.uk. Regional commercial television.

Teletext Ltd (Scottish Editor): 39 St Vincent, Glasgow G1 2QQ; ☎0141-221 4457; www.teletext. co.uk; www.teletext.co.uk. Television and internet information service.

D. C Thomson & Co Ltd: 2 Albert Square, Dundee DD1 9QJ; ☎01382-223131; fax 01382-322214; www. dcthomson.co.uk. Newspaper and magazine publishing.

Public Transport

British Airports Authority (BAA): Edinburgh Airport, EH12 9DN; ☎0870-040 0007; fax 0131-344 3470; www.baa.co.uk. Airport management.

British Airways: Waterside, PO Box 365, Harmondsworth UB7 0GB; ☎0870-850 9850; www. britishairways.com. Domestic and international flights.

Caledonian MacBrayne: The Ferry Terminal, Gourock PA19 1QP; ☎01475-650100; fax 01475 637607; www.calmac.co.uk. National ferry services.

easyJet: easyLand, London Luton airport, Bedfordshire LU2 9LS; ☎0871-7500 100; www.easyjet. com. Domestic and international flights.

Great North Eastern Railway: Station Road, York YO1 6HT ; ☎08457-225 333; fax 01904 524532; www. gner.co.uk. Train services.

Highlands and Islands Airports (HIAL): Inverness Airport, Inverness IV7 2JB; ☎01667-462445; www.hial. co.uk. Airport management.

Lothian Region Transport Ltd: 1-4 Shrub Place, Edinburgh EH7 4PA; ☎0131 554 4494; fax 0131 554 6038. Bus services.

National Express Coaches: Ensign Court, 4 Vicarage Road, Edgbaston, Birmingham B15 3ES; ☎0121-625 1122; fax 0121-456 1397; www. nationalexpress.com. Long distance coach services.

First Scotrail: Caledonian Chambers, 87 Union Street, Glasgow G1 3TA; ☎0845-601 5929; www.firstgroup. com/scotrail. Railway infrastructure.

Scottish Citylink Coaches: Buchanan Bus Station, Killermont Street, Glasgow G3 2NP; ☎0141 332 9644; fax 0141 332 4488; www.citylink.co.uk. Medium and long distance coach services.

Stagecoach: 10 Dunkeld Road, Perth Scotland PH1 5TW; ☎01738-442111; www.stagecoachbus.com. Bus and coach services.

Virgin Trains: PO Box 713, Birmingham B5 4HH; ☎0870-789 1234; fax 0121-654 7500; www.virgintrains. co.uk. Train services.

Research & Technology

Hannah Research Institute: Hannah Research Park, Mauchline Road, Ayr KA6 5HL; ☎01292-674000; fax 01292-674003; www.hri.sari. ac.uk. Research into the biology of lactation and the use of milk in food products.

ICI Nobel Enterprises: Ardeer Site, Stevenston, Ayrshire KA20 3LN; ☎01294-487000; fax 01294-487230; www.ici.com. Automotive, aerospace, nitrocellulose, enterprise.

Macaulay Land Use Research Institute: Craigiebuckler, Aberdeen AB15 8QH; ☎01224-498200; fax 01224-311556; www.mluri.sari.ac.uk. Research into rural land use and development.

Moredun Research Institute: Pentlands Science Park, Bush Loan, Midlothian EH26 0PZ; ☎0131-445 5111; www.moredun.org.uk. Research into infectious diseases of sheep and other ruminants.

Rowett Research Institute: Greenburn Road, Bucksburn, Aberdeen AB21 9SB; ☎01224-712751; fax 01224-715349; www.rowett.ac.uk. Research into human nutrition.

Scottish Crop Research Institute: Mylnefield, Invergowrie, Dundee DD2 5DA; ☎01382-562731; fax 01382 562426; www.scri.sari.ac.uk. Crop research, including genetic modication.

Tayside Optical Technology: Kinnoull Street, Dundee DD2 3ED; ☎01382-833022; fax 01382-833824; www.totl.co.uk. Thin optical film coatings.

Online Company Directories

The following websites include searchable databases of companies based in a geographical area or a particular field of business.

Companies House: www. companieshouse.gov.uk. Database of all UK companies.

*Dundee Chamber of Commerce:*www. dundeechamber.co.uk/directory/ search.cfm.

Glasgow Chamber of Commerce: www.glasgowchamberonline.org/ memberdir.asp.

Inverness Chamber of Commerce: www. netmedia.co.uk/users/chambers/ members.html.

*Scottish Oil and Gas Industries:*www. oilandgas.co.uk/.

*Perth & Kinross Council:*www.pkc.gov. uk/business/businessdirectory.htm.

Useful Publications & Websites

Writers' & Artists' Yearbook, published annually by A&C Black (London).

The Writer's Handbook, published annually by Macmillan (London). Both the above list UK publishers and other media companies together with contact details of newspapers and magazines.

Times Top 100 Graduate Employers, ed. Martin Birchall (High Fliers Publications 2004).

EURES (European Employment Services): http://europa.eu.int/eures/.

British Employment Law: www.emplaw. co.uk.

STARTING A BUSINESS

CHAPTER SUMMARY

- ○ EU nationals have the right to move to the UK to set up in business without any restrictions.
- ○ 22 Local Enterprise Companies across Scotland provide help to people who wish to set up their own businesses.
- ○ There are no great legal difficulties to starting a small business.
- ○ You may operate your business as a sole trader, a partnership, a company or a franchise.
- ○ If your business is to run from a property which needs alterations for the purpose, you will have to apply to the planning department of the local council for permission for 'change of use'.
- ○ You can run your own home as a bed and breakfast without notifying the authorities.
- ○ If you employ somebody in your business, you must tell the Inland Revenue.
- ○ Businesses pay non-domestic (business) rates to the local authority based on the rateable value of the property and the non-domestic rate poundage.

Traditionally, Scotland has created fewer new businesses than the rest of the UK and many other industrialised countries. Latterly, this has been identified as undesirable for the Scottish economy, and a concerted effort has been made to improve the situation. It seems to be working: the number of business start-ups has increased steadily since the 1990s while the number of failures decreased. This is partly as a result of the 'Enterprise System', a network of local enterprise companies (LECs) set up to assist the formation and continuance of new businesses.

If you choose to move to a rural area of Scotland for the quality of life, you will find that, because of the small population density, the chance of finding 'a job' is limited. Certainly, the traditional 'nine to five and weekends off' form of employment is very thin on the ground. To make a living wage, many people take a number of short-term, seasonal and part-time jobs. An alternative is to start your own business, a less daunting prospect than it may at first appear. There are an increasing number of very small businesses in rural areas, many of them designed to start and stay small and local, others with the potential to grow into far larger companies.

As a result of recent efforts to encourage entrepreneurship in Scotland, there has been a growth in the number of small businesses within the country. Although Scotland as a whole is still below the UK average for the numbers of new businesses created, this disguises great regional variation in the figures between different Scottish locations: the rural parts of Scotland are in fact above the UK average. The highest numbers of businesses relative to their populations are in the Orkney and Shetland Islands, with high business densities also in Grampian, the Highlands, Borders and Dumfries and Galloway. The lowest densities of businesses are found in the Central Belt.

Part of the reason for the higher percentage of businesses in rural areas is that, although the population is low, they need the same range of services as people in more populous areas. This means there may be more 'gaps in the market' which can be filled by a local business. The residents of these economically marginal areas are generally enthusiastic about supporting local businesses rather than going further afield for services, even if it means paying a slightly higher price for a product or service. The 'use it or lose it' mentality is strong so you may find it possible to compete against businesses which, on paper, can undercut you. Many rural residents, for example, will make a point of buying groceries in their small local shop, rather than travelling to a larger town where they could buy the same goods slightly cheaper.

New technology has created far more opportunities for entrepreneurs to set up small businesses. With no more than a computer and a website, you can set up and carry on an e-commerce business from the most remote areas. In the publishing industry, more and more functions are being carried out remotely by freelance writers, editors and indexers. Copy is produced and sent electronically with no need for long, expensive trips to a publisher based in Edinburgh or Glasgow – or indeed, New York or Lausanne.

The tourism industry presents plenty of opportunity for small businesses. Scotland has long been a popular holiday destination both for foreign and UK visitors. They all need accommodation, food and drink, and 'things to do' during their holidays. And they all want to spend money on good value products and services.

Businesses which are less likely to do well in remote rural areas are those which incur expensive transport costs. Traditional agriculture is becoming hardly viable in many remote areas, although with some imagination and the willingness to try something new, there are markets to be tapped in this area too. With concerns about the genetic modification of foods being much in the news, small-scale organic farms and market gardens are finding new customers among catering businesses and residents looking for good quality, local produce. In the late nineties the bottom fell out of the Scottish livestock market, with signs that it was never likely to recover to previous levels, particularly in remote areas where less fertile land and high transport costs made animal farming uncompetitive. Some who switched to keeping rare and unusual breeds of animal, such as Hebridean sheep and goats found they could make a better living, both by inviting tourists to visit their animals and by producing premium-priced animal products.

Residence Regulations

EU nationals have the right to move to the UK to set up in business, to buy an existing business or to provide services without any restrictions, and do not need a visa.

Businessmen and self-employed persons from other countries are free to visit the UK and transact business during their stay (as long as they have the necessary visa and/or entry clearance). Those who want to come permanently to the UK to set themselves up in business or self-employment, or to join as a partner or take over an existing business, must satisfy certain requirements. Most importantly, they must bring at least £200,000 of their own money to invest in the business and they must show that the business will create new, paid full-time employment for at least two people who are already settled in the UK. For further details see the chapter *Residence and Entry Regulations*.

CREATING A NEW BUSINESS

It is not difficult, legally, to start your own business. In most cases, there is little to stop you setting up in business overnight. But this would be foolhardy without having done plenty of groundwork first. There are two broad approaches to identifying an idea for a business, which depend on personal circumstances and requirements. If you are committed to living in a certain part of Scotland, you need to survey the locality to identify services which are lacking and those which are well-supplied, and from this come up with a business which is needed and which you can provide. Alternatively, if you already have your business idea, the best approach is to decide in which area of Scotland it will work best. This will depend on such things as where you are likely to find your customers and suppliers and whether you need good transport infrastructure for your business to work efficiently, or whether this is irrelevant for your particular product or service.

There is a third way which does not depend at all on the area in which you live and work. Knowledge-based occupations using computers and the internet as their supply route can run from a remote island with no road access as easily as from the centre of a busy city. Obvious areas of work ideally suited to teleworking include writing, editing, indexing, website design and other computer-based services.

If you are considering a more conventional area of business, changing trends are an important factor to bear in mind. Many people who move to tourist areas of Scotland assume that they will be able to make a reasonable income from offering bed & breakfast in their houses. Although this is one of the easiest businesses to set up – the legal and planning requirements to make this sort of use of your family home are minimal – it is not necessarily the sure-fire income-generator it once was. Long-term Highland residents look back fondly to the 1970s and before, when there was a shortage of places to stay. Almost every household offered their spare room to visitors, and once those rooms were full, visitors were happy to sleep on the floor. Or so the story goes, anyway. Today the picture is very different. Most visitors who are staying in an area now prefer self-catering cottages, so the bed and breakfasts mainly attract those who are touring the area. Tourists who travel around, stopping for one or two nights at B&Bs en route tend to prefer those with en suite facilities, and features such as a private lounge for guests. Larger B&B establishments on main travel routes which can offer private facilities are thus able to generate a reasonable income, while the small family home with a spare room or two and shared bathroom facilities now loses out.

When researching an area, it is wise to keep in mind the community relations implications of your proposed venture, as well as its business prospects. For instance, if you plan to move to a small community, setting up in direct competition with an existing business is not guaranteed to get you off on the right foot with your neighbours.

Planning Permission

If your business is to run from a property which needs conversion or alterations for the purpose, you will need to investigate the planning implications. Unless the property was previously used for the same purpose, you will have to apply to the planning department of the local council for permission for 'change of use'. Where the business is open to members of the public they will take into account such things as parking provision and health and safety considerations. In the end, it may be that you are simply not allowed to run that sort of business from the premises you have in mind. So it is wise to do your research first – ideally before you've even bought the property. Planning department officials will advise you on the chances of obtaining planning permission.

It can be frustrating that at times planning regulations seem somewhat arbitrary: if, for instance you buy a small cottage and let it out for self-catering, there is no requirement to apply for change of use nor to ensure parking arrangements or health and safety considerations comply with local council regulations. If you buy the same cottage and turn it into a small café or shop you do need planning permission and the requirements regarding parking and health and safety are stringent.

BUYING AN EXISTING BUSINESS

One way of avoiding planning problems, and of avoiding the pitfalls of starting a business completely from scratch, is to buy an existing business. This affords the obvious benefits of being able to walk into a business and take up where the previous owner left off. However, it is advisable to do some research locally to discover why the business is being sold, and how long it has been on the market. If it didn't do well, you need to work out whether you could make a go of a similar business in the same place. The viability of the business is generally reflected in the price asked, of course – a thriving business with 'a genuine reason for sale' is likely to cost you far more than one which has been struggling to make a profit.

Buying a franchise is another way into business, which takes some of the risk out of setting up on your own. Franchises have the advantage of offering, in most cases, a tried and tested name and product, training and back-up support. The pros and cons of franchises are discussed further below.

Finding Premises or an Existing Business

Properties suitable for conversion into business premises, as well as existing businesses, can be found for sale and to rent from the same sources as domestic properties. Estate Agents and Solicitors Property Centres have commercial properties on their books. Details can be obtained from the local office, from their newspapers and through their websites. See *Setting Up Home* for a full list of contacts.

Local newspapers also advertise businesses and business properties, as do regional advertising newspapers, such as *Scot-Ads* (☎08457-434343;www.scot-ads.com).

Cost of Buying a Business

When considering businesses for sale or to lease, the price asked will depend on a number of factors. Bear in mind that some are sold simply as premises, previously used for a certain purpose, while others are selling the entire business, together with fixtures and fittings, stock and 'goodwill' – i.e. you are paying an element for the existing customer base that hopefully will continue to patronise the business after it changes hands. Location is, of course, another important element of the asking price.

Always try to ascertain how long the property has been for sale, as this is generally a good guide to whether the price being asked is reasonable or not. If it has been on the market for at least a year it is generally worth making an initial offer below the asking price. Where they are selling a business as a going concern, the vendors should make copies of previous accounts available to you. If they will not, or say they have none available, it is wise to be cautious – it may not be such a thriving business as they imply. There are few regulations in relation to bed and breakfast providers, so it is rare to find that such businesses maintain full accounts.

It may be possible to find mortgage schemes specifically tailored to your particular needs. For instance, the Scottish Building Society has a 'Flexible Guest

House Mortgage' designed for those who wish to buy or refinance a guest house or bed and breakfast business.

Useful Address

Scottish Building Society: 23 Manor Place, Edinburgh EH3 7XE; ☎0131-220 1111; www.scottishbldgsoc.co.uk.

Prices of Business Premises

Prices of business premises vary greatly depending on location. Generally, the closer to centres of population, the more expensive the property.

SAMPLE BUSINESSES FOR SALE IN SCOTLAND IN NOVEMBER 2004

Type	Place	Area	Price
Post office & shop	Dornoch		Offers over £120,000
Book shop	City centre	Aberdeen	Offers over £30,000
Bar & Nightclub	Kilmarnock	Glasgow	Fixed price £380,000
Coffee shop & gift shop	Kelso	Borders	Offers over £245,000
Hotel with public bar	Hopeman	Moray	Offers over £325,000
Shop	Dumfries	Dumfries & Galloway	Offers over £49,950
Restaurant & Takeaway	Newington	Edinburgh	Offers over £355,000[

PROCEDURES INVOLVED IN STARTING A BUSINESS

People who work for themselves on their own or in partnership with one or more people are classified as self-employed. You must inform the Inland Revenue and your local Tax Office if you are self-employed, and if your taxable turnover (total sales) is more than £58,000 in a 12 month period, you must also register for value added tax (VAT) with Customs and Excise. All three bodies can be notified simultaneously through filling in form CWF1 Notification of Self-Employment and returning it to the Inland Revenue. The form is available from your local Inland Revenue office or can be downloaded from their website www.inlandrevenue.gov.uk.

There is a very useful series of factsheets at www.bgateway.com/ .

Business Structures

There are a number of different structures you can adopt for a business, which vary in the number and type of regulations the owner is required to observe.

Sole Trader. The simplest form of business. As its name suggests, this is a 'one-man' or 'one-woman' business. There is no need to register it with anybody, other than notifying the Inland Revenue that you are self-employed. You will be liable to pay National Insurance contributions unless your earnings are very low, in which case you may be able to elect not to pay contributions until your earnings reach the statutory level. For details of rates of National Insurance, see *Daily Life*.

There is risk involved if the business should fail, because a sole trader is personally liable for all debts, which means he or she could lose all their assets, including their house.

Records of all income and outgoings should be kept, together with relevant receipts, because these details must be entered on the self-assessment tax return, sent each year in April. This asks for the information required to calculate income tax and capital gains tax for the year. Once the form is completed, it is returned to the Inland Revenue, who will calculate the tax owed if they receive it before 30th September. Alternatively, the business owner or their accountant can calculate the tax bill, in which case it must be returned by 31st January. There is no requirement to send receipts with the tax return, but the tax office may ask to see them to check the submitted figures.

If a sole trader trades under a name other than that of the owner, the owner's name and address must legally be displayed at the business premises and on stationery.

Partnership. Where two or more people run a business together, they may set up a partnership. Partners can set up a business as informally as a sole trader, but this may not be advisable. Even the best of friends or colleagues who work well together might have disagreements once entering business, and this could lead to disputes in the future unless financial arrangements regarding the business are clearly laid out in the first place. For this reason, a formal deed of partnership, drawn up by a solicitor, should be considered, although it is not mandatory.

A self-assessment tax return is completed in April by each of the partners. The tax bill for each is calculated as if their share of the partnership is a profit that they have made on their own.

If a partnership is trading under a name other than that of the owners, their names and addresses should be displayed. Partners are each personally liable for all the debts of the business should it fail.

Company. Setting up a company is a far more complicated procedure than starting a business in the ways listed above. It may not be necessary or worthwhile to turn it into such a formal and highly regulated structure, at least in the early days when the business is small and still finding its feet. Company officers have wide responsibilities and obligations in law, so it is a good idea to take advice from a solicitor or an accountant as to whether an incorporated company is the best way to run your business.

One of the biggest advantages of a company is that, in most cases, a director's or member's liability for debts is limited, so personal assets are not at risk if the company is wound up.

There are four main types of company:

O *Private company limited by shares.* Members' liability is limited to the amount unpaid on shares they hold.
O *Private company limited by guarantee.* Members' liability is limited to the amount they have agreed to contribute to the company's assets if it is wound up.
O *Private unlimited company.* There is no limit to the member's liability.
O *Public limited company (PLC).* The company's shares may be offered for sale to the general public and members' liability is limited to the amount unpaid on shares held by them.

Briefly, a private company must have a minimum of one director and a company secretary, while a public company must have at least two directors and a formally qualified company secretary. The business of the company and the way it will be run is laid out in a memorandum and articles of association. These itemise such matters as the minimum and maximum number of directors it should have, how many of these constitute a quorum at meetings and the procedure should the company be wound up at any time. Companies are legally obliged to hold regular, minuted meetings for members, and to deliver full annual accounts and an annual return to Companies House. The names, addresses and occupations of all directors must be notified to Companies House, and any changes must be notified immediately. These details are available for public inspection by anyone who asks.

It is possible to buy ready-made companies from company formation agents, and company registration agents will help with the work involved in forming a new company. Addresses can be found in Business Pages, Yellow Pages and www. yell.com. Agents include:

First Scottish Formations: Bonnington Bond, 2 Anderson Place, Edinburgh EH6 5NP; ☎0131-554 6006; www.fsss.co.uk/services/formations.html.

Scotts Company Formations: 5 Logie Mill, Edinburgh EH7 4HH; ☎0131-556 5800; www.millar-bryce.com/.

Alternatively, you can incorporate a company yourself by sending the following to Companies House:

O A *memorandum of association* including the company's name, the address of the registered office, and what the company will do (its object.) This may be stated as simply as 'to carry on business as a general commercial

company.'
- *Articles of association* which set out the rules for running the company's internal affairs.
- *Form 10* listing personal details of the company's directors and secretary.
- *Form 12*, a statutory decollation of compliance with all the legal requirements relating to the incorporation of a company.
- A *registration fee* of £20. (A premium 'same-day service' is also available at £80 which guarantees incorporation on the same day documents are received at Companies House offices as long as they are received before 3pm).

The rules governing the four different types of company are fairly complex, so full details should be obtained from Companies House (Companies House Scotland Office, 37 Castle Terrace, Edinburgh EH12EB; ☎0870-333 3636; fax 0131-535 5820; www.companieshouse.gov.uk) which issues a range of guidance booklets which are sent free of charge on request or available from their website.

Franchise. The full term for this way of doing business is 'business format franchising'. It is the granting of a licence by one person (the franchisor) to another (the franchisee) which entitles the franchisee to trade under the trade mark/trade name of the franchisor and to make use of an entire package, comprising all the elements necessary to establish a previously untrained person in the business and to run it with assistance of a predetermined basis.

The franchisor receives an initial fee from the franchisee, payable at the outset. This is followed by on-going management service fees, usually based on a percentage of annual turnover or mark-ups on supplies. The franchisor has an obligation to support the franchise network with training, product development, advertising, promotional activities and management services.

A formal contract must be made between franchisor and franchisee, and legal advice is essential. It is also strongly recommended that any franchise you consider should be run by a member of the British Franchise Association (Thames View, Newtown Road, Henley-on-Thames, Oxon RG9 1HG; ☎01491-578050; fax 01491-573517; www.british-franchise.org.uk) the regulatory body for franchising in the UK.

SOURCES OF FINANCE

There are a number of sources of funding to assist with the formation or expansion of a business, although unless you have some personal capital to invest, whether from your savings or through financial help from friends and relatives, you may find it difficult to lever further funds from external sources. Broadly, the formal sources of finance are banks, venture capitalists and the public sector. As part of the move to encourage the formation of businesses of all sizes in Scotland, a variety of public bodies have funds available to assist new businesses to get off the ground and to develop or expand existing businesses.

Enterprise Companies

These were set up in 1991, largely funded initially by the Scottish Office and latterly by the Scottish Executive. The two main enterprise companies are Scottish Enterprise (SE), whose area of operation is southern and central Scotland, and Highland and Islands Enterprise (HIE) who cover the north. Their purpose is to work in partnership with both the public and private sectors to encourage and develop business growth, to enhance the skills of the Scottish workforce through offering a wide range of training courses and business advice, and to promote Scotland's international competitiveness. Scottish Development International is an arm of SE which works to attract international companies to Scotland. If you have a business which you wish to move with you to Scotland, they may be able to assist with finding premises and may negotiate a relocation package as an incentive to bring your business here.

SE and HIE carry out their functions at a local level through a network of Local Enterprise Companies (LECs), which offer a range of services including advice and finance, in the form of grants and loans under a variety of schemes.

Useful Addresses

Scottish Development International: Enquiry Desk,,SDI Headquarters, Atlantic Quay, 150 Broomielaw, Glasgow, G2 8LU; ☎0141-228 2828; fax 0141-228 2089; www.scottishdevelopmentinternational.com.

Scottish Executive: St. Andrew's House, Regent Road, Edinburgh EH1 3DG; ☎0131-556 8400; fax 0131-244 8240; www.scotland.gov.uk.

Scottish Enterprise: 5 Atlantic Quay, 150 Broomielaw, Glasgow G2 8LU; ☎0141-248 2700; fax 0141-221 3217; www.scottish-enterprise.com.

Highlands and Islands Enterprise: Cowan House, Inverness Retail and Business Park, Inverness IV1 7GF; ☎01463-234171; fax 01463-244469; www.hie.co.uk.

There is a network of 22 local enterprise companies across Scotland. Generally, you should approach the LEC in your geographical area in the first instance for advice and information about grants and loans which may be available. It is difficult to give guidance on the sort of businesses different LECs might be prepared to fund, because these vary between areas depending on perceived local needs, and vary from year to year depending on political pressures to concentrate on certain forms of business at the expense of others. For instance, while e-commerce is new and therefore fashionable, funds are more likely to be available for internet businesses than for more traditional tourist businesses such as the setting up of a self-catering cottage. But the converse could be the case in a few years time in the face of changing circumstances. It is always worth asking the enterprise companies what schemes they are currently funding. Indeed, it may be that you choose a certain area for your business because the LEC has a scheme to assist just that sort of venture, while the neighbouring LEC is less keen.

Addresses of Local Enterprise Companies

Argyll & the Islands Enterprise: The Enterprise Centre, Kilmory Industrial Estate, Lochgilphead, Argyll PA31 8SH; ☎01546-602281; fax 01546-603964; www. hie.co.uk.

Caithness & Sutherland Enterprise: Tollemache House, High Street, Thurso, Caithness KW14 8AZ; ☎01847-896115; fax 01847-893383; www.hie.co.uk.

Inverness & Nairn Enterprise: The Green House, Beechwood Park North, Inverness IV2 3BL; ☎01463-713504; fax 01463-702002; www.ine.co.uk.

Lochaber Enterprise: St Mary's House, Gordon Square, Fort William PH33 6DY; ☎01397-704326; fax 01397-705309; www.hie.co.uk.

Moray, Badenoch & Strathspey Enterprise: The Apex, Forre Enterprise Park, Forres, IV36 2AB; ☎01309-696000; fax 01309-690001; www.scottish-enterprise. com.

Orkney Enterprise: 14 Queen Street, Kirkwall, Orkney KW15 1JE; ☎01856-874638; fax 01856-872915; www.scottish-enterprise.com.

Ross & Cromarty Enterprise: 69-71 High Street, Invergordon IV18 0AA; ☎01349-853666; fax 01349-853833; www.race.co.uk.

Scottish Enterprise Ayrshire: 17-19 Hill Street, Kilmarnock KA3 1HA; ☎01563-526623; fax 01563-543636; www.scottish-enterprise.com.

Scottish Enterprise Borders: Bridge Street, Galashiels TD1 1SW; ☎01896-758991; fax 01896-758625; www.scottish-enterprise.com.

Scottish Enterprise Dumfries & Galloway: Solway House, Dumfries Enterprise Park, Dumfries DG1 3SJ; ☎01387-245000; fax 01387-246244; www.scottish-enterprise.com.

Scottish Enterprise Dunbartonshire: Spectrum House, Clydebank Business Park, Clydebank, Glasgow G81 2DR; ☎0141-951 2121; fax 0141-951 1907; www. scottish-enterprise.com.

Scottish Enterprise Edinburgh & Lothian: Apex House, 99 Haymarket Terrace, Edinburgh EH12 5HD; ☎0131-313 4000; fax 0131-313 4231; www.scottish-enterprise.com.

Scottish Enterprise Fife: Kingdom House, Saltire Centre, Glenrothes, Fife KY6 2AQ; ☎01592-623000; fax 01592-623149; www.scottish-enterprise.com.

Scottish Enterprise Forth Valley: Laurel House, Laurelhill Business Park, Stirling FK7 9JQ; ☎01786-451919; fax 01786-478123; www.scottish-enterprise. com.

Scottish Enterprise Glasgow: 50 Waterloo Street, Glasgow G2 6HQ; ☎0141-204 1111; fax 0141-248 1600; www.scottish-enterprise.com.

Scottish Enterprise Grampian: 27 Albyn Place, Aberdeen AB10 1DB; ☎01224-252000; fax 01224-213417; www.scottish-enterprise.com.

Scottish Enterprise Lanarkshire: New Lanarkshire House, Strathclyde Business Park, Bellshill ML4 3AD; ☎01698-745454; fax 01698-842211; www.scottish-enterprise.com.

Scottish Enterprise Renfrewshire: 27 Causeyside Street, Paisley PA1 1UL; ☎0141-848 0101; fax 0141-848 6930; www.scottish-enterprise.com.

Scottish Enterprise Tayside: Enterprise House, 45 North Lindsay Street, Dundee DD1 1HT; ☎01382-223100; fax 01382-201319; www.scottish-enterprise.com.

Shetland Enterprise: Toll Clock Shopping Centre, 26 North Road, Lerwick, Shetland ZE1 0DE; ☎01595-693177; fax 01595-693208; www.shetland.hie.co.uk.

Skye & Lochalsh Enterprise: Kings House, The Green, Portree, Isle of Skye IV51 9BS; ☎01478-612841; fax 01478-612164; www.sale.hie.co.uk.

Western Isles Enterprise: James Square, 9 James Street, Stornoway, Isle of Lewis HS1 2QN; ☎01851-703703; fax 01851-704130; www.hie.co.uk.

Local Councils

Local councils too have their own financial packages to assist in the improvement of properties and the creation and expansion of businesses. Generally these would be administered by the Economic Development Department or the local equivalent. (Department names vary between councils, so the best thing is to enquire via the switchboard or reception as to who would deal with your particular enquiry.) See the full list of local councils in the *General Introduction*.

In the Highlands, there is an additional Enterprise Trust, incorporated in 1986 and now funded solely by the Highland Council. It provides support, grants and loans for businesses.

Useful Address

Highland Opportunity Ltd: 81A Castle Street, Inverness IV2 3EA; ☎01463-228340; www.highland-opportunity.com.

Crofters Commission

If you are buying a croft or becoming a croft tenant, the Crofters Commission (4-6 Castle Wynd, Inverness IV2 3EQ; ☎01463-663450; fax 01463-711820; www.crofterscommission.org.uk) has its own grant and loan schemes to assist with approved business ventures. If, for instance, you wish to set up a market garden on your croft, you may be able to get grants for a percentage of the costs of fencing and of purchasing polythene tunnels in which to grow your produce.

However – and this is an important however – these public bodies have limited funds, so whether you will actually get the assistance you require is another question. It is a myth that grants are freely available for businesses in Scotland: only around six per cent of money for new businesses comes in the form of grants. Although guidance is provided regarding the sort of projects that may be funded and the form in which a business plan should be presented, even if you follow these to the letter there is never any guarantee assistance will be forthcoming. In the end, all you can do is apply, backing up your application with a well thought-out, well-presented proposal and business plan in respect of what you wish to do. But you would be taking a big risk if your business idea relies on getting financial assistance. Look at the possibility of grants as an opportunity to start out a little more ambitiously than you would if you needed to rely solely on your existing resources and maybe a bank loan.

Loan Finance

Most new businesses which receive external finance get it mainly in the form of loans, usually from the banks. Loans account for 40 per cent of total external funding for new businesses. Loans are available at competitive rates from some other sources. LECs, local authorities and the Crofters Commission may offer low interest loans for certain items or buildings. The Princes Scottish Youth Business Trust (6th Floor, 53 Bothwell Street, Glasgow G2 6TS; ☎0141-248 4999; www. psybt.org.uk) specialises in loans to under-25s who have a viable business idea.

Whether you can obtain a loan from any of these will depend on the quality of your business plan, the amount of revenue your business will generate, the security you can provide and your own personal credibility. As the main concern of any lender will be your ability to repay the loan and meet the interest charges, your main concern must be to convince them you are a 'safe bet'.

Those businesses which apply for, and receive, a loan are in the minority. In fact, fewer than 30 per cent depend on loans, whether because they do not wish to take on the risks and costs involved, or whether they are unable to raise external finance. It is very often those which do rely on this sort of financial assistance that get into trouble, so you need to think carefully about whether you actually need a loan or can manage without.

Equity Capital

This is the core capital of the business, which helps to set it up in the first place and keep it going. If you have a good equity base it can help to unlock other funds such as loans or grants. You may have enough capital for this purpose from personal and informal sources. If not, there are other sources of equity capital, but they are not easy to obtain, and may involve you in losing some control over your running of the business.

Private individuals, venture capitalists and the public sector may inject funds if you can convince them your business is a sure-fire winner. However, their risks are high, so they will generally expect a high return. Where a substantial up-front investment is required, banks may be unable to finance such a project due to lack of security or cashflow – the high street banks are not in the business of risk-taking, which is perhaps why so few new businesses obtain funding from this source. Venture capitalists are professional investors looking for a good return on their money, and will therefore only back businesses capable of earning significant financial returns. Many of them avoid start-up businesses, seeing them as too big a risk and instead concentrate on developing existing businesses with a strong track record.

A more promising route for a new business is to approach public sector venture funders. Scottish Equity Partners, linked with Scottish Enterprise, may be prepared to invest where a private venture capitalist would not. Some LECs can also assist in this area. Not only can they inject funds but they may also play a role in encouraging other private-sector investors to take part.

Useful Addresses

Information on sources of venture capital is available from the following:

The British Venture Capital Association: 3 Clements Inn, London WC2A 2AZ; ☎020-7025 2950; fax 020-7025 2951; www.bvca.co.uk.

Scottish Equity Partners: 17 Blythswood Square, Glasgow G2 4AD; ☎0141-273 4000; fax 0141-273 4001; www.sep.co.uk.

LINC Scotland: Queens House, 19 St Vincent Place, Glasgow G1 2DT; ☎0141-221 3321; www.lincscot.co.uk.

Scottish Development International: Enquiry Desk,,SDI Headquarters, Atlantic Quay, 150 Broomielaw, Glasgow, G2 8LU; ☎0141-228 2828; fax 0141-228 2089; www.scottishdevelopmentinternational.com.

WRITING A BUSINESS PLAN

Before deciding whether to lend or grant you monies for your business, potential funders require a business plan which lays out in detail your proposal together with your projected costs and income.Whether you are applying for finance to a private or a public sector organisation, they will need to be assured that they will generate a return on their investment, either in the short or the long term – although the nature of the return may vary: in the case of a bank or a venture capitalist this will be seen in purely monetary terms, whereas a public organisation such as a local enterprise company or a local council may classify a good return on investment in other ways, such as the creation of a number of new full-time jobs, or the provision of a needed service in a particular geographical area.

Both groups will be looking to avoid risk, and they are also likely to be choosing between a number of business ideas, of which yours is just one. So a business plan which sets out your proposal clearly and predicts a good return on investment is essential to help beat the competition.

A business plan would normally include the elements in the chart below –

although the names and order of the subjects might vary from plan to plan, they should all be covered somewhere in the document.

CONTENTS OF A BUSINESS PLAN

1. Commercial section:

Title page	Products and services
Table of contents	History of you and your team
Introduction	Objectives of the business
Description of the business and market	

2. Financial section:

Profit budget	Past accounts
Cash-flow forecast	Future accounts
Current financial circumstances	
Financial requirements:	amount requested
	purpose of financing
	use of funds
	description of security (if seeking a loan)

3. Appendices and supporting documentation:

e.g. Photographs, samples, letters, forms, documents.

Things to bear in mind when writing the plan are that it should be clearly laid out and easy to understand. Excluding appendices, aim for a plan of about ten to 12 pages. While putting forward the 'best case scenario' regarding the prospects of the business, don't be tempted to exaggerate. Funders may hold you accountable for any statements which prove false or untenable. Try to see the funders' point of view, which is likely to be far narrower than your own. Focus on those aspects of the business which will be important to them. Most importantly, get the figures right. Providers of finance will want to know how much the business will make after paying expenses and salaries, how long it will take you to break even, and will compare your personal finances with the proposed business finances. It is advisable to have your figures verified by a qualified accountant – this in itself will carry weight with the funders.

Advice on producing a business plan that works is available from various sources. Local enterprise companies may have advisors who will help on an individual basis, or they may offer a business planning course you can attend. Business Gateway, a partner of Scottish Enterprise, has interactive business tools on its website at www.bgateway.com/interactive – zone.asp.

There are also business planning computer software packages available, although these are not cheap. 'Business Plan Pro 2005' is one which will set you back about

£100-150. See www.paloalto.co.uk.

Useful Address
Business Gateway: First Floor, Haymarket House, Clifton Terrace, Edinburgh
EH12 5DR; ☎845-609 6611; www.bgateway.com. There are offices all across
Scotland. See the website for local addresses.

IDEAS FOR NEW BUSINESSES

Tourism

The Scottish tourist trade offers many opportunities for businesses, and if done
well they can achieve a good return on investment. With visitors coming from
all over the world, whether to view the historic sights of the country, to enjoy the
stunning scenery, to take part in the many outdoor activities, or to research and
experience their Scottish ancestry, with a little imagination you can tap into this
multi-million pound industry yourself.

Because of the seasonal nature of tourism, it is unreasonable to expect a small
business in the sector to provide year-round earnings large enough to support a
family without other sources of income. However, B&Bs and self-catering cottages
can offer an attractive way to augment your income. Many retired people, for
instance, choose to offer holiday accommodation in order to boost their pensions,
while residents who work at other jobs can receive additional income from offering
accommodation during the summer months.

If you choose an area such as Aviemore, which is one of the few genuinely
year-round tourist attractions of Scotland, you should find that your income is
far more evenly spread throughout the year. Even in other areas, however, there
are signs that the tourist season is getting longer, as people's holiday habits change
and the traditional two-week holiday in the summer is becoming less common.
With a little imagination and sensible marketing, you can aim to attract visitors
from spring through to autumn, with welcome additional bookings at Christmas
and New Year.

Although B&Bs are a less popular form of holiday than in the past, with visitors
preferring to self-cater or to stay at a purpose-built guesthouse or hotel which has
a higher standard of facilities than a basic B&B, if you are on a main tourist route
and offer en suite facilities and extra services, you can still attract healthy numbers
of guests. Consider aiming at niche markets: for example, if you are in an area
popular with mountain-climbers, advertise in magazines they will read, and offer
facilities which will attract them – hot showers all day, a place to leave dirty boots
and wet clothes, packed lunches; or aim at the 'grey panthers', retired people
with time and money to spend in comfortable surroundings with proprietors
who are prepared to pamper them, feed them excellent food, maybe drive them
round the area and generally treat them like old and valued friends for a week or

a fortnight.

If operating a self-catering cottage, remember that people look for comfort and quality. It is almost certain to rain at some time during their stay, so make sure your cottage is warm, comfortable and well-equipped with plenty of hot water, and extras such as books, board games, videos and computer games for the days when they can't – or don't want to – go out. A 'games room', whether in the cottage or in a shed in the garden, providing such things as a pool table or dart board, footballs, tennis rackets and the like for outdoor activities, maybe even exercise equipment for the fitness conscious, is an 'add-on' which will attract guests.

Caravans and chalets too are an option. Although the return per unit will be smaller than from a self-catering cottage, if you have two or more, they can be a viable option, aiming at the budget end of the holiday market. A relatively new feature in areas which attract backpackers, walkers, climbers and cyclists is bunkhouses, offering basic but clean facilities, often in the form of bunk-bedded dormitories with showers and communal kitchens.

Not only do all these visitors need somewhere to stay, they also need things to do while they are on holiday. Holidays offering a wide range of activities are popular and are something which may allow you to utilise any skills you possess: painting, writing, sailing, photography, horse riding – anything you can do which you can teach to others could be the basis of a business. You may wish to offer accommodation as well as tuition, or you may arrange accommodation for your students in other local establishments.

If you live in an area which already has plenty of accommodation, consider offering a service for those visitors. For instance, provide chauffeur-driven day tours of the area, taking in the historical and scenic 'must-see' sights. If you can obtain an unusual vehicle – a classic car, or an old bus, maybe – even better.

And while they are out and about during the day, or want to relax in the evening, these visitors need places to eat, drink and be merry. Hotels, bars, cafés and restaurants are businesses which, although notoriously hard work, can bring good rewards. If you can reflect your own ethnic background in the meals you provide, this will make your establishment stand out from the crowd. In the Highlands, apart from the ubiquitous Indian, Chinese and Italian restaurants, mainly in the towns, ethnic food is hard to find.

It may be a good idea to join the local area tourist board, as this will help to maximise advertising of your business, particularly abroad. See *Employment* for addresses of all the area tourist boards.

Retail

Shops aiming at local residents or at holidaymakers, and ideally at both, can make a viable business. Market research is essential, to ensure that you won't be opening yet another mini-supermarket in an area already well-supplied with them. Arts and craft shops do well in tourist areas, especially if you aim for the quality market and are not selling the same cheap and cheerful souvenirs as the shop next door.

You may wish to set up a retail outlet for your own art and craft works, but if you are living in a rural area you may have a problem finding suitable premises. Empty shop units for sale or to rent are like gold dust, especially in popular tourist areas. An alternative option in this case is to consider running a mobile shop, which has the advantage of reaching a wider customer base by travelling to small communities on a weekly rota. Currently there is a 'Mobile Art Studio' touring the Highlands, which is simply a caravan from where the artist works and sells his paintings. Other mobile shops which regularly tour the Highlands include butchers, clothes shops, a wool retailer and fish-sellers.

Garages

Garages selling petrol and diesel, and carrying out vehicle repairs and MOT tests are essential even in the remotest areas. However, they often struggle to survive. But just like any other business, if run well and offering a good standard of service, they can be viable. The difficulties of running such a business are evident from the fact that there always seem to be garages and filling stations for sale; the plus side of this is that you might pick one up at a bargain price. Always look at the full cost implications carefully: a filling station which has been inoperative for some time will need to have its fuel tanks checked and passed as suitable before you can trade. Upgrading or other work may be required to satisfy the regulations, and this will inevitably be a costly process. Buying a going concern rather than a garage which has not been trading for some time would therefore be a better option in this respect, however the purchase price will inevitably be higher.

Franchises

Franchising is a technique used by a variety of businesses in retailing, business services, domestic services, car repairs and fast food. This is one of the fastest-growing areas for new businesses in the UK, which has come relatively late to the technique compared with the USA.

The main advantages of franchising are that the business concept and name is already established and works well, and that the franchisor offers a complete package of support including advertising, training, assistance to launch the business and instructions about its day to day running.

The disadvantages are that they require quite a large amount of capital to begin with and that you do not have total control over your business. If the franchisor gets into difficulty this can affect you through no fault of your own. Generally, franchise agreements involve up-front support for the initial period, with this support reducing after the initial period, however the fees and royalties you pay to the franchisor continue for the full length of the franchise agreement. This can mean that the returns on the business are not as good as the returns you would get on a totally autonomous business.

Make sure you do your homework before going into this sort of venture. The Scottish Enterprise website has useful advice at www.scottish-enterprise.com/franchises/. The British Franchise Association have a telephone helpline on 0870-161 4000, or visit their website at www.british-franchise.org.uk.

Franchises for sale can be found advertised alongside other businesses for sale in newspapers and estate agents' publications.

Consultancy

If you have expert knowledge and qualifications, you could set yourself up as a consultant. The demand for consultants in all sorts of fields is clear from a look at the Scottish Business Pages telephone directory. It lists entries under the following: building consultants; business enterprise agencies; employment agencies & consultants; health & safety consultants; hotel & catering consultants; management & business consultants; marine consultants; marketing & advertising consultants; noise & vibration consultants; personnel consultants; public relations consultants; publicity consultants; quality assurance & control consultants; science & research consultants; consulting engineers, financial advisers.

Computer Services

With ever-increasing use of computers and the internet, there are opportunities for those with hi-tech skills in such areas as hardware and software design and production, website design and support to home and business computer users. Although technology is improving, computers are still notoriously prone to crash, and in order to keep up with latest developments, computer-users are regularly upgrading their hardware. Local computer wizards who can supply and fit new hardware, or offer assistance and advice at the end of a telephone or on e-mail, are a valuable asset to a community, particularly in areas remote from large towns.

Trades

Skilled tradespeople are in demand just about everywhere. Builders, plumbers, hairdressers, gardeners, painters and decorators are needed in both urban and rural areas, so there are opportunities to transfer your existing business to Scotland with you. See *Employment* for details on how to obtain a Certificate of Experience in certain trades.

Working as a Freelance

There is a wide range of work you can do from home, making use of new technology to find and keep in contact with clients. Such occupations as writing, editing, proof-reading, data input, indexing, translating, technical authoring, abstracting, distance teaching, graphics, illustration, web design, programming, music composition can all be carried out successfully by individuals working from their own homes. This way of working has the advantage that you can adjust your working hours and work-rate to suit your own situation, either working full time or fitting the work around your other commitments as a part-time source of income.

If you have talents in these areas but are not formally trained in them, there are distance learning courses you can take from home, completing assignments which are sent to you either through the mail or across the internet. If you prefer more personal contact with tutors and fellow students, there are short and longer term day and residential courses available in all manner of creative fields. Some courses allow you to work towards a formal qualification or diploma, which will assist you in finding work once you are qualified. Others are very practically-based, concentrating from the start on assisting you to find markets for your work, aiming by the end of the course for you to be launched on the freelance path, already making money from your chosen field. Here are just a sample of companies and institutions running courses:

Distance Learning Courses

Eston Training: 5 Mannofield Court, 456a Great Western Road, Aberdeen AB10 6NP; ☎01224-311992; www.estontrg.com. Technical authorship.

Chapterhouse: 2 Southernhey West, Exeter EX1 1JG; ☎01392-499488; fax 01392-498008; www.chapterhousepublishing.co.uk. Copy-editing and proofreading.

College of Technical Authorship: PO Box 7, Cheadle, Cheshire SK8 3BY; ☎/fax 0161-437 4235; www.coltecha.u-net.com. Technical authorship.

Institute of Copywriting: Honeycombe House, Bagley, Wedmore BS28 4TD; ☎01934-713563; fax 01934-713492; http://www.inst.org/copy/. Copywriting.

The Society of Freelance Editors and Proofreaders: Riverbank House, 1 Putney Bridge Approach, Fulham, London SW6 3JD; ☎020-7736 3278; fax 020-7736 3318; www.sfep.org.uk. Copy-editing and proofreading.

The Society of Indexers: Blades Enterprise Centre, John Street, Sheffield S2 4SU; ☎0114-292 2350; fax 0114-292 2351; www.socind.demon.co.uk. Indexing.

The Writers Bureau: Sevendale House, 7 Dale Street, Manchester M1 1JB; ☎0845-345 5995; fax 0161-236 9440; www.writersbureau.com. Creative writing and journalism.

Estate Agency

It is possible for anybody to set themselves up as an estate agent, assisting others to buy and sell property. Although the more heavily populated areas of Scotland are well-catered for in this respect, in the experience of the author, remote rural areas can benefit from locally based property selling services. In recent years the business of buying and selling property has changed greatly: with the advent of the internet, individuals can now advertise their own properties to the world, via their own websites or through commercial sites which advertise properties for sale throughout a region or the country. For a very small investment, you could provide such a service for your local area, finding local keyholders for vacant properties, arranging visits to properties where required and ensuring properties are locally as well as nationally advertised, to catch the eye of visitors who are so impressed by the area they decide they want to live there.

Food & Drink

Scotland has a world-wide reputation for high quality food and drink products. Venison, beef, salmon, raspberries, shortbread, fudge, heather honey and whisky are just a few of the products instantly and inextricably linked with Scotland. The list goes on: haggis, Dundee cakes, marmalade, Drambuie. You can build on this reputation by producing quality food or drink products with the cachet of being 'made in Scotland'.

If you come up with a winning product, there is potentially a thriving export and domestic market for it. Local enterprise companies, particularly in the Highlands & Islands Enterprise area, are keen to encourage new food production businesses.

For many years, Scotland was renowned for poor quality vegetables, but this is an area which has improved dramatically in recent years. There is an increasing demand from consumers for good quality organic products, which can be produced cost-effectively even on a small scale. Local tourist businesses as well as local residents will pay a premium price for produce if they know it is fresh, local and organic.

Exporting

Scotland's 'brand image' is strong throughout the world, and you could cash in on this. Think about what people in your home country connect with the country: tartan and tweed, heather and thistles, history and romance, whisky and shortbread. Whatever it may be, there is possibly a market for products which play on these connections. With your knowledge of your home country and compatriots, you could build an export business bringing a taste of Scotland to them.

Miscellaneous

One of the most important rules of creating a business which has a good chance of success is to identify a 'gap in the market'. In rural areas there are still surprising gaps which you could fill if you have the right skills or are prepared to learn them.

Jill Blackhurst of Wester Ross says
I found, much to my surprise, that there was no commercial videographer based in the Highlands, so I learned to use a digital video camera and was soon much in demand for weddings.

Kennels and catteries are few and far between in rural areas, yet people always need somewhere to leave their animals when they are away. If you like working with animals, this is a possible business to establish.

The Scots love music and dancing, so if you are skilled at playing an instrument or singing, you will always be in demand for local ceilidhs, weddings, dances and other functions.

Look at the area with an open mind and with imagination and there are all sorts of opportunities – you just need to be prepared to give them a try.

E-COMMERCE

Whatever business you set up, effective marketing is important to make it successful. The internet has opened wide new marketing opportunities. Even the most traditional businesses can make good use of the new technology to reach a wider, and international customer base. Those which have set up their own websites are reaping the benefits of easy, cheap and direct overseas access. For even the smallest B&B or self-catering cottage, setting up one's own website or advertising on a community or commercial site is cost-effective. For larger businesses, the returns are potentially even greater.

If online credit card facilities are provided, this makes booking a holiday from the other side of the world no trouble at all. Small businesses often find, however, that the costs of providing such facilities are too high for the return. However, the speed and ease of use of email, together with simple devices such as a downloadable booking form, can work almost as well to make booking easy and thus attract more foreign visitors.

As well as adding value to traditional businesses, the internet opens up whole new fields of enterprise. Successful businesses can be built which would not be possible or viable any other way. Internet auctions are becoming popular worldwide, and increasing numbers of people are finding they can make a good income by dealing in goods across the internet. If you can find a source of desirable Scottish products which you can sell through internet auction sites and ship across the world, this is another potential success story.

The beauty of many internet-based businesses is that they need little initial investment – in some cases just the time and cost involved in setting up a website is all that is required. Janis MacLean of Dingwall did just that, as a result of an idea which came to her after being asked to witness the wedding of a German couple in her local registry office. She set up, practically overnight, a highly successful business called Highland Wedding Belles. Through the use of the internet and a home computer she began to organise weddings for clients from all over the world, arranging weddings large and small, formal and informal, in venues as diverse as castles and lighthouses. Within a year it was a phenomenal success.

RUNNING A BUSINESS

Taxation

If you are running a company you must pay corporation tax on company profits, rates varying on a sliding scale depending on the amount of profit made. In the 2003-2004 tax year the corporation tax main rate was 30 per cent. There are discounts for small businesses, with the small companies' rate set at 19 per cent. This is for companies with taxable profits between £50,000 and £300,000. The starting rate is zero for companies with taxable profits of £10,000 or below.

Marginal relief eases the transition from the starting rate to the small companies' rate for companies with profits between £10,000 and £50,000. Marginal relief also applies to companies with profits between £300,000 and £1,500,000.

Capital expenditure, expenses and outgoings of the company can be offset against tax payable. Capital allowances against tax are made on items purchased for the company such as machinery and plant, cars, industrial and agricultural buildings, scientific research and information and communication technology equipment.

Sole traders and partners pay income tax on a sliding scale as detailed in *Daily Life*. Tax liability for each tax year is calculated on the basis of information provided on the self-assessment tax return. Outgoings, expenses and purchases of capital equipment and other supplies for the business may be offset against the tax bill, so it is important to keep records of all outgoings and enter these on the tax return. If you work from home, you can claim a percentage of the costs of running your home against tax. The Inland Revenue will accept your estimation of the proportion of your electricity, gas, telephone and house insurance costs which should be put down to your business, as long as you are reasonable about it: while they might be happy with an estimate of 20 per cent of costs, they are likely to look very closely at your actual expenses if you claim 90 per cent.

Company cars are taxable, with an employee paying tax on a percentage of the list price of the car each year, depending on the business mileage per annum and the age of the car. If the employer provides free fuel this will be taxed based on the car's engine size and whether it is petrol or diesel powered. Employers are also liable to pay Class 1A NICs on these benefits. In order to protect the environment, the use of cleaner, more fuel efficient cars is rewarded by linking the tax and NICs charge to the car's exhaust emissions, in particular its carbon dioxide (CO_2) emissions. For full details see Leaflet IR172 Income Tax and Company Cars. Available from www.inlandrevenue.gov.uk. Capital Gains Tax is payable on profits made from selling land, property or businesses, other than one's own dwelling house. In 2004-2005, any profits made on the transaction over £8, 200 are taxed at ten per cent for the first £2,020; 22 per cent between £2,021 and £31,400; and at 40 per cent above this. If profits made are invested in another business, however, capital gains tax may not be payable.

If your business turnover (i.e. taxable supplies to customers) exceeds a certain amount you must register for value added tax (VAT) with Customs and Excise. In 2004-2005 this amount stands at £58,000, but it is reviewed annually. You must register if at the end of any month the total value of the taxable supplies you have made in the past 12 months or less is more than £58,000, or if at any time you expect that your annual turnover will exceed £58,000 in the next 30 days.

If your turnover is less than this, and you supply goods and services which are not exempt from VAT, you may choose to register if you wish. This may be to your benefit, because it means you can claim back VAT you have paid out on purchases. However, advice should be taken on this from an accountant or tax adviser. If you run a company which is registered for VAT, only the company is liable, but if you are a sole trader or partnership and you register for VAT, it is the individual who is liable. This means that, if you have more than one source of income you are liable for VAT on all your business activities, even those which do not exceed the VAT threshold and this could work to your disadvantage. See *Daily Life* for details of VAT rates for different goods and services.

Inland Revenue Enquiry Centres

Aberdeen: Ruby House, 8 Ruby Place, Aberdeen AB10 1ZP; ☎01224-401700.

Ayr: Russell House, King Street, Ayr KA8 0BD; ☎01292-615000.

Buckie: Moray House, 17 East Cathcart Street, Buckie AB56 1AN; ☎01542-837300.

Coatbridge: 2 Muiryhall Street, Coatbridge ML5 3EZ; ☎01236-441000.

Dumbarton: 15 Meadowbank Street, Dumbarton G82 1JR; ☎01389-744550.

Dumfries: 161 Broom Road, Dumfries DG1 3EX; ☎01387-245700.

Dundee: Caledonian House, Greenmarket DD1 4QX; ☎01382-424200.

Dunfermline: Merchiston House, Foundry Street, Dunfermline KY12 9DE; ☎01383-843200.

Dunoon: Auchencraig, Argyll Road, Dunoon PA23 8ED; ☎01369-708800.

East Kilbride: Queensway House, East Kilbride G79 1AA; ☎01355-275000.

Edinburgh: Elgin House, 20 Haymarket Yards, Edinburgh EH12 5WS; ☎0131-346 5600.

Falkirk: 45-47 Vicar Street, Falkirk FK1 1LJ; ☎01324-604100.

Galashiels: 53 Market Street, Galashiels TD1 3AH; ☎01896-663500.

Glasgow: Cotton House, 7 Cochrane Street, Glasgow G1 1HY; ☎0141-285 4100.

Glenrothes: Saltire House, Pentland Park, Glenrothes KY6 2AL; ☎01592-222500.

Greenock: 99 Dalrymple Street, Greenock PA15 1LN; ☎01475-553400.

Hamilton: 1 Barrack Street, Hamilton ML3 0HS; ☎01698-206200.

Hawick: Crown Building, 51 North Bridge Street, Hawick TD9 9QH; ☎01450-

365200.

Inverness: River House, Young Street, Inverness IV3 5BN; ☎01463-256700.

Irvine: Marress House, Friars Court, Irvine KA12 8XG; ☎01294-317902.

Kirkcaldy: 26 Victoria Road, Kirkcaldy KY1 1DS; ☎01592-209900.

West Lothian Connected: Unit 16A, Almondvale Centre, Livingston EH54 6NB; ☎01506-431144.

Motherwell: 43 Civic Square, Motherwell ML1 1TJ; ☎01698-787100.

Paisley: Gilmour House, 26 Gilmour Street, Paisley PA1 1EQ; ☎0141-840 5600.

Perth: 1-3 Water Vennel, Perth PH1 5UD; ☎01738-492100.

Peterhead: Keith House, 4 Seagate, Peterhead AB42 1HF; ☎01779-474861.

Rothesay: 9 King Street, Rothesay PA20 0DE; ☎01700-505047.

Stirling: 8 Spital Street, Stirling FK8 1AT; ☎01786-457100.

Wick: Government Buildings, Girnigoe Street, Wick KW1 4HL; ☎01955-673100.

Inland Revenue website: www.inlandrevenue.gov.uk.

Employing staff

If you decide to employ somebody in your business, you must tell your Tax Office. They will send you a New Employee's Starter Pack which contains all the instructions, tables and forms you will need.

If you employ staff, you must deduct tax and Class 1 National Insurance contributions from the pay of your employees under the Pay As You Earn (PAYE) scheme. It is the employer's responsibility to work out the tax and NI due each pay day and pay it over to the Inland Revenue Accounts Office each month. This can be done quarterly if your average monthly payments of tax and NI contributions are below £600. You must tell your Tax Office at the end of each tax year how much each employee has earned and how much tax and NI contributions you have deducted, and give each employee a statement showing these details.

Further information on PAYE and National Insurance can be found in *Daily Life*.

Your local Tax Office or Inland Revenue Enquiry centre have information leaflets on a variety of aspects of employing staff. Their addresses are in local Phone Books under 'Inland Revenue'. Most offices are open to the public from 8.30am to 4.30pm from Monday to Friday.

Employers also have a number of responsibilities to their employees under employment legislation, regarding such things as contracts of employment, working hours, conditions of working, health and safety, and sexual and racial equality of opportunity. For fuller details of these, see *Employment*. The Department of Trade and Industry website contains leaflets and factsheets on these aspects of employment. www.dti.gov.uk.

Rates

Businesses pay non-domestic (business) rates to the local authority based on the rateable value of the property and the non-domestic rate poundage. The rateable value of every property is determined by the Assessor for the local authority area, who is independent of both local and central government, and is his estimate of the annual rent which that property would command on the open market. Non-domestic rates for a particular property are calculated by multiplying the rateable value by a value called the 'rate poundage'. Small business relief is given in parts of Scotland: in the Highland Council area, small businesses including self-catering cottages are allowed a 50 per cent discount. These figures and allowances are regularly reviewed so are subject to change from year to year.

As a guide, in 2004-2005, the rateable value of a small holiday cottage in the Highlands was £900, with a rate poundage of 48.8.8 pence, making a total of £439.20. With 50 per cent Small Business Relief, the amount payable for the year is £219.60. The rating year runs from 1st April to 31st March and can be paid in one lump sum on or before 30th September in the rating year; in two instalments, the first on or before the 1st August and the balance on or before 1st November; or in ten monthly instalments. Direct debit arrangements are available for the payments to be made directly from your bank account.

If you work from a room in your home, it is possible to class your office as business premises, paying non-domestic rates on that amount, although you are still liable for council tax on the rest of the property. If your office is distinct from the rest of the house, this might be feasible, and would allow you to claim the whole of any expenses relating to that portion of the property. However, you would be liable to pay business insurance in that case, and if you ever sold your house you would also be subject to capital gains tax on a proportion of the sale price. In most cases it is probably best to claim just a proportion of allowable household bills against your business, as described in *Taxation*. An accountant or tax advisor will be able to give you advice on the best arrangement in your personal circumstances.

Insurance

Insurance for most types of small to medium sized businesses is available from the main insurance companies. If you need specialist insurance for your particular business, an insurance broker should be able to source a company giving the cover you need at a competitive price. Insurance for self-catering cottages is one area which some companies are wary about providing, presumably because they are perceived as being a bad risk. Other companies, such as Pearl Insurance, may insure a holiday property as long as you take out the insurance on your own dwelling house with them. There are some companies which offer policies specifically for holiday properties, but ensure that the cover is sufficient and that the company is reputable – as a holiday cottage owner you are likely to be direct-mailed by obscure companies offering cover. As a general rule of thumb, the better known companies are probably a safer bet as far as the business owner is concerned. If your letting property is close by your own house you may find that the insurance premiums are lower than if you live a distance away so cannot easily keep your eye on the property. If you offer bed and breakfast in your own house you may be required to take out business insurance, as a normal domestic policy probably would not cover you in the event of a claim.

Apart from insurance cover for buildings and contents, you can cover your business for a range of other eventualities, including business interruption, employer's, public and product liability, stock and goods in transit, personal accident and sickness, and insurance for commercial vehicles.

Insurance Companies

AXA Direct Insurance: 107 Cheapside, London EC2V 6DU; ☎0845-300 0489; www.axa-direct.co.uk.

J.C Roxburgh (Insurance Brokers): 151 Glasgow Road, Clydebank, Dunbartonshire; ☎0141-952 0371; fax 0141-952 0255; www.jcroxburgh.co.uk.

Royal & SunAlliance: St Mark's Court, Chart Way, Horsham, West Sussex RH12 1XA; ☎01403-232323; www.royalsunalliance.com.

R.J. Shawcross (Insurance Brokers): 139 Market Street, Atherton M46 0SH; ☎01942-891891.

Eagle Star Insurance: The Small Business Team, Eagle Star, 3000a Parkway, Whiteley, Fareham, Hampshire PO15 7JY; ☎0800-015 0151; www.eaglestar. co.uk.

Data Protection

If you keep computer records of names and addresses and other personal data regarding people you employ and do business with, you may be required to notify the Data Protection Commissioner. If you are classed as a data controller who is processing personal data you must notify unless you are exempt. Exemptions may be allowed for some not-for-profit organisations; if you are processing personal data for personal, family or household affairs; if you only process personal data for the maintenance of a public register; or if you only process personal data within your own business for the purpose of staff administration, advertising, marketing and public relations, accounts and records.

If you are required to notify, you are legally obliged to ensure any data you hold on computer is up to date and accurate. Individuals have the right to examine those records, and fines or compensation may prove to be payable if the information is incorrect. Failure to notify where required is a criminal offence. If you keep only manual records, there is no requirement to notify.

Further details can be found on the Information Commissioner's Office website, which also includes an easy to use self-assessment section which helps you to identify whether you need to notify. If you are required to do so, you must complete a form which you can obtain by phoning the notification helpline 01625 545 745 or print out from the website. Notification must be accompanied by a fee of £35 for the first year, and a continuation fee of £35 must be paid annually.

Useful Address

Information Commissioner's Office – Scotland: 28 Thistle Street, Edinburgh EH2 1EN; ☎/fax 0131-2256341; www.informationcommissioner.gov.uk.

The Euro

Although at the time of writing Britain has not yet joined the Euro, the single European currency introduced on January 1 1999, it may well happen in the long run. Until the UK joins the European Monetary Union (EMU) the euro will be a foreign currency in the UK and will not be legal tender. This means that UK businesses will not have to accept it unless they agree to. However, businesses may use it in their transactions with member states within EMU if they wish to.

The single currency is already directly affecting many UK based businesses, particularly those which buy and sell products throughout Europe. Those exporting into the euro zone have at times found a competitive disadvantage because of the relatively strong pound. Some have therefore begun to trade directly in euros. This has implications for their accounting systems, which need to handle the euro. Most UK retail banks offer euro accounts for businesses which require them.

The sorts of businesses most affected by the euro, even before the UK joins, are exporters and importers, multinational firms, UK firms in supply chains headed by multinational companies, and wholesale financial markets, which are already using the euro instead of the currencies it replaced on 1 January 1999.

The UK government has a website which contains all the latest and advice and information for UK businesses. www.euro.gov.uk.

Useful Address

Euro Information: Floor 3/S1, Euro Preparations Unit, HM Treasury, 1 Horse Guards Road, London SW1A 2HQ; www.euro.gov.uk.

Accountancy Advice

A good accountant can help you to order your business affairs most efficiently, and can prepare your tax return on the basis of information you supply. The amount of tax they may be able to save you is usually well worth what they would charge in fees. Despite the promise of the Inland Revenue that the self-assessment tax system would be clear and simple for lay people to follow, since its introduction the annual return form appears to have become more complex every year, so a good accountant can be worth his/her weight in gold.

Qualified accountants will be members of the Institute of Chartered Accountants of Scotland (ICAS) or the Association of Chartered Certified Accountants (ACCA). Addresses of accountants in your area can be obtained from them, or from the local Phone Book, Yellow Pages or Business Pages.

Useful Addresses

Association of Chartered Certified Accountants: 83 Princes Street, Edinburgh EH2 2ER; ☎0131-247 7510; fax 0131-247 7514; www.accaglobal.com. The ACCA website includes a small business section with useful information and publications.

Institute of Chartered Accountants of Scotland: CA House, 21 Haymarket Yards, Edinburgh EH12 5BH; ☎0131-347 0100; fax 0131-347 0105; www.icas. org.uk. The ICAS website includes a searchable database of accountants across Scotland.

Tax Advice

Specialist and general tax advice can be obtained from members of the *Chartered Institute of Taxation:* 12 Belgrave Street, London SW1X 8BB; ☎020-7235 9381; fax 020-7235 2562; www.tax.org.uk. They can provide details of tax advisers in your area.

Legal Advice

Any contracts relating to your business should be drawn up or vetted by a qualified solicitor, and any purchase of property must be handled by a solicitor. All solicitors in Scotland must be members of the *Law Society of Scotland:* 26 Drumsheugh Gardens, Edinburgh EH3 7YR; ☎0131-226 7411; fax 0131-225 2934; www.lawscot.org.uk.

OTHER SOURCES OF ADVICE & ASSISTANCE

There are a number of sources of support for those who are running or wish to start a business.

Business Gateway: First Floor, Haymarket House, Clifton Terrace, Edinburgh EH12 5DR; ☎845-609 6611; www.bgateway.com. There are offices all across Scotland. See the website for local addresses.

Highlands & Islands Enterprise have a network of 'Business Information Sources'. Contact the relevant local enterprise company (details above) or see http://www. hie.co.uk/case/bis.htm.

Local Councils may be able to provide advice and assistance. See *General Introduction* for contact details.

Chambers of Commerce throughout Scotland represent business people in their local area. For details of your local branch contact *Scottish Chambers of Commerce:* 30 George Square, Glasgow G2 1EQ; ☎0141-204 8316; fax 0141-221 2336; www.scottishchambers.org.uk.

Scottish Development International: Enquiry Desk,,SDI Headquarters, Atlantic Quay, 150 Broomielaw, Glasgow, G2 8LU; ☎0141-228 2828; fax 0141-228 2089; www.scottishdevelopmentinternational.com.

Relocation Agencies can assist companies to find premises for their businesses and homes for their staff to rent or buy when moving to Scotland. *The Association of Relocation Agents* (ARA) can provide a full list of their members. PO Box 189, Diss IP22 1PE; ☎08700-737475; fax 08700-718719; www.relocationagents. com.

Small Business Associations throughout Scotland represent the interests of local businesses. *Federation of Small Businesses:* Scottish Office, 74 Berkeley Street, Glasgow G3 7DS; ☎0141-221 0775; fax 0141-221 5954; www.fsb.org.uk.

How To Books publish a number of guides to setting up and running a business, including *Becoming Self-Employed* and *Starting A Business From Home.* For further information contact How To Books, Head Office, 3 Newtec Place, Magdalen Road, Oxford OX4 1RE; ☎01865-793806; fax 01865-248780; www. howtobooks.co.uk.

PERSONAL CASE
HISTORIES

PERSONAL CASE
HISTORIES

CLARE AND ALLY WRIGHT

Clare and Ally moved from Cambridgeshire, England in 1999, with their two young sons, Callum and Ruairdhri. They now live in the north west Highlands, both working freelance, Clare as a writer and editor, Ally as a musician and composer.

Why did you move to Scotland?
Clare. There were a lot of reasons for our decision, but the main one was our wish to find a more integrated lifestyle where our family could live and work together rather than on different, sharply delineated careers. The village where we lived was fast turning into a suburb of Cambridge rather than the rural bolt-hole it was originally. I was already self-employed as a journalist and editor, working mainly via the internet, and I felt I could pursue that just as well somewhere else. Modern technology meant I didn't need to maintain some kind of umbilical link to London and the south-east any more, and I wanted the children to grow up in a genuinely rural environment.
Ally. Once I'd given up my day job in England to look after the children and we were surviving perfectly well – better actually – on what Clare was earning over the internet, it soon became obvious that the one unquestionable rule we'd grown up with, that you had to live near London, simply didn't pertain any more. God bless the internet! Suddenly the whole world was our oyster, we could go anywhere and live how we wished and make it work financially. It was very liberating. I'd been to university in France and we both loved the place but we decided on the Highlands because I have family connections there. We also thought it would be selfish to expect the boys to learn another language at ages six and four. Younger or older perhaps but not at that age. And now, of course, they're learning Gaelic!

How did you begin the process of finding somewhere to stay?
Clare. We'd been on holiday in the Highlands several times and had visited three

main areas – Wester Ross, Skye and Lochaber. We liked all of them and we house-hunted in each area. However, we'd made some friends in Wester Ross who were setting up a relocation agency. They had a lot of information which helped us greatly, and pointed us in the direction of the property we eventually bought.

Were there any difficulties with the moving process?
Clare. The most difficult thing about it was selling our house in England. That took seven months from when we made the decision to move, and it was a real anti-climax sitting around and waiting, having made that decision. We finally sold the house in May 1999 but it took until September before the sale got to completion. Once we had a moving date, though, everything turned into a blur. We had about a fortnight to sort out some temporary accommodation and arrange a 700 mile move!

Moving from England to Scotland can be tricky because of the differences in the legal system, you daren't even make an offer on a house in Scotland until your sale is completed in England, because an offer in Scotland is legally binding. Once we'd completed down south, of course we had to move, and luckily our friends in Wester Ross found us a house to rent very near the property we had our eye on. There was a lot of interest in it and the sale went to sealed bids! It was all pretty nail-biting stuff, but luckily our bid was accepted and we bought the property – a six-acre croft with a derelict house on it. We're now renovating the old house, which we plan to rent out to tourists, and we're having a new house built for ourselves on the croft.
Ally. Much is made of the difference between the two legal systems. However, in England you would make an offer subject to satisfactory survey which gives you a get out, and there's nothing to stop you stipulating that an offer is also subject to the satisfactory conclusion of your sale south of the border, which gives you another.

How would you describe your current work?
Clare. Journalist, editor, teacher, crofter, horticulturalist, craft-worker, mother. Not necessarily in that order.
Ally. A bit of this and a bit of that. The way it's always been in the Highlands, it's just my list of activities includes a large hi-tech element.

Is it what you envisaged when you moved here, or has it changed or developed in any way?
Clare. It's really developed – don't come to Scotland looking for a quiet life, whatever you do! I'm working harder than I ever have. My work as a journalist is as healthy as ever, I've taught an evening class in teleworking skills at the local school, and we're growing organic vegetables on the croft for sale locally. I'm also making craft items to sell in the local market and through shops in the district. I'd

only ever made things for amusement before, but here there are so many natural materials – driftwood, shells, feathers, stones – that it's really easy to have good ideas.

Ally. We didn't move from an urban environment so life in Wester Ross was not much of a culture shock after life in East Anglia. I can imagine moving from a city would require more conscious effort to deal with the change. We were already used to dodging livestock on the roads and having to travel significant distances to the supermarket with a cool box in the back of the car to prevent everything defrosting on the long journey home.

Now that you have been here for some time, what are your feelings about living in Scotland?

Clare. I wish we'd done it years ago.

Ally. Well, I've lived in London, Brighton, Grenoble, Bonn, the wilds of Norfolk and less wild Cambridgeshire – all great places. Scotland's just another place. I have ties here but it's not Nirvana. I wouldn't go back but I don't feel my time elsewhere was wasted and that this is where I should have been all along. One thing I would say is that I'm glad we were within reach of Addenbrooke's Hospital in Cambridge when the boys were born. They were both complicated births and I'm not sure what would have happened if the nearest hospital had been 75 miles away over the mountains.

Would you recommend it to other English people?

Clare. Yes – as long as they realise they're emigrating. Scotland is quite definitely a different country to England, with different ways. You can't come here and carry on as though you were still in Surbiton or St Albans.

How do you find the Scots – do they seem different from the English?

Clare. Yes. It's a much more matriarchal society in the Highlands. The women pretend to defer to the men, but it's plain that they're really the ones in charge of the families, especially the older women! They're a much nicer people than the English in general – gentler, more generous, more trusting. They don't have the driven work ethic of the English, which is wonderful in lots of ways but can also be frustrating when you want something to happen in a hurry. The pace is slower and less aggressive.

Ally. Well, my mother is a Highlander so I grew up with a lot of this culture bottled and shipped down south (like so much else!) Scots tend to be much more direct which may jar a little with southern English particularly. Often I find things are said very openly here simply as an observation with no pejorative overtones, things which would go unspoken down south. There's little of the southern English sense of reserve or keeping up appearances. Up here things don't necessarily look so perfectly turned-out but people are a lot more genuine and warm-hearted.

Did you find it easy to make friends?

Clare. Yes, people were very welcoming. Perhaps a little shy of us at first, but it wasn't snobbery or disdain, more that they didn't want to look pushy. Highlanders aren't instantly outgoing people, but they are basically really friendly. We're getting more and more involved in local and community activities, like the market and the village Fun Day. We made sure we didn't push ourselves forward though, we didn't want to be seen as trying to take anything over. It's nice when you're asked, though.

Have you come across any 'anti-English' feeling from people?

Clare. Only one remark from someone who's locally renowned as a fool and a mischief-maker! Every district has one. Apart from that, none whatsoever. The people here tend to take you as they find you. If you're an idiot, you're an idiot – no matter what nationality you are.

Do you think moving with children made things easier or harder?

Clare. Easier. We got to know other parents through the local school, and the teachers were a very useful local point of contact straight away. Adding two children to a 12-strong school also probably made us more popular locally!

Ally. Mostly easier, although I do feel because we've got young children and we can't just drop into the pub any time we fancy, that we had a great introduction to one part of the neighbourhood but may have missed out on another. Other folk in the district have grandparents for ad hoc babysitting, we don't.

How long did it take you and the boys to acclimatise to both the way of life and the climate?

Clare. I really don't know the answer to that. I felt fine about it all from the beginning, although sometimes I can get frustrated by people's passivity – they sometimes accept things like lousy service from companies as if they don't think they can complain or ask for improvements. As a southerner born and bred, I tend to scream and shout when I don't get the service I want. Our satellite dish was a good example – when a storm brought it down, we were told we'd have to wait a month for a service visit. Other people in the district had similar problems. I made such a fuss eventually the satellite company flew someone up from London to install a higher-spec dish – and I could tell the whole episode made ripples locally. I ended up feeling rather self-conscious about it! Things like not working on a Sunday take some getting used to – you can't just go out and clean the car or paint the house, some people would find it offensive.

As for the climate, I didn't find it significantly worse than Cambridge. Certainly no colder in winter – living on the coast, we have the benefit of the gulf stream.

Windier and rainier, but hardly horrific. We didn't find ourselves putting on extra layers, and so far we haven't been snowed in. The worst thing is the insects. I'm mildly allergic to bites and stings and when the midges and clegs (horseflies) come out in the summer I look like I've got plague.

Ally. The way of life – no time at all, except the religion. I confess I do find it rather oppressive but I'm the incomer so I have to respect it. As regards the climate, everyone was expecting us to be shocked at the winter. Well, it's a bit windier than East Anglia I suppose, but not much. I don't have a problem with the wind and rain but I've found a greater difference in the summer. I'm not referring to the midges – they're considerably less of an annoyance than you would think – but rather that the summer's definitely significantly cooler than I'm used to and there's much more cloud cover.

What do the boys think of it now?

Callum (now aged 7). The weather changes a lot here. The sheep are sweet, especially the lambs. I like the look of the mountains but I don't like climbing them because Mum and Dad walk for too long and our feet get really tired. I am looking forward to learning how to go sailing. I miss some of my old friends. I made a good friend here called Calum but he moved away and now I am friends with Ross and Judith and Iain, who is the funniest boy in the school.

Ruairdhri (now aged 5). I like looking at the sea. I like the beaches, but I miss my friends in England. I like my school because it has got lovely things in it like pictures on the wall and computers we can play games on. I like doing painting at school and I liked learning the Gaelic action song for the Mod.

How do you find the standard and cost of living in Scotland?

Ally. Petrol is ludicrously expensive and, of course, you get through a lot of it but you just have to accept that as a consequence of living here. After all, property's cheap. Generally, we spend less because there's other stuff to occupy our time and we go to the shops less often so we have less opportunity to buy stuff we don't need! You might have to make a bit more effort and occasionally accept some quaint compromises, but you can have everything you had down south and life up here does work on all the usual practical levels: schools, supermarkets, healthcare, car servicing, hairdressing, digital television etc. It's not some weird eco-hinterland. However, the standards by which people live are very different, there's much less emphasis on possessions.

Have you any advice for others thinking of moving to Scotland?

Clare. If it's what you really want, do it before you get too old to enjoy it. Don't wait for 'retirement' – there are mountains to climb and seas to swim in. Bring your children and keep the rural schools open. Bring derelict land back into use. Renovate ruins. Choose life.

BOB GRAYSON

Bob (not his real name) moved from Dublin to Edinburgh in 1996 when he was 22 to take an Edinburgh-based position with an Irish IT/management consultancy firm.

I had only been to Edinburgh once before, on a school trip, but moving over for what was meant to be a six month period did not hold any real worries or fears. I had just finished an 18 month stint in the eastern US, so being comparatively close to home, with the promise of frequent work trips back to Dublin, softened the pill.

Now, three years after those six months elapsed, I'm still here – how did that happen? Well, I settled into work immediately and found a place to live without too many problems. Work put me in a B&B for a few weeks and I did the rounds of the letting agencies. One thing I didn't really have a good appreciation of were the various different residential areas of Edinburgh but I managed to find a two bedroom flat in Murrayfield which I shared with another Irish guy who started in the same job with me. I found the rent reasonable enough, but got a wee surprise when I got a council tax bill – I'd never heard of it before!

There were some teething problems moving over – setting up bank accounts and credit cards was particularly frustrating. I needed to supply letters from bank managers in Ireland and the US who would never have laid eyes on me. For a while, having no UK credit history was a real pain, but it gradually built up, more through having my name on the electoral roll, I guess. Funnily enough, while the bank was reticent in minding my money, the taxman had no such compunctions – gladly setting my tax codes with the minimum of fuss.

I moved flats a few times over the last few years and in 1999 bought my own place close to the city centre. This is something which I wouldn't have been able to do had I stayed in Dublin – house prices, even in Edinburgh, are far more affordable than in Ireland. I moved jobs a few times too, both times through personal contact, and have remained in IT.

I find Scotland, and Edinburgh in particular, a great place to live – I often have friends visiting from Ireland, and they really enjoy the city and the surrounding countryside. I found it quite easy to settle, helped by having a good friendly social crowd in work. I have never come across an anti-Irish feeling; in fact at times (especially during the summer) Edinburgh seems to have more Irish people in it than natives.

I'd recommend moving to Scotland – even if you don't have a particularly pressing reason. The pace of life in Edinburgh is unlike that in other capital cities, but gives access to far greater amenities. Living and working here is easy to do – plenty of jobs and accommodation available if you look at the right time of year (avoid festivals and start of terms).'

RAINER THONNES

Rainer, a German national, came to Edinburgh in 1973, aged 18, as a diplomat's child, having just completed school in Germany. His father had just been appointed German Consul-General for Scotland, and Rainer was able to take up studies at Edinburgh University the same year.

At the time the family had no idea how long they would stay. Previous foreign postings had been around three to four years. In the event, they ended up staying 15 years until Rainer's father retired.

After Rainer graduated he stayed on as a post-graduate student for a year, in the same University department, and was then offered a temporary post there. This was followed by another temporary extension, and so it went on until somewhere along the line he was made permanent.

Were there any difficulties with the immigration process or was it all plain sailing?
Diplomatic status had its advantages, of course, and I'm not sure how easy it would have been without it in those days. All this business about equal rights for EEC nationals was just starting then, but today there should be no difficulties whatever in that respect for nationals of EU member states, though it's more difficult for non-EU Europeans and for Americans.

What are your feelings about living in Scotland?
I'm glad enough I came, and that it never crossed my mind to move away again. I would recommend it to anyone, but just because it's OK for me doesn't mean it'll suit everybody. Edinburgh is just the right size to have aspects of both small town and big city life. I don't think I could stomach London, if anything I'd move to somewhere more remote. It's nice to be within reasonable reach of places where you can unwind away from people.

How do you find the Scots – do they seem different from Germans?
On the whole they're not too different – all peoples have their own little differences, but deep down the similarities are more evident. The Scots are a particularly friendly lot.

Have you come across any 'anti-European' feeling from people?
Not seriously, not any more at least. The old enmity from the war has largely decayed and Scots are apt to be more anti-English than anti-European, and in a good humoured way at that.

How long did it take you to acclimatise to both the way of life and the climate?

The way of life is pretty laid back. I felt that life in Germany was in many ways more regulated.

The climate? Well, if you're used to being hot, you'll be disappointed, but if you like variety, this is the place to be, where you can often experience four seasons in one day. On the other hand, you could say there's lack of variety, as expressed by one of those funny postcards you can get. It shows two identical drawings, of a sheep standing in the rain. One is titled Scotland in Summer, the other Scotland in Winter. It takes a little getting used to, but it's nothing serious.

How do you find the standard and cost of living in Scotland?
A bit difficult to say, never having lived elsewhere as a money-aware adult. Food is probably cheaper in Mediterranean countries, and certainly accommodation in Edinburgh is pretty expensive, but that doesn't hold true for most of the rest of Scotland.

Have you any advice for others thinking of moving to Scotland?
Stay away – we don't want you spoiling it for those of us already here!

SAMUEL WHITE

Sam came to Scotland from the USA in September 1998 to study at the university of St. Andrews. He moved alone from Houston, Texas at the age of 18 and has no family in Scotland. He graduated in June 2002.

I originally applied to read History but changed my degree to Modern History and Middle East Studies. The course costs about £7,000 pounds a year, which is roughly the cost of studying at a state university out-of-state in the US. It is without doubt a far better bargain, as I get a masters degree after four years at a prestigious university while most Americans might study for five years to get a bachelors degree at a mediocre university. I really don't understand why more Americans don't take advantage of opportunities to study overseas, particularly at Scottish universities, which seem to welcome Americans more than the English.

I found most of my information on Scottish universities over the internet – advisors and administrators at my high school were completely ignorant of overseas universities, and I was the only one of a graduating class of 640 to study abroad. I found the admissions process much easier and more objective than that of most American universities.

Immigration was pretty easy, but it's important to bring written proof of your acceptance to university and financial details proving you can pay your own way without taking full-time employment. I received a one-year visa to start with, extended to a four-year the next year. None of the other Americans I have talked to have reported any difficulties passing immigration.

I took up university accommodation my first year, and was assigned to a beautiful old house near the golf course and sea with about 20 other students. I then took private accommodation costing £210 per month plus bills, but then again St. Andrews is more expensive than most other Scottish towns. Finally I lived in Edinburgh, where accommodation was both cheaper and easier to find, but as always I started looking in advance, and I wouldn't recommend it to any American just arriving in Scotland without a place to stay. There are plenty of internet sites and university and other accommodation services offering places.

A recent law now permits all full-time overseas students to find temporary work in Britain without express permission. This is not at all obvious for most students arriving in Britain, and the fine print on most visas still seems to contradict this. I only heard of the change when my university sent out a letter to all the overseas students last year. I don't work during the academic year, but I took up temporary work at an insurance agency in Edinburgh in the summer. The work was easy to find, there were no bureaucratic obstructions, and I was paid a pretty decent £5 pounds per hour. The cost of living in Edinburgh was higher than in the US, but only about half that of London, where most foreigners go to work.

I've found the Scottish pretty welcoming on the whole. I've met a lot of ignorance and stereotypes but very little hostility. The biggest changes for me have not really been the culture and society, but the move from a big city to a small town and the move from a hot humid climate to a cold windy one. It took about two weeks to get used to the accent, and I'm still not used to the food. One warning I would have to make to other Americans is how prominent drinking is here. I can only imagine how difficult it must be to socialise at university or at work if you don't like to have a few pints on Friday nights.

All told, it's been a good experience moving to Scotland, and I would strongly recommend it to other Americans. The culture shock is not too great, and life is much more relaxed than back in the States.'

PAM AND TONY SHINKINS

Pam and Tony first discovered the Highlands in 1980, when they were living in Yorkshire, England. One day in a pub Tony picked up a home-produced leaflet for 'A Highland Holiday with Yorkshire Relish', advertising a bed & breakfast in Wester Ross, the owner of which had once been a barmaid in the pub.

'The photo was stunning – azure blue sea, golden beach – it looked like the Caribbean,' Tony recalls. 'We couldn't believe it was really like that in the Highlands – so we thought we'd better go and find out for ourselves.'

After their first stay in that B&B they became addicted to the area and returned as often as possible. 'The natural politeness and hospitality of the Highlanders really made us fall in love with them – we'd already fallen in love with the scenery and the laid back way of life.'

They both had stressful jobs and got away to the peace of the Highlands as often as possible. After about five years of holidays Tony decided he'd like eventually to retire to the area, so they began to look for a holiday home which they would move to full-time one day. There was no great rush to find a property. Tony still had some years to go before he could think about retiring, Pam even longer.

Once they bought the house, in 1986, Tony was just working towards being able to 'escape'. He had moved to a more stressful job, and Pam's was getting harder too. They spent their own holidays in the bungalow and rented it out the rest of the time as self-catering holiday accommodation.

'At that time,' Pam recalls, 'Tony was happier with the idea of retiring than I was. I couldn't quite see what we'd do when we stopped working so hard. And the idea of moving so far away was a little worrying too. But I was running out of the stamina to cope with the job.' Working until Tony was 65 and Pam was 60 came to seem an undesirable option. 'Finally we had to ask ourselves the question, what were we working for?'.

In 1991 the opportunity arose for Pam to take early retirement, and Tony put in his resignation at the same time. They left Yorkshire to set up their home permanently in the Highlands. 'Well,' says Pam, 'That was Tony's plan. I kept my thoughts to myself, but I had decided, if Tony died tomorrow, I'd move back to England straightaway. I don't feel like that any more – I'm well and truly settled. But it did take me 12 months to get over that feeling.'

Pam and Tony avoided many of the uncertainties that beset those moving to the Highlands because they'd got to know the area over eleven years and had made some good friends. So they'd have a support network, they knew about the local infrastructure and services, and knew that they would be able to survive.

For the first few years they augmented their pensions by offering bed and breakfast in their home – at which they were so successful that when Pam reached 60 and they chose to give up the B&B, they found several previous guests still insisted on coming each year, even though they were no longer advertising accommodation. 'They had now become friends, and it was difficult to say no to the extra money, so we continued to have paying guests for several weeks every summer,' says Pam.

When they moved to the Highlands, they did so accepting that their standard of living would inevitably drop. However, this didn't prove to be the case. They live as well, or better, than they ever did before. 'We've come to see that it costs a great deal of money to go to work. The costs of what you wear to work, travel expenses, attendance at social functions and, if you're in a stressful occupation, the costs of holidays to get away from the daily grind. Now we're here, we rarely go away on holiday – we don't find the need for them.'

STUART AND SANDY NAIRN

Although Stuart and Sandy were already living in Scotland – in Falkirk – before they moved to Ross-shire, their experiences throw into relief the differences between living in the Central Belt and the Highlands.

Why did you decide to move?

To improve our quality of life. We spent our time working to pay the bills, leaving no time for ourselves.

What made you decide on this area?

We spent a lot of time in the Western Isles and thought about moving there, but it was just too far – any travel would involve either a ferry or plane and we decided that was not suitable for us. We always wanted to be in the west, and wanted to be by the sea. When we stayed here for holidays, we spent a lot of time driving around the west coast & Skye, but always felt that coming to Wester Ross was coming home.

What job(s) were you doing previously?

Sandy was a management accountant for a small company involved in metal fabrication work and the biotech industry. Stuart was a system architect with a US based international electronic design consultancy.

Did you have set ideas on what you intended to do when you moved to the Highlands?

Stuart was involved in a new start company based in Livingston and would work part–time for them and part-time for our own company still doing system architecture work. Sandy would build up an accountancy business gaining local clients and doing some telephone support work for her replacement at her previous employer's offices. We also planned to buy a small croft to grow veg, keep a few chickens, & maybe a couple of pigs.

Has it turned out as you visualised or are you doing different things than you intended?

Work-wise it has turned out reasonably as planned: Sandy spent more time than expected working for her previous employer and has also been doing some waitressing at a local restaurant, Stuart has done a few jobs for people in their homes – electrical/plumbing etc. We have become involved in more community projects such as a local organic food co-operative and the community renewable energy project. Stuart has been providing help for the Community Council on communications issues as well as doing cookery demonstrations organised by the local Healthy Hearts Co-ordinator. We never did buy a croft and we still don't have the chickens or pigs – but we have got two spaniels.

How long did it take you to find accommodation and set yourself up in work?

Friends in the area told us of a house which would be available to rent at about the right time for us to move. We rented that from March 2003 to September 2004 when we moved into our own house. In the meantime we tried to buy two crofts, but were unsuccessful each time.

Workwise: Stuart had already agreed to work remotely with the company in Livingston, and had contacts for other work so that kept him busy from the start; Sandy was kept busy by her previous employers for quite a while and the local clients have been steadily coming from early days here.

Describe your way of life in the central belt?

Wage slaves! Leaving the house at 7.30am each weekday morning to go to work, and returning at anything between 6.30-8.00pm at night. Eat, sleep & off to work again the next morning – just to pay for the diesel and mortgage. This did not leave much time or energy for social life, and being out all day, we never really got to know our neighbours and make friends locally.

Describe how it is different in the Highlands?

We don't have to travel to work, can work different hours if we want, e.g. be out during the day & work in the evenings when it's dark. We can plan our days to suit whatever work or other jobs need to be done at the time.

How different is the social/community side of things in the Highlands?

The sense of community is very strong here, whereas it was non-existent in the central belt. People are willing and able to help out whether it be picking up shopping or moving house. There are more social events organised here for the benefit of something in the area e.g. the school, and these are always well supported and provide a great opportunity to meet people.

What are the benefits and disadvantages of a) your central belt lives b) your highland lives?

Central belt

Advantages: salaries were higher, availability of work was greater, infrastructure (roads, telecoms etc) better looked after, easier access to larger shops.

Disadvantages: too busy, cost of living/housing much higher therefore higher salary soon swallowed up, crime rates and antisocial behaviour, pollution levels, too much traffic.

Highlands

Advantages: slower pace of life, strength of community, scenery, more flexibility for working hours, less busy.

Disadvantages: poor telecoms, smaller client base, distance from existing clients.

On balance, are you glad you made the move?

Absolutely – yes.

Compare a) your standard of living b) your quality of life with what it was before.
Standard of living: no significant change – the income has reduced, but so have the costs.
Quality of life: much improved. We spend more time together, we spend time walking the dogs instead of sitting in cars in queuing traffic on the daily commute.

Complete guides to life abroad from Vacation Work

Live & Work Abroad

Live & Work in Australia & New Zealand	£11.95
Live & Work in Belgium, The Netherlands & Luxembourg	£10.99
Live & Work in China	£11.95
Live & Work in France	£11.95
Live & Work in Germany	£10.99
Live & Work in Ireland	£10.99
Live & Work in Italy	£10.99
Live & Work in Japan	£10.99
Live & Work in Portugal	£10.99
Live & Work in Russia & Eastern Europe	£10.99
Live & Work in Saudi & the Gulf	£10.99
Live & Work in Scandinavia	£10.99
Live & Work in Scotland	£11.95
Live & Work in Spain	£11.95
Live & Work in Spain & Portugal	£10.99
Live & Work in the USA & Canada	£10.99

Buying a House Abroad

Buying a House in France	£11.95
Buying a House in Italy	£11.95
Buying a House in Portugal	£11.95
Buying a House in Scotland	£11.95
Buying a House in Spain	£11.95
Buying a House on the Mediterranean	£13.95

Starting a Business Abroad

Starting a Business in Australia	£12.95
Starting a Business in France	£12.95
Starting a Business in Spain	£12.95

Available from good bookshops or direct from the publishers
Vacation Work, 9 Park End Street, Oxford OX1 1HJ
Tel 01865-241978 * Fax 01865-790885 * www.vacationwork.co.uk

In the US: available at bookstores everywhere
or from The Globe Pequot Press (www.GlobePequot.com)